PENGUIN BOOKS

MEDIC

Praise for the authors' previous books:

'Splendid, fascinating, gripping, moving' *Mail on Sunday*

'A riveting and revealing account of World War II bravery' Andy McNab

'Humanity shines through. A sensitive account of the best and worst of human behaviour' *Daily Telegraph*

'Gripping, moving and thoughtful. The excellent team of Nichol and Rennell have done it again' Patrick Bishop

'Impressive scholarship but with all the pace of a novel' Andrew Roberts

'Compelling, powerful, gripping, revealing' *Daily Mail*

'Wonderfully vivid, with neither a dull nor a sentimental page and crammed with anecdotes which stretch the imagination'
M. R. D. Foot, *Spectator*

'Powerful and compelling, the untold story of a largely ignored dimension of the war' *Washington Post*

'Scrupulously researched and deeply moving' Sir Raymond Carr

ABOUT THE AUTHORS

John Nichol is a former RAF flight lieutenant whose Tornado bomber was shot down on a mission over Iraq during the first Gulf War in 1991. He was captured and became a prisoner of war. He is the bestselling co-author of *Tornado Down* and, with Tony Rennell, *The Last Escape*, *Tail-End Charlies* and *Home Run*, and author of five novels. He is also a journalist and widely quoted military commentator. His website is www.johnnichol.com

Tony Rennell is the author of *Last Days of Glory: The Death of Queen Victoria* and co-author of *When Daddy Came Home*, a highly praised study of demobilization in 1945, and, with John Nichol, *The Last Escape*, *Tail-End Charlies* and *Home Run*. He is a former deputy editor of the *Sunday Times* and writes regularly on historical subjects for the *Daily Mail*.

Medic

Saving Lives – from Dunkirk to Afghanistan

JOHN NICHOL AND TONY RENNELL

PENGUIN BOOKS

PENGUIN BOOKS

Published by the Penguin Group
Penguin Books Ltd, 80 Strand, London WC2R 0RL, England
Penguin Group (USA), Inc., 375 Hudson Street, New York, New York 10014, USA
Penguin Group (Canada), 90 Eglinton Avenue East, Suite 700, Toronto, Ontario, Canada M4P 2Y3
(a division of Pearson Penguin Canada Inc.)
Penguin Ireland, 25 St Stephen's Green, Dublin 2, Ireland (a division of Penguin Books Ltd)
Penguin Group (Australia), 250 Camberwell Road, Camberwell, Victoria 3124, Australia
(a division of Pearson Australia Group Pty Ltd)
Penguin Books India Pvt Ltd, 11 Community Centre, Panchsheel Park,
New Delhi – 110 017, India
Penguin Group (NZ), 67 Apollo Drive, Rosedale, North Shore 0632, New Zealand
(a division of Pearson New Zealand Ltd)
Penguin Books (South Africa) (Pty) Ltd, 24 Sturdee Avenue, Rosebank,
Johannesburg 2196, South Africa
Penguin Books Ltd, Registered Offices: 80 Strand, London WC2R 0RL, England

www.penguin.com

First published by Viking 2009
Published in Penguin Books 2010

1

Copyright © John Nichol and Tony Rennell, 2009

The moral right of the authors has been asserted

Printed in Great Britain by Clays Ltd, St Ives plc

A CIP catalogue record for this book is available from the British Library

ISBN: 978–0–141–02420–2

www.greenpenguin.co.uk

For Sophie and Harry

This book is dedicated to our country's exceptional military medical personnel. Their courage is an inspiration.

Contents

PART V: AFGHANISTAN

PART VI: AFTERMATH

List of Illustrations

Maps

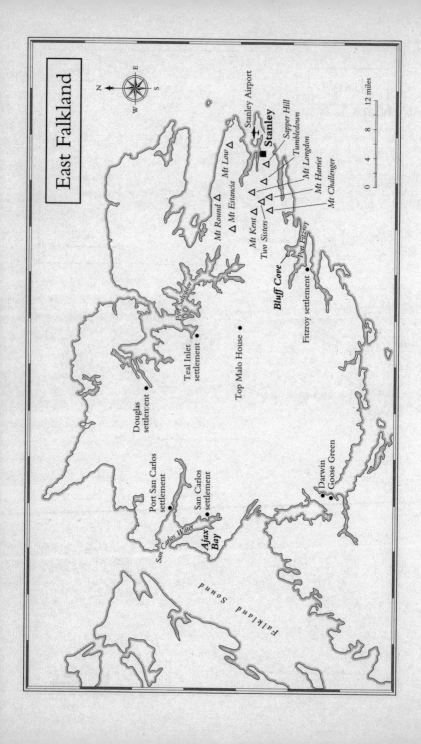

East Falkland

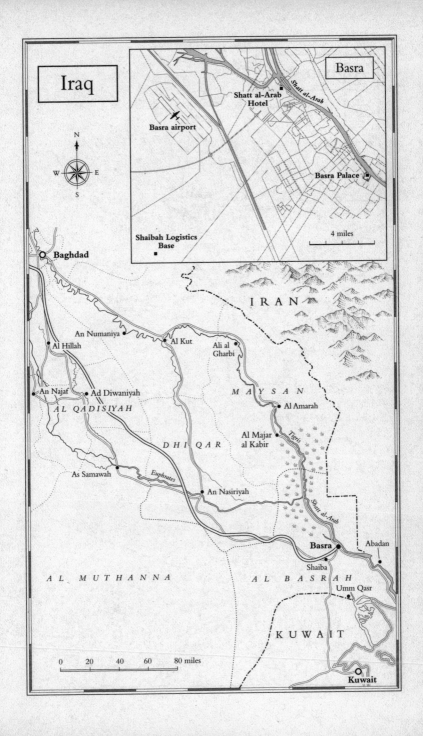

Iraq

Basra

N
W   E
S

Shatt al-Arab
Hotel

Basra airport

Shatt al-Arab

Basra Palace

Shaibah Logistics
Base

4 miles

Baghdad

IRAN

An Numaniya
Al Hillah
Al Kut
Ali al
Gharbi

MAYSAN

An Najaf
Ad Diwaniyah
Al Amarah

AL QADISIYAH

Al Majar
al Kabir

DHI QAR

Tigris

As Samawah
Euphrates

An Nasiriyah

Shatt al-Arab

Basra
Abadan

Shaiba

AL MUTHANNA
AL BASRAH
Umm Qasr

KUWAIT

0 20 40 60 80 miles

Kuwait

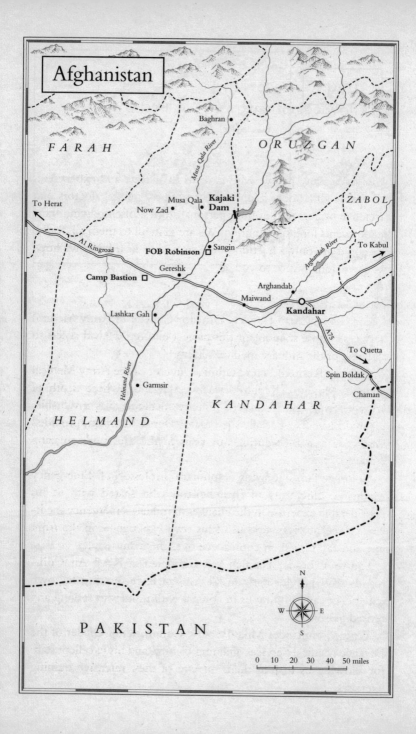

Acknowledgements

There are many people who gave us their time and expertise as we wrote this book. Hundreds of medics, nurses, doctors and stretcher-bearers told us their personal stories, often reliving traumatic events long since buried. We are grateful to them all. Sadly, we could use only a fraction of the stories we heard, but we hope we have done justice to you all.

Particular thanks also go to:

Major General Alan Hawley, Director General of Army Medical Services, whose support for this project ensured we had access to all levels of the military medical system.

Captain (Retired) Peter Starling, Director of the Army Medical Services Museum, Keogh Barracks, Aldershot, whose depth of knowledge of the history of military medicine was invaluable. He and his staff, especially the curator Derek Marrison, provided unstinting assistance during our visits to the museum's amazing archive.

Colonel Tim Hodgetts, Honorary Professor of Emergency Medicine, University of Birmingham, who shared with us his considerable expertise in the changes in military emergency medicine in recent years, told us of his own experiences in the front line and cast his expert clinical eye over the manuscript.

Squadron Leader Damien van Carrapiett at RAF Air Command, who provided invaluable assistance, recounting his own experiences and putting us in contact with numerous serving and retired personnel.

Wing Commander Mike Priestly, Commanding Officer of the Defence Medical Services Training Centre, and his excellent staff, for allowing us to join them on one of their intensive training exercises.

The administrators and members of the Army Rumour Service and Rum Ration websites, for access to inside information, contacts and expertise. The good-natured banter of all those involved was a welcome reminder of the strength of character and camaraderie of our military personnel.

Frank Garside from the British Limbless Ex-Servicemen's Association, Major (Retired) Marie Ellis, Regimental Secretary Royal Army Medical Corps, and Captain Bill Anderson of the Queen Alexandra's Royal Army Nursing Corps, all of whom provided contacts to many serving and retired personnel.

Cathy Pugh, General Manager of the Second World War Experience Centre in Leeds, who searched out accounts from the centre's archives, and Rod Suddaby of the Imperial War Museum, London.

Patrick Bishop, Max Arthur and Hugh McManners for allowing us to tap into their knowledge and expertise of the Falklands war and operations in Afghanistan. Paul Carter for his matchless critique of the manuscript. Sarah Helm, David O'Reilly and Brian Mac-Arthur for help and encouragement.

Group Captain Andy Bowen, Mark Pillans, Sam Harrison and Laura Kerr at the Ministry of Defence, who facilitated contact with serving military personnel and clearance for them to tell their stories.

Our agent Mark Lucas and our editor Eleo Gordon, and the team at Penguin Books.

Finally, and perhaps most importantly, our wives, Suzannah and Sarah, for their constant love, support and advice.

Preface

Although it is November the fifth, the sharp crackles and bangs snapping out over the cold, wet Hampshire countryside are not fireworks. They are gunfire, blanks admittedly, but still aggressive in intent. Along a forest trail, local walkers with their dogs are ushered away in a different direction, back to cosy, safe homes. Here a batch of young men and women are learning about war. Soon they will be off to join it, in Afghanistan, a hot and dry place as different from this soggy wood on the edge of the garrison town of Aldershot as it is possible to imagine. What makes the day even chillier for those of us watching them at the Defence Medical Services Training Centre at Keogh Barracks is the very real prospect that some will not return in one piece and some not at all. A patrol is coming our way, creeping in and out of the trees in their khaki coveralls, Bergen rucksacks on their backs, SA80 assault rifles held across their chests, fingers twitching, eyes alert. Ambush! A seasoned Scottish sergeant leaps out into their path and blasts at them with rapid fire from his automatic weapon. They return fire, scatter, hug the ground, call out instructions and guidance to each other. Casualties! Two men are down, simulating the wounds they were assigned for the exercise. One is very quiet, just lying there, not moving. The other is screaming, moaning, groaning, calling for help, swearing like . . . a trooper. 'Medic! I need a sodding medic, for effing sake!' he yells. He is in luck. They are close by, ready to go into action, just as medics have been through centuries of warfare. This is what these particular youngsters are here for. They are members of the Royal Army Medical Corps and they are training to go into combat and save the lives of their comrades under fire.

The drill they follow is well defined and precise. First they must see off the enemy and secure the ground. Defensive pickets are posted, spreadeagled in the wet bracken with clear firing arcs through the trees and down the forest path.

If you look closely at the faces under the helmets of those gripping the rifles, softer features and a few straggles of longer blonde hair identify the girls. It is a surprise to find them in such a combative situation, armed and ready to fight. Theoretically, women are not allowed on the front line in the British Army, denied jobs where the primary duty is 'to close with and kill the enemy face to face', as the Ministry of Defence defines it. They are thus excluded from the infantry, the cavalry and the armoured corps. But they are now a large and much valued part of the military medical system. They get no special treatment and nor would they ask for it. As medics, they are every bit as exposed to danger as the men and every bit as courageous in the line of fire.

With the area secured, the medical work begins. The noisy casualty needs calming, but his swearing indicates that he is awake and has no problem breathing. The priority is the quiet one. He is rolled into the recovery position – face down, head to one side – and methodically examined. Is he bleeding? Check. Is he breathing? Check. Does he have a pulse? Check. It's vital not to panic, to keep your head, to follow procedures even when it's cold and confusing and all hell is breaking out around. The instructors ram home the point. Heroics and hysterics will not save lives. Calm assessment and the right action will. Talk to the casualty, the instructors urge, ask him his name, what happened, how he feels, where it hurts. As with any GP in a surgery or doctor in a hospital casualty department, information is the key to diagnosis and treatment. The 'casualties', though fellow trainees, are well briefed in their pretend injuries – some have already served in Iraq and Afghanistan and may well have seen them for real, in the flesh, as it were. One is acting as if he had a sucking chest wound. The real thing would have air leaking dangerously from his lungs like a punctured tyre and could kill him in minutes. It needs a special air-tight dressing from a medic's professionally packed Bergen. The other casualty is haemorrhaging badly, fake blood spurting feet into the air from a plastic pouch and spattering red across the autumn leaves on the ground. As he thrashes about in pain, the medics struggle to get a tourniquet around his beefy thigh. Rain is falling heavily now and a bitter wind has sprung up. Patching up people is taxing enough on the nerves in a ward or consulting room, as the high stress levels in doctors and nurses show. Down here in the cold and the mud, with a battle, albeit a simulated one, raging around them, it is an entirely different experience, calling on every last fibre of resolve.

Now comes the hardest part of the exercise. The company aid post, which sounds grand but in reality is just a largish, stand-up tent with room for two stretchers on trestles, is a mile away. There is a field ambulance to take the casualties there – as, on an actual operation, there might be a helicopter – but it cannot get any closer to them. It is parked 600 yards away, at the top of a steep and muddy hill, and there is no stretcher. Brute strength is the answer. The biggest of the medics stoops and hauls the casualty across his shoulders in a fireman's lift. He totters under the weight – who wouldn't? – and we all smile, because there has just been a story in a newspaper about a fire brigade in the Home Counties banning this manoeuvre for health and safety reasons. Apparently it's been ruled unsafe because someone might get hurt. Perhaps we should send the health-and-safety brigade to Afghanistan and unleash them on the Taliban, someone suggests. The medic in question isn't finding any of this funny as he begins to make his way to the ambulance. He starts at a good pace but quickly slows as the 15 stones of soldier on his back take their toll. He staggers a little, stops, starts again, then puts down his man and thinks about having a rest. It's only an exercise, for God's sake. The instructors harry him. Come on, laddie, this isn't a game. This is for real. Keep going When you're in Afghanistan, you won't be able to take a rest. Someone's life will be down to you. Are you going to let him die? Keep effing going!

And he does. He picks up the casualty again and sets off, though his legs are buckling now. He is carrying more than his own weight uphill over slippery stones, and the strain is immense. He is breathing hard. He is *hurting*. But, in fits and starts, he gets to the waiting ambulance, hands over his casualty, and then collapses on a log. His Olympian effort has paid off. The look on his face as he gasps for air and holds his aching side is half grimace, half smile of satisfaction. He knows that if he ever has to do this for real – and the odds are he might – then he will be up for it. He can be relied on.

The other casualty, it should be said, is already there. At the bottom of the hill, the trainee medic in charge of him had come prepared with a piece of American kit he found in an army supplies store and bought with his own money. It is a lightweight, roll-up canvas stretcher, easy to stow and carry and a godsend in this situation. The instructors, all hardened NCOs and not given to unnecessary praise, are impressed – by the equipment itself, which they have never seen before, and by the youngster's initiative in seeking it out.[1] It is important that, as well as doing everything by the book, a good medic knows instinctively when to throw the book away and do what needs to be done. The stretcher is laid out, the casualty is eased on and, with a medic at each corner, they virtually charge up the slope. The girls join in now. Some are a foot shorter than the men and physically couldn't carry a casualty single-handed, as their lanky male colleague has done. But they can share the load of a stretcher, another point in favour of this revolutionary roll-up version. We all wonder why it has taken so long to come up with this simple and obvious answer to a perennial battlefield problem. In the Falklands conflict, troops took to using their waterproof poncho capes to evacuate the wounded from the battlefield, and this is really just a purpose-made version of that makeshift solution from a quarter of a century ago. We all wonder too why the MoD isn't making them standard issue – and why our young soldiers are having to shell out from their own pockets to equip themselves to do their job properly. Surely no such expense – and this is a small one – should be spared on kit that will save lives on the battlefield? It is hard to resist the conclusion that, as a society, we are shortchanging those we send to war on our behalf and those we task to save their lives

Everyone is now collected at the top of the hill, where the

casualties are loaded into the field ambulance, essentially a Land Rover with a long wheel-base and a high cabin on the back. It is unwieldy and basic, verging on the obsolete. It bears the same relationship to the top-notch civilian ambulances on our streets as the army's Green Goddesses do to modern fire engines. As it bumps along the forest track and grinds through the gears on its way to the aid post, the medics appear unfazed by any Fred Karno comparisons. At the aid post they cluster around the casualties, apply dressings, practise emergency CPR (cardio-pulmonary resuscitation), discuss the use of painkillers and putting in lines for intravenous fluids. Soon enough they will be in Iraq or Afghanistan and what becomes second nature now in the drizzle of a grey English winter will stand them in good stead on a red-hot, sun-burned street in Sangin or Musa Qala when bullets are flying and bodies falling. This is a serious business and they take it seriously, focussing, learning, preparing for the real thing.

The tradition these young people are heir to is a long and honourable one, though often overlooked. The garlands of war are usually awarded to those who win battles or die in the attempt to do so. Those who go on to the battlefield not to take life but to save it attract less attention. Their deeds are what this book is about. It is a story worthy of telling, not least because it is not often told. As one experienced medic told us, not with rancour but with a sigh of resignation, 'We tend to get ignored, even sneered at, by the rest of the military – until the shit hits the fan.' Then all of a sudden we become a popular commodity. The fact is that we have the most difficult job in the army, but this is not a truth that is often acknowledged.'[2]

As the history we tell advances from the Europe of 1940 to the Afghanistan of 2009, the very nature of modern warfare changing radically along the way, what binds together the individuals in it is an amazing humanity and compassion, a selflessness that, in the worst of circumstances, seeks out and finds the best in people. Medics experience war at its rawest. Gore, not glory, is their stock in trade. They deserve our respect and our admiration but also our understanding of the extra courage it takes to do the supremely testing job they have volunteered for. What I do, one veteran medic told us, is to run into the middle of a firefight to help someone else, and that is neither easy nor natural. It takes a conscious decision. It is a personal battle every time. 'But the plain fact is that someone is hurt and may be dying and you have the skill to help him. Are you going to go to him or not?' On that question hangs what you are about to read.

The battlefield is not a pretty place, and in what follows the authors have not pulled any punches. What a high-velocity bullet or a roadside bomb does to human flesh and bone is horrendous and not for the squeamish. That horror, though, is what we expect our servicemen and women to face on our behalf and the military medical services to deal with. Their bravery cannot be properly understood if the truth is softened, and we have not sought to do so.

1. Saving Sergeant Major Stockton

He was out in the open, alone and exposed on a dusty Afghan road, and the full moon seemed to search him out like a spotlight. *Crack!* So did the enemy snipers. *Crack!* He felt as if the whole world was shooting at just him. *Crack! Ping!* What he recalled most vividly later, what embedded itself in his memory, was that sound of bullets exploding from unseen rifles, then glancing off the metal sides of the armoured trucks he was running past as fast as his legs would carry him and his medical pack. *Ping!* Such a puny noise for something so deadly, no different from the tinkle of pellets in a fairground rifle range. *Crack!* But this shoot-out was not for amusement. It was in deadly earnest. Those were Kalashnikovs, not air-rifles, and everyone else in the patrol kept low, seeking cover from the murderous volley coming at them from the trees on the other side of a canal, lifting their heads only to fire back a burst and then duck down again. Lance Corporal Gary 'Loz' Lawrence of the Royal Army Medical Corps (RAMC) stayed on his feet. He had a special job to do, whatever the danger. The hard hat on his head offered some protection, as did the Kevlar body armour. But all that really kept him alive was the poor shooting of the Taliban that particular night. The Afghan insurgents had lured his patrol of British soldiers into an ambush on a narrow tow-path in the desert town of Sangin, bandit country, a no-go area where the writ of the Afghan government and its allies from Britain and the United States meant nothing. They were now pinning down the patrol with fire from all sides. A man was down, struck by an RPG, a rocket-propelled grenade, the Taliban's deadliest weapon. He was badly wounded, *very* badly. Down the radio net had come the soldier's call from time immemorial: 'MEDIC! We need a medic! Here! Now!'

Lawrence had responded instantly. This was what he was trained for, his calling. He grabbed the Bergen rucksack containing his supplies and was out of the truck, dancing his way through the bullets, racing back down the convoy, dodging from vehicle to vehicle to where a comrade needed his help. At one stage the line of Humvees and Land Rovers lurched forward and, before he caught them up, he was left even more exposed, a lone figure in the middle of the night in the middle of nowhere with mayhem and murder breaking out around him. 'You're a medic, and you think you're bulletproof,' he said in explanation. 'But that night people out there were trying to kill me. At one point, I was running along, and there were bullets flying all around me, and I was thinking, "What am I doing here? I could die, I really could." Oh yes, that feeling was real, very real.'[1]

And yet the day that led to this nightmare had begun pleasantly enough. 'Loz, I'm making a brew. Do you want some?' Lawrence had stirred from his pit and said yes. A cup of tea made by the captain himself, Jim Philippson . . . no bad way to start another long, hot, dusty day in the featureless scrubland of Helmand province in southern Afghanistan. Camaraderie like this, mucking in together regardless of rank, helped make life a little more bearable here in Forward Operating Base [FOB] Robinson, a sorry, fly-blown outpost in the desert that was home to the British detail. Sitting in the Snake Pit, a shaded dug-out scraped from the sand and circled by the rusting metal hulks of freight containers that made up this makeshift mini-fortress, Lawrence contemplated the hours ahead, as featureless as the surroundings. He would take a sick parade of his own blokes, if any had ailments that wanted treating, then he would wander over to the neighbouring compound of the ANA, the Afghan National Army, and supervise a similar parade there. As resident medic in a unit whose specific task was to tutor and mentor the Afghan soldiers, that was his main job. It was dull work in a hateful climate and a landscape that well earned the name the locals gave it – the Desert of Death. 'You tried to keep busy,' he would recall, 'tried to occupy yourself. But there was not a huge amount to do during the day because it was so hot. We kept in the shade as much as possible.'

Conditions were spartan. Some men, the lucky ones, bunked inside the stifling, sand-scarred containers. Newcomers – and the base was now bursting at the seams – had to doss down in improvised lean-tos, thrown up in shanty-town style against the giant wire mesh and canvas sandbags that formed the six-foot-high bomb-proof perimeter wall. With one washroom for 120 men, many chose to dunk themselves in a huge barrel fed by a well in the corner of the compound, jumping in fully clothed and washing their combat fatigues at the same time. For exercise, there was some gash gym equipment cannibalized from old tins and a broomstick. As billets went, there weren't a lot worse than this. It made Camp Bastion, thirty miles away, the main base for the British, American and Canadian forces who made up the NATO task force, seem almost palatial, with its neat rows of tents, vast communal marquees, solid flooring and air-conditioning. But Lawrence could comfort himself, perhaps, with the knowledge that he and his detachment were where it mattered. What they were doing was central to why the British Army was back here on the ground in Afghanistan in 2006 – as trainers and instructors rather than combat soldiers, helping the locals learn how to carry on their own fight against the Taliban insurgents threatening their country.[2]

But that day, Sunday 11 June, everything was about to change. What had started out as a hearts-and-minds operation – one, indeed, that the politicians in London who sanctioned it hoped could even be completed without a single shot fired in anger – turned deadly. By the time night fell on the desert and the harsh terrain began to cool, a real war, hot and horrific and deadly, would begin, and Gary Lawrence would be wondering whether he would ever see home again. There had been 'contact' with the enemy before, firefights in which the Paras and the Gurkhas, with their superior weaponry, had come out on top. The Taliban – a clever and brave enemy, not to be underestimated – had taken substantial casualties. But apart from a few broken bones and shrapnel wounds, the British forces deployed in Helmand had come through unscathed. No longer. That day the very first British soldier would die. As the death count rose inexorably in the coming months and years, first into double figures, then into hundreds, it fell to medics – from the various grades of combat medical technicians such as Lawrence, right up to the most highly skilled cutters, the surgeons – to keep the tightest possible lid on that toll of British soldiery.

They displayed skills that are often taken for granted, even by the military themselves, until the dire moment, the life-or-death emergency, when they are needed. Then they are called on to perform miracles – and they do. Medics and military doctors fight their wars with stretchers and splints, saws and scalpels, but also with superhuman endeavour and courage. Their importance is not just that, in the thick of the action, they are there to save lives. Without the promise, the *pledge*, of their presence and commitment, few troops would care to advance into battle. The much-vaunted 'covenant' between society and its soldiers begins with medics, the unsung heroes of modern warfare. The tragedy that first fatal day in Afghanistan was that a brave soldier died. For us, the story is that another one was brilliantly saved.

It was evening, and Lawrence was once again hanging around the Snake Pit when the shout went up from the Ops Room (another container). A patrol was in trouble. Help was urgently needed. Earlier that day, a miniature robotic spy plane carrying high-tech video equipment had been sent flying out over the area around Sangin, a Taliban stronghold, to send back pictures of the build-up of enemy forces. The Desert Hawk UAV (unmanned aerial vehicle) was the military's latest star turn, a relatively cheap – at £12,000 each – and safe way to gather intelligence. But this Hawk, instead of flying back home at the end of its hour-long surveillance, lost height unaccountably and ditched out in the desert. A patrol was about to go out from Robinson on a routine sweep and it was re-directed to recover it.

'I watched them go,' said Lawrence. 'There wasn't any sense that they were going into a major contact.' The patrol found nothing at the coordinates they had been sent to and widened their search before learning from locals that the Hawk had been captured and spirited away. Frustrated in their mission and with the sun setting, they started back to base. They had had to cross to the far side of the Helmand river, which they now re-crossed. On the bank, the Taliban were waiting. Tracer bullets lit up the night sky. The crackle of machine-gun fire – not unlike the sound of plastic bottles being crushed underfoot, as one soldier recalled – shattered the desert silence. A soldier took a bullet through the chest. The patrol radioed frantically for back-up.

Back at Robinson, the whole base came alive. Orders were barked out and men rushed to kit up, grab helmets, throw on body armour. Captain Philippson – commando-trained, extrovert, enthusiastic, popular – was one of a number of officers putting together a rescue force. Lawrence wanted to go with them. His unit, his comrades, 'my guys', were going. He should be with them. But the incident sounded serious and the unit's doctor decided he was going himself. Lawrence was ordered to stay behind and prepare for incoming casualties. In eight lightly armoured Land Rovers, the rescue force roared away, headed for the river, parked up near the ambush site and advanced on foot. It was a trap. Once again, the Taliban were waiting. Under fire, the rescuers made it to where the wounded soldier was lying and began to carry him to safety. But in the eerie half-light of the full moon, Philippson was shot dead. Hearing over the radio the news of a death but not the name, Lawrence, for all his medical experience, felt gutted. 'It was the first death. We were all desperate to know who it was. We were a small detachment, just twelve of us, all close, colleagues and comrades, all on first-name terms. And now one of us was dead. But who?' In another container was his medical centre. 'It was pretty basic – a stretcher and trestles with some bits and pieces of medical gear.' He prepared it as best he could to receive casualties – and a corpse.

The rescue force retreated under withering fire, then fought their way back to recover the captain's body. That was part of the military covenant too. No man wanted to be left to rot or, worse still, for his body to be abused, trailed in the dust as a trophy, as dead American soldiers had been in Somalia not so many years before. Whatever the illogicality, the guarantee of a decent laying to rest was important to morale. So the captain was brought back to FOB Robinson in the back of a Humvee. It was Lawrence's job to receive him. 'I opened the door to the vehicle and saw straight away that it was Captain Philippson. I laid him on a stretcher and took him into the med centre. His face was grey and ashen. There was a gunshot wound to his head. It was a shock. I had to be professional about it and I was, but I couldn't stop thinking how only that morning he'd made that brew for me. Here, staring me in the face, was the stark reality of war.'

That shocking reality was soon registering itself in many other quarters – with the twenty-nine-year-old Philippson's devastated parents and girlfriend, mourning 'a wonderful and brave son'; with those politicians who had ordered men into the political and military quagmire of Afghanistan in the hope that none would die; with other British servicemen who had believed they were there strictly as advisers and trainers of the Afghan Army and now found themselves on the front line of a full-out war. And one for which they were not properly equipped. Later, a coroner would blame the Ministry of Defence for starving the troops of essential equipment. Philippson's group had gone into battle with no night-vision kits to spot the enemy in the dark nor the Minimi light machine guns and grenade launchers to outgun them with. The captain's father put the responsibility higher up the chain of command – to Gordon Brown, then Chancellor of the Exchequer, for starving the MoD of cash.

But the recriminations were for the future. For now, there was a job to do at FOB Robinson. There were still men out there, the remainder of the rescue force, plus the original patrol, fighting for their lives, in danger of running out of ammunition and of being overrun. Another rescue operation had to be mounted. The unit doctor, who had returned with Philippson's body, desperately trying all the way to revive him, turned to Lawrence. 'Right, Loz, you're the next one out.' The lance corporal sprang into action, pulling off the red cross armband he wore around the base. Out in the field, it offered him no protection. The enemy took no notice of such niceties, whatever it said in the Geneva Convention, and it might even expose him to extra danger. Its white background would stand out in the dark, while the cross would be a red rag to a bull for fanatical muslims. He was about to face the supreme test, and he could not help wondering, like every soldier who ever went into battle, if he had the balls for what lay ahead.

As a young adult, he had drifted. Tried a couple of years at college, then stacked supermarket shelves. Tried some more studying, then decided on the military. 'I wanted to be doing my bit for my country. I'm sentimental like that.' Even then, he continued to drift – tried the RAF but was turned down for pilot training (he was too tall), then applied unsuccessfully to be a PT instructor (didn't have the right sporting credentials). 'So I joined the army instead.' He opted to be a medic because this was where he felt he could make a real contribution. He was about to discover whether he was man enough for the dangerous job he'd chosen for himself. 'Until you go into action, until you actually face it, you just don't know whether you're going to cope or not. I was worried about just one thing: what if I can't handle this, what if I can't do my job properly?' He was not alone in his apprehension that night, far from it.

*

'S'arnt major, we've got you a truck!' Here at last was the shout Andy Stockton of the Royal Artillery had been waiting for. It was his Hawk that had gone down in the desert and prompted an operation now escalating by the minute into a pitched battle. A simple recovery mission had spiralled into two firefights, one dead officer, badly wounded soldiers. And it was not over yet. Four men from his own detachment – 'one of them younger than my own son' – had gone in the first search party and were still out there. A professional soldier for fifteen years, intelligent and well informed, he had feared this eventuality ever since arriving in Afghanistan – not for himself but for the young recruits under his command. He had never bought into the idea that this could be a campaign in which not a single shot would be fired.[3] He knew all about the toughness of Afghan guerrillas. For a promotion exam, he had researched and written a paper on the *mujahedin* resistance to the invasion by the Soviet Union in the 1980s. The superpower had been worn down and eventually kicked out. 'I had a good idea of the sort of people we were up against. Fighting was their bread and butter. I knew what they were capable of.'[4]

He had known too, as his artillery unit trained for Afghanistan with grenades and ammunition usually reserved for combat troops, that the Hawk's limited radio range meant they would be operating, if not on the front line, then as close behind it as to make no difference. 'We heard rumours that 16 Air Assault Brigade, to whom we were attached, were packing enough body bags for losses of one in six. So we didn't scrimp on first-aid training! At FOB Robinson we were nearer the front than artillery men ever expected to be. But the lads loved it. We felt as though we were manning an outpost of the Empire in the early 1900s. It was real soldiering. Even so, I never expected to be fighting with an enemy just a few *metres* away.'

The day the Desert Hawk was lost it was being used to observe ferry crossings on the Helmand river during the Sangin evening 'rush hour', monitoring which vehicles were using them and where they headed when they got to the other side. 'We could see it going down on our screens and we knew exactly where it was. We had its grid reference.' Nothing seemed easier or more routine than recovering it. And then everything turned pear-shaped as the search patrol was ambushed – ironically, at one of the very crossings the Hawk had been spying on – and then the rescue force. Stockton felt helpless – and guilty. 'These guys were under fire, and I'd sent them out there. I felt really responsible. I should have been out there with them.'

He pleaded with the ops officer to be allowed to go with the second rescue force that was now assembling at top speed at the gates of FOB Robinson. 'At first he ordered me to remain behind and to prepare to receive any casualties when they returned. But then he changed his mind. They needed anyone who could be spared, and I got that shout I had been so desperate for. So off we went. Such is fate!' He was apprehensive as the convoy of five heavily armed Land Rovers and two American Humvees drove out into the desert night and on into the outskirts of Sangin. 'I had always wanted to see action. This was what I had joined for. But there was still a knot in my stomach.'

They moved slowly down a track so narrow it was impossible to turn or to reverse. On one side was an irrigation ditch, on the other a canal. On the far bank, trees were clearly visible in the moonlight, but there were ominous dark shadows between them, ideal hiding places for ambushers. They came to a halt by a bridge, watching silently in a limbo of apprehension, the uneasy stillness before the storm. 'Movement front right!' yelled a voice through the radio receiver in Stockton's ear, and he heard the loud woosh of an RPG rocketing from the other side of the canal. He hurled himself out of the vehicle. 'Bullets were going across our heads and tracer was flying out into the night. Our top-cover gunners blazed back. I crouched behind the bonnet of my Land Rover, saw people through my sights running alongside the canal and opened up on them.' His fear was gone. He was in his element, the adrenalin pumping through his body, his heart thumping with excitement. 'There was a lot of fire going down, and it was really noisy. I was shouting orders at the guys and radio messages were pouring into my ear.' The last of these was another urgent warning – 'Movement rear left . . . *Contact* rear left!'

Stockton swung round to the back of his vehicle, trying to spot where this fresh enemy attack was coming from. He saw nothing, turned back to the Land Rover, '. . . and I felt a blow to the upper part of my left arm – as if somebody had hit me hard with a sledgehammer.' An RPG had struck him. Amazingly, it had not exploded – if it had he would have been dead – but the force of it threw him to the ground. 'I had no idea I was injured until I rolled over, reached for my arm and it wasn't there. I had grabbed the stump, which felt like a piece of warm, sticky steak. I knew straight away my arm had gone.' He managed to haul himself off the ground, 'and what was left of my arm came up with me, dangling on a thread of tissue. There was not much pain, just a dull ache. I could see the grenade, lodged in the side of the Land Rover, its tail protruding. My first thought was how lucky I had been – another couple of inches and it would have been my chest, and that would have been goodbye! Then I realized blood was spurting everywhere and I knew I had to act fast if I wanted to stay alive. I shouted into the radio: ' "I'm down! MEDIC!!" '

★

A thousand miles and four and a half time zones away, it had been a sweltering summer's day in England. Stockton's girlfriend, Emma, spent much of it on a lounger in the garden of their house in Wiltshire, playing with their Westie dog. In the evening, for some reason, she found herself reading through the pile of 'bluey' airmail letters they had sent to each other in the three years they had been together. She was 'Army' too. They had served together in Iraq during the first phase of the invasion, she as the military clerk in his battery and one of just a handful of British women in the entire operation. 'I ended up being everyone's mother, auntie, sister, someone that they can tell their troubles to and confide in.'5 She left in 2004 when her tour was up. 'I'd done four years in the army and I was ready to move on. I was in a relationship with Andy and we'd bought a house in Wiltshire. He had another four years to go and then the world would be our oyster – we could travel, or start a family, whatever we wanted.'

Afghanistan stood in the way of her dreams. They both knew it was going to be a tough mission, the intensity of the pre-operation training indicated as much. 'He told me: "Where we're going, it's going to be bad." We talked about the worst, if he didn't come home. He went over his will with me. We were both realistic and practical. You have fears, of course, but there's no point in voicing them.'

They talked on the telephone, and emailing was an easy option, but both of them preferred to communicate the old-fashioned way with handwritten letters. 'They take a little bit longer, but they're more personal, aren't they?' Their whole life together was measured in 'blueys'. These had been their main form of communication even when they were in Iraq together. 'It was difficult to have a proper relationship out there,' she explained, 'so we'd write to each other and leave the letters on each other's desk, or even post them in the internal mail to each other. So that evening I was sat out in the garden and reading all the ones he'd ever written to me. I was thinking about him . . .' She didn't know it but 'the stark reality of war' (as Gary Lawrence had put it) was about to change her life for ever.

*

As the blood flowed from his shattered arm, Stockton pinched the artery underneath to try to staunch the flow, 'squeezing for all I was worth'. Surprisingly calm and practical in the circumstances, he yelled to his stunned driver to find something to tourniquet the stump. In training, they had been given new instructions about the use of tourniquets. For years, doctors, both military and civilian, had gone round in circles of debate about this most fundamental of first-aid techniques. Tourniquets were disapproved of (if not actually banned) in general medical practice and in hospital Accident and Emergency departments because, if applied too rigorously or for too long, they could starve limbs of blood, causing serious long-term damage and leading to unnecessary amputations. But a battlefield had different priorities, as RAMC doctors had come to appreciate. 'Tourniquets had been off the map for a long time,' said Stockton, 'but now we'd been instructed that the benefits outweighed the risks. They were life-savers.'

The sergeant major's life certainly needed saving. A traumatic wound like this could kill, and quickly. 'But my driver could find nothing to tie round my arm so I told him to help me back into the Land Rover in case the convoy started moving again. The bottom of my arm was hanging on by a sinew, and I placed it on my lap. As he climbed over me into the driving seat, I remember yelling at him to watch out in case he broke the fingers of the hand, as if that mattered any more. Then I tried to shut the door, and my arm fell off my lap and was hanging down. It got trapped, so I picked it up and placed it between my knees to keep it out of the way.' Another soldier appeared from the back of the Land

Rover holding up a 'Plasticuff' he had found, a loop of thin plastic normally used like handcuffs to restrain detainees. He tied down Stockton's shattered arm with this, leaving the sergeant major's other hand free to grip his rifle, jam it into his armpit and prepare to shoot anyone who came too close.

For what seemed an eternity, they remained stationary while gunfire continued to crackle all around them. Then the order came to drive on and they lurched forward, but the gunfire followed them, as fierce as ever. 'We were being pursued, and the situation looked pretty dodgy. The RPG tail was sticking out of the shattered window and I worried that it might detonate.' He stuck his foot hard against it just in case. It was then, as they drove on down the narrow track, that real pain first began to kick in. An increasingly dizzy Stockton cracked a few tasteless jokes at his own expense, anything to take his mind off the agony of his arm. 'I suppose this means I'm going to have to cancel my guitar lessons,' he grunted. They crunched to a halt again, and seconds later he saw a breathless Gary Lawrence at the window, un-slinging his Bergen.

The medic had been in the second vehicle in the rescue convoy, sitting behind the driver. The seat next to him, he remembered all too vividly, was still covered with Captain Philippson's blood. 'We were going along by the canal when suddenly it all kicked off. I saw a fizz of orange light and the streak of an RPG coming across the back of us. It hit a wall and exploded. "What the fuck's going on here?" I thought. Then I realized we'd been ambushed and we were in a real battle.' Almost immediately, he heard the call for a medic. There was a casualty in one of the vehicles behind. 'I had to get to him. I could hear the gunfire and see the tracer, but it didn't seem to register. My job was to get to him.' He had worried about this moment of truth. To his relief, the training and the adrenalin kicked in together. 'I didn't have time to be scared,' he remembered. He dropped out of the Humvee as the furious firefight raged around him. But the track was so narrow and the American vehicle so wide he was pitched straight into the canal.

It was fast-flowing and the only thing that stopped me being carried away was that my Bergen got caught on the Humvee. I dragged myself up and started heading back along the convoy. I'd gone about 20 yards when the vehicles began to move again, leaving me out in the open. I sprinted back and jumped in. The convoy halted again and I was out once more, dashing the longest 40 yards of my life, being fired on from all directions, until I got to Andy Stockton's Land Rover. He was holding his arm in his lap. A dark, wet patch was seeping out around it. He wasn't totally with it.

The dazed sergeant major was alert enough to register Lawrence's arrival and feel the sense of relief all soldiers seem to experience, no matter how badly wounded, when they are in the hands of a trained medic. 'I didn't know Gary at the time, but he was a welcome sight. I knew now I'd get some proper treatment,' Stockton remembered, though Lawrence's recollection is that the last thing he felt at this moment was a safe pair of hands. 'To me it seems I stood for ages, thinking about what I had to do and what needed to happen. But the guys who were there said, no, I got on with it straight away. Andy's arm was almost totally amputated mid-bicep, held on by a bit of skin and muscle little more than an inch thick. But in the dark I didn't realize that, and when I tried to loop the tourniquet over the stump, it kept getting tangled up. I finally managed to get the tourniquet on, but he was still bleeding heavily. I wound the tourniquet as much as I could and also pulled the Plasticuff tighter.'

Over the radio net, a voice asked: 'Is the medic in the vehicle?', and someone mistakenly replied, 'Yes.' At that point the convoy started up again. In fact, Lawrence was out of the Land Rover and kneeling on the ground getting more kit out of his bag.

I thought, 'Fuck, what's happening?' I was afraid they were going to disappear without me, and the last thing I wanted was to be stuck out here on my tod. I picked up my bag and hot-footed it back to my own vehicle. I was running as fast as I could, with bullets pinging all around me. Fortunately, the convoy was moving slowly and I was fairly fit, and as I reached the Humvee, the American soldier on top-cover spotted me. I heard him shout down the hatchway: 'Tommy, that medic of yours, he's not in another vehicle, he's running behind us!' Sergeant Major Tommy Johnson opened up his door and looked out at me. 'Loz, what the fuck do you think you're doing? Get back in, you tube!' And I did.

It would have been funny, a soldier's Carry On anecdote to savour, if it hadn't so nearly been the death of him.

The convoy found shelter under some trees and paused as Lawrence braved the gunfire again to get back to his patient. 'I turned my torch on him and for the first time could properly see the damage. He had lost a lot of blood – he was drenched in it. It was vital to get some fluids into him as quickly as possible.' He found a vein and put in a line for a saline drip – not easy to do while on the move across rough terrain, under continuous fire and with only the dim glow from the vehicle's interior light to work by. Stockton himself was impressed by the skill with which it was done. Lawrence, on his admission, was improvising. 'In training, we're told to administer a maximum of 250 millilitres of saline, but my guess was that Andy had already lost three or four pints of blood, and 250 millilitres was nothing. So I followed my instinct and gave him as much as I thought he needed. Forget the textbook stuff; you're having to make these decisions in real time with the best knowledge you've got. He asked for morphine, but I kept him off it for now, because the only pain he was complaining about was that the tourniquets were too tight. I told him, "Look, if that's all you're worried about, you're fine!"'

But the problems were piling up as the wounded sergeant major's condition deteriorated.

He was drifting in and out of sleep. His face was grey, he was cold, he was shivering, he was thirsty – all classic signs of shock, and that's a killer. Then, with the fluids inside him, his arm started weeping again, which meant the tourniquet wasn't working. I had to tighten it even more, or else he was going to bleed to death in front of me. I also needed to put something round the stump, but he was a big guy with large biceps, and none of the normal limb bandages I had fitted. In the end, I had to use an abdominal dressing to wrap round it. I thought of cutting the strip of flesh that was holding the lower part of his arm but didn't want the severed bit to get lost. I put a plaster on his other arm. He had a deepish cut there, but it was just a scratch compared with what had happened to the left one. But he was complaining about it, so I patched it for him.

Stockton was even more concerned for his army-issue watch, which he had signed for and would have to account for to some pen-pusher, to whom his injury in the line of duty would be no excuse for losing it. It was still on the wrist of his semi-detached arm. He asked Lawrence to take it off and take care of it for him.

The medic worked on, nudging the inert Stockton, swearing at him, insulting him, anything to stop him sinking into a coma. 'Oy, sir, fucking wake up, sir,' Lawrence bellowed. The sergeant major rallied enough to remember his rank. 'You talk to me like that again, Lance Corporal, and I'll fucking kill you,' he growled. The goading had done the trick. Lawrence kept up a stream of conversation. They small-talked about Stockton's sons and how he liked playing football with them. 'It was all just a means of keeping him going. It was like one of your mates is having a bad time and you go down the pub, you have a drink, you have a fag, you chat . . . anything to keep them up and running.' Lawrence was buying time. He had done all he could to contain the problem. Now the sergeant major's life was out of his hands. It hung on a simple issue – stuck out in the wilderness, with the enemy still on their tails, the battle not yet over, how long would it be before he could get to a surgeon?

*

At the hospital in Camp Bastion, the four-man airborne Medical Emergency Response Team (MERT) was on standby – in the sort of relative luxury and crew comfort that the lads of FOB Robinson could only dream of. They had their own tent, strewn with newspapers and magazines like any officers' mess, a kettle, fridge and a television on which they watched DVDs of war films. *Platoon* and *Hamburger Hill* were favourites, along with *Black Hawk Down*, the story of a search-and-rescue mission that went horribly wrong. Their kit was already stowed in a Land Rover waiting outside, ready to rush them to the helicopter take-off and landing site half a mile away, when the call came.

Flight Lieutenant Damien van Carrapiett relaxed while he could. He had years of experience in emergency medicine. He had worked in an NHS casualty department and then for an air-ambulance company, neither of which was challenging enough for the action man in him. As an RAF nurse, he had served in Sierre Leone, the Balkans and Iraq. But Afghanistan was turning out to be different, by far the riskiest of all. He knew the dangers, though he kept them from his wife. Not wanting her to worry, he told her his four-month tour there was behind a desk, far from the action. 'She didn't know I was spending my time in the back of a helicopter under fire, coming down in the middle of hot landing zones, and that somebody right next to me had been shot. My dad knew the truth, so when I needed to get some of the tension off my chest, I wrote and told him.'[6]

It was twenty past midnight when the phone rang from Joint Operations Command Centre, and they scrambled into the Land Rover and raced fast down a gravel track to the landing site, where a Chinook was squatting, its rotors already rolling. The force-protection squad, whose job was to throw a defence cordon around the helicopter the moment it landed, were already on board in flak jackets and helmets, and gripping their rifles. Yellow plugs were stuffed in their ears to drown out the roar of the engines. The air crew arrived from their briefing. 'We didn't have much information,' van Carrapiett recalled. 'We all knew there was a big fight going on, a TIC, Troops In Contact. We were told there was a casualty with an arm injury, and that was all that we had to go on as we took off.'

The Chinook is a wonderful workhorse of a helicopter in a war where the front line is constantly shifting. It can ferry in dozens of troops in battle order and take out casualties. It is a huge beast, the size of a couple of double-deckers, but travelling in it is no bus ride. It lurches and yaws like an out-of-control Underground train, and the noise batters the senses until eyes glaze and nerves strain. It is also vulnerable. Its bulk makes it an attractive target for any enemy, as inviting to a gunman as a barn door. The men who fly in it are fully aware of the danger, particularly on landing and take-off, when it is wide open to an RPG attack. If this happened in Afghanistan, the disaster would be twofold – not just the catastrophic loss of life but the immense boost in morale the Taliban would derive from such a score. To down a helicopter was a prized ambition of theirs. It would mean history was repeating itself. Every Afghan guerrilla knew that it was acquiring the means to knock gunships out of the air (with Stinger missiles, supplied, ironically, by the Americans) that had brought victory over the Russians. 'If an RPG hit us, we were toast,' said van Carrapiett. The guerrillas would also blaze away with their rifles and, though bullets alone were unlikely to bring down a Chinook, they could pierce the sides and cause serious injuries, even death.

As the Chinook scooted across the desert towards Sangin, the medics, shouting through the bells-of-hell din from the howling engines and the massive rotors front and back, drew up a plan of action. With just one casualty to pick up from a site that was known to be 'hot', it made sense not to go for the full landing procedure. The protection force would not be deployed. Instead, as soon as the ramp went down, van Carrapiett and the anaesthetist, Colonel Griffiths, would run off with a stretcher, shove the casualty on it and be back inside in seconds. The Chinook came to ground and, as it settled, they dashed out into the pitch-black night. Dust from the down-draught was swirling everywhere. They were all but blind. The loadmaster, hanging from the rear door, pointed them into the gloom, towards a figure he had spotted. A soldier was waving his hands in the air, but not to guide them towards him but to tell them to go away! 'Get back on the fucking helicopter,' he yelled. They had come down in the wrong place, into a contact zone. Fortunately, the man signalling at them was friend not foe – he could all too easily have been a Taliban fighter, with disastrous consequences. 'We got back on, the helicopter took off again and we spent forty-five minutes in the air, circling. Sitting in the back, we didn't know if we were lost or what was happening.'

In fact, they were in the right place but the area was simply not safe to land a Chinook. Taliban gunmen were in the woods bordering the pick-up zone and sniping at the picket line of soldiers that had fanned out to protect Stockton until he could be 'cas-evaced'[7] out. There was a delay, therefore, until an Apache gunship arrived from Camp Bastion and raked the edge of the trees with machine-gun fire. Stockton and Gary Lawrence cowered in the back of the Land Rover as, for twenty minutes, the air outside shook with the 'phenomenal noise' of the gunship in action. 'An Apache hovering above you with the chain gun going is pretty scary,' said Lawrence. But it was also a welcome noise because it meant rescue was near. The firing ceased after twenty minutes, and then they heard the Chinook. Suddenly, Lawrence recalled, Stockton was all action again. He snapped out of the advanced stage of shock he had been in and stepped out of the vehicle, a cigarette glowing in his good hand, as the helicopter, like some giant insect, touched down on the ground.

For van Carrapiett, it was the same drill as before. 'The ramp dropped and we dashed out into the dark. I was on the front end of the stretcher, the colonel on the back.' Only afterwards did it occur to anyone what an astonishing spectacle this was, one that confounded centuries of military tradition. Two officers, one of them a colonel, racing to the rescue of a front-line casualty – it was unheard of in previous conflicts but, in twenty-first-century warfare, was now normal practice. 'We spotted a Land Rover and sprinted towards it. I saw a guy and I reached out to grab his arm so I could lean towards him and shout in his ear above the deafening noise from the helicopter. There was no arm there! I found myself shaking his humerus, his bone. This had to be the casualty, then. He refused the stretcher. He walked towards the helicopter, which was quite remarkable, considering.'

Before reaching the Chinook, Stockton stopped and turned.

'Cheers, Loz,' he called back to Lawrence. 'Thanks very much.'
Then he walked up the ramp. Once inside he was made to lie
down on a stretcher and strapped in as the Chinook took off and
headed to Bastion, 'head down and fast, because this guy obviously
needed to get to an operating theatre quickly'.

Back on the ground, Gary Lawrence ducked down against the
blast of wind and dust from the helicopter. He was relieved to see
the sergeant major on his way. He had done what he could, and
done it well. Crucially, he had contained the bleeding. Otherwise,
Andy Stockton's bones would have quickly joined those of the
thousands of other British soldiers whose blood, over the centuries,
has seeped away 'on Afghanistan's plains', as the poet of British
imperialism, Rudyard Kipling, put it. As the sound of the helicopter died away, the medic still had work to do. The rescue force
was strung out in defensive lines, waiting for the chance to make
the dash back to the reinforced walls of FOB Robinson. Lawrence
moved from man to man, 'checking on the guys to see if there's
any injuries, if anybody needs anything. It wasn't until I'd gone
down one side and was just coming back up the other side that an
officer stopped me and asked me, "Loz, have you eaten, have you
had anything to drink?" I hadn't, so he ordered me to take a rest.
I lay down and just collapsed. I was absolutely knackered. I'd gone
four or five hours without food or water, running on adrenalin.
In the heat of it all, you just forget about those things. It was
Andy's life that mattered.'

That life, and the preservation of it, was also now concerning
van Carrapiett. As the helicopter bumped and bucked its way to
Camp Bastion, 'I checked his ABC – airway, breathing, circulation
– which may sound silly, since his problem was obvious: his arm
was hanging off. But there is always the danger that a gross injury
like this sidetracks you from some other life-threatening problem,
gunshot wounds in the chest, for example, something that he may
not even be aware of. You have to make sure he's not leaking
blood from another hole.'

Small metal fragments were devils. Undetected and left in the
chest, the risk was peritonitis; in the buttocks and the result could

be a perforated rectum; in the neck and the patient might die from a blood clot. So van Carrapiett checked thoroughly en route. It was not as easy a procedure as it sounds. Lawrence had had enough difficulty treating Stockton in a slow-moving Land Rover. In the air, in the vibrating hull of the Chinook, with no lights and the deafening noise blotting out everything else, it was next to impossible. 'You're wearing a helmet and, for most of the time, you can't hear anything,' said van Carrapiett.

A stethoscope isn't much use because you have to be able to hear the heart beating or the lungs inflating, and at 50 feet off the ground and more than 100 miles per hour, that's just not going to happen. Even taking a pulse, the most basic of clinical checks, is incredibly hard. And these difficulties are multiplied tenfold when it's the middle of the night or when you're under fire. I was proud of myself just for getting a cannula [a needle for delivering fluids] into a wounded soldier. In a casualty department in the NHS, it's fairly simple. In the dark in the back of a helicopter, believe me, it's bloody difficult.

He managed to get a line into Stockton and put him on an intravenous drip of pain relief and antibiotics. 'After that we just did our best to make him comfortable and to reassure him. We talked to him, told him he would be all right. It was a couple of hours since he had been hit. If people are going to die from unsustainable injuries, then, generally speaking, they do so within the first thirty to forty-five minutes. That he was still with us was an important clinical indicator that he was going to make it.'

But, even now, nothing could be taken for granted. The injury was a catastrophic one and needed urgent attention. The Chinook was hardly the most soothing of ambulances to ride in, but the sergeant major, with the morphine kicking in, recalled the flight back to Bastion as 'pretty comfortable', though, not surprisingly, he was hazy about the detail.

The medics moved around me, making sure I was okay. As we landed and the ramp came down, I saw an ambulance backing up to the door, so I made to get up off the stretcher, whether from shock or bravado, I'm not sure. I remember thinking that stretchers were for sick people, not me! They made me lie down again, and they carried me off. Suddenly, I felt really cold, and as I got into the emergency room, my legs started to shake uncontrollably as delayed shock set in. The doc stood over me and introduced his med team. It seemed bizarre. I had just been airlifted out of a firefight where people were trying to kill me, and the next moment I'm in this place where everyone is so civilized, calm and professional, no shouting or screaming or yelling of orders. The doc explained that they were going to have to take me straight to theatre and that it didn't look good for my arm. 'Do what you have to do, Doc,' I said. The anaesthetist leaned over, and told me I would soon be asleep . . . and then everything went black.

The 'Doc', as Stockton called the surgeon about to wield a scalpel on him, was Lieutenant Colonel Paul Parker. The thing about soldiers, he remarked to his colleagues as they took up their positions around the sergeant major's comatose body, was that they were 'like lab-rats, they're very difficult to kill'.[8] They were young and fit and capable of handling the sort of trauma that would completely pole-axe others. 'They're muscular, and their arteries are muscular too. When an arm is blown off by an RPG or a mine, the little muscles in the artery walls constrict and go into spasm, and that can save them. A shot in the groin or the armpit is much worse and can be a killer, because you can't easily get to the artery to control the bleeding.' Stockton's injury, for all its obvious gore (not to mention the devastating implications for him and the rest of his life) was a classic war wound, an injury that could have been sustained any time in the past four hundred years – 'a musket ball could have done it, or a cannonball.'

There was no chance of saving the arm whatsoever, Parker concluded. 'The hand was cold and blue and facing the wrong way. It had to be amputated, and you just get on with it.' (Just to be on the safe side, however, he had photographs taken showing that the arm was completely unsalvageable. 'I didn't want him going back to the UK and some fancy young surgeon, far from the battlefield, saying, if I'd been there, I could have saved your arm.') Parker now snipped the sinew still holding the lower arm and a medic carried the severed limb away. Then Parker removed the combat tourniquet – which, for all the trouble Gary Lawrence had had with it, had proved very effective – tied off the artery, then went to work with a saw on the bone, just as army doctors did under similar circumstances in the Crimea or the American Civil War a hundred and fifty years ago. He cut swiftly through the bone, then turned his knife on the raw pieces of traumatized muscle. 'Anything that looks like hamburger is bad, it has no blood supply and is dead and has to be cut away. Fillet steak is best – well-defined tissue with a good blood supply!' It was all done in forty-five minutes. Parker tidied up the skin around the stump but left it unstitched for now. Finally, the wound was loosely dressed. It was not stuffed with swabs or tightly bound, as a lay person might expect an injury of this severity to be and as surgeons would have done before the Second World War. Modern military medicine dictates that the flesh be left open to the air and given a chance to heal naturally. 'I was taught,' Parker declared, 'that wounds of war need to be packed lightly and with soft, fluffy things, like a lady's handbag'. Cotton wool, gauze and a crepe bandage now covered the spot where Andy Stockton's lower arm had once been.

★

In the home in Wiltshire she shared with Andy, Emma had gone to bed with the dog for company. It was a hot summer's night and she slept fitfully.

Then I thought I heard a knock at the door, but the fan was on and making a racket and the dog didn't stir so I thought, no, I'm half asleep, dreaming. But the knocking was persistent. I looked at the clock and it was 3 a.m. I was a woman alone in the house and thought, 'I'm not going down to answer it. I'll peep out of the bedroom window.' On the porch below was a man in a suit – and for the life of me I couldn't think what he was doing there, in a suit, at 3 a.m. I shouted down:

'What do you want?' And then from out of the darkness I saw a young lady in military uniform. That woke me up. I could see that the man in the suit was a captain Andy and I'd served with in Iraq. Then I knew – this is the moment we all dread.

From her window, Emma called out the question that instantly formed in her mind. 'Oh my God, is it the worst?' The captain shook his head. Relieved, she ran down the stairs and let them in.

I was shaking and I had gone all cold but I wasn't hysterical. He said that Andy had been shot. 'Shot, where?' I asked. 'In his arm.' 'Which arm?' 'I don't know.' 'Is his arm still there?' 'I don't know.' I thought, 'He knows, but he's not telling me.' Being ex-military, as I am, it's worse, because you know what a bullet can do. My mind went into overdrive, trying to think through what was happening. I didn't scream or cry. I was just sitting on the corner of the sofa and I was shaking. He said he'd just spoken on the phone to the chief surgeon out in Afghanistan and that Andy was stable and just about to go into the operating theatre. They didn't tell me at that point that he was going to lose an arm.

The captain and his colleague didn't stay long. Emma told them to go. She wanted to be on her own to digest the news. ' I sat out in the garden in the dark, back on the lounger. The dog was pottering about and I was just sitting there thinking, "Oh my God, what's just happened?" I was holding on to what they'd told me – "He's stable." I remember telling myself, "He's stable, so that's all right . . . even though it could go one way or the other, at the minute he's stable . . . and I'm sure he's going to be fine . . . he's going to be fine."'

And Stockton was indeed fine, and proving himself as hardy as any laboratory rat. He had woken from the operation as the orderlies loaded him on to the trolley to take him to a ward. There he asked the nurse: 'Can I have a fag, please?' Not surprisingly, the request was denied, and it was a while before he managed to wangle a smoke. Lt-Col. Parker got up for breakfast after snatching a few hours back in his bunk after the operation. 'Outside the entrance to the hospital, I saw Mr Stockton calmly smoking a cigarette. One of his mates passed by and called out, "Hey, Andy, what's the time?" He made to look at his watch, but of course it wasn't there, and they both fell about laughing. Typical squaddie black humour!'

Flight Lieutenant van Carrapiett saw him too, later the same day, and could hardly believe it. 'He was outside, having a fag, having a chat. It was great to see him, because it meant the whole medical system was working. He was in a bad way when we brought him in, and a few hours later he's on his feet, having a ciggie and a laugh. I read a few months later that he'd taken up one-arm water skiing. Brilliant – that's what our job is about.'

In England, the phone rang in Emma's house at 9.30 that morning. She'd already been on to the army welfare staff and thought it was them calling back. Instead, she heard a familiar, chirpy voice: 'Hiya, babe, it's me.' On the other end, Andy was chatting away as if nothing had happened. 'He didn't say anything about being shot – he was making small talk.' Finally, she asked him outright about his arm, though she didn't actually use the word. 'Is *it* still there?' 'No.' 'It's gone then?' 'Yeah.' 'Are you all right?' 'Yeah, yeah, I'm fine, it's gone, I'm all right, really lucky, could have been dead. I'm fine, I'll be coming home soon.' 'How much has gone?' 'Just below the shoulder.'

'He didn't seem down or anything,' said Emma. 'My initial reaction was Thank God he's still alive. He's lost an arm, but that doesn't matter at the minute. A little bit selfishly, I also thought, "He won't be going back there to Afghanistan again now." A pretty hefty price to pay, mind.' It was after she put the phone down that, for the first time since that 3 a.m. knock at the door, she began to cry. 'I was wandering round the house and seeing all the pictures of him. There was one in the lounge with both his arms round me, and I was thinking, "Oh, that arm's not there now. He's never going to put both his arms around me again." And that's when the tears came.'

Stockton was on an immediate evacuation flight back to England and, a matter of hours after the RPG crashed through his arm beside a canal in Afghanistan, he was lying back in the calm atmosphere of Selly Oak Hospital in Birmingham. An anxious Emma arrived with his mother to see him.

He was in a side room and, at first, we walked past him. Then I saw him in the corner of my eye, in lovely salmon-coloured pyjamas! There were two St John Ambulance women with him – he was charming the ladies, as usual! I rushed into the room, but I didn't know what to do. Do I give him a hug? Would he be able to hug? Would it hurt him if we did? I'd expected him to be lying in bed, but he was standing up, and I was very conscious of looking at his arm, and then worried that I was staring at it. 'What do we do? What do we say to each other?' I thought. Then he asked: 'Are you coming outside for a cigarette?' and I knew he was still the same Andy. We managed a hug. The partner who'd left me to go to war was back, just minus an arm.

★

War is a brutal business with terrible physical consequences, and Andy Stockton had been at its cruel cutting edge. His departure from Camp Bastion coincided with the arrival of a British government minister on one of those heavily orchestrated whirlwind tours to rally the troops. They met briefly, and one observer noted laconically that the visitor from Westminster 'at least had the good grace to look embarrassed as he shook the sergeant major's *good* hand'. Blushes apart, it is right for those who make the decisions that put other men in the firing line to see at close quarters the results of what they ordain, to confront the butcher's bill. That bill is the stock in trade of medics. It falls to them to witness the terrifying consequences of combat, to deal with inhumanity in its starkest form.

Young doctors joining the Royal Army Medical Corps in 1941, perhaps the bleakest period of the Second World War for Britain, when catastrophic defeats in Africa and the Far East left little to be optimistic about, were offered this prospectus for what lay ahead for them: 'In battle you will live dangerously and you will feel the grip of fear. You will be unarmed amid violent, indiscriminate lethality. To you, the hurt and the frightened will turn for easement and comfort. The work that you do – under conditions that will range from the merely inconvenient to the utterly impossible – will be of the very greatest importance.'[9]

Sixty-five years later, Gary Lawrence, Damien van Carrapiett, Paul Parker and all those working with them were doing exactly that in Afghanistan. Their courage and dedication were the saving of Sergeant Major Stockton.

2. Inhumanity

Medics are not to be taken for granted, as if they had always existed, their presence on the battlefield assured. On the contrary, historically, men going to war have seldom been able to rely on medical intervention to save their lives. Indeed, if the history of humanity were measured by the way it treats those who fight its battles, then it is only in the last hundred years that we have come out of the Dark Ages. Since time immemorial, ordinary soldiers, professionals and conscripts alike, have been treated as cannon-fodder – and, before artillery was invented, as bow-fodder, sword-fodder, club-fodder, fist-fodder. Even into the twentieth century, their welfare has been of little importance to their commanders or to those people whose interests they fight to defend. It was Rudyard Kipling who, in his poem 'Tommy', captured the hypocrisy of a society that delighted in the glory of war but turned its nose up at the warriors, until they were needed to do the dirty work.

> O it's Tommy this, an' Tommy that, an "Tommy, go away";
> But it's "Thank you, Mister Atkins", when the band begins to play
> Yes it's Tommy this, an' Tommy that, an' "Chuck him out, the brute!"
> But it's "Saviour of 'is country" when the guns begin to shoot.[1]

If ordinary soldiers were snubbed when able-bodied, then their position was hopeless when wounded. The accounts of wars and great battles give short shrift to the maimed. They often have to slink home to a society whose gratitude and forbearance all too quickly dry up. The world moves on, yet they are left with their scars, physical and, increasingly these days, mental. Men blinded by chlorine gas in the First World War sold matches in the street. After the Second, there were few jobs for the one-legged victims of anti-personnel mines, one of its most pernicious (and, sadly, most enduring) innovations. In the United States, wounded veterans of Vietnam returned to a nation that was embarrassed by their existence. And so it has gone on into the twenty-first century. Iraq and Afghanistan are whirlwinds of human tragedy, the full consequences of which we are yet to reap. If the dismissive reaction of some people to troops returning from those conflicts is any indication, then the future may not be much better.

Saving lives rather than destroying them has rarely been a priority of the battlefield. Surgeons travelled with Julius Caesar's legions and, a millennium later, with William the Conqueror when the Normans invaded Britain. In the countless wars in the intervening centuries, there was no such help, and wounded men were left to die where they fell, saved only if camp-following wives came to their rescue. In medieval times, the Knights of St John of Jerusalem provided hospitals for the Crusaders – though their medical skills were rudimentary compared with those of Saladin's doctors. But what medical support existed was for the high-born. One of the duties of a knight's squire was to carry dressings and ointments such as arnica to treat his lord in battle. But the common soldiers could rot.

Not that rank was a guarantee of survival. Richard I died of his wounds after the clumsy extraction of an arrow from his shoulder. Another king, however, Edward I, was saved by a surgeon who cut away the morbid flesh around a deep wound (not that very different from the way in which Sergeant Major Andy Stockton's arm was debrided and cleansed in Afghanistan in 2006). Henry V had twenty physicians in the army he took to France in 1415. They were overwhelmed, as medics so often are in warfare. Dysentery swept away soldiers in their thousands, but surgeons did manage to save the Duke of Gloucester, successfully binding up a potentially fatal stab wound in his abdomen and sending him back to England. Again, the common soldiery were not so privileged. The hopelessly wounded were put out of their misery, their throats cut, while those with survivable injuries were paid off and abandoned to find their own way home.

Slowly, the importance of trying to save lives was realized, out of practicality as much as philosophy. Fighting men were a commodity not to be wasted – patch up the wounded and send them back into the fray. But the methods employed were gruesome in the extreme and often hastened death rather than preventing it. Wounds – particularly from gunshots, the consequence of increasing use of gunpowder – were treated with boiling oil to stem the bloodflow. The patient screamed in agony until he passed out, sometimes never to wake again. Shattered limbs, liable to become gangrenous, were hacked off with knives and saws, and a red-hot iron was used to seal the blood vessels. The better sort of surgeon sewed up the arteries and even put on a tourniquet first, a French innovation of 1674 which proved an enduring (if controversial) life-saver over the succeeding centuries. A French treatment that did not last was sucking wounds to cleanse them and then packing them with chewed pieces of paper.

The courage of soldiers undergoing any of these procedures without anaesthetic can still catch the breath, all the more so because such drastic remedies were happening far more recently than, in our ignorance, we might imagine. Take this spine-chilling account from Henry Durant in 1859, just 150 years ago, after the Battle of Solferino.

With one knee on the ground and a terrible knife in his hand, the surgeon threw his arm around the soldier's thigh and with a single movement cut the skin around the mangled leg. A piercing cry rang through the hospital. The young doctor, looking into the suffering man's face, could see the frightful agony he was undergoing. 'Be brave,' he said under his breath. 'Two more minutes and you will be all right.' The surgeon began to separate the skin from the muscles under it. Then he cut away the flesh from the skin and raised the skin about an inch, like a sort of cuff. Then, with a vigorous movement, he cut through the muscles with his knife as far as the bone. A torrent of blood burst from the opened muscles, covering the surgeon and dripping on to the floor.

The patient, in an ecstasy of pain, muttered weakly, 'Oh let me die,' and cold sweat ran down his face. But there was still another minute to go through, a minute that seemed like eternity. 'An assistant counted the seconds, looking from the operator to the patient's face and back again, trying to sustain his courage and seeing him shaking with terror. It was now time for the saw and I could hear the grating of the steel as it entered the living bone and separated the half-rotten limb from the body . . .²

The young soldier somehow survived, but his ordeal and that of the other thirty thousand dead and wounded on that single day – and as many again succumbing in the following two months from disease, infection and exhaustion – so shocked Dunant that he devoted himself to founding the International Red Cross organization.

But it was a struggle to get military commanders to think in humanitarian terms. Wellington was, at best, lukewarm about his men's suffering and the need for doctors, at worst, contemptuous. His chief of medical services, James McGrigor, dared to disagree with the Iron Duke's indifference. 'In the proper execution of their duties,' he wrote, 'medical officers are frequently under fire. Some were killed and many lost limbs in sieges and battles. Yet it has been ignorantly advanced by some military men that the medical men have no business in exposed situations and they would deny the medical officer a pension for the loss of a limb. Yet the cases are numerous wherein the lives of officers and soldiers have been saved by the zealous medical officers of their regiments being on hand to repress haemorrhage.'

Napoleon put Wellington to shame. His armies were the first to develop ways of getting quantities of wounded men off the battlefield, while also bringing the best of medical care to them as soon as possible. The Emperor's medics went to war, a dozen at a time, in specially designed carriages drawn by six horses. Chests held dressings for more than a thousand injuries. All this was at the behest of his surgeon-in-chief, Baron Percy, who was 'distressed at seeing the deaths of so great a number of soldiers whose lives might have been preserved and limbs saved. One cannot too often repeat that the chief consolation and the assistance of first importance to a wounded man is for him to be carried promptly and properly from the scene of conflict.' This was a big advance on leaving men to die where they fell, the practice of millennia past.

All the crucial steps in battlefield medicine at this time were French. The innovators, Percy, and his colleague, Baron Larrey, were never far from the front line. Larrey saw action in all of Napoleon's campaigns – at sixty battles and four hundred skirmishes. On the retreat from Moscow, he performed two hip-joint amputations (the most difficult and dangerous of this type of operation) and put himself in such danger as he arranged passage for the sick that the soldiers in his party had to restrain him. In one battle he commandeered 150 wheelbarrows to trundle the wounded to safety.

The British Army closed its eyes and shut its ears to such advances, as was cruelly and disastrously exposed in the Crimean War. The scandal, every bit as significant as the diabolical hospital conditions that Florence Nightingale alighted on at Scutari, was that British generals had mounted an expedition to Russia with little thought for the treatment of casualties or any equipment for dealing with them on the battlefield. Medical wagons along the lines of the French model were available and indeed were landed from supply ships. But the horses to pull them were not. Officers, their eyes on military glory, were blind to such needs, giving cavalry mounts precedence. The commanding officer of one regiment took one look at the panniers of medical supplies and dismissed them as 'useless encumbrances'. He left them on the quayside, where they stayed, while the soldiers whose lives they could have saved died of cholera, and all the doctor could offer them was a sip of brandy mixed with cayenne pepper.

The Crimea was a disgrace for the British Army. There were no stretcher-bearers, no hospital ships, no sense of the value of saving life. Nonetheless, the doctors did what they could, and magnificently. Three won Victoria Crosses for treating the wounded under fire. Afterwards, there was supposedly a change in attitude to medical care of troops, but how much the generals really cared was still debatable. When Kitchener took an army of nearly ten thousand to the Sudan in 1896, he could only be bothered to include five medical officers. In the Boer War a few years later he drastically cut back medical supplies when it suited him.

And yet the ability to inflict injury was increasing exponentially. The second half of the nineteenth century was remarkable for a boom in weapons technology, each device that little bit more lethal than the one before as slaughter moved on to an industrial scale. The American Civil War of 1860–64 was crucial, the breeding ground for an array of new killing machines and their accessories – repeating rifles, land mines, booby traps, revolving gun turrets, flame throwers, trench periscopes and the first machine gun. Medicine struggled to keep up. At Gettysburg there were fifty-five thousand casualties, and the makeshift operating tables, often just a barn door or plank of wood, ran red with blood. Severed limbs were tossed aside until the pile was level with the tables. But at least there was now ether or chloroform to dull the pain, for some. There was not enough to go round, and the lightly wounded had to grit their teeth, bite on a piece of wood or simply scream and sob.

The sciences of medicine and war have advanced, one behind the other, ever since. The Franco-Prussian War dealt out death as never before. The latest machine guns had 25 revolving barrels spitting out 125 rounds a minute. But, then, the victims of their salvos had a better chance of surviving because chemists Lister and Pasteur had done the research that led to the development of antiseptics. Disease had always killed more men than bullets or blades. Now there was a chance of tackling gangrene and other deadly wound infections. As for those machine guns, what came out of their multiple barrels were thin, coned bullets, which passed through human flesh and made cleaner wounds than the exploding musket balls they replaced.

The First World War was not the revolutionary event it is often deemed to be. In the techniques of inflicting human suffering, it was the culmination of all that had gone before but magnified to obscene levels. The casualty *rate*, in fact, was no different from wars before and since, but with armies counted in millions and offensives that lasted for weeks, the *numbers* of dead and injured were simply astronomical. To those taking part, it felt like the end of civilization. In many ways it was – living in trenches, bombed, gassed, advancing through minefields and into machine guns, dying in foxholes, drowning in mud.

The medical services had – like the rest of the military – gone into the war with a plan. Getting the casualties out was what mattered. There was a well-defined chain of evacuation, from regimental aid post to dressing stations, casualty clearing stations and field hospitals well behind the front line, the latter staffed by members of the Royal Army Medical Corps, which had been set up as a separate, specialist military unit twenty years earlier. The idea was that there would be little surgery on the front line, just a patching and dispatching. The theory didn't survive the reality for a minute. In the offensives, when men with fixed bayonets marched in lines against machine guns, the regimental first-aid posts became butcher's shops where the already dying were cast aside and the maimed but just viable operated on in extremis to give them the barest chance of reaching hospital alive.

Often, writes historian John Laffin, that first-aid post 'was no more than two orderlies crouching in a shell-hole or behind a pile of sandbags with a stretcher beside them. At best, it was a low-ceilinged shelter in a dug-out with just enough room for a doctor, his assistant and a table. In the heat of an action, their clothing would be saturated with blood. There would be men holding their intestines in both hands, broken bones tearing flesh, arteries spurting blood, bared brains, maimed hands, empty eye sockets, pierced chests, skin hanging down in tatters from a burned face, missing lower jaws. The only light was from acetylene lamps, flashlights or candles. Sometimes it was necessary to work in the dark, with doctors groping to wind or unwind a bandage.'

Further along the evacuation chain, conditions were marginally less frantic but every bit as harrowing. Chloroform was a boon and so was morphine, but 'there was so much to be done and so many soldiers for whom surgery could do so little – the abdominal cases, who died quickly; the brain cases, who took a long time to die.' And of all the dreadful wounds in war, the lacerating brain wound was the hardest to treat. 'Restless, noisy, delirious, the victim struggled with the orderlies, babbling incoherently, crying for water and yet spitting it out when brought.'[3]

For First World War medics, the tidy idea of surgeons operating in some safe, calm, sanitized spot away from the sights, sounds and smells of war was a Dr Finlay-type fantasy. To save lives most effectively, doctors had to get as close as they could to where those lives were in danger. Ninety years on, the same discussion takes place. Should medical services be concentrated on the front line or behind it? Military doctors in Iraq and Afghanistan can't decide whether the priority should be faster evacuation – with, say, a dedicated helicopter fleet for the wounded – or sending the very best of surgeons right into the heart of the fighting and risking them being killed and their critical life-saving medical skills lost. The difficulty in this debate is that, in today's wars against terrorists and insurgents, there is no front line nor any safe haven behind it. But, in reality, it was always thus. More often than not, medics of all degrees have had no choice in the matter of where they did their duty. The front line not only came to them but sometimes totally overwhelmed them – as it did most memorably on the beaches of Dunkirk in 1940.

3. Overwhelmed

Major Ralph Brooke, a surgeon in the Royal Army Medical Corps, had much to think about as he set off from Southampton for France at the beginning of 1940 with the 400,000-strong British Expeditionary Force to bolster the French and Belgian armies against Adolf Hitler. What was preying on his mind was a lecture he had listened to by a surgeon in the Spanish Civil War, which had ended just a year before.

Josep Trueta had been a doctor with the defeated Republican forces, operating on those wounded in air raids and ground attacks in a beleaguered Barcelona. He had fled Spain after General Franco's victory, and in London had introduced an audience of doctors at the Royal Society of Medicine to the horrors of modern warfare. What imprinted itself on Brooke's mind was the picture Trueta painted of a never-ending stream of casualties, and of doctors having to choose to treat only those they thought could be saved. 'The surgeon,' Brooke wrote, 'was forced to turn a deaf ear to the pleadings of the hopeless cases.'[1]

This life-and-death dilemma fascinated and horrified him. As a qualified barrister as well as a doctor, he found this an affront to the rights of the gravely injured. Yet he knew such choices lay ahead for him when what so far had been a phoney war with Germany turned into the real thing. Much responsibility would fall on people like him if lives were to be saved and the fighting men properly supported in the way they deserved. 'It is not a comforting thought that our sons may be left to die after the battle because there is such a press of work and the number of surgeons is so small,' Brooke mused. 'If they are not to be denied their chance of survival, there must be sufficient personnel to deal with a sudden influx of cases as efficiently as at home. An enormous demand will be made on the medical services. Will this be met?' It was a good question.

He himself was giving up a lot to do what he perceived as his duty. Leaving behind his private consultancy on the Sussex coast meant a drastic drop in pay, from £6,000 a year (well in excess of £250,000 today) to an army officer's salary of £800. He could only hope that other established doctors like him would follow his lead, forego their comfortable lives at home and not flinch from the colours. He also knew he would have to put his life in serious jeopardy if he was to do his job as an army surgeon effectively. 'One of the most important lessons we have learned from the Spanish War is that the wounded must be treated in the first four or five hours after they have been wounded, if they are to be saved. This can only be achieved by pushing the operating centres up to as near the front line as possible. Surgeons must themselves be prepared for sacrifices and the medical profession for a high mortality amongst its more skilled members.'

In even thinking about such matters, Brooke was streets ahead of his military commanders. The extensive medical service built up in the First World War had been dismantled afterwards in the vain hope that 'the War to End All Wars' had done precisely that. The regular ranks of the Royal Army Medical Corps were cut to a little over five thousand officers and men, but even more drastic was the pruning of the Territorials. The number of TA field ambulance units was slashed from forty-five to fifteen, general hospitals from twenty-three to three, and the fifteen casualty clearing stations axed completely. It would not be the last time that, in some post-conflict economy drive, Britain's military medicine machine would be stripped to the bone.[2] Nor was any attention given to the next generation of military doctors. RAMC doctors not only lagged way behind their civilian contemporaries in earning potential but, for unfathomable reasons, were on a lower pay grade than officers in fighting regiments. The result was that, in 1924, only seven candidates applied for forty new commissions and the entrance examination was cancelled.[3]

As for the work itself, it was less battlefield and more bureaucratic, its emphasis switched very much from surgery to hygiene and general health. Beneficial and important as this was, it meant that regimental medical officers were generally more skilled in siting latrines than in amputating limbs. Things did change as Britain woke up to the threat from Nazi Germany, and there was a sudden expansion of Territorial units, though to still only a fraction of its 1918 complement. With the outbreak of war in September 1939, frantic efforts were made to plug the gaps. Ralph Brooke was among those called from their hospital rounds and consulting rooms to do their duty.

The thoroughness and high expectation with which he approached his responsibilities were dented when he arrived at Camiers, near Boulogne, to find a shanty-town of Nissen huts and tents masquerading as a hospital capable of treating four thousand casualties. The lack of running water was just one problem, though there was plenty of it soaking the ground, where the spaces between beds were ankle-deep in mud. In the makeshift operating theatres there were tarpaulins on the floor instead of boards, and naked gas burners hung above the tables for light. Of this and other tented army hospitals in northern France, Brooke wrote, 'Sepsis everywhere. It is quite unsafe to open the abdomen or the knee joint under such conditions.' The military medical services, he concluded, had been allowed to lag behind every advance in medicine. 'We have the equipment of the last war. We will just have to do the best we can.' He could not believe how the follies of 1914–18 were being repeated. There had been a hospital at Camiers then, and it had been bombed frequently, because it was beside the railway line to Paris. Hundreds of nurses had been killed. 'Now we are at war again, and the same incredibly foolish mistakes are being made again.'

As usual, the generals and the politicians had based their forward planning on how the last conflict had played out. The Maginot line would keep the Germans at bay and, if they did manage to pierce it, the war would quickly settle into a repeat of the static lines and trenched stalemate of the Western Front *circa* 1916. The military theorists who prophesied a fast-moving, tank-driven war with *blitzkrieg* – literally, 'lightning war' – thrusts of startling aggression and daring were ignored. The orthodox view prevailed, which, in terms of medical dispositions, meant a familiar staged structure of 1) regimental aid posts and advanced dressing stations in the front line, 2) large and generally fixed RAMC field ambulance units consisting of up to 250 doctors, medics, orderlies, drivers, etc., who would stabilize casualties so they could be evacuated to, 3) even more massive casualty clearing stations, from where the wounded would be filtered and funnelled to 4) base hospitals such as Camiers or by hospital ship back to England.[4]

The German strike through Belgium in the second week of May, bypassing France's defences and dashing for the Channel coast, swept aside such tidy notions. In the disaster that was about to befall the British Expeditionary Force, doctors, orderlies and stretcher-bearers, with lives depending on them, would be the ones to stay at their posts and to keep their heads while, in the largest retreat in British military history, all around were losing theirs.

*

In a village in Belgium near the historic battlefield at Waterloo, Corporal R. H. Montague was in charge of a four-man RAMC stretcher party at an advanced dressing station. He watched kilted Cameron Highlanders, bayonets fixed on their bolt-action Lee Enfield rifles, heading forward cheerily to meet the advancing German forces. One tapped the blade and said, 'Jerry does'na like this.'[5] They never got close enough to find out the truth or otherwise of this proposition: bayonets were useless against tanks and crack infantry armed with rapid-fire Schmeisser machine pistols. Casualties were soon staggering back into the aid post, which itself came under fire from heavy-calibre mortars. Shells broke against the cobbled street and sent showers of lethal shrapnel into the air. It was time to move, and fast. The wounded were shovelled into ambulances, supplies into a 30cwt truck, and Montague stood on the rear step and clung on to the door handle as the 6th British Field Ambulance retreated at speed towards Brussels. There, they and two other medical companies arrived at the fashionable Hôtel Haute Maison, where, to their amazement, smartly dressed Belgian army officers and their ladies were sitting down to a formal dinner and dance.

It was a scene reminiscent of the Duchess of Richmond's famous ball on the eve of Waterloo a century and a quarter earlier – except that this time what was staring everyone in the face was not a famous victory but abject defeat. 'They seemed blissfully unaware that their country was being overrun by a ruthless and well-equipped enemy,' Montague recalled. 'We, on the other hand, were straight from battle with fifty casualties in need of surgery.' The hotel manager took one horrified look inside the ambulances pulled up outside and called a halt instantly to the party. As the Belgian officers and their *mesdemoiselles* were hustled out into the night, the ballroom was turned into a reception area for stretchers and the dining room into an improvised operating theatre. Napkins and tablecloths were torn up for theatre linen and, by the light of the chandeliers, two medical officers performed twenty operations, with the dental officer as anaesthetist.

The German divisions forged on, and as they broke through into the outskirts of Brussels, Montague's outfit checked out of the hotel in a hurry, packing their supplies into wicker panniers, which they tossed into the trucks. The casualties, a dozen of them newly out of theatre, were loaded into the ambulances, and the convoy was off again. This was not how anyone had ever envisaged running a battlefield medical service but, as Montague noted matter-of-factly, 'The rapid advance by the enemy and the fluid state of the front line rendered the old system of evacuation of the wounded impossible.'

One night they set up in a convent, the next in a school, then in an old brewery, a château and a farm. At an abandoned shoe factory, 150 casualties turned up at 11 p.m. Captain Ian Samuel, a GP until just a few months ago, and another doctor, performed eighteen operations over the next ten hours, including several amputations. A lull in the work at mid-morning gave them a short breather, but more casualties arrived and they were back at the table, cutting out a length of damaged bowel, closing up chest injuries and plugging liver wounds.[6] Then they were on the move again. This was medicine on the run in what was turning into a full-scale rout.

Fighter planes flew overhead and buzzed them, strafing and bombing. The Englishmen had a grandstand view of the latest in weapons technology as dive bombers obliterated a town. Wave after wave of Junker 87 planes plunged to within a couple of hundred metres of the tops of buildings to release their loads. 'The planes and the bombs emitted a high-pitched scream, which had a shattering effect on the morale of those below. We found ourselves caring not just for badly wounded British and French soldiers but local civilians. Many of the women and children were quite demented and very difficult for us to pacify.'

Here was the sort of mass-casualty situation the Spanish doctor Trueta had described in his lecture in London just a few months earlier. Now, every pocket of resistance was subjected to a Guernica bombardment from the air, with terrible consequences. Huge numbers of casualties were building up at the dressing station, which was handling as many as five hundred new cases a day. Samuel was so tired after hours of operations that he fell asleep leaning against a barn wall and only woke up when he fell over.

Whenever the medical convoy moved, it did so at night, slowly making its way down narrow roads clogged with fleeing refugees and retreating soldiers. 'We were utterly weary, unpacking the equipment, dealing with casualties, repacking our ever-diminishing supplies and on the move again.'

Where precisely to stop and set up was a recurring problem. It was no good having a dressing station that casualties could not find or be directed to, but the situation was so fluid that any location was a matter of chance and last-minute choice. They tried to pick sites near churches and then post red crosses and arrows at the nearest crossroads. At night, a four-gallon petrol drum was upended, the shape of a cross cut in the middle and covered in red paper and a hurricane lamp placed inside. In the darkness of a blacked-out landscape, it would be a beacon of hope for the wounded, but also a tempting target for an enemy, who, many BEF medics feared, had little regard for such sanctuaries, whatever the strictures of the Geneva Convention. One ambulance unit identified itself as open for business by planting a large red cross flag in the ground. Within minutes it took a direct hit from a bomber. A clearly marked hospital ship, the *Maid of Kent*, was sunk in Dieppe harbour by German bombers, and an ambulance train that had pulled up on the quay next to her was flattened.

Montague found himself having to cope with sights and smells and sensations beyond anything he had ever experienced. In a matter of days, death had become commonplace in his world, but he was particularly moved by a nineteen-year-old second lieutenant whose bullet-shattered and gangrenous leg had to be cut off. He died in the night, and his burial in the morning was shot up by machine-gun fire from a passing German plane. Nothing, it seemed, was sacred any more. At another stop, a distraught army driver brought in an English officer whose entire lower jaw and tongue had been shot away. 'But the most horrifying part was that he was still alive and conscious, though he could not speak, only move his eyes from side to side.' They sent away the driver, reassuring him they would do their best, but they knew the officer had no chance of surviving. 'Nothing could be done surgically and I knew we would probably be moving quite soon,' Samuel said. But he could ease the man's suffering. The doctor filled a syringe with morphine and injected him. With much relief, the watching Montague recalled, 'we saw him lapse into unconsciousness and after about twenty minutes he died peacefully without any further trauma.' But the trauma carried on for those who had been unable to save him. 'When I think back on those terrible days,' said Samuel, 'I see that half face and know how ghastly war can be.'

The German machine rolled on relentlessly, pushing the re-treating armies and fleeing civilians into an ever-tightening corner in northern France. Movement along the blocked roads towards the Channel coast was increasingly difficult, the traffic halting whenever planes appeared overhead and everyone flinging themselves into the ditches alongside. For the remnants of Corporal Montague's 6th British Field Ambulance unit, it was not just from overhead that the attack was coming. Enemy infantry had forged ahead and now mounted an ambush on the column. Rapid machine-gun fire was spraying over them from either side. The impatient paid with their lives. Montague watched helplessly as a French soldier, tired of crawling along in the ditch, rose to his feet and began to run from the bullets. He kept his body bent low, 'but to no avail, because another burst of fire knocked him flat into the ditch. I crawled to him but it was too late. He must have died instantly.' The Englishman looked up from the body, chanced a glance behind him and saw that all the ambulances in the convoy were in flames. He was shocked. The vehicles were clearly marked with red crosses and yet they had been deliberately fired on, in complete defiance of the Geneva Convention.

But at least he now knew where he stood – or, rather, crouched. He, a medic, could take up arms in self-defence. He picked up the dead French soldier's ancient carbine rifle – later, it proved to be a relic from France's late-nineteenth-century colonial wars – and some clips of ammunition from his bandolier. 'It appeared that the Germans did not intend to respect the red cross. I felt comfort in having something I could shoot back with.'

But there was little comfort to be found elsewhere as he looked around him at 'destruction and desolation, bombed-out houses, some still burning, others flattened to heaps of rubble'. It was a fine early summer's day, but the sky was black with smoke, which was even darker in the direction of the coast. At a village jammed with cars and lorries and thronged with thousands of British and French soldiers on foot, 'the word went round that we should make for the port of Dunkirk.' As they trudged in that direction, they picked up leaflets dropped from enemy planes with a map showing the areas the Germans already occupied. 'We were virtually surrounded, with the sea as our only means of escape. From a military point of view, the situation looked hopeless.' But the mood was defiant. 'The consensus among us was that we would get home, though we had no idea how.'

*

Equally defiant was Major Ralph Brooke. He was staying put, determined not to leave the hospital in the French town of Rennes, to which he had been posted from Camiers, until he had done all he possibly could. His gloom at the news that Brussels had fallen to the Germans was compounded by his misery at the shattered young bodies he was having to repair. He was treating RAF pilots and crew, who from airfields in France were fighting against impossible odds to try to slow the enemy's advance. 'I am working at full pressure with wounded coming in all the time. I saw one of our machines soon after it had been brought down. It had burst into flames and two of the bodies were just charred masses with a heel bone sticking out. Even their identity discs were burnt beyond recognition. The third man has nearly every bone in his body broken and his back is one large burn. I have been working on him for two days. He has had three blood transfusions. Why he continues to live it is difficult to say.'

Like all military doctors, Brooke did not confine his caseload to those in uniform, and there was an increasing flood of civilian casualties to treat. He rushed to a refugee train, full of women and children, that had been machine-gunned and bombed. At the scene he found 'two small mites quite dead, and one with half her face blown away. It was all very quiet. The women mostly sat looking into space like dumb animals. It was horrible beyond all conception.' Streams of bullet-riddled cars pulled up outside the hospital, disgorging 'bloodied, tired and hungry humanity'. The work was feverish and frenetic.

Surprisingly in these dire conditions, he was managing to put some new medical procedures into operation. Instead of gaping wounds being stitched, a process that locked in infection, they were first to be 'debrided', the technique by which all dead tissue and foreign bodies are removed and the muscle cut away until it contracts under the scalpel and bleeds healthily. The wound was then dressed lightly with gauze (not packed) and left undisturbed because 'this affords the best chance of cure.'[7] This was another lesson Trueta had brought from the infirmaries of the Spanish Civil War – excision of the wound, loose suture (if any at all) and immobilization in plaster of Paris or splints. It was an answer to gas gangrene, the fast-spreading infection of decaying human tissue that had been the deadly plague of the dressing stations and wards in the First World War. An RAMC officer had tested this new technique on the trickle of wounded he had to deal with from skirmishes around the Maginot line in the quiet weeks before the full-out German attack. Out of twenty-five cases, only two went septic. The word spread along the grapevine of junior doctors.

Introducing these new methods of treatment was not easy. Brooke had to restrain nurses of the old school from constantly re-dressing injuries, as they had been trained to do. He had to force them against their instinct to leave bandages in place, even if they had begun to smell. Even the presence of wriggling maggots under a bandage could be ignored as nature's way of cleaning deep wounds, however revolting to witness or repulsive for the patient to endure. 'As long as the patient is a good colour, not in undue pain and his temperature and pulse are normal, he should be left alone,' he told the nurses, though he could tell they were not all won over. Another doctor told a patient who complained that maggots were crawling out from under his plaster, 'That's good! We like that,' but agreed to change the dressing because the man was so distressed. When the plaster came off, maggots and flies fell out, but the wound itself was salmon-pink, whistle-clean and infection-free.

However, the major problem with the Trueta method was logistical. Its clinical success depended on patients being immobilized – and in what was now a war of intense mobility, with most medical units constantly on the move and overwhelmed by the number of casualties needing urgent treatment, that was a luxury that had to go by the board. Instead of letting nature take its slow course, many doctors out on the road – literally cutting, then running – were reduced to slapping on antiseptic, doling out morphine and hoping for the best.

Other doctors, though, had new medical weapons to deploy. At the Atlantic coast resort of La Baule, where operating tables were set up in the casino, RAMC Major J. S. Jeffrey swore by the new anti-bacterial agent sulphonamide for controlling infection. This was a recently developed synthetic chemical, from the laboratories of the pharmaceutical firm May and Baker in Dagenham, Essex. Its original military use had been as a treatment for gonorrhea, the army's biggest scourge, as tens of thousands of boys away from home for the first time in their lives were suddenly thrust into manhood in the brothels of northern France before the fighting began. But sulphonamide was equally effective for battlefield injuries if packed, in its powder form, into infected wounds and fractured joints. Jeffrey plugged a hen's-egg-sized cavity in a man's brain tissue with it, with good results. He was delighted when his resourceful colonel devised a foot-activated air pump that could spray the powder into the corners of even the deepest wounds.

Another life-saver was stored blood, donated back in England and kept in pint bottles for up to a fortnight. It came from the Army Blood Transfusion Service, which had been set up in Bristol just a year earlier. Here was another breakthrough in military medicine being tested for the first time. To historian Mark Harrison, this development was crucial. 'Britain was the only nation that went to war with a fully functioning transfusion service.'[8] The Germans had nothing to compare with it. The promptness with which donated blood could be given saved many lives.

*

Twenty-five miles outside Dunkirk, an outer defensive ring was being established. Here, the 1st Bucks battalion of the Ox and Bucks Light Infantry was ordered to stand its ground and delay the enemy as long as possible to protect the retreat. As the men knocked slits in farmhouse walls and mounted Bren guns, the medical officer, Lieutenant Trevor Gibbens, who had qualified as a doctor a little over a year ago, set up his aid post in the basement of a girls' school. While there was time, he toured the deserted town and stocked up with whatever supplies came to hand. In a doctor's house he found an American Red Cross basket from the First World War. Inside were the finest linen bandages, cut on the cross-weave in such a way that they would lie flat and unwrinkled against the patient's skin. He consoled himself with the thought that, in the battle ahead, his casualties would at least be perfectly bandaged.[9] Their first use was on an officer who drove up in a jeep and said quietly, 'I seem to have got one in the elbow, Doc.' Gibbens cut off his sleeve and saw that his elbow joint had been completely shot away, leaving a two-inch gap between the bones. 'I put a long wire splint on the whole arm and sent him off in the last of the ambulances.'

For the defenders, the waiting went on for another two days, and then, coming up the road, they saw their first German tanks. The battle was furious and lasted days. The Bucks' CO was shot down while trying to run across the road and the second-in-command killed by a burst from a machine gun. Floor by floor, the four-storey girls' school was reduced by mortars and shells. Down in the cellar, Gibbens could hear the rumble of falling masonry overhead as he did what he could for the wounded and eased the pain of those beyond help. 'I soon learnt the First World War trick of putting the dying at one end, and at quiet times I did the rounds, giving them plenty of morphia and sips of water.' In that confined space, where the cries of broken men were drowned out by the boom of the bombardment outside, he felt himself like a surgeon below decks on one of Nelson's ships.

One man was brought down with his abdomen completely opened up and his bowels pouring out. 'There was nothing I could do but put wet, warm packs on him and fill him up with morphia. He died quietly the next day.' But Gibbens's surgical inexperience was cruelly exposed when another soldier was carried in with blood pumping from a wound below his shoulder blade. It could be stopped only by pressing the artery against his top rib, but the moment the pressure was released, it spurted again. The doctor had a terrible decision to make. 'If I had been an experienced surgeon, I could have cut down on the artery and tied it off or clamped it with forceps.' But this was work beyond his ability. 'The man was virtually unconscious and I decided it was hopeless. We maintained the pressure, each of us in turn, but his life ebbed away.' Of the fifty men he treated in that hell-hole of a cellar while a battle raged above, this was the death that would always haunt him.

By now, bodies were piling up around him as the Germans continued a merciless barrage, 'trying to shell us out of existence'. The Bucks had put up incredible resistance, but when darkness fell it was time for those who could to make a break for it and try to reach Dunkirk. Gibbens opted to stay. 'The fifty wounded were my responsibility, and there was nothing much that I could do by dodging about the fields in the night.' The next day, as the roof collapsed, showering rubble over the men left on their stretchers on the floor, he walked up the stairs and out into the open air. Everything was deathly quiet. Around him, in the blinding sunlight, was a moonscape. Tentatively, he held up his haversack, a red cross on it. 'A German officer with forage cap and a grey mackintosh was in the middle of the road, and he waved for us all to come out. I went up to him and said in my best German, with great urgency, "*Fünfzig Verwundeten im Keller*". He nodded and sent a young lieutenant back down with me to check.'

When the doctor resurfaced with his wounded, they were waved to a wall and made to line up. Three soldiers faced them with tommy guns. Gibbens thought they were about to be shot – a realistic fear given that some British troops who resisted to the end had been massacred in cold blood by Waffen SS units. But these were regular Wehrmacht soldiers, 'and after a few minutes we were ordered off to various trucks'. They had survived, but they were prisoners of war, and a long incarceration lay ahead.

Elsewhere along the line, Private B. C. Miller's 10th Casualty Clearing Station had also been overrun and forced to surrender. After days on the move, stopping and starting, the unit had set up in a small village and taken over virtually every building to house the wounded. The operating theatre was in the school, seven stretchers laid across the desks and, with fierce fighting nearby as the BEF struggled vainly to stem the German tide, in almost constant use. 'Time for me ceased to exist,' recalled Miller, a theatre orderly. 'My days blurred into an endless pattern of work, sleep, work. We were strafed, the cook was killed and I went to my bed to find bullet holes in it.'[10] Theatre debris was cleared only when it actually obstructed movement around the stretchers. Discarded ampoules of Pentothal, used as an anaesthetic, piled up three feet high in a corner. Then a cruel order was passed down the line: 'Bridgehead at Dunkirk can take no further wounded,' it read. 'Therefore, the 10th Casualty Clearing Station will remain where it is. It is realized that this will mean inevitable capture but it is hoped that the traditions of the Royal Army Medical Corps will be upheld.' The women nurses were ordered to leave, and reluctantly they did. The Germans were not going to get their hands on them. But as for the men, 'we carried on treating the wounded,' said Miller, 'easing the pain of the dying and burying the dead.' Retreating troops passed by in trucks and offered lifts to the coast. 'Not one of us took advantage of them. We had a job to do, and to the best of our ability we did it.'

After everyone else had gone, a deep but unnerving silence settled over the unit. Then the Germans rolled by in large numbers, with scarcely a glance at the field hospital, now behind the lines. A German officer eventually took charge but left Miller and his colleagues to complete the job until all their patients were well enough to go to a prison camp or into a German hospital.

*

The time the rearguard had bought – thousands with their lives, thousands more with their freedom – had been a godsend for those *hundreds* of thousands who had made it to Dunkirk and the wide beaches that ran for a dozen miles northwards and over the border into Belgium. One of these was Corporal Montague, who on reaching the outskirts of the port came across a Signals sergeant with a long shard of shrapnel in his eye. He cleaned the wound with the last of his water and led him to a French hospital. The scene that greeted him was horrific – 'every corner and passageway was filled with wounded and dying.' The sergeant lay on the floor to await his turn for a doctor. Stepping outside, Montague surveyed devastation. 'The town had been subjected to attack of every kind from the air. The roads were blocked with vehicles on their sides, burnt out and useless. Overhead billowed dense black smoke from a burning oil refinery near the docks.' Not a single building had escaped damage, but still the planes continued their unceasing attacks.

Standing on Dunkirk's esplanade, its once-grand hotels now shattered behind him, he stared out to sea. 'Just off shore was a Royal Navy destroyer with a broken back, smoke pouring from her and no signs of life aboard.' His eyes took in the beach and the untidy rows of soldiers, some standing, others sitting, all with nowhere else to go, at the end of the line. Queues stretched out to the edge of the docks and along the concrete breakwater, the Mole, jutting three quarters of a mile out into the sea, which was the only place the big evacuation ships could berth. Dive bombers wheeled over, their wing-mounted machine guns peppering the sand and the helpless troops with thousands of bullets every minute.

In rare lulls in the lethal onslaught, Montague went to work. He got down on his knees and dug with his bare hands in the sand, carving out shallow graves for the growing piles of dead. 'We stuck each man's rifle into the sand at his head and tied his identity disc to the trigger guard.' Night and a thick mist off the sea halted the planes, and the thousands of soldiers – their ranks swelling constantly as more and more desperate stragglers ducked and weaved their way through the shattered streets of Dunkirk and crowded on to the beach – tried to sleep through the cold and damp and the hunger in their bellies. Many had had nothing to eat for days.

A few miles along the coast from Dunkirk, the promenade of the pretty holiday resort of La Panne[11] had transformed into 'a sort of military Harley Street', in the words of Colonel C. M. Finney of the RAMC.[12] A large force of field ambulances and clearance stations congregated there at the end of their retreat and set up for the last time in seafront hotels. Their lobbies became giant casualty areas, the floors a carpet of stretchers and human misery. The kitchens became operating theatres. Every room and corridor on every floor was filled with bandaged bodies and the groans of men in pain. Hospital ships were anchored offshore and were taking away as many casualties as they could, but with no proper pier the operation was slow, difficult and dangerous. Lorries had been reversed into the water to form makeshift jetties, but generally stretcher-bearers had to struggle out through the waves and put their patients on to small boats for transfer to the bigger ships. Others were dispatched in ambulances to the Mole at Dunkirk, where stretchers could be more easily manhandled on board. Some of the ambulances turned round and came back for more. But not all. Some were ditched as their drivers and orderlies joined the evacuation, putting self-preservation first, to the disgust of those who believed their duty lay in staying, not fleeing.[13] Not everyone, it seemed, wanted to be a hero.

One of those who stayed was RAMC Corporal F. C. Adams of the 11th Casualty Clearing Station, whose diary was a frank admission of how tough it was, both physically and mentally, to treat the ceaseless flow of wounded under these conditions. There were no beds or sheets, and the blankets covering the patients were soaked with dead men's blood. The doctors were fully occupied in carrying out surgery, and all the difficult post-operative care had to be left to orderlies like him. Inside, the noise of hurt, bewildered and angry men was constant. Only the unconscious slept. From outside, the sound of guns and bombs shredded what few nerves were still intact, and some patients went mad with fear when planes roared over. He took to subterfuge to keep some semblance of order. He would pretend to be the wife of a soldier who kept calling out for her in his delirium. Another was loudly and disruptively demanding an operation for a bladder wound. Adams gave him morphine, put a plaster on the wound when he fell asleep and told the man when he woke that he had had his operation. It calmed him, which in many cases was the most the medic could hope to do. Adams appalled himself by wishing that the hopelessly wounded would hurry up and die so that space would be released for the hundreds waiting outside for treatment. How had he become so callous, he wondered to himself.[14]

But now La Panne was about to be overrun, and it fell to the

RAMC's Colonel Finney to order those under his command to make for Dunkirk to be evacuated. Not all could go, however. There were wounded who were not fit enough to be moved again, let alone go through the ordeal that lay ahead on the beaches. They would have to stay and be captured, and so would a certain number of medics to look after them. The colonel visited the units one by one with written instructions to that effect. It was, he knew, 'a terrible order' to have to give to anyone, but one doctor and ten orderlies would remain for every one hundred patients. The choice of who stayed was settled by drawing lots.

Similar situations had arisen (and would continue to arise) in clearing stations and hospitals all over northern France and Belgium. At the Chapeau Rouge château just outside Dunkirk, surgeon Philip Newman's heart pounded as papers were shuffled for the ballot. Three of the seventeen officers were to stay. He had a pretty good chance of getting away. It wasn't to be. 'I was number seventeen and down the drain.'[15] As the others made their preparations to leave, he tried to look efficient and 'don't care-ish'. He noticed that every one of them guiltily avoided catching his eye. At La Panne, the lucky ones lined up and trudged off towards the smoking ruins of Dunkirk away in the distance, the medics among them with rifles in their hands, aware that they might have to fight if they wanted to survive. Into his haversack, Major L. J. Long packed his ambulance unit's admissions book with the names of all those they had treated and the one hundred graves registration forms he had accumulated, each marked either 'brought in dead' or 'died of wounds', his very own book of the dead. Those medics who had drawn the short straw settled down with their patients to await their fate in what was now the BEF's last casualty clearing station, in the casino. Given how many lives had been gambled and lost in the past three weeks, it seemed appropriate.

At Camiers field hospital outside Boulogne, Sergeant W. Simpson was awaiting his fate too. As the hospital was evacuated, six officers, three NCOs and twenty-seven men were required to stay, and volunteers were called for. He stepped forward. He was single, and he felt it only right that married men should have first chance at getting back to their families. Besides, he ruminated, there was still hope of an ambulance train turning up to evacuate them all in time. He was wrong about that. There was no escape. As he sat with his patients, waiting for the Germans to arrive, he had 'an overwhelming sense of desolation'.[16] Medics who stayed behind had some consolation in being protected by the Geneva Convention as non-combatants. Theoretically, they could hope to be repatriated once the wounded soldiers they were looking after were well enough to go into a PoW camp. Simpson had no confidence that this tradition would be respected. 'It was clear from what we had seen and heard that the Germans were trigger-happy and shooting at anything that moved. Our chances of survival seemed very small. I recall the regret I felt that I had not really lived and that my parents might never find out what had happened to me.' But there were patients to treat, and he put his fears to one side and did what so many medics do at times of greatest stress – he got on with his job.

When the Germans arrived he was surprised by the correctness of their behaviour, though they seemed inordinately concerned to establish if any ordinary soldiers were masquerading as medics. In his office, Simpson secretly collected all the pay books and endorsed each one with an official-looking certificate of his own devising confirming their status. The ruse worked. It also may have saved lives. The unit included a number of Jews, and Simpson, with an inkling of what dangers might lie ahead for them if their identity was known, destroyed their pay books and issued new ones stating their religion as 'C of E'.[17]

Meanwhile, on the beach in Dunkirk itself, a morning mist was slowly clearing, to reveal a miracle. Corporal Montague and what was left of his field ambulance gazed out to sea. 'We could see hundreds of small craft of every description moving in as close to the shore as possible. Many of our fellows were wading out to these cabin cruisers, motor barges and lifeboats, climbing on board and being ferried out to cross-Channel steamers, fishing vessels, river pleasure boats and yachts lying in deeper water.' From one of those steamers, medical officer Malcolm Pleydell looked out at 'black clusters of men swarming like a disturbed ants' nest on the sands. We steered gingerly between the wrecks of ships, their masts leaning over at drunken angles, and could hear a grating noise as we grazed past them.'[18] Small craft were zipping backwards and forwards 'like water beetles', he recalled, in this 'macabre regatta'. But for all the size of this armada and the incredible courage of those at the wheels and tillers, it was clearly going to be a very slow process to get everyone away.

What dismayed the waiting and watching Montague was that, however many men braved the deep water and the waves to get from shore to ship, 'the khaki multitude along the beach did not appear to diminish, and, if anything, seemed to swell by the hour.' Men threw caution aside in their desperation to escape. Liverpool-born Len Brown was a bugler in the 1st battalion of the South Lancashires and doubled up as a stretcher-bearer. But the prowess he drew on now was neither musical nor medical. What mattered was that he was a swimmer in the battalion water polo team. 'I saw this ship anchored 600 yards out, and I said to my mate, "Shall we have a go?" We waited until the next air raid was finished, took off our clothes and went in.' Sailors on the ship spotted their heads bobbing in the water, lowered a small boat and came for them. 'They helped us in and gave me a cigarette, and a pair of brown overalls, because I had no clothes on.'[19]

By the time night came, Corporal Montague had not had his chance to get away and, with the many tens of thousands left on the beach, he drifted towards the Mole, where long queues were still forming. There was no respite from the bombardment. The Germans had taken Calais, and their heavy guns there had got the range of the Mole and its approaches. He realized with alarm that 'the enemy is clearly closing in on us.' But discipline was maintained. A brigadier in a red-banded, soft-peaked cap was calling out instructions, Montague recalled, 'as coolly and calmly as if he was coaching a rowing eight at Henley'. The men formed themselves into groups of fifty and, on a command, raced through gaps in the shellfire across the beach and on to the Mole. 'We were ordered not to stop once we had started. The group ahead of us slowed down, and a shell landed in the middle of them, leaving many dead, dying and wounded. We were directed past them and arrived safely on the Mole.' Montague scrambled along a plank towards a waiting ship, a Dutch ferry. He looked down nervously at the black oily water some 30 feet below before the strong hands of two Royal Navy ratings seized him and hauled him on board. He was going home. Eight hours later, the ship pulled into Folkestone harbour 'under a clear blue sky, without any gunfire'.

Many ships, crammed with evacuees, never got that far. The destroyer HMS *Grenade* was blown apart by a bomb while she was tied to the Dunkirk Mole. Nineteen-year-old sickbay attendant Bob Bloom was hit with such a blast and was in so much pain from burns that he wanted to die. 'The skin was hanging from my hands as if I was trying to pull off gloves. My face was stinging, my lips were swelling and my nose had all but disappeared.'[20] He jumped into the water, then climbed up on to the Mole and over to a paddle steamer berthed on the other side. But she too was hit, and he found himself back in the water. 'By now my face was so swollen I could hardly see. But I was saved by two soldiers who were hanging on to what looked like a barn door with a ring fixed to it.' They kicked with their legs, and he sat clinging to the ring until, hours later, they were picked up by a passing ship and taken to Ramsgate.

★

Back in France, tens of thousands were still waiting for their chance to escape. Many of them were medics, invariably among the last to leave any of the dwindling number of defensive positions around Dunkirk. In his aid post in a cellar in a village six miles from the sea, Richard Doll, with just one orderly and two stretcher-bearers to help, had a continuous stream of casualties, whom he was patching up and sending off in ambulances to the port. When he finally managed to poke his head out of the door, he saw that the battalion of Lancashire Loyals he had been retreating with had all disappeared, and the message left for him was that he should 'do what I thought best'. All around him were burning ruins. He decided it was time to get out. The wounded who could still fire a rifle were armed and put in the back of a lorry. The others were crammed into his car. 'Before starting, I gave all of them a last dose of morphine,' he recalled.[21]

Headed by a stretcher-bearer (a conscientious objector – one of many who would not fight but who bravely went to war anyway to save lives) on a motorbike, the mini-convoy headed for Dunkirk. They came on the Loyals again, who were dug in along a canal bank. Doll sent off the lorry with the wounded towards the beaches –'the last I saw of it' – and set up a new aid post in a barn. The last bridge over the canal was about to be blown, but a deserter was lying drunk in the middle. Doll, ever the life-saver, ignored orders to leave him, revved up the engine of his car, accelerated on to the bridge, heaved the man into the back, turned and fled. Only afterwards did Doll grasp how reckless he had been and took a swig of tea and brandy to calm his nerves. Then he got back in his car and toured the area for genuine casualties. All the while, shells were bursting around him. He sent off more fully laden ambulances towards the beaches and was heartened when all the drivers dropped their loads and came straight back, though it would have been the easiest thing in the world for them to have taken the chance to flee. That night, the battalion was finally given permission to withdraw under cover of darkness. 'I had one wounded man with me in my car, and I gave a lift to two others with blistered feet as we headed for the Mole, which was lit up in the distance by a pillar of fire.'

When they could go no further, they ditched the car and began to walk the last half-mile. 'The Mole was full of French troops, who were moving slowly out along it into the dark, ignoring the shells falling all around. To us it seemed too dangerous even to try, and we found spades and dug a shallow shelter for ourselves among the foxholes and craters on the beach. But it was soon obvious that we could not just sit there. We must either push on along the Mole and get to a ship that way or else wander off and look for boats along the beach.' There was a rumour that empty boats had been spotted a mile or two along the sands, and Doll decided to take a chance and head with his men in that direction. It could have been a wild goose chase, and a fatal one at that. In fact, he had made the right call. 'We had walked for about ten minutes when we saw a dark mass ahead of us and found to our joy that some two hundred to three hundred British soldiers were standing in the water while out beyond them were a couple of rowing boats. We lined up to wait our turn and, as the boats returned to the shore, we waded out to them. The water came up to my chest before I was pulled over the gunwales and aboard.' A motorboat tugged the now overflowing dinghy out to a waiting paddle steamer. Doll stood soaking wet and exhausted in a crowded gangway but did not mind the discomfort and the cold. 'This was the boat that was going to take me back to England, and that was the only thing that mattered.'

The doctor's work, though, was still not finished. There were a dozen stretcher-cases in the sick bay for him to treat. Doll was utterly done in, but he was revived with steaming cups of tea, Oxo and bread and butter and knuckled down to the task. 'Some were so terribly wounded I didn't know how they had got on board. One Coldstream Guard, a survivor from a platoon that had been hit by a shell on the beach, had six separate leg fractures, and he died before the boat got back. A sergeant from the Loyals looked unhurt, but when I cut away his shirt I saw that his right shoulder was almost blown away and the arm was held on by a few pieces of muscle and skin. I splinted it by pinning pieces of bandage to the back of his coat, over his arm and on to his chest.' Now Doll could sleep, and when he woke, the steamer was in Ramsgate harbour.

★

It was 2 June when Doll got back to England and, by then, close on 300,000 British and French troops had been brought back across the Channel. 'Dynamo', as the operation was called, was wound up two days later, having rescued eight times as many men as those masterminding it from underground headquarters inside the cliffs at Dover had ever thought possible. In France, 30,000 British soldiers were dead, never to return, or wounded, and a further 35,000 already in the bag as prisoners of war. But another 150,000 were still at liberty and, with the fall of Dunkirk, Calais and Boulogne, were heading westwards along the coast in the hope of finding a means of escape.

Among those still at liberty was Major Ralph Brooke, who had stayed at his post in the hospital at Rennes with one other doctor and a handful of orderlies while France was collapsing around them. The town, through which thousands of refugees were pouring as they headed towards the Atlantic ports, came under attack from the air. The hospital was hit and he was thrown down a flight of stairs and showered with broken glass. He vomited, sick with fear. 'But then I began to pull myself together' – which was just as well, because an ammunition train had exploded next to two troop trains in the railway station and hundreds of casualties were arriving. 'We picked up the up-ended operating table, swept as much broken glass as we could from the floor and set to work.' The window frames had all been blown out and there was a large gap in the wall through which, on this hot mid-June day, the sun streamed brightly. A second table was rigged up, two patients were anaesthetized at a time and Brooke moved between them as fast as he could.

'There was no time for proper sterilization,' he recorded in his diary, which was extraordinary for a doctor who had warned so stridently (and correctly) about the dangers of sepsis in army hospitals when he was first posted to France. The realities of war changed all that. 'One just washed one's hands and went from one table to the other, working with bare hands, lopping off limb after limb, tying arteries, sewing torn bowel. No sterile towels, only a macintosh sheet. Instruments flung into a boiler between cases sometimes, sometimes the bloody ones used from the previous case.' He went on for hour after hour. 'No stop. Limbs piled up in buckets and when the buckets were full the limbs were thrown into a corner.' As soon as patients came off the table, they were loaded, some still under the anaesthetic, into ambulances waiting outside and driven away. He counted later that he had carried out forty-seven operations and removed fourteen legs and six arms.

'Then word came through that the Hun was only two hours away and coming fast. We were ordered to leave at once and make for the coast.' By then he had collected more than two hundred seriously wounded men, and the hastily assembled convoy joined the exodus of cars and carts crawling out of the wreckage of Rennes along streets strewn with bodies. Out in the country, they came under attack from the air. 'I was riding in the first ambulance, there was a huge flash behind and I turned to see that the two behind me had been hit. We stopped and searched for injured, but all of them had been killed.' Ten men had been blown to smithereens, with nothing left except pieces of mangled flesh and torn clothing. A large crater was now blocking the way of the rest of the convoy, and the ambulances had to detour through ploughed fields to get back on the road. 'I can still hear the groans from the poor fellows as the ambulances lurched over the furrows. I gave morphia to as many of them as I could.'

In the early hours of the morning, they crept into St Nazaire. When they opened up the ambulances, Brooke found that six more patients had died. At the port, ships were casting off and about to sail, already full to the brim. There was no room. Brooke lined up his ambulances on the quayside and, as dawn broke and enemy bombers came swooping over the water, he felt utter despair. 'All hope left us. So nearly away and yet so far.' A British naval officer came to the rescue. He dashed up in a car and told Brooke that a Norwegian cargo boat carrying copper bars in the hold was leaving from another part of the harbour. 'If we could get there, the captain would take us, but he would not wait.' They raced over and were given fifteen minutes to load as many stretchers as they could. 'A fearful struggle against time began. We worked like navvies carrying the stretchers up a single, steep gangway and stowing them on top of the copper.' From somewhere, he found superhuman strength as he toiled away 'as I had never done before in my life. I discovered I could lift a stretcher with a heavy man on it with ease, whereas in cold blood I could not have contemplated such a thing, let alone done it. The last man was being loaded as the ship moved away from the quayside.

We had carried eighty-two stretcher-cases on board in fifteen minutes.' How close a call it had been was apparent as the ship cleared the lock gates. 'We could see the Boche tanks coming down the hill into the town. We were the last out. The ship following us was caught at the lock gates.'

★

The rescue of the BEF had concentrated on bringing home the able-bodied, who would form the nucleus of the army that, in time, would return to France and do to the Germans what they had done to the British Army. Out of necessity, many of the wounded had had to be left behind. But there were still many thousands of injured men[22] who made it back home, thanks to the doctors, orderlies, ambulance drivers and stretcher-bearers who had stayed resolutely by their side. It was now down to medical staff on the home front to take over from them. Each ship arriving in port with casualties was met by a naval medical officer and two sick-berth ratings, whose first job was often to release tourniquets that, in the panic and horror of the evacuation, had been left on too long. 'We saw many cases of congestion of the limbs due to prolonged application of tourniquets,' reported Surgeon Captain A. R. Fisher, the senior medical officer at Dover. One soldier he came across had had his wounded arm strapped tight for thirty-six hours, and the limb was completely dead. Fisher put the case for windlass-operated tourniquets –'easy to apply, easy to release and easy to re-tighten, and can be controlled by the patient'[23] – but it would be the next century before such devices were standard.

From the south-coast ports, the wounded were whisked by rail to hospitals around the country. Artist Keith Vaughan, a conscientious objector who volunteered for medical work, met one such train in Yorkshire. As he climbed on board with his stretcher, he was hit by the smell of wool, urine and sickly-sweet flesh. But the sight that greeted him was vindication of his deep loathing for warfare. Here were its unforgettable victims.

Three tiers of bunks lined the white walls, each with a face that stared out quietly and expressionless. Some turned to look at us, visitors out of the night, from another planet. Others were still locked in their prisons of pain, where we had no admittance. No one spoke. We held our stretchers up to the bunks and coaxed the men to brave the crossing on to the steel meshes. They dragged across those parts of their bodies they were able, the rest we carried for them, grotesque shapes of wool and splint and bandage, joined to them only by pain. In a bunk near the door a pale boy watched our approach with an open, curious gaze and turned his face away when he saw we were coming for him. A nurse whispered something in his ear and wiped his forehead with some wool. We asked him if he could ease himself across a bit. He tried and couldn't. 'It's his leg, poor laddie,' the nurse said, and gave him a quick little pat and a smile. We drew back the blankets and saw that his arms finished at the wrists in two logs of yellow-stained wool and bandage. His right leg was a shapeless ball of bandage supported on pillows. He worked himself across slowly on his elbows, lay back a moment with closed eyes and lips trembling in despair. Then, drawing together the last fibres of courage, he forced himself too quickly on to the stretcher so that the leg twisted in our arms. His face broke open with silent tears.[24]

Ann Reeves witnessed even greater agonies as a student nurse in a London hospital when some of the worst of the wounded arrived. She remembered a man whose face was shot away and having to feed him 'through what was left of his mouth, either by a tube or a tea spoon, and somehow spare him the ignominy of dribbling. I had to remove long lengths of congealed ribbon gauze from huge cavities, before packing them with clean dressings soaked in Eusol [a solution of chlorinated lime and boric acid]. It was like bleach, and he just looked at me with large, hurt eyes. He was still a person, but shattered beyond recognition.' Burns victims could be even more traumatic. 'They made my flesh creep,' she admitted. 'Most of them had been covered in flaming oil and were indescribably, horrifically, burnt.'[25]

She recalled a Scots corporal named Jock who had been enveloped in thick burning oil when the rescue ship he was on was bombed. He was 'a living torch' as he jumped into the sea and was now 'an unrecognizable bulk of burnt flesh'. She put his charred arms and legs into cellophane Bunyan bags filled with saline and treated the rest of his body with tannic acid. 'He was never free from pain except when mercifully drugged with morphine.' Like all burns cases, he needed urgent rehydration, but his lips and tongue were too corroded and swollen for him to drink. Doctors tried an intravenous infusion of saline, 'but they could not find a vein in Jock's charred body and so he died'. But a suffering world had a long, long way to go before, like Jock, it would be out of its misery. And, though it didn't bear thinking about and didn't seem possible, on the other side of the world, a whole new dimension in man's inhumanity to man was soon to begin.

4. Bamboo Surgeons

Making his way back from a foxhole on the beach at Dunkirk, Irish-born RAF doctor Squadron Leader Aidan MacCarthy had every reason to believe his life was charmed. Not only had he fled across northern France just a matter of miles ahead of the German front line but when the ship he boarded was holed on the waterline by a mine, he (and the boat) survived. 'The captain ordered us all to the opposite side,' he recalled, 'and thus tilted, with the hole clear of the water, we made safe but slow progress across the Channel.'[1] Back in England, he was posted as senior medical officer to an air base in East Anglia, where two hundred WRAFs, members of the Women's Royal Air Force, were paraded before him in a hangar for an FFI (Free From Infection) inspection. 'They were lined up in four ranks with an elderly officer standing in the front, and every one of them was stark naked!' He ordered bras and pants back on at the double, but the story made him the envy of the base. The doctor's good fortune was not to last, however. In the winter of 1941, he was sent to the Far East, where the forces of Japan were on the march against British strongholds.

Another medic on that long sea voyage to the tropics was Private George Temple of the RAMC, who had taken a course as a theatre orderly and, more importantly, stayed on his feet the first time he stood around an operating table. 'It was the removal of a gall bladder and all I could see was this heaving mass of raw red flesh. The lad next to me excused himself but I managed to stick it out.'[2] He would 'stick out' a lot worse in the years ahead and perform more than the surgeon he watched that first day could ever have imagined from a mere orderly. The war with Japan would unleash unspeakable horrors and be the most testing time that any medically trained man or woman could ever experience.

It would be very different from the European theatre of war, where captured doctors and medics had a reasonable expectation of being respected. Those who surrendered to the Germans at Dunkirk in order to take care of their wounded comrades did so with the knowledge that, under the rules of war, medics were entitled to be returned home once their job was done. It was some consolation for those who volunteered to go into captivity. There was no guarantee at the time that this agreement would be honoured, and few men could stake their lives on this pledge with absolute conviction. But, as the war went on, there were indeed a few repatriations from PoW camps in Germany, and, though life behind the wire was hard, medics in the *stalags* and *oflags* were generally allowed to do their jobs, albeit in very difficult circumstances and with limited resources. Not so on the Pacific front. Japan was not a signatory to the Geneva Convention on the humane treatment of prisoners. It applied the *Bushidō* code of the warrior, in which those who surrendered on the battlefield were beneath contempt. Nor did it see any honour in the work of those seeking to save the lives of men it considered to have forfeited their right to exist.

From the very start, the Japanese showed no compassion. When Hong Kong, the British crown colony off mainland China, was overrun in Christmas week of 1941, British Army medical staff and their patients were among the first to feel the lethal and barbaric thrust of Japanese aggression. The Salesian Mission was the main medical store holding supplies for all the military hospitals and aid posts in the colony and was manned by a dozen RAMC orderlies, doctors of various nationalities, stretcher-bearers and nine women nurses, mostly from the St John Ambulance Brigade. Japanese combat troops took the building without a shot being fired or any resistance offered, and at first it seemed as if the red cross flag hanging in the entrance hall would be respected. Everyone was lined up outside and marched away. The women went in one direction and were released unharmed. But the men were ordered to halt and take off their shoes and tunics. Their identification cards, each marked with a red cross to indicate their status as medics, were taken from them, cursorily examined, then tossed aside, and the men were marched a quarter of a mile up a steep, wooded hill.

In a small clearing, the killing began. Some were bayoneted and slashed with swords, others shot down as they tried to run away. The massacre was witnessed by Captain Martin Banfill, commander of the RAMC unit, who had been separated from the others and kept alive to be interrogated later. He lay on the ground, a Japanese boot in his face, listening to his men being slaughtered, the sounds of Japanese chatter and laughter mingling with blows and shots and the screams of the dying. He was threatened with the same fate as his men before being dragged away from the scene and, unaccountably, reprieved.

Another survivor was RAMC Corporal Norman Leath, who had been struck by a sword on the back of his neck in an attempt to behead him. 'It shot me into the air and spun me completely round,' he recalled. 'I fell to the ground face downwards, blood pouring into my eyes, ears and mouth.'[3] His neck muscle was almost severed in two, several vertebrae were badly damaged, but his spinal chord was miraculously intact. He lay beneath the pile of corpses in a drainage ditch and played dead until it was safe to crawl away.

After the war, apologists for the Japanese would argue that the Salesian Mission massacre was a one-off incident by a rogue officer. But a week later, as the fierce fighting for Hong Kong continued, there was not merely a repeat performance but an even worse atrocity at St Stephen's College, a boys' school that the British had turned into an emergency 400-bed hospital. It had around a hundred patients in the main hall and adjoining classrooms when, just before dawn on Christmas Day, two hundred Japanese troops broke in. The senior medical officer bravely tried to bar their way while also attempting to make a formal surrender. He was shot in the head and stabbed as he lay on the ground. Then the troops went from bed to bed plunging their bayonets into the helpless occupants. Fifty were dead within minutes. This time, the women nurses did not escape. A dozen of them were herded into an upstairs room and then taken away in threes and fours to be gang-raped. Some were murdered and their bodies muti-lated (whether before or after death was never established). The men too were locked in a room and then brought out in pairs. 'After the door was closed and locked again, the remaining prisoners would hear screams and shots, followed by more shots. Then silence until the next selection in half an hour or an hour.'[4]

The Japanese 'excuse' for the killings at St Stephen's was that troops had come under fire when they approached the building, and there was evidence that retreating British soldiers may indeed have had machine-gun emplacements made from piled-up mat-tresses and hospital blankets in the grounds and on the veranda. But the argument that this nullified the protection that doctors, nurses and patients were entitled to falls away in the light of the degree of brutality they were subjected to. They were non-combatants by any definition, and they were willing to surrender. They were dispatched and degraded with an indifference to human suffering that would be a remorseless feature of the Japanese con-quest of the Far East. In doing this, they defied their international obligations. It is well known that Japan had not signed up to the clauses of the Geneva Convention on the treatment of prisoners of war and felt no obligation under that code. But it had ratified the articles of the convention explicitly protecting medical person-nel (in 1907) and those agreeing to humane treatment of the sick and wounded (1929). Its cold-blooded flouting of these inter-national obligations was deliberate – as those caught by Tokyo's next onslaught against the British empire were finding out. As Japanese troops fought their way down the Malaya peninsula in a campaign of aggression, courage and ingenuity that had British and Australian defence forces in a full-scale fighting retreat, it was once again the wounded and those tending them who were easy prey, helpless as lambs to the slaughter.

At a village called Parit Sulong, an Australian commander had no choice but to withdraw through the jungle, leaving behind 150 badly wounded men on stretchers. It was a tough decision to make, but there was no reason to think it would be a deadly one. Until then, there was a reasonable expectation that, as in the battles against the Germans in Europe and North Africa, the wounded would be treated humanely. The men lay waiting, wary but optimistic, some looking forward to the prospect of at least being able to wash and get out of the filthy, bloodstained battledress they had been in for weeks. Japanese troops drove up in trucks and immediately bayoneted and clubbed those who lay on the ground and were not quick enough or fit enough to dodge out of their way. The rest were herded, hobbling and helping each other as best they could, into a circle and made to strip naked. Requests for water were ignored as the captives were crammed into a shed, 'a stinking, scrambling hell-hole, full of tortured, groaning, delirious wounded soldiers', as one of the few survivors put it.[5] Water and cigarettes were offered to their outstretched arms, snapped by a Japanese photographer for propaganda purposes – and then snatched away once he had his picture. The butchery took place on a riverbank, to which the men were brought roped together by the neck in a long chain of misery. Some were shot, some beheaded with samurai swords. Some were still alive when petrol was thrown over the pile of bodies and set alight. What was even more ominous was that these Japanese soldiers were not a rabble momentarily out of control but the Emperor's elite, his Imperial Guard, as prestigious a regiment as Britain's Grenadiers or Coldstreams. Mercy, it was now clear, was not on the Japanese agenda.

This dire message was now getting through to the British command in the island of Singapore, at the tip of the Malaya peninsula. Word had also arrived there of the hospital massacres and rapes in Hong Kong. With a siege about to begin, the decision was taken that the many army nurses on the island must not be allowed to suffer the same fate. They were ordered to join the exodus of civilians clamouring for places on the ships in the harbour, and did so, many reluctantly, none too soon. Just a mile behind them, Alexandra Hospital and its eight hundred bedridden patients, with red crosses prominent on its roof, lawns and hanging from the windows, was in the path of the advancing Japanese imperial army. A hopeful and brave British medical officer, Lieutenant Wilson, fashioned a white flag of surrender and went to meet the invaders as they entered the hospital grounds. A bayonet in the stomach killed him, and a systematic slaughter began, ward by ward. In one of these, Gunner Ferguson Anckorn was drifting out of the anaesthetic after an operation on a badly mangled hand, saw Japanese soldiers and thought he was dreaming. He turned to the man in the next bed and asked what was happening. 'He said, "They're taking people out on the front lawn and killing them." I said, "Oh I see," and then went off again. The next time I woke up the Japanese were going from bed to bed with fixed bayonets.' He was certain he was going to die and, as they got closer to him, he put his head under the pillow. 'I was lying there, I couldn't move anything and I didn't mind being killed as long as there was no pain. But I didn't want to see it happen.'

For him, it didn't. 'When I came up for air they'd gone, and there were four people left alive in the ward.' He survived, he believed, because he had his hand on his chest, the hand had a massive hole in it from his wound and blood was pouring from it. 'They must have thought I'd already been bayoneted and moved on.' Another survivor was an orthopaedic surgeon who stood up to a dozen rampaging Japanese when they pushed through the doors of his operating theatre. 'We were lined up against the wall and they set upon us with bayonets.'[6] A jab cut into his hand and leg, but his cigarette case miraculously deflected what should have been the fatal thrust. 'I decided to pretend to be dead,' he recalled, 'and lay there for quite a while before they moved off.' But, in all, more than three hundred men were killed in the atrocity. One of them, a corporal, was even impaled on the operating table. Ninety RAMC doctors and orderlies were among the dead, cut down while selflessly trying to protect their patients.

As Singapore's demoralized garrison surrendered, those who had fled were not out of danger. Sister Margot Turner of the Queen Alexandra's Imperial Military Nursing Service[7] was one of the nurses ordered to leave, and sailed in a small ship, the *Kuala*. As they slipped out of the harbour at twilight, she looked back at a skyline smeared black from burning oil and petrol tanks. The nurses were remarkably steadfast and brave amid the horrors of war. One had recently written home to her parents: 'Don't worry about me. I have no fear for myself and look on life as a great adventure with the unexpected round every corner.' But the 'unexpected' was worse than any of them could have imagined. The next morning, the captain anchored off a small island and camouflaged the ship with branches and leaves to sit out the daylight hours. The disguise didn't work. Planes found the *Kuala* and bombed her. With the ship on fire from bow to stern, Turner leapt overboard, without a lifejacket. 'As I jumped, some man took off my tin hat, which was a helpful and kindly act,' she recalled.[8] It saved her life. 'I went down very deep but I came up, unlike Miss Russell [her matron], who jumped with me, but I never saw her again.' Around her as she surfaced the sea was full of dead, dying and swimming people, targets for the Japanese planes that swept over, their machine guns blazing at those in the water. Every time they came, she dived deep and, when they had gone, she struggled to land against a swirling current and crawled out exhausted. Though very groggy, there on the beach she nursed a wounded British soldier who had been hit by a bomb splinter and was unconscious. 'I stayed with him until he died, then I slipped his body into the sea. I never discovered his name.'

There was much work to do. With seven other nurses, all that remained of the fifty who had gone on board the *Kuala*, she tended the many wounded and sick among the three hundred survivors. They tore strips from their dresses to make bandages and fashioned tree branches into beds. They had a few morphine tablets, 'which made the last hours of the mortally wounded more bearable'. For three days they kept going on rations of one biscuit and half a cup of water a day before a small tramp steamer passed by and picked them up.

The joy of their deliverance was short-lived. In the night, this ship too was bombed. Hundreds of women and children were asleep down in the hold, but Turner was lying out on deck when a searchlight glared from the sky and, without any warning, there were two violent explosions. 'All around us, people were dead and dying.' Struggling up the gangway from below was a fellow nurse, her dress covered with blood. 'She said the hold had taken the full force of one of the shells and was absolutely smashed.' By now the ship was almost on its side and, once again, Turner found herself in the sea and fighting not to be sucked down to her death as it sank. 'The cries and screams of the wounded and the helpless in the dark were terrible; dead bodies were floating everywhere; mothers wailed for their children.' She and another sister found a couple of small life rafts and went looking for survivors.

'We managed to pick up fourteen people, including six children, two of whom were under one year old. There was room for two people to sit back to back on each raft, each one of them holding a child in their lap. The rest were in the water hanging on to the lifelines. I instilled into all of them the importance of never letting go, but when dawn broke I found that two had disappeared. That day, with the tropical sun beating down on us, two more of the women let go and were carried away.' Worse was to come. 'On the second day the children went mad. We had a terrible time with them, and lost them all. I examined each of them with great care before committing their small bodies to the sea. The last one was a very small baby and it was difficult to know if it was dead or not. I thought, "This is some woman's precious child; I must not let it go until I'm sure." But in the end there was no doubt and it had to go with the others.'

By nightfall, just Margot and one other woman were left, adrift in an utterly empty ocean. 'We sat back to back on a single raft with our feet in the water. Our lifejackets had rubbed our chins absolutely raw, so we took them off and trailed them behind. The afternoon of the next day, our third on the raft, we saw some islands and paddled feebly towards them using pieces of driftwood. Mrs Barnett [the other woman] let her paddle slip from her grasp and, before I could stop her, she had plunged into the sea after it. I was much too weak to swim after her. I called and strained my eyes to catch sight of her, but there was just nothing. I was alone.' But she was fiercely determined to live. 'I would hold on to life as long as it was humanly possible.' That meant staying awake and focussed. She collected raindrops in the lid of her powder compact and ate seaweed that floated by. 'Night came and I watched the stars and soaked up the rain that beat down on me. I thought of home and my family and the happy things in my life.'

On the fourth day, she spotted a ship on the horizon. It came towards her, a warship – a Royal Navy one perhaps? But as it got closer, she saw Japanese faces. Hauled on board at the end of a rope, she was surprised to be treated in a kindly fashion. She was given tea and a drop of whisky, then bread and milk. Her painful sunburn was treated. She was left to sleep. Then, when the ship arrived at an island off Sumatra, she was carried gently ashore because she was unable to walk. On dry land, she heard English voices and realized she had been brought to a PoW camp. She had been through hell since fleeing Singapore a little over a week ago, 'so much death, so much suffering'. But she was alive and, after dangerously infected boils in her leg were lanced (albeit painfully with a blunt scalpel), well. Moreover, as she listened to the stories of other nurses who had been brought to the camp at Muntok, along with civilian internees from more than sixty refugee ships the Japanese had sunk in the waters between Singapore and Sumatra, she realized that her ordeal had not been the worst.

Sister Vivian Bullwinkel was an Australian nurse, one of sixty-five who had left Singapore on a ship named the *Vyner Brooke* which appeared to have escaped detection until Japanese planes found and bombed it. Less than a third of the three hundred passengers got away, in a pair of leaky boats, and drifted on the currents until they came ashore in small groups on Sumatra – now, like Singapore, in Japanese hands. Realizing they could not hope to survive on their own in this desolate land, a naval officer from Bullwinkel's group went looking for help and returned with a patrol of Japanese soldiers. Ominously, they had brought no stretchers with them for the wounded. What was going on?

The Japanese strode into the group and separated off the able-bodied men and the walking wounded. The twenty-one nurses and a dozen stretcher-cases laid out on the sand remained behind, watching as the men were marched away along the beach and out of sight. After a little while, the soldiers came back, and the women saw they were wiping blood off their bayonets. They then lined up the nurses and ordered them to walk into the surf, just as they had done with the men. 'Chin up, girls, I'm proud of you,' called out their matron, Irene Drummond,[9] in a low voice as machine guns opened up, shooting them in the back. Bullwinkel was hit in the waist, but the bullet went clean through her body and out the other side. She floated face down in the water, pouring blood and apparently dead. The Japanese turned away, bayoneted the stretcher-cases and marched off.

When she realized they had gone, the nurse struggled ashore and hid in the jungle, where she came across a British serviceman who had managed to survive the massacre of the stretcher-cases, though a bayonet had punctured his lung. They kept each other alive for two weeks, living off scraps from a native village, until they had no choice but to give themselves up. They were brought to Muntok internment camp, where she now whispered her story to Margot Turner. 'We decided in the camp that we would never mention this incident as, if it got to the ears of the Japs, Vivian's life might have been in danger. But what tremendous courage she had shown.'[10]

*

Courage of a similar order would be needed by the fifty thousand men who, back in a blazing and devastated Singapore, had surrendered to the Japanese forces of General Yamashita. To begin with they were treated surprisingly well, given the contempt in Japan's military culture for men who chose to live in captivity rather than die in battle or by their own hand. While hundreds of Chinese were massacred by vengeful Japanese soldiers, the British and Australian captives were marched in a long, dreary line – but with bagpipes playing and singing 'Tipperary' – to Changi, an area in the east of the island with a barracks, bungalows, a jail and the sea on three sides. There they were surrounded by barbed wire and pretty well left to get on with their internment.

Conditions deteriorated when the men refused en masse to sign undertakings not to escape and some who did try to escape were callously executed. Then the food supplies the surrendering soldiers had brought with them ran out and they were left to rely on meagre rations of reject rice from their captors. Illness on a major scale set in, and the task for the doctors and medical orderlies was immense. In the first three months at Changi, the camp's makeshift hospital admitted sixteen thousand patients, more than half of them with dysentery. Deaths were soon past the two-hundred mark, and accelerating. RAMC trooper George Temple was on duty in one of seven hundred-bed wards filled to overflowing with dysentery sufferers. 'The conditions were appalling,' he recalled. 'Gross over-crowding, no running water, no lighting, no proper steriliz-ation, no existing arrangements for the disposal of hospital and human waste.' Drugs were scarce and medical equipment non-existent. The only medicine was Epsom salts, to try to purge the germ from their intestines, followed by chalky kaolin solution to line the stomach. 'Men were relieving themselves twenty or thirty times a night, which was debilitating enough for them. But then there was no nourishing food to sustain them from further attacks in the future. At night, we would hear the sound of terrible hiccups and retching and know that a man had not long to live and we would be carrying his body out before dawn.' Semi-starvation brought a host of other problems. Lack of protein and calories sapped strength, while vitamin deficiency caused the skin to peel painfully from men's most vulnerable parts – their feet and their genitals. Royal Artillery medic Sergeant Joe Blythe reckoned that half of the six hundred men under his care were suffering from malnutrition, and the only supplement he could offer them was a smear of Marmite in hot water.

But Changi, for all its problems and hardships, would be looked back on as a paradise and its hospital a haven compared with what came next in the prisoners' lives. Thousands were transported to work camps in conquered Thailand to build a railway line to Burma, through two hundred miles of the toughest mountain and jungle terrain on earth. They were cruelly conned from the outset. RAMC orderly David Jones recalled being told they were going to a sanatorium in the hills that would be especially beneficial for the sick.[11] The reality was a five-day trip in a goods train through stifling heat to a jungle hell. Here, in primitive living conditions, worked as slaves, starved and subjected to extreme and arbitrary violence, they would be stretched beyond human endurance.

What puzzled the prisoners was the lack of common sense on the part of the Japanese. 'Had they fed us reasonably well and refrained from brutality, the railway would have been built much sooner,' Temple noted. As it was, a third of them were to die, and the survival of the rest was largely because the doctors and medics among them performed miracles untaught in medical schools or hospital wards back home. Against a backdrop of barbarism and indifference, they would carry out feats of outstanding bravery and inventiveness.

It took immense courage to stand up to slave-driving Japanese camp commanders who demanded that the sick should join the work parties carving a passage through jungle and bare rock, digging out boulders, building viaducts and embankments, laying track. Doctors such as the Australian Lieutenant Colonel Edward 'Weary' Dunlop took regular beatings to prevent the flimsy bamboo huts that passed for a hospital being raided for men who had been felled by malicious guards, malaria, dysentery, beri-beri, diphtheria and flesh-eating tropical ulcers and could barely raise their heads, let alone toil in the heat. The Japanese would demand fifty; the doctor would offer ten and then stand his ground. At night he would smuggle reasonably fit men into the hospital so he could produce them on demand the next morning and keep their captors happy. He took huge chances with his life by hiding the illicit camp radio – possession of which was punishable by death – in his medical supplies. He paid for his guile and his guts. On one occasion, Dunlop was made to stand at attention for two whole days outside the guardhouse in an attempt to break his spirit. Then they made him kneel for another twenty-four hours, but still he grinned – literally, according to many witnesses, his smile infuriating the guards even more – and bore every indignity, every beating.

His defiance lifted the spirits of skin-and-bone men on the brink of caving in mentally and physically.

Jack Chalker, a fellow PoW, thought Dunlop the most valiant man he ever met. 'He was tall, and the Japanese didn't like that so they made him kneel to beat him up. But, knowing very well he was going to get beaten up, he would still go to them again and again to try and get better conditions for us or to stop their brutality. For somebody to do that continuously, on our behalf, for three years, deserves ten Victoria Crosses, because it was not in the heat of battle but very real, deliberate courage. He had ulcers from being knocked about by the guards and he suffered from typhus and dysentery, just as we did, but he was like a human dynamo.' The light Dunlop generated was an inspiration. In these dreadful camps, where life sank to a humdrum of cruelty and death, doctors and medics – with little more than Epsom salts and quinine to dispense – were the last link to a better world of hope and humanity.

With virtually no proper equipment, the operations the surgeons among them carried out were remarkable, from amputations to brain surgery.[12] With a complicated appendectomy to perform, Captain Stanley Pavillard laid out his instruments – a cut-throat razor, a pair of rusty scissors, three pairs of artery forceps and some catgut. No scalpel, not even a knife. At another camp, a doctor extracted a deeply embedded wisdom tooth with a chisel. Out in the jungle and under canvas, Dunlop operated on a soldier with a perforated peptic ulcer in the middle of the night because the patient would otherwise not have made it to morning. The only light was from a hurricane lamp and a torch. As he bent over his patients, there were times when the doctor, as susceptible to disease as the men he served – perhaps more so, since he was constantly in contact with infection – was so sick himself he could barely stand. He carried on despite the difficulties because he was that sort of man. For Dunlop and the scores of doctors like him, the call of duty was a cry for help that never ended and which they never shirked.

Some of the worst problems to deal with – for patient and

doctor alike – were ulcers from wounds that would not heal in the fly-blown, disease-laden jungle heat. Some were the result of savage beatings by guards, but even simple scratches from working bare-legged in the thick undergrowth or an insect bite could turn black overnight, fester and deteriorate dangerously. Flesh decayed, exposing bone, then flies laid eggs in the bone and their maggots ate away at the marrow. Once the rot had set in, only radical surgery could stop it spreading.

Lieutenant Colonel Albert Coates – a man of nearly fifty who had turned down the chance of evacuation from Singapore in order to stay with his Australian troops – had five hundred such cases at a camp in Burma and had to have each man held down physically while he gouged away the flesh, without anaesthetic. Those who watched found it hard to decide who was braver, the doctor or the patients. 'Tears ran down their cheeks, they would curse and bite their hands and hold on to their mates like grim death,' one recorded. 'Their courage was astounding and their confidence in the colonel absolute.'[13] But even this torture too often proved not radical enough to save their lives, and Coates had to resort to amputation. That same witness recalled him bending over a hopelessly eaten-away leg and saying, 'It's no good, laddie. We'll have to take it off for you and give you a chance. When would you like it done?' More often than not, the patient would give him the nod there and then: 'Let's get it over with, sir.' Under a bamboo shelter with a leaf roof, Coates, clad in shorts with a sweatband on his forehead, would go to work with a scalpel and a saw borrowed from the kitchen, and an hour later the soldier would be back in his bed, drawing on the cheroot the colonel had given him, minus the diseased limb but with a prospect of survival.

Success was far from guaranteed, however. In the second half of 1943, Coates carried out more than a hundred full-limb amputations (as well as snipping off countless fingers and toes). One man in ten died on the operating table and half of the rest within two months. It was not a hit rate that Coates, a professor of anatomy, would have been content with back home in Melbourne, but in the jungle it was close to miraculous. Many men who otherwise would have died would eventually be able to hobble home on crude prosthetic legs made out of wood, leather from a Sam Browne belt and elastic from a pair of braces.

Another 'miracle worker' was the RAMC's Captain Jacob Markowitz, who borrowed his saw for amputations from the camp carpenter. An officer who watched one of his open-air operations recalled gusts of wind blowing eddies of dust over the patient 'while flies and bluebottles in their hundreds buzzed incessantly around and were flicked off when they settled'.[14] Markowitz was surgeon at the Chungkai hospital, a collecting point in a jungle clearing for casualties from all the work camps in Thailand. When he arrived in May 1943, there were already seven thousand patients there, stacked on wooden platforms in huts without walls, on top of pools of stagnant, mosquito-infested water. Twenty patients a day were dying, but each day more wrecks arrived from the work camps to add to the numbers. To treat them he had a stethoscope, a spattering of antiseptic and enough chloroform for just two operations.

While he set his overwhelmed orderlies to root out whatever tools they could find or fashion for surgery, he concluded that blood transfusion was essential to save lives. But how could blood be collected in the absence of sodium citrate, the chemical additive necessary to stop it instantly clotting? From experience in a blood laboratory years earlier, he recalled the answer – keep stirring it with a spoon. With a needle, a few old bottles and the tubing from his stethoscope, he soon had his transfusion kit, and his first success. Blood from a willing donor flowed into the veins of a man dying from anaemia brought on by malaria. He came out of his coma. After that, Markowitz recalled, 'we gave transfusions for every-thing. Men dying with dysentery often recovered. Men suffering from vitamin deficiency became more cheerful and regained their will to live. Tropical ulcers healed more quickly.'[15] In time, Marko-vitz would also come up with an answer to the problems caused by the lack of vitamins in the constant diet of polished rice.[16] A strange brew of rotten bananas, rice and human saliva[17] produced health-giving yeast. 'This new elixir worked miracles,' he reported, 'as swollen stomachs, sore eyes and ulcerated mouths responded to the magic of our cure'. In another camp, an equally ingenious doctor managed to transform a four-gallon kerosene can and some rubber hosing into a plant to produce distilled water, which could then be used as an intravenous fluid for cholera victims.

Over the next year, Markowitz – 'a knife, fork and spoon surgeon', as he styled himself – would perform 1,200 operations in his bamboo theatre, in conditions that reminded him of what he had read about surgery in the Crimean War. He was assisted by illicit supplies of the anaesthetic Novocain, smuggled into the camp by Thai villagers, and the ingenuity of an orderly who scrounged the materials to make retractors, a rectal speculum, a rib-cutter, a quadruple needle for skin grafting, a tracheotomy tube and spinal and hypodermic needles. He operated on a man gored by an angry elephant and another who fell from a tree and had skull fragments in his brain. He repaired a lot of jaws broken by Japanese rifle butts. For gaping tropical ulcers, he preferred skin grafts to amputation, first scraping out the wound with a spoon and then grafting skin from the patient's thigh to cover it. A soft dressing impregnated with pig fat was applied, and the whole leg then encased in sponge rubber from a mattress until it healed.

Another doctor, Stanley Pavillard, used the Trueta method of debriding the wounds made by ulcers and encasing them as best he could to heal themselves. He would apply a little of his precious stock of iodine or sulphonamide and then bind the limb in bandages made from old sheets and bark from banana trees. But there were times when amputation could not be avoided, as Markowitz learned the hard way after a sergeant major pleaded for more time to allow his ulcerated leg to heal on its own. 'Give it another week, Doc,' the man pleaded, and the doctor reluctantly held off. It was a kindness that killed. 'On the evening of the third day, he died in his sleep.'

★

In every Japanese PoW camp, there were outbreaks of almost all known diseases, which were liable to spread like forest fires in the unsanitary conditions and among men weakened by overwork and chronic underfeeding. Hospital huts were more like charnel houses – 'pitiful places, the stench of putrefying flesh and sweating, emaciated bodies huddled together on bamboo slats and tormented by bugs which came out in their thousands to feed on them', as medical orderly George Temple recalled. At night they were even more fearful places of pain, panic and death. One doctor used up a precious half-grain of morphine to quieten down a man whose loud and violent delirium was distressing the other patients. 'It is difficult coping with cases in a dark and crammed hut by the light of an oil flare,' he noted.[18]

Once an infection took hold among the men, it was impossible to contain, especially since the guards tended to hang on to any medicines to dose themselves. At his camp, Temple was caught up in an outbreak of diphtheria and had neither the drugs to combat it nor the means to perform the tracheotomies – incisions in the throat – that would enable choking patients to breathe. 'All we could give them were gargles of permanganate of potash and then, with a pair of long forceps, try to remove the fungus-like growth from their throats.' As he prodded inside their mouths, the patients would invariably cough and splutter over him. He protected himself as best he could with a face-mask made from an old rag soaked in carbolic, but inevitably he caught the disease himself. He survived it only because the medical officer somehow procured an anti-diphtheria drug. 'He injected it into my buttocks, and the next morning, as I gargled, the membrane peeled from inside my throat like a large lump of jelly. I was as weak as a kitten but that saved my life.'

He survived only to be sent to another camp, where water-borne cholera, perhaps the most feared of all tropical diseases, had broken out. 'It could turn a perfect physical specimen into a living skeleton in a few hours, his kidneys ceasing to function, his voice a mere croak, oozing continuous fluid from his back passage and doubled with terrible cramps in the stomach until dehydration of the body was complete.' The victims were isolated in tents away from the main camp. 'The stench of faeces, mud and slime pervaded the air.

Deaths were a daily occurrence – 130 in 10 days – and all bodies had to be burned on a pyre to stop the epidemic spreading. The guards wouldn't come anywhere near us. Our ration of rice and jungle stew [a concoction of leaves] was left outside the compound, and I used to take mine into the jungle to eat, away from the flies, which were deadly carriers of the disease.' Temple and his fellow medics sprayed each other with disinfectant as they bravely moved from tent to tent, and he was lucky. The epidemic petered out when the rainy season ended.

Not all prisoners showed the same selflessness as their doctors and medics. With 350 cases of malaria, diphtheria and dysentery in his camp, Dr Robert Hardie pleaded for a blanket for a man suffering from all of these conditions. 'One of the officers in his battalion, who had three, refused to lend him one,' the appalled and disappointed medical officer, trying to do his job with just some quinine, some magnesium sulphate and flavine solution at his disposal, recorded in his diary.[19] Against this, 'Weary' Dunlop paid tribute to the staff sergeant on his medical team, 'himself reduced to a near-naked skeleton and shivering with chronic malaria, yet who, when confronted with a man naked and tormented with cholera, dropped his last shred of comfort in the world, his blanket, over the dying man. Only those ill, emaciated and thin, who slept on exposed and rough surfaces in all weathers, could comprehend the depth of his sacrifice.'[20]

But, all too often, in that jungle nightmare, sacrifice and dedication were not enough. Nothing was or could be. Medical orderly Temple, his worldly possessions down to a loincloth, a banana-leaf sunhat and a pair of wooden clogs, felt helpless most of the time. If a man went down with cerebral malaria he would rave and groan until he either died or recovered, 'and there was nothing we could do about it.' Under these awful conditions, without supplies and subject to uncaring captors, many medics found themselves at a loss – without the consoling thought that they were at least saving lives. Sergeant Joe Blythe was one of these. The 'Death Railway' was not the only place the British prisoners had been sent to work, and Blythe ended up in one of the myriad of other slave camps around Japan's Pacific gulag. He was the sole medic among a work detail of eighty men from the Royal Artillery on the island of New Britain, off Papua New Guinea. His diary, written in secret and hidden from the Japanese under a pile of bloody bandages he knew they would not search, was a litany of death as, one by one, his comrades succumbed to illness. With nothing but first-aid training in the St John Ambulance to call on, he could do little medically but ease their passing.

On Good Friday, 1943, a significant day for the strongly religious man that he was, he recorded the death of Gunner B., 'only a young man of twenty-two, who died in his sleep, another victim of beri-beri. He has been ill a long time and also had severe attacks of malaria. He had a lovely tenor voice and would try to entertain us with a few songs. Our total of dead is now forty-two, more than half.'[21] At their Good Friday service, Blythe, who was a lay preacher at home in Nottinghamshire, took as his text Jesus's words on the Cross: 'It is finished.' But it wasn't. On Easter Saturday he was forced to record two more deaths, one of a man with beri-beri and malaria who had lost his reason and been out of his mind for a month. 'We had tried to get a tarpaulin from the Japanese to make him a small tent so he could be separated from the other lads who were seriously ill and distressed by his condition. But in vain.' The countdown of deaths continued remorselessly. 'We all begin to wonder if and when it will end. Who will be next? Shall I fall victim? Will any of us survive?' Six weeks later, the party of eighty was down to just twenty-six. Sickness caught up with Blythe himself, first malaria, then an outbreak of ten tropical ulcers on his legs and a deep abscess on his back. 'I cannot stand but managed to crawl to a patient to give him his injection. What am I going to do? I cannot neglect them.'

Even the little comfort doctors could offer was often snatched away. RAF medical officer Aidan MacCarthy – who had escaped one enemy at Dunkirk only to be imprisoned by an even more vicious one in Java – was nursing an airman dying of dysentery. 'Severe abdominal cramps make this a most painful way to die, and I watched as his wasted body stiffened with each spasm. There was no medicine to be had and all that I could do was to pray and hold his hand and whisper encouragement.' A Japanese guard entered the hut and, lost in his terminal task, MacCarthy failed to stand up and bow. 'He rushed towards me screaming, with his rifle raised. In a mixture of Japanese, Malay and English, I explained that the patient was dying, but he smashed his rifle butt on to my elbow and fractured all the bones in the joint.' The injured doctor was taken to a civilian hospital for repairs. 'A Japanese surgeon examined me and seemed reasonably competent. He said he needed to operate. In the theatre, I was told to lie on the table and an orderly strapped my legs and arms to the table. I thought this a rather odd preliminary to the anaesthetic – and then discovered there was to be *no* anaesthetic.' The surgeon, who MacCarthy later learned was a third-year medical student, began to make his first incision, 'when I suddenly realized he was making it in the wrong place. Then the blinding pain hit me and I fainted. When I came to, I saw this butcher proudly holding half the head of my radius bone in his forceps.' The cut was stitched and dressed, the arm put in a sling and MacCarthy was swung off the operating table and marched back to the ward. He survived this ordeal and learned never to trust Japanese medicine. When he and other doctors were ordered to inject fellow prisoners with a vaccine they were told was for their benefit but which they suspected was a guinea-pig trial for an untested anti-plague drug intended for Japanese troops, they pinched the skin into a fold and pushed the needle harmlessly though it and out of the other side.

It was hard to come to terms with the obscene cruelty routinely carried out in the camps. One of MacCarthy's first experiences was being paraded past a prisoner who, for some minor infraction, was buried up to his neck and then left bareheaded in the sun. 'The Japanese refused to let me offer him any relief. Instead, they insisted that we walk past him dozens of times each day. In forty-eight hours he changed from a young man to a decayed geriatric. Insect bites set up immediate infection, his eyes closed and his lips set in a permanent snarl. It took two days and a night for him to die.' Nor was the doctor allowed to help when what he called a procession of 'scarecrows', 249 blind men, hands on the shoulders of the one in front, arrived at the camp gates led by the only sighted one left among them. 'Their blindness was the result of optic papillitis, brought on by prolonged vitamin deficiency. They were emaciated, dirty, and completely demoralized.' The doctor and his men were not allowed any contact with them, 'but from our own limited resources we managed to pass clothing, soap and even a little food over to them'. They were all that was left of a working party of a thousand who had been shipped off to a remote coral island to build a runway for Japanese aircraft and been worked and starved to death. More than seven hundred had died, two hundred of them packed into the hold of the tramp steamer bringing them back to Java.

Soon MacCarthy was to experience one of those 'hell ships' for himself as he was transported to Japan to be a slave labourer. The men were sealed below decks in horrific heat. 'When the air raid alarm sounded, we sat terrified in the steaming darkness, expecting a torpedo at any moment.' They survived, drew within sight of the Japanese mainland and thought they were safe. Then they were hit. 'The torpedo exploded right underneath us, blowing off the front length of the keel. The lights went out, and I called to the officers on each side of me, amazed that the noise had not woken them. Then I realized they were dead. The explosion had had a whiplash effect on the iron deck, and the vibration had fractured their necks. The fact that I was sitting up and struggling with a large rat that had been gnawing at my feet saved my life. It was an incredible escape and one that continues to haunt me.' The ship, its engines still turning at full revolutions, was plunging beneath the waves, and MacCarthy made his way up a ladder as water cascaded into the hold over him and almost knocked him off.

I felt someone's hand clasp my ankle and, spurred on by terror, I managed to pull the two of us to the top. Then I swam for it, putting as much distance as possible between me and the rapidly sinking ship. A small island of wreckage floated by and I clung to it in thankful relief. Cries and screams came from all around me. I heard an Australian voice calling

'That you, Doc?' I swam towards the voice and found two bedraggled Aussies, one of whom was badly injured. It was the beginning of a most unusual sick parade. I swam from one piece of wreckage to another, binding broken collar bones, roughly splinting broken arms and legs, using bits of rope and string and timber picked up from the drifting flotsam. The surrounding sea was a heaving oily swell, and as we clung to the wreckage our bare feet often touched a soft yielding mass, the bodies of women and children whose refugee ship had also been sunk. I had a great shock when I dragged the first of them to the surface and found myself looking into the staring and sightless eyes of a dead child, with its mouth forever fixed in an eternal scream.

The doctor was in the water for twelve hours, 'human flotsam, dumbly bobbing up and down', before he and about twenty others were picked up by a Japanese destroyer, and he thought he was saved. 'We were given rice balls and a drink of water. But then they turned on us, beat us up and began throwing us back overboard.' MacCarthy jumped rather than wait to be pushed. 'We swam back to the wreckage, now some distance away, and reached it exhausted and terrified.' He had almost given up hope when a Japanese whaling boat came by, stopped, picked them up and brought them to a port. 'The authorities there wanted the whalers to go back to sea and drop us back where they had found us, but the crew were anxious to see their families and refused. Grudgingly we were allowed to disembark, eighty-two of us standing naked on the dock, a strange-looking bunch covered with cuts and abrasions from the nails and sharp edges of the wreckage. Salt encrusted our bodies and our skins were wrinkled like new-born babies.' They were marched through the streets, some dragged on makeshift litters, others on sticks. Japanese crowds jeered at them as they were led to a flea-infested labour camp outside a steel factory. It was only later that MacCarthy realized the ominous significance of the place that was to be his home – Nagasaki. As a doctor at war, it seemed he was destined always to be a participant in the very worst of human suffering.

5. Desert Doctors

In the past century, weapons of war have changed out of all recognition, but what has stayed much the same throughout this explosion of ever deadlier arms is the experience of being wounded, which, it seems by most accounts, is initially not always a matter of searing pain. That comes soon enough. But, to begin with, there is a blow like a jolt of electricity that can hurl a man to the ground or drop him slowly and gracefully in a heap. The chief sensation as he lies there is usually neither resignation nor anger but utter surprise – which seems odd, given the dangerous environment he knew he was entering when he went to war. Yet few soldiers, airmen or sailors go into battle thinking about being wounded. Killed, yes. That's the occupational hazard. But the half-way house of being damaged, badly, often seems harder to contemplate and so is ignored – until it happens. After the surprise comes the shock, which is numbing, and many will remember the calmness of that almost matter-of-fact moment when they looked down and saw a mangled leg or felt their insides tumbling out. Then the realization sets in and, with that, possibly the pain begins, but more likely the fear, sudden and overwhelming, particularly if he is alone and with no one to call on. With fear comes stress, heightened to screaming pitch by the noise of battle around him. Then the human reaction is the same as with any hurt animal – to want to crawl away to some quiet place.[1] Except that, to your horror, you cannot move.

Private Maiki Parkinson's experience was a classic case. In the battle for Tunis, in North Africa, the New Zealand soldier – one of Montgomery's 'Desert Rats', who were confronting Rommel's apparently invincible Afrika Korps – was caught by the blast of a German mortar that landed next to him and knocked him over. One leg was hanging on by a thread, 'and blood was pissing out everywhere, just pumping away'[2]. He tried to get up, but his strength was ebbing and the weight of his pack, his tommy gun and his ammunition was holding him down. He wanted to take off his belt but could not undo it. 'I just lay there,' he recalled. 'I had my hand inside my groin and I could feel the bone. I wasn't in pain. They say your life swims before you, and I found myself thinking of home.' Two stretcher-bearers picked him up and carried him along a trench, ducking bullets the whole way, to an aid post, which was where he finally passed out. He woke in a military hospital in Tripoli, still not grasping what had happened to him. In the next bed was a young soldier whose leg had been amputated at the thigh, and Parkinson commiserated with him. 'At least we'll get decent pensions,' the soldier said. *We?* The truth suddenly hit him every bit as hard as that mortar shell had done. 'I looked down and realized my leg had gone too. It was the most devastating thing that ever happened to me.'

The doctors who had to deal with the tens of thousands of casualties like Parkinson had had little or no specific training for the work they were required to do. Malcolm Pleydell had been thrown into the deep end professionally at Dunkirk[3] and swam rather than sank, but it was a close call. 'I honestly was scared,' he told his girlfriend in a letter. 'The noise is the worst thing when you aren't used to bangs.' But at least now he had 'a rough idea' of what to expect next time. A rough idea – that was as much as most of them ever got beforehand about the business of saving lives on the battlefield. Martin Herford's exploits were to encompass Alamein, the conquest of Sicily and Italy, Arnhem, escape from a prisoner-of-war compound and the liberation of the Belsen concentration camp, and make him the RAMC's most decorated doctor of the entire war.[4] Yet at the outset he was a greenhorn graduate from university medical school in Bristol with just a year's surgical experience as an ear, nose and throat houseman in a hospital. He was, in his own words, 'guileless', and so far removed from the grizzly realities that he took his tennis racket with him when he went to war.[5] His graduation from tonsils to traumatic amputations was a crash course at the university of life (and death).

And he, unlike many of his contemporaries, at least had an inkling of war's horrors beforehand. As a student he had been to Barcelona with a Quaker aid mission during the 1936–39 Spanish Civil War, come under shell fire, watched lines of hard-pressed doctors operating on victims of bombing, seen ribs removed under nothing stronger than a local anaesthetic.

For Robert Debenham, at forty older than most of the others, and a lieutenant colonel, the steepest do-or-others-die learning curve was in a network of damp and dirty sea caves, a truly bizarre site for a hospital. He was at Suda Bay on the northern coast of the Greek island of Crete, which, in May 1941, was about to fall to the Germans. An advance force of paratroopers had dropped from gliders and captured his hospital in the town of Canea. While he watched from a slit trench in the grounds, the red cross flag and the union jack were hauled down and replaced with a swastika. The conquest was short-lived, because Commonwealth troops fought back and ejected the invaders. But this was only staving off the inevitable: the Germans would be back in overwhelming numbers. And this was why Debenham had relocated to the caves, with several hundred patients and staff, to hide and carry on as best he could. 'All hospital work now done in caves,' he recorded in his diary.[6] Stretcher-cases were brought in along the beach or via a tunnel from a ledge in the cliffside. There were good caves and bad. 'Cave 5 is difficult to approach and only walking wounded can get to it, through a rather winding crack through rocks,' he noted. 'But when reached it is a good cave and opens out right on to the sea.' The dysentery cases were all sent to a special 'isolation' cave, some way off from the others. Outside, on the main part of the island, more German parachutists were dropping and enemy planes were shooting up anything that moved.

The doctor was ensconced in what had been designated the surgery cave and, with his caseload increasing by the hour, hardly left it. The operating table was set up close to the mouth, because this was the only source of light. The floor sloped beneath his feet and was so fouled with goat droppings that he and the other surgeons frequently lost their footing in the slimy mess. In the confined spaces of the 'wards', the fetid stench of decomposing wounds was overpowering. At least British Red Cross nurse Joanna Savridi was able to get some respite from this. As a new recruit to medicine, she had wondered whether she would be able to stand the smell of ether and the sight of blood and gore. Now she had no time to think about such niceties or turn up her nose. There was a monumental job to do, and she got on with it fearlessly. She did get to leave the shelter of the caves, risking the constant bombardment outside. As she darted away to fetch badly needed medical supplies from the town, she breathed in the fresh air as if it were pure oxygen.[7]

Wounded men were arriving all the time, two hundred in one night alone. Breaking off from a non-stop stream of surgery, Debenham pulled down his face mask, wiped the sweat from his brow and gazed out at the savage blitzing of the island. Yet more 'customers' would soon be on the way. He could see the hospital buildings they had so recently evacuated taking a terrible pounding from the air. He had not been able to get all the patients away to the cave, and he knew some were still there. Lying in their beds, how could they survive the raking machine-gun fire and the bombs? But at least his underground sanctuary was being respected. He had decided to gamble and advertise its presence with a huge red cross made from white hot-water-bottle covers and red hospital screens laid out on the clifftop. It appeared to be working. To underline that this was a place for non-combatants, when out in the open 'between caves', he and his staff took off their steel helmets so they wouldn't be mistaken for soldiers by marauding German fighter pilots, and held up their arms to display their red cross bands. But the enemy's ground troops were closing in. Their line was now just four miles away. 'Things don't look too good,' the doctor noted. 'Capture seems very likely.'

They had not been abandoned, however. Word came that rescue ships were on their way from Egypt, four hundred miles away. With the caves about to come under assault from the ground, Debenham assembled a line of walking wounded and loaded stretcher-cases on lorries to cross the island's southern shore. Not everyone could go. Four hundred patients were unfit to be moved, and thirty orderlies stayed behind to look after them. As in northern France at the time of Dunkirk, there were agonizing decisions to be made and tough orders given to those medics whose duty was about to cost them their liberty. Debenham had to choose men to stay behind knowing that, as senior surgeon, his own duty was elsewhere, with the main body of evacuees. He left with them to trek to the other side of the island, but there was no let-up in the demands made on him. The Germans were superbly well armed, with sub-machine guns and the latest field artillery. He set up a temporary dressing station in a little church among the olive groves and performed twenty operations beneath the altar. 'The font was an excellent receptacle for scrubbing up,' he recorded, 'but water was in short supply so we could only change it once.' From the church wall he prised out a six-inch nail to use as part of an improvised splint for a broken leg. It was pushed through the sole of the man's boot as an aid to traction and worked well, 'with the help of a bit of string', just as wood from the pews made good tops for crutches.

For days, they either marched or hid up in the hills, until they reached a small bay on the south side of the island. Then, as they waited their turn for a boat, he was faced with another tough decision. It was decreed from on high that only the WWs, the walking wounded, could be guaranteed a place. There would be no room for the many stretcher-cases who had been lugged across the interior of the island. They would have to stay, as would more medics to look after them. Debenham agonized again – 'horrible job' – and opted to sacrifice the least experienced of his men in order to hang on to those he thought would contribute the most to the war effort afterwards. 'Finally, I left with the WWs' – and later he was cross with himself that he had allowed an undeserving case, a man with gonorrhea rather than a battle wound, to get away among them. In a destroyer, they were whisked away – it was 'like an express train at 40 knots, with many twists and turns' – and fifteen hours later disembarked in the safe haven of Alexandria.

Already in the Egyptian port was that young RAMC lieutenant

from Bristol, Martin Herford, who had made an equally traumatic exit from mainland Greece a month earlier. British forces had been deployed there to stave off the defeat of the Greek army by invading German and Italian troops. His job had been to coordinate transport between forward medical units and casualty clearing stations, which had meant his criss-crossing the rugged countryside and pot-holed roads on a motorbike, an Enfield 250. But now the Allied expeditionary force was in full-scale retreat down the Greek peninsula, under constant bombardment from enemy planes. Growing numbers of casualties were in danger of being left behind. From the town of Levadia, near the front line, Herford, a new-comer to the army and a mere junior subaltern, ignored military protocol, grabbed a phone and rang the staff officers at headquarters in Athens to demand loudly and indignantly that an ambulance train be sent up the line at once. His cheek brought a positive response, and a train was dispatched. But, before it could arrive, Levadia was blitzed. Fighters, descending like hornets, strafed the roads and railway line, and the station was reduced to rubble as a nearby ammunition dump exploded. The train had made it only as far as Thebes, thirty miles away, and Herford needed to get there to organize the evacuation.

He jumped on his motorbike and took off along a road already littered with wrecked vehicles, dead mules and craters. Over a hill in front of him, a Dornier fighter-bomber appeared and swooped in at tree-top level, spitting bullets. A bomb erupted behind him, then another one ahead, and the twin blast knocked him over the handlebars and into the dusty road. He lay there, too frightened to move, certain he must have been badly wounded, just waiting for the pain to kick in. It didn't, and he realized that, somehow, he was still in one piece, as, equally miraculously, was his bike. As the air raid continued, he rode on into Thebes.

There, amid chaotic scenes, he found the ambulance train, the windows of its carriages shot out by bullets from the air. The prominent red cross painted on its roof had clearly given it no protection. Hundreds of stretcher-cases had already been loaded on board, but they were going nowhere. The line had been cut by bombing five miles out of town, and the way south to Athens was blocked. The casualties would have to go by road, and he helped to unload them, stretcher by stretcher, amid their cries of pain, on to the platform to wait for lorries to arrive. But Herford had another concern. The ambulance train, one of only a handful in Greece and a valuable asset for saving lives, was a sitting duck and needed to be moved into cover if it was not to be destroyed. First he needed to hook up the carriages to an engine, and the driver of the only spare was nowhere to be seen. The doctor went looking and found him in a shelter, cowering from the air attack. He refused to move, until Herford took out his gun and forced him and his fireman back on to the footplate. The doctor then stood shotgun over the man as he shunted stray wagons out of the way of the ambulance carriages. A quick learner, after watching the driver for a short while, he even took a turn at the controls himself. Doctoring . . . train-driving . . . it was all in a day's work.

All the time, Messerschmitts were buzzing overhead, their guns blazing down. Eventually, the empty ambulance carriages were hitched up and, through a barrage of bombs, the engine pulled them to comparative safety down the line. Over the next twenty-four hours, a gang of navvies repaired the break in the track, the ambulance train was loaded up and the latest collection of casualties, more than two hundred of them, were eventually on their way to Athens. Back in Thebes, Herford, having waved it off, switched back to being a doctor again. One of the German fighter pilots whose low-level attacks had been making his life hell had been shot down and was wounded. Without a second's thought, he treated his enemy as he would any British soldier.

By now, the Greek army had surrendered to the invading Germans, and the remains of the Allied expeditionary force were heading, in a degree of panic, to ports in the south to be evacuated. Herford was picked up by a navy cruiser and taken to Crete and then on to Alexandria. It was the end of the first phase of his war, one in which, in truth, he had made little use of his medical skills. He had hared around organizing the evacuation of the wounded, at constant risk to his own life. But in his dedication and his flouting of danger, he had demonstrated that, for a doctor at war, there were no boundaries. It was his moral duty to put the safety of his patients above his own, and if that meant driving a steam train through an air raid, then so be it.

★

With the fall of Crete and Greece in 1941, the battlefield switched to the deserts of North Africa, an unnatural habitat for soldiers from the temperate climes of northern Europe, uncanny and unsettling. The landscape was vast beyond imagination, the front lines uncertain and often non-existent, supply lines always at breaking point. The terrain was sometimes achingly beautiful but more often harsh and ugly. Emptiness stretched in every flat, arid direction. Underfoot, there was as likely to be stones and grit as soft sand. Tank attacks took place over hundreds of miles, outflanking was routine and the enemy could be (and often was) camped in the next wadi or over a nearby dune, and you never knew until you heard a German or an Italian voice drifting over the night breeze and caught a glimmer of a fire. In this 'bleak, barren, virgin, stony desert', the RAMC's Malcolm Pleydell was dug in, sleeping under the stars in a slit trench, as he revealed in a letter home. 'A hot wind comes from the Sahara and is very trying. It brings a sandstorm in its train, grit in the hair, in the eyes, in the mouth, down the shirt, everywhere. How I miss England with its soft greens and blues and its changing skies. Damn these flies!'[8]

For doctors in these conditions, the enemy was more often not so much the Axis forces but the environment. Hygiene was paramount – keeping men clean and healthy and warding off flies and disease, particularly dysentery. Here, that pre-war RAMC training on where to site the latrines came into its own. 'Mobile bogs' were constructed from petrol tins and wooden frames, topped with the vital component – a lid. This was a war the Allies won hands down. Sickness rates among British troops were consistently well below half those of German troops throughout the North Africa campaign. Some strategists argue that the war in the desert was so finely balanced that the extra men the Allies were able to deploy were crucial to the outcome. On the eve of the second battle at Alamein, sickness cost Rommel a fifth of his forces.

A new generation of drugs proved important. Inoculation against typhoid was almost universal, while sulphaguanadine, introduced in 1942, transformed the fight against dysentery by slashing recovery times. Those with the disease could be treated in camp instead of having to be shipped back to a main hospital for three weeks of nursing on a liquids-only diet. But what made the biggest difference was that the British buried their human waste, whereas the enemy tended to leave theirs littering the surface.

The Tommies were well schooled medically in the prevention of the spread of infection from hand to mouth to stomach and then by hand to others.[9] They were bombarded with blunt messages on cleanliness. 'Don't Murder Your Mates' urged one poster. Injunctions like this worked – but not when it came to sexually transmitted disease. Men threw caution to the desert wind as they tramped in their thousands through the whorehouses of Cairo and Alexandria. The condoms that could have saved at least some of them from debilitation were the subject of much moral/military debate. The Archbishop of Canterbury denounced the distribution of prophylactics on the grounds that it would invite fornication. Montgomery, on the other hand, was all for his boys having a good time when they deserved it, and most of them agreed with their commander. The dilemma for doctors was that they were often too busy dealing with battle casualties to find the time to lecture the men on the dangers of venereal disease or to carry out health inspections of authorized brothels, another of their supposed duties. But, as a result, their wards were over-burdened with clap cases. At Robert Debenham's military hospital in Alexandria, two hundred of the seven hundred beds were occupied by VD patients.

It was to these hospitals in the rear that casualties were brought from the fighting hundreds of miles away in the desert. Out there, clashes were intermittent but brutal. When a tank was hit and 'brewed up', the injuries from fire were horrific. An armour-penetrating shell could shear off a man's head as cleanly as a guillotine. Mines, scattered like seeds over mile after mile of sand, blew off limbs. Initial surgery was done as close to the action as possible, in highly mobile field medical units. Just behind the fighting, two desert-camouflaged, hard-top lorries would back up to each other and park a few yards apart. When the gap between them was covered over with canvas, a big enough space was created for an operating theatre. Here, complex abdominal and chest operations were attempted. Even 'Max Factor' (maxillo-facial) procedures such as skin grafting were started on to meet a growing problem. In the heat of the desert, sweating tank crews tended to discard their anti-flash protective clothing, with the result that more than a quarter of casualties were now burns cases. Surgeons at the front jumped smartly to meet all these new challenges.

To help them, they had an increasingly efficient supply of the battlefield's number-one life-saver – blood. Initially, it had to be transfused for each patient, sometimes arm to arm, directly from the donor, but the introduction of mobile transfusion units transformed all that. They arrived at the front carrying bottled blood stored in oil-burning refrigerators. As he watched the life pouring back into a badly wounded corporal from the Nottinghamshire Yeomanry, 'his blood pressure rising, his colour improving', RAMC surgeon Captain J. C. Watts could see with his own eyes that this was 'one of the most outstanding advances in war surgery'.[10] In this particular case, it meant a life-saving operation to amputate the soldier's crushed leg could begin immediately. If the doctor had had to wait for a live donor to be found, his blood cross-matched and then extracted before it was available for use, then he was sure the patient would have died. Stored blood, on the other hand, brought quick results when speed was of the essence, as, in war surgery, it so often was.

Less of a success story were the logistics for evacuating the wounded from the battle area to hospitals in the rear. The distances involved presented huge problems. Planes were rarely an option, to the disgust of the army's adjutant general, who was appalled to discover there was not a single dedicated air ambulance in use. His protestations – 'it is impossible to get accurate figures as to the number of lives lost and the suffering inflicted through the non-provision of ambulance aircraft'[11] – went unheeded. The Axis forces were routinely evacuating their wounded by air, the Germans in specially adapted Junkers planes attached to each medical unit. But the best British casualties could hope for was to be loaded on to transporter planes returning to base after delivering supplies to the front.

Generally, their journey to hospital was overland and arduous. An RAMC report likened the situation to having a base hospital in London, casualties in York and the area in between not only uninhabited and uninhabitable but served by one narrow road and a single-line railway. Every train and ambulance convoy was a tempting target for enemy planes. Nonetheless, across the desert wastes they trundled back, many of those with leg fractures immobilized for the uncomfortable journey in what became known as a 'Tobruk splint'. This was based on a traditional metal-framed Thomas splint – much used in the First World War and whose origins went back to its eponymous inventor, a Welsh-born doctor, who treated badly maimed dockers in Liverpool in the 1870s and then navvies building the Manchester Ship Canal. But in the 'Tobruk', an equally inventive (and unknown) RAMC medic of the Second World War, treating casualties in that besieged city, added a cast of plaster of Paris around the splint. It became a standard technique for safely transporting those with broken legs.

As fighting in the desert intensified, casualty numbers sent back to hospitals on the Nile rose to more than thirty thousand in one six-month period alone. During the big set-piece encounters, such as Rommel's victory at the first battle of Alamein, so many casualties arrived at hospital that, in the theatre, instruments were laid out on a central table cafeteria-style, and surgeons, with their different patients, grabbed what they needed. Debenham thought that war surgery was generally 'very crude' and not very interesting to perform, a view shared by a surprisingly large number of army surgeons. There was a tendency for the work to be fast and pressured but otherwise routine, 'an endless round of cleaning, shaving, trimming, packing and plastering', in the words of one medical historian.[12] No great intellectual challenges were posed or inventiveness required – unlike, say, the demands made on doctors in the jungle prison camps in the Far East. But on occasions when the casualty convoys were coming in a non-stop stream from the front, Debenham rose to the occasion. Work then was very satisfying, he declared, 'because we are achieving something'.

★

Out in the desert, Malcolm Pleydell was a medical officer with the Brigade of Guards and found his regimental aid post suddenly caught in the middle of a fierce battle. From out of nowhere, there was 'a big circus' of fifty German planes in the sky above him, and he witnessed a vast dog-fight as half a dozen Hurricanes took on the Stukas and Messerschmitt 109s. 'Some came pretty low over our heads,' he recorded in his diary, 'and there was a good deal of machine-gunning. Five planes brought down – three of theirs and two of ours.' For all his non-combatant status, he was not averse to taking pot-shots at the low-flying enemy himself. 'I knew pilots disliked small-arms fire, and I often had a rifle to hand. The deliberate Axis bombing of Tobruk hospital in daylight destroyed completely any confidence I had in the Geneva Convention.' The following day he was at the heart of the battle himself as the Germans attacked. 'Much consternation, with trucks dashing round. Shelling very hard on both sides. Suddenly there were thirty German tanks on our doorstep. Several shells landed close. Walking with the padre when one banged down about 80 yards away. Went flat. Dust and earth pattering all around.' The attack was beaten off, 'with plenty of bangs and smoke' . . . for now.

Soon Pleydell was on the move with his ambulances, setting out in a bitterly cold wind and seeing fires blazing on the horizon where an enemy ammunition dump had blown up. There was no let-up from the action. 'Machine-gunned by five ME109s. One man wounded in the genitals, forearm and wrist.' In the early-morning fog – another hindrance to visibility – he lost contact with the rest of the column, a frequent occurrence in this vast terrain, and drove around aimlessly until the chatter of their Bren guns steered him in the right direction. He was lucky. He could just as easily have crossed some invisible front line and found himself in enemy hands. After a tank battle with Italian forces, he drove out to pick up casualties. 'Very bad. Chloroformed one who was mad with pain, and he died. Shattered leg and eye blown out. Treated about seven. Then followed wire back through minefield to battalion HQ. Treated wounded there. One vomited over me – very messy.' On another occasion he went out to a shot-down Hurricane burning in the sand. 'Pilot dead a few yards off with fractured skull. Not very nice. His parachute had failed to open.'

There were many dangers peculiar to desert warfare. First was the very real risk of getting lost. Pleydell recalled wandering off from the bedded-down and darkened column one night to relieve himself and then realizing that, in the pitch black all around him, he did not have a clue where they were. He forced himself not to panic. 'You have to sit down, light a cigarette and keep your head. After what seemed hours, a noise gave their location away. But without that indication, any step I took might be leading me further and further into solitude.' Another problem was the weather, which could change in an instant. 'Dust storm blowing up,' he reported, 'and trucks around are slowly slipping out of sight. The sand blows along in rapid waves like a fire licking along the ground. The sky is turning a dirty yellow. Men lean against the wind as they walk, with their heads down, shielding their eyes. The trucks look ghostly and my slit trench is slowly filling up with sand. My red cross flag flaps wildly, torn in half by the wind.'

And if the sand wasn't getting in your eyes, then a heat haze was clouding your vision, making it difficult to discern whether the half-track looming into view was one of yours or one of theirs. Pleydell treated the buttock wounds of an officer who had sworn the approaching armoured car was friendly – until its occupants opened fire. The mistake wasn't fatal this time, but it was uncomfortable and undignified. On other occasions, he found to his horror that the enemy had sneaked so close he could almost touch them. 'Suddenly very surprised to see German troop transport about 200 yards to my left. We opened up on them and moved on.' It was easy to find yourself surrounded. 'German column moving up on us from the south, another to our west, another to east. We moved north, and met a large concentration of Germans in front of us. They shelled us. Our position seemed hopeless and I thought my last hour of freedom had come, but we slowly zig-zagged away. German vehicles followed in parallel with us on flanks and shelled us. Dusk came to our rescue.'

It wasn't just with the enemy that the doctor had problems. He sometimes had to face down his own army superiors and their tendency to believe that he – along with all MOs, probably – was a soft touch. He was presented one day with a deserter, a man who would have been court-martialled and shot in the First World War. That sanction had disappeared, erased from the Army Manual by an act of parliament in the inter-war years. Pleydell was asked for his professional opinion, sat the reluctant soldier down in the back of an ambulance and, as shells flew by outside, tried to persuade him back into battle. 'You must go,' he said. 'We're all in the same boat, and if everyone does the same as you, we will all be in the bag [captured].' But the only thing the man could say was: 'I can't, I just can't.'

The doctor reported to the colonel that he was going to evacuate the man 'with a bad case of battle fatigue', a diagnosis that was greeted with undisguised contempt and hostility. The second-in-command's suggestion was that the man should be forced into the front line ahead of men with bayonets drawn 'so that he advances in front of them, minefields or no minefields'. To send him back down the line to safety would destroy morale and encourage more deserters, Pleydell was told in no uncertain terms. 'They'll *all* be going off sick.' The doctor stuck to his guns, 'right or wrong', as he remembered it. He turned out to be right. After the man was sent away, it became a daily ritual for the colonel to taunt him, 'How many deserters have you sent back to-day, Doctor?' But, Pleydell recorded, in vindication of himself, there were no more, 'and slowly the colonel forgave me'.

The fact is that he knew how easy it was for courage to desert a man. 'We were all scared in different ways and at different times. The sound of machine-gun fire at first light was unnerving. My courage was flickering, present one second, absent the next. Just a matter of trying to control fear, panic and cowardice.' He remembered when his unit was surrounded and shells had come very close, and two officers beside him threw themselves to the ground. 'For some reason, I remained standing. The expressions on their faces as they looked up and saw me looking down on them were priceless. For one brief second, I felt ten feet tall. The next minute, I was a coward again!' But Pleydell was doing himself a disservice. It was not the act of a coward to volunteer, as he now did, for secret behind-the-lines operations, with L Detachment of the Special Air Service Brigade, the newly formed SAS.

He joined in June 1942 as medical officer of the hundred-strong unit after a taste of life in a military hospital at Suez, which he found unexciting to the point of depression. Doctors en masse, he decided, were 'such a dull lot, with a self-satisfied air of stupidity. Few of them know what fighting is. They forget there is any excitement in life, any thrills. Just sit around on one end of a microscope or stethoscope.' That wasn't the life for him. He craved action, and got it in a series of daring raids that took the fight into the enemy's backyard. For weeks they would motor in modified jeeps packed with machine guns, ammunition clips but little else, through remote seas of sand and across mountains, to bypass the enemy's defences. Then they would pop up as if from nowhere to destroy an airfield or a vital fuel dump. 'It was a hit-and-run, hide-and-seek type of war,' Pleydell recalled.

We would make long detours south of the battle line and then loop up north to within striking distance of our target. In the deepest parts of the desert, the distances were so immense and maps so unreliable that we took our bearings by sun and stars and plotted our routes from tables based on Greenwich Mean Time. Camouflage had to be expert so that when we hid we were not detected, even at close distance. Slow-flying enemy aircraft would follow our tracks to our hiding places, and they presented a real threat. Water discipline was essential as supplies were sometimes very limited. You had to eke out your water bottle in sips.

In his letters to his girlfriend, Pleydell revealed as much as he was able to about this new clandestine life of his. To his delight, he told her, he had total medical responsibility for the lives of the men in his troop – 'odd after hospital, where you had to sign six forms before you looked at a patient!' Evacuating the wounded from the depths of the desert was next to impossible, and, apart from a single orderly, he was on his own. If he had to operate, he would administer the anaesthetic himself before getting on with the job in the back of a truck parked in the middle of nowhere, 'with very little shade and no shelter from sand or wind'. But he had the very latest in medical science to draw on. There was plaster of Paris for binding wounds Trueta-style and, for transfusions, 'dried' plasma – not as good as 'whole', oxygenated blood for instant powers of healing but easier to keep and transport and still a powerful tool. 'I get priority in my demands,' he reported. Most revolutionary of all, he had what he described to his girlfriend as 'a very rare drug for injecting into abdominal wounds which it is hoped will save lives'. He was referring to penicillin.

They drove over every different type of desert terrain. Across the vast sand seas, they stuck to a steady and monotonous 40mph for hour after hour through the night until they lost all sense of motion. The sight of a discarded cigarette-end in the sand was the only sign of progress. 'Occasionally a driver would fall asleep and you would see the lights of his vehicle drift away, before he could be recalled.' Then there were towering dunes to negotiate. 'You had to drive fast up the slopes without somersaulting over the top. Fatalities could and did result in this way, since there were no shadows to indicate the peaks of the dunes, which followed each other in huge successive waves. The dunes were usually packed hard on the windward side and soft and falling on the leeward side. A drift of sand would blow from the peaks, so that they fell in small avalanches.' But then they came to mountains and caves where, when they stopped to rest, the doctor found prehistoric paintings, a neolithic arrowhead and Greek and Roman pottery. All this brought out the philosopher in him. 'The greatest solace in the immensity of the desert was the sense of communion with the universe, and the stars as they rose and set. There were vast Wagnerian sunsets, which reminded one of Turner, and which mesmerized the senses. The feeling of the insignificance of our existence came as a balm which soothed anxieties and, perhaps, helped us to come to terms with life on our tiny planet.'

Coming to terms with death, however, was tougher. A highlight of SAS operations – for all the wrong reasons – came in September 1942, with a 200-man attack alongside French special forces, the Long Range Desert Group and the Special Boat Section (SBS) to blow up ships and dock installations in the Italian-held port of Benghazi. It was a disaster. The men trekked 1,500 miles through the desert but news of the raid had leaked, and their column of forty heavily armed jeeps ran into an ambush on the outskirts of the town. They were forced to retreat and then pursued into the desert by fighter planes and bombers. Fifteen jeeps and twenty-four trucks were lost. Four men were killed and a number wounded as they battled their way out.

With the aid of morphine, Pleydell fixed a broken thigh bone in the back of a lorry covered in camouflage netting and dealt with the second-degree burns on the chest, abdomen, arms and legs of a man who had driven over a mine. As wind rattled through the canvas cover of the lorry and dust swirled around, he amputated a leg – a remarkable feat in such a confined and unsterile space – fed two pints of plasma into the patient's veins and then had to drive like fury to catch up with the rest of the convoy as it made its escape. The men he had just operated on were lying in the back of the lorry in front of Pleydell's red-cross-emblazoned jeep, 'and each time the lorry hit a bump I could see three legs and one stump being flung up in the air and falling back.' He had to stop, climb in the back and tie their legs down with a rope. They drove on, but the men's faces were caking over with yellow dust thrown up as they sped across the desert and he had to stop yet again to bathe their faces and allow them to breathe.

With the convoy still under attack, Pleydell had more casualties to deal with. 'I had a case of multiple wounds, not too bad; another through the lung, for which there was little I could do; one with a compound fracture of the humerus, radius and ulna, with the arm shattered in two places. I left the arm on. All the bad injuries had two pints of blood plasma and I waited until they were stronger before operating.' His most difficult case was a man who couldn't pee – 'retention of urine due to the perineal urethra being shot away'. The doctor struggled. 'Because I was unable to find the proximal end of the urethra, I eventually had to perform a suprapubic cystotomy [cut a secondary drain from the bladder]. It was the devil. I was wondering if I should open the peritoneum but I had two scalpels and two Spencer Wells [artery forceps] and I was alone. With nobody retracting, it's damned difficult to see what you are doing. I did not dare risk any bleeding, as I could hardly have reached the bleeding point and tied it off. I did muscle splitting with blunt dissection and luckily got down to the bladder with no bleeding.' The medical jargon in his letter to his girlfriend would not have disguised the drama from her nor his bland assertion that 'the responsibility of being in sole charge of the wounded is quite a mental strain, you know.' As a nurse, she would have known every move he made, felt his dilemma. A man's life was in his hands. He had to operate to save him, but the operation, in poor light in the back of a truck and with no one to assist, could well be fatal if he got it even slightly wrong. Pleydell had wanted excitement rather than the dull routine of a hospital, but this was more than he could ever have bargained for. His skill and his nerve were stretched to the limit.

He pulled it off, only to be hit by an even greater dilemma. When he rejoined the convoy, it rapidly became clear that, with so many vehicles put out of action by the bombing, there was no room for stretcher-cases. Four of the wounded would have to be left behind. It was the Dunkirk and Crete dilemma all over again. The doctor's natural instinct was to stay with them. But common sense told him this 'wasn't my job'. As the sole medical officer on the trip, his duty was to remain with the main fighting force in case of more casualties up ahead before they made it back to base. He left the four wounded men in the care of his orderly and, with the rest of the convoy, he drove off into the night for the long trek home. All the walking wounded he took with him made it back, and he was happy about that. Only later would he discover that the four he had had to leave behind were picked up by the Italians, as he had hoped, but all died from their wounds. The medical orderly who stayed with them died too, in a prisoner-of-war camp.

That long-distance raid took its toll on the doctor. His eyes had taken a hammering on the drive and were now constantly bloodshot. 'After all those night drives, the dust whipping in behind your goggles, and the glare of the sun on the white sand in the day, I had solar conjunctivitis.' He was transferred to a base hospital to work, hated every minute of it and hankered for the desert he had fallen in love with. What kept him going was the sparkling morale of the wounded men he treated, but he feared for their futures.

They treat me as one of themselves and they rag me quite a bit, but to hear them joking and laughing though their arms and legs are shattered makes me want to ensure that they don't get the same treatment as their fathers had after the last war. I don't want to see any more men at street corners with last war ribbons and an old gramophone to keep them company. If people living in luxury at home could see these men, then stop and think for a moment and consider what the future holds for them, I think it might bring a lump to their throats. But, in a few years' time they will be forgotten and people will think what a nuisance they are – and why remind us of a war that is over and done with? Please God, I shan't forget.

★

For the Allied forces, the desert bloomed. It was here that, after the multiple defeats and retreats of Dunkirk, Singapore, Greece and Crete, the first indication came that the tide of war was turning. Montgomery's defeat of Rommel at the second battle for Alamein was, in Churchill's thunderous phrase, 'the end of the beginning. The bright gleam of victory – a remarkable and definite victory – has caught the helmets of our soldiers, and warmed and cheered all our hearts.'[13] The grand rhetoric cut no ice with the nurses who had seen with their own eyes the cost of that victory arriving at Cairo hospitals in convoy after convoy of ambulances from the front. 'We had far too many mutilated young men in our care for us to feel like celebrating,' said Sister Margaret Jennings.

The poor, wretched, dirt and blood-caked casualties were carried in, stretcher after stretcher of them. Some had been half roasted alive in their tanks, others so badly mutilated that it was amazing they were still alive. Our training had scarcely prepared us for the horror of it all – some with parts of their face missing, others with deep abdominal wounds, legs hanging by threads of tissue with bones protruding. The urgency of the task lent skill to our fingers. One by one we worked our way through them all, washing them, dressing their wounds and putting them between clean white sheets. Bleeding was stopped, transfusions given, plaster of Paris applied over Thomas splints, and pain-killing injections given. The expressions of relief and gratitude on their faces as they saw they were being tended by female nurses was unforgettable. They never complained. We were working night and day but the courage and fortitude of those lads was such an example and inspiration to us that we forgot our weariness.[14]

But a strategic corner had indeed been turned in the war, and attack now replaced defence in Allied military planning – and, as the fight was taken to the enemy, medics were right up in the vanguard. From North Africa, Captain Martin Herford took his place in 200th Field Ambulance in July 1943 for the invasion of Sicily, 250 miles away across the Mediterranean Sea, the first stage in the re-conquest of Europe. After his flight from Greece two years earlier, it felt good to be going in the opposite direction at last. It was half past midnight, the sky red with phosphorus flares put up by the German defenders, when he and his unit clambered down into one of thousands of landing craft and made for a beach close to the town of Syracuse. The opposition, softened up by a naval barrage from out at sea, was slight. He had expected to find himself pinned down by German fire. Instead he was able to stand at his leisure and drink in the sight of fields of ripening grapes and tomatoes ahead. There were apples and figs on the trees, the early morning sun shone brightly and the smell of jasmine hung in the air.

He sensed that this was the lull before a very bloody storm, and he was right. Two miles off the coast lay a hospital ship, the SS *Talamba*, white-hulled and fully illuminated with prominent red crosses on each of her three funnels. She had been receiving a steady flow of casualties from the shore all day. That evening, a flight of German dive bombers, having been beaten off by the guns of a British cruiser they were attacking, picked on her instead. She sank, with doctors and nurses scrambling to get their patients into lifeboats. A surgeon who was amputating a soldier's leg as the bombs fell bandaged up the stump at top speed, strapped the man to a stretcher and in desperation lowered it over the side into the water. He hoped it would float, and it did, unlike the *Talamba* herself, who slid stern-first to the bottom of the sea. On land, resistance was growing. Having surrendered the beach areas, the German forces were massing on the hilltops in the mountains ahead. Those fields and vineyards, the sight of which had brought out such rapture in Herford, proved close up to be sown with a deadly crop of land mines.

With a lorry and two light ambulances, he went forward with the first wave of the assault on the German positions. A procession of tanks, heavy artillery and infantrymen crept along narrow and winding mountain passes where every village was a stronghold and the fighting was long and fierce with heavy loss of life. Though he could have chosen to be in the safety of a casualty station in the rear, Herford got on his motorbike, just as he had done in Greece, and went looking for casualties to treat and evacuate. Mortars exploded around him as he sped along tracks and struggled over rough ground. Showers of earth and gravel hit him, stinging his face and hands, but his luck held. His presence was an undoubted tonic to the fighting men and, by being so close to the action, his prompt treatment was credited with saving many lives.

Sometimes, he was too close. He was evacuating casualties from a wooded hill held by Canadian infantry when German soldiers rushed them. Weaponless, he could only throw himself to the ground as the Canadians fought off the attack. 'Bullets whistled overhead; the air was thick with the acrid smell of gunpowder as spent cases sprayed from the breaches of the Canadian guns,' wrote his biographer.[15] 'His ears were deafened by a barrage of thunderous rifle cracks.' The attack was repelled and the Germans pulled back, leaving several corpses behind. In the nearby forest, stretcher-bearers found a number of Allied soldiers wounded in the initial assault, and Herford was able to put to good use the blood-transfusion equipment that was now for the first time being carried in army ambulances.

In that fierce, inch-by-inch battle for Sicily, it took six weeks in the hot summer sun before the German and Italian forces finally abandoned the island. The Allies lost close to five thousand men killed, with a further nineteen thousand wounded. But this was just the start.

The next step was to cross the Straits of Messina to mainland Italy. Herford and his men stocked up their medical supplies and equipment for an even tougher battle. He came ashore unopposed at night at Pizzo, 80 miles north of the main landings at Reggio, and established a dressing station on a hillside overlooking the bay. Once again, he had been lucky, because in the morning he discovered that his unit had landed ahead of everyone else. The main assault force was only now arriving on the beaches – and was in trouble, under a continuous barrage from German gun emplacements and peppered with bombs from the air. As the troops struggled ashore, casualties were high. In the dressing station, the doctor and his team worked frantically on the wounded who were brought up to them.

From his vantage point he looked down and saw one particular landing craft take a terrible pasting. Bodies were everywhere and the stretcher-bearers were overwhelmed. Down the hill Herford raced, on to the beach and out, waist-deep, into the water, to the landing craft wallowing in the waves. Badly hurt men were lying inside, and, as gunfire splattered the sides, he climbed on board, treating and soothing them until the overworked stretcher-parties could return to carry them to safety. Once they had been taken away, he jumped back into the water and, still under fire, scoured the beach for casualties before returning to the dressing station. On the way back up the hill, a bomb nearly got him, and he took cover behind a stone wall. As chunks of debris thudded into the ground around him, he covered his head with his hands. In the rush to get to the beach, he had forgotten to put on his steel helmet. He really was pushing that luck of his.

The shelling was showing no sign of easing, and an ambulance outside the dressing station was hit, causing several fatalities. The whole brigade was pinned down and wounded soldiers were being brought in all the time. Politics saved the day. Just when all seemed lost, over the radio came the news that the Italian government had surrendered. A large force of American troops had also landed, 150 miles along the coast at Salerno. The German forces ceased firing and withdrew, to fight their key battles further up the peninsula. The battle here was over, and Herford and his medics joined the swelling Allied army heading northwards to pursue the enemy. There was still much fighting – and much saving of lives – to do before this war would be over. A bigger invasion than Sicily or Italy was on the planning boards, one in which the medical services would be instructed to prepare for a possible bloodbath. Their biggest test was yet to come.

6. Stout Hearts

The mighty force of 'stout hearts' – as General Montgomery called his troops in his commander-in-chief's address to them on the eve of D-Day – crossed over from England to the Normandy beaches in June 1944 protected by the prayers of half the world and the promise of penicillin. Carried in the task force's medical packs, the newly mass-manufactured, quick-acting antibiotic meant that more of them had a good chance of returning alive, of *not* dying from their wounds. The 'very rare drug' that SAS medical officer Malcolm Pleydell had been entrusted with on his secret missions in the Western Desert eighteen months earlier was now in general use. It proved an extraordinarily important life-saver that gave the Allied armies an edge over their German adversaries.

Discovered in 1928 by the British scientist, Alexander Fleming, the drug's practical uses had been developed in wartime by an Australian-born Oxford professor of pathology and adviser to the British Army, Howard Florey. In trials on wounded soldiers in North Africa in 1943, he established that penicillin did a better and quicker job of killing infections than sulphonamides, and with none of the toxic side effects that sulphonamides could have. Large-scale manufacture in powder form (and later as a liquid for injection and intravenous drip) got underway in the United States, and Allied soldiers fighting their way up through Italy were the first to benefit.

'Marvellous stuff,' declared RAMC colonel Robert Debenham as he watched a casualty with the usually fatal gas gangrene in his thigh sitting up and eating a hearty breakfast. Here was the 'Holy Grail', as one leading bacteriologist called it,[1] a wonder weapon against the greatest killer of all on the battlefield – infection. In their field hospital in Italy, Lorna Bradley and her fellow nurses hailed it as 'gold dust'. As they puffed the powder into wounds with a special 'gun', sparingly because it was still in short supply, they felt privileged to be using it. 'We could see it was going to alter the whole treatment of the wounded and save millions of lives.'[2] It even gave a chance to the 'abdominal' cases – those with guts spilling out, on whom surgery was so complex and time-consuming that they were often put to one side so doctors could concentrate on patients with simpler problems and a better chance of survival. Crucially, the Germans did not have penicillin – an irony given that Florey's co-researcher, Ernst Chain, was a Jew from Berlin who had fled to Britain to escape Nazi persecution. As a result, their wounded troops were slower to recover and get back to the front line. Advantage to the Allies.

Winning the war was the thought in everyone's mind in that spring of 1944, but first there was a massive hurdle to climb, a Channel to cross. Getting a foothold back on the north European mainland was not going to be easy. One hundred and fifty thousand Allied troops were assigned to take part in the initial assault. Back home, civilian hospitals throughout Britain were emptying wards to make space for as many as a *third* of them. Beds were stripped of their white sheets and spread with grey blankets on which to lay soldiers in dirty, bloody uniforms, as one nurse recalled. 'A large trolley was ready with piles of towels, soap, flannels, razors and pyjamas for men with no possessions.'[3] The medical preparations and provisions were bigger and better than in any other military operation – or so the generals and the official histories came to believe. 'Never before in history has a British expeditionary force left the country so well equipped medically,' one senior medical officer stated.[4]

The men on the ground were more sceptical. Dr Bill Helm, joining the RAMC from a casualty department at Middlesex Hospital in London, was not so confident about his own preparation. He had found the military training hard going. There were tough assault courses and terrifying mock-battle exercises using live ammunition in which he was warned that sometimes there were fatalities. 'I was horrified that I might have to face some terrible casualty,' he remembered, and what he had not been given was specific medical instruction in what to do.[5] His training was in how to be a soldier but not in being a battlefield doctor. It was assumed he knew how to treat wounds but, like so many drawn into the fight for the first time, he had to learn the essentials as he went along. The only practical advice he ever got was from his father, who had been a doctor in the trenches in the First World War: never move a wounded man without splinting him first.

The ranks were getting more help than Helm did. The War Office issued a folded card of first-aid instructions for 'the fighting man' to carry into battle, 'to help him to go on fighting and to aid his friend in that cold interval between getting hit and getting help'. With a cartoon on the cover of a smiling Tommy and a heavily bandaged Hun, it was part manual, part propaganda. 'Courage in disaster,' it demanded. Don't panic, was its message. 'Wounds can look frightful. Be prepared for this. Remember modern surgeons can do wonders. Nature does her best to heal all wounds. But give Nature a chance. Stop wounds getting worse. That is your job. That is First Aid.' Think first, it urged. 'There may be three men wounded at once. Treat the most urgent first. Keep under cover. If mechanized, turn off petrol. Look out for falling walls. Any fool can be brave and get killed. Be brave, don't get killed, and save your friend instead.'[6] It advised on how to stop bleeding ('put your fist into the wound'), how to apply (and ease) a tourniquet and how to tie down a broken limb. Don't give water to a man with a belly wound, it instructed, because it will kill him. To carry a wounded man off the battlefield under fire, 'tie his wrists together, crawl on hands and knees on top of him, put your neck under his wrists and drag him underneath you'. You can go a long way like this, it told its perhaps less than convinced readers, aware now of the hell they were about to descend into and rightly concerned whether, once in this inferno, they would have the time or the cool presence of mind to consult the instruction card's wise words and follow its diagrams.

More tangible help was the sheer weight of trained medics lined up for the operation. The service had been massively pumped up, and it was decreed that there would be at least one medical orderly with advanced knowledge of first aid in every landing craft that approached the beaches. Seventy landing craft were reserved exclusively as water ambulances for evacuating the wounded. Doctors, accompanied by stretcher-bearers and blood-transfusion units, would be going in just behind the very first assault teams to set up instant dressing stations on the beaches. The biggest uncertainty was that almost all these newly recruited medics, from doctors to stretcher-bearers, were going into action for the first time. However well trained they were, how would they react under fire? Would they perform or collapse? The brigadier in command of one beach dressing station hit the nail on the head. 'There remains a world of difference,' he said, 'between handling and caring for an exercise casualty labelled "GSW [gunshot wound] abdomen" and a real man with his intestines protruding from a gaping wound in his stomach.'[7]

The time to put that difference to the test had come. Bugler and stretcher-bearer Len Brown – whom we last came across swimming to a rescue ship at Dunkirk[8] – had, like Helm, been through some arduous training, jumping into the water in full kit in a cold Scottish loch and wading ashore. Now he was crouching in the belly of a rolling and pitching landing craft as it raced with hundreds of others towards Sword, one of the five assault beaches on the Normandy coast. He was the first-aid man, with two medical kits on his back and no weapon. Behind him, rocket ships – 'marvellous' – were hurling salvoes at pill-boxes on the shoreline ahead, but he had already had his first casualty. A soldier had dropped his spring-loaded Sten gun, accidentally set it off and shot himself dead.

The landing craft slowed as it reached shallow water, steering round concrete obstructions and lethal mines attached to hop-poles that poked up through the waves, and as the bottom scraped against French sand, the front ramp went down 'and we just ran off'. Some of his unit were hit instantly by the volley of bullets coming from machine-gun nests on shore and pinging off the craft before it even came to a halt. Another soldier had a vivid memory of racing down the ramp of the landing craft that day into water already dark red with blood and seeing the man ahead of him cut down by machine-gun fire. 'He screamed for a medic. One of the aid men moved quickly to help him and he also was shot. I will never forget seeing that medic lying next to the wounded soldier and both of them screaming. They died in minutes.'

Those still on their feet and in one piece crept in behind tanks with flails that were beating a path through the barbed-wire barricades and buried mines on the beach. Brown tried to stay on track, but he saw men who strayed to one side trigger explosions that blew them apart, and he had to risk setting off a mine himself to go to help them. He knelt in the sand with a soldier whose leg was hanging off. 'I cut the trousers off him and put a bandage and a tourniquet on. I marked a "T" on his forehead and the time the tourniquet was applied so the medics coming behind me would know when to release it. Then I went on to the next man. We were under orders not to stay with the wounded too long but to keep going forward with the front troops as they tried to get off the beach.' The presence of a comrade with a red cross on his helmet seemed to give the fighting lads an extra impetus to keep going, to stand up and burst forward, guns blazing, through the vicious shell fire falling down on them. 'It's nice to have you up with us,' they told him as they lay in the sand together, waiting for the next dash forward. 'And I was. I was right up there with them,' Brown recalled. 'When they went forward, I went forward. I thought it was necessary. A bad wound needed to be tourniqueted straight away. Then a jeep could come up over the rough ground and take him away. But treating them quickly in those first few minutes after being wounded was vital.'

Over on Omaha, hemmed in with high bluffs, and the most heavily defended of the beaches, US regimental surgeon Major Charles Tegtmeyer was face down in the shingle after struggling waist-high through water criss-crossed with submarine obstacles and booby-traps just to get ashore. He had already 'done' opposed landings in North Africa and Sicily, but this was in a new league of lethality. He cowered behind a small shelf of sand and could hear nothing but the explosions of shells and the sharp whistle of bullets. What he could see as he lifted his head was even worse.

In every direction were the huddled bodies of men, living, wounded and dead, as tightly packed together as cigars in a box. Some were frantically attempting to dig in, a few were raising themselves and firing towards the concrete-protected enemy on the cliff above, but the majority were huddled together, face downward. Artillery shells exploded. Bullets, like a million angry hornets, buzzed over and plunged into the water behind us with sharp hisses or whined away into the distance as they ricocheted off stones. At the water's edge, floating face down with arched backs, were innumerable human forms, eddying to and fro with each incoming wave, the water about them a muddy pink in colour. Floating equipment rolled in the surf, mingling with the bodies. Everywhere, the frantic cry, 'Medics Hey, medics,' could be heard above the horrible din. Crouching, running, crawling and stumbling, my men and I slowly worked our way up the beach, answering the cry.[9]

The doctor had to make snap decisions. 'The number of dead, killed by mines, shell fragments, machine guns and sniper bullets was appalling. I examined scores as I went, telling the men who to dress and who not to bother with. My men were superb as time and time again they went back and plunged into the surf, regardless of the hail of steel fragments whistling about them, to pull wounded ashore.' He had to restrain them from crawling into a minefield to haul out the wounded until he could get a sapper with a mine detector to clear the way first.

Slowly, the Germans on the clifftop were being knocked back, the attack proceeding. But the cost was horrendous. Tegtmayer had eighty-four casualties laid out on the beach around him, and more arriving by the minute. 'An infantryman was brought in with a traumatic amputation of the right leg and multiple fractures of the left leg. He was conscious and cheerful but his only hope was rapid evacuation, and at this time evacuation did not exist. An hour later he was dead.' Some could, however, be saved. The doctor examined a man with a terrible chest wound who looked as if he was about to die. 'I called for plasma but the God-damned bottle had no vacuum and would not draw up the sterile water [to dilute it for transfusion]. I called for a second, and the same thing happened. But the third bottle worked and we were able to get the stuff into him. A few minutes later, his pulse improved and he felt better.' Availability of blood was, like penicillin, a key life-saver for the Allies. Against the Germans' almost negligible blood service, from the start the British forces alone had five transfusion units and more than a thousand bottles of refrigerated whole blood on the Normandy beaches.

The replacement blood was a drop in a dreadful ocean. The scale and the horror of the casualties – the blood-*letting* – was deeply distressing to many of the less experienced medics who found themselves on the beaches. One medical officer recalled the overwhelming crush in and around his beach dressing station, with sixty men lying on stretchers waiting for emergency blood transfusions and hundreds of walking wounded. Medics worked non-stop – hours on end, with little or no rest. One young surgeon claimed to have woken up in England at 5 a.m. on Monday (5 June) and not stood down from duty until midnight on Thursday (8 June). Many popped Benzedrine tablets to keep themselves going, just as RAF night bomber crews did for long-distance raids. The pep pills came in the rations.[10] But even more debilitating than exhaustion for some tyro medics was the trauma of seeing hideous injuries. This, says historian Mark Harrison, was especially true of unseasoned stretcher-bearers, who, as bandsmen, cooks and clerks, were unused to the gore they were now steeped in. One regimental medical officer, Dr Aitken of the 24th Lancers, a conscript on a short-term commission, felt queasy enough himself during D-Day and could only imagine what his inexperienced stretcher-bearers were feeling at their first sight of real injuries. Some 'hesitate to lift a stretcher unless they can turn their backs on the injured', he noted.[11] That the buglers and batmen stuck to their task was to their lasting credit.

*

While the furious fight was going on to capture and hold the beachheads, there were other contingents of Allied troops already behind the enemy's lines and battling hard for an advantage. Hours ahead of the main frontal attack, airborne forces had dropped by parachute and glider. Dr John Vaughan of the Oxfordshire and Buckinghamshire Light Infantry was in the very first wave, medical officer for a glider strike force detailed to capture the key bridges over the River Orne and the adjacent Caen canal three miles inland and hold them until elements of the main force arrived from the coast.

They had begun the operation in the knowledge that they would be the very first troops to land in Occupied France – but also that they might be isolated and quickly eliminated. If, that was, they got anywhere near the target in the first place. Sitting, his face blackened, in the narrow fuselage of the third of six all-wooden Horsa gliders as they were tugged silently through the night sky and over the French coastline, Vaughan realized that a single searchlight from the ground below and an ack-ack shell would end the mission and his own life in a trice. 'I was appalled by our helplessness in this flimsy contraption,' he recalled. It was his first time ever in a glider and he longed for a parachute, for which he was fully trained. 'We all of us knew that anybody who survived this day would be very lucky.'[12] He peeped through the Perspex windshield and saw the town of Caen below, just as the tow rope was released, 'and down we dropped, gathering speed. The pilot made two right turns, there was a loud splintering sound directly underneath . . . silence (we had bounced) . . . and then *nothing*.'

When he came to in a marsh beside the wreckage of the crash-landed glider, Vaughan had no idea where he was. He thought for a moment that he had woken up in his bed in the officers' quarters back in barracks on Salisbury Plain. The sound of automatic fire disabused him of that comforting notion. As he rubbed mud from his eyes, 'I realized the area I had landed in was bristling with offensively disposed Germans.' He heard terrible groans – 'the like of which I will never forget' – and staggered to the wreckage, where a man was trapped. Though still groggy, his hand went automatically to the pocket in his battledress where he kept his syrettes (single-dose, disposable syringes) of morphine, and he jabbed a needle into the casualty. 'I tried to reassure him and told him I was going to go and find a stretcher-bearer. I staggered off.' Vaughan looked around and saw other upended gliders. He also spotted the bridges – already, he was glad to see, in British hands, but not totally secured. From the second of these, a metal roll-up-roll-down contraption over the canal,[13] the sound of shooting was coming . . . and also the chilling heavy rattle of an approaching German tank. On the roadway, an airborne sergeant knelt, aimed his anti-tank gun and squeezed the trigger. The tank stopped in its tracks and burst into flames. But others were queuing behind it. The battle to hold the bridges was on.

The doctor set up an aid post and tended some of those already wounded, though, sadly, most were beyond his help. Suddenly a Mercedes staff car came hurtling towards the bridge. A German officer, refusing to accept the truth of what was happening, was attempting to get a close-up view of the situation. The car was quickly cut to ribbons by a Sten gun, and a snarling Major Schmidt was pulled from the wreck and taken prisoner, promising that the impudent British invaders would soon be thrown back into the sea. His badly wounded driver wasn't going to be throwing anyone anywhere, though. Both his legs were appallingly shattered, and there and then Vaughan amputated one of them, using a pair of scissors. It was his first battlefield operation – and it was on an enemy. It was not a success. 'Not having a couple of bottles of blood for transfusion about me at the time, I wasn't in the end able to save the poor fellow's life,' he noted later.

Dawn broke over the Orne that morning accompanied by the boom of big guns from the direction of the coast. Naval ships were bombarding German defences. D-Day proper had begun, and soon those swarms of landing craft would be beetling across the water to Sword, Omaha and the other beaches. As the day wore on, the Germans were desperate to destroy the bridges, which would hold the key to the Allied advance. The doctor watched from his aid post as a Luftwaffe fighter-bomber swooped in and dropped a bomb, which hit the canal bridge but failed to go off. German frogmen were spotted swimming towards it with explosives and were dealt with. A gunboat full of soldiers was sent packing by the anti-tank gun. But gradually airborne resistance around the bridge was being worn down, ammunition was running out and the doctor was at full stretch, with growing numbers of casualties. 'Suddenly I became aware of the most absurd sound – bagpipes!' A file of Royal Marine commandos was approaching along the road from the coast, led by its commander, the flamboyant Lord Lovat, striding along with a walking stick and a piper. The relief had arrived. The doctor went to greet a young commando, 'and he dropped before my very eyes, slid down into the ditch, and lay still. He had been shot through the head by a sniper.' The line between victory and defeat, life and death, was paper-thin, a heartbeat.

Now, more gliders were arriving in the area, some bringing in jeeps and trailers to form field ambulances. Captain J. C. Watts, surgical veteran of North Africa and Italy, commanded one such unit and made sure he had plenty of the magic ingredient that he knew from experience would save lives. Each of his men carried two bottles of blood plasma in his pouches, giving the doctor an opening store of two hundred pints for the emergency operations that began almost as soon as he had landed. He set up his advanced dressing station (ADS) in a large and grand country house and chose the cellar for his operating theatre – dark and dismal, maybe, but safer from bombardment. Soon Primus stoves were roaring away with hot water to sterilize instruments and the first casualty was on the table, an officer of the Royal Ulster Rifles with severe mortar wounds that once would have cost him his arm. Watts cut out all the damaged muscle and fixed the limb with plaster of Paris so he could be evacuated without suffering more harm in the move. The next soldier was not so lucky. His foot had been pulped in the same mortar attack and it had to be removed completely. But, where another doctor might have been tempted to amputate the rest of the man's leg, Watts opted to leave it intact. Out on the battlefield, he felt, it was right to do whatever was strictly necessary to keep a man alive, and no more. Haste was dangerous. In the less frantic atmosphere of a hospital ward, surgeons were better able to make the decisions that would so drastically affect the patient's future and his quality of life.

The cases piled up. A man with a fractured femur was brought in, and Watts introduced the novices in his surgical team to the Tobruk splint. He had picked up such tricks of the trade over a number of years but, as he was very aware, his men were learning war surgery the hard way, 'under terrific pressure'. He was astonished by their prowess. 'I never had to show them a procedure twice. They were veterans in an afternoon.'[14] A medical student administered anaesthetics, while triage – the initial sorting out of casualties according to the severity of their injuries – was skilfully undertaken by an orderly who had been a barber in civilian life but who now sifted out the priority cases and kept the flow of patients moving smoothly into theatre.

The battle was never far away. Suddenly, the Germans launched a counter-attack in the area and shells shook the house. Windows smashed, plaster rained down, but in his cellar Watts kept his head down, eyes firmly fixed on the table and whichever lacerated human was on it. When he did manage to take a short break, he went upstairs, looked out of the window and could clearly see German soldiers on the march across open fields nearby. To his horror, he realized they were to the *west* of his dressing station, in the direction of the sea – which meant he must now be behind enemy lines. His position was surrounded and could be overwhelmed at any moment. In the event, this German counter-attack was pushed back, but the truth was that, for a while, he, a doctor, had not only been up in the front line but way beyond it on the other side. Medics, so often the Cinderellas of the military services, were as exposed as the next man to danger – if not more so. With casualties to tend, they could not manoeuvre their way out of trouble or run and hide. The doctor returned to his table and carried on.

An exhausted Watts now had to deal with a complicated case. It was late at night and, by the light of a hurricane lamp, he examined a patient with almost no pulse and dressings over his stomach.

When I removed these, I saw a ghastly sight. He had apparently been almost eviscerated. There was a deep trench furrowing across his abdomen from side to side and no bowel to be seen. All through the busiest times of the North African and desert battles I had never had to refuse a case, but I had ten cases awaiting operation, all of them with a reasonable chance if they were operated on in time. This man's plight seemed so desperate that even if operated on he would have little chance of survival. Despondently I arranged for him to have a large dose of morphia to ease his pain, and instructed the stretcher-bearers to put him in a corner to die.

Watts worked through the night, cleared his cases and was astonished next morning to find the same man still lying on his stretcher, very much alive and complaining that no one was treating him. 'I inspected his enormous wound again and, by the light of day, I could see that he was an immensely fat man, and that an anti-tank shell had furrowed across his belly wall, inflicting the deep trench I had noted. But so thick was the fat that the shell had not actually opened the peritoneal cavity. The injury, which in my tired state and in the poor illumination of the previous night I had conceived to be hopeless, was merely a large (and easily stitched) flesh wound.'

But, despite this fortunate outcome, Watts never lost his wariness of belly wounds. He was comfortable treating limbs and chests in the front line but, as he observed, 'the abdominal wound presents a very difficult problem for the war surgeon. The patient's chances of survival are slight without operation, but after operation he must be held and nursed for about ten days until normal bowel function is restored.' This was difficult to do in the confines of an advanced dressing station, especially if a battle was raging outside. 'We were severely mortared one day when we had some abdominal cases still with us four or five days after their operations. Shelling is unpleasant enough when one is fit, but its effect is disastrous on a desperately wounded man lying on a stretcher unable to move, a tube in his nose leading to his stomach, and another giving him saline through a needle in his arm. Two of these poor patients, who had been progressing well until this shelling, deteriorated, paralysis of the bowels set in, and in spite of all measures they died from toxaemia within twenty-four hours.'

Most patients were evacuated as quickly as possible from the ADS to casualty clearing stations that, as promised, had now been set up on the beaches. Stretcher-bearers and ambulance drivers in any vehicle they could seize were constantly on the go, back and forth, dashing along unfamiliar roads in darkness and wet weather and through mortar and shell fire. On the day of the German counterattack, a convoy of seven ambulances, led by a motorbike, was on its way to the beaches and, at a crossroads, was waved on by a sentry. Only as they passed and he took pot shots at them did they realize he was German. So quickly was the situation changing that, on the way back, they saw German bodies lying at the roadside at the same spot after the successful British fight-back.

The fighting continued to swirl close to Watts's house for the next fortnight, causing endless problems. 'Spasmodic sniping and stray machine-gun bullets restricted our movements, even when we were not the object of any concerted attack,' one medic remembered.[15] Stretcher-bearers risked their lives constantly to bring in casualties. They would crawl forward into the heart of contact zones in twos, one carrying a stretcher, the other waving his red cross armband in the air. Many of these stretcher-bearers were conscientious objectors, who, on religious and moral grounds, refused to fight or carry weapons but were willing to save lives and ease suffering. Lieutenant David Tibbs, a doctor in the Parachute Regiment, had six of them in his unit and thought them 'excellent men'. He was touched by their strong faith, even when it was foolhardy. One, he recalled, sat in a deckchair outside the regimental aid post to read his bible, fully exposed to enemy fire, and when the doctor advised him to get inside, replied stoutly, 'If it is the Lord's will that I shall die, then I shall die!' He changed his mind when the first seriously injured casualties arrived and he could see close up the reality of the risk he was taking. Piety could go too far. 'He quickly moved his deckchair inside and never sat out there again.'[16]

In that desperate post-D-Day battle to consolidate the landing against an enemy equally determined not to give ground, no one was immune from danger and death. Tibbs was put in charge of a large barn filled with wounded paras, many of them dying in the straw where they lay. Their only 'protection' was a large red cross flag but, since a British anti-tank-gun position had been set up close by there was little chance of it being respected. German shells and mortars came in, followed by the rat-tat-tat of small-arms fire close by. A panicking ambulance driver burst through the door of the barn and shouted, 'German soldiers are at the bottom of the lane, fifty yards away!' A badly wounded Glaswegian sergeant pulled himself up, pointed his Sten gun at the driver and snarled, 'Stop yer blathering, ye fucker, or ye'll be the first to get it!' What astonished Tibbs was how all the wounded men now struggled to lay their hands on their guns. By rights they should not have had them inside the aid post. But they did, 'and here they were fully prepared to shoot it out, even though one grenade tossed in by the Germans would set the straw ablaze and all would die.'

The doctor wondered what *he* should do, where his ultimate duty as a medic lay. 'I had a 9mm automatic which I could use well. Should I join in the shoot-out, or try to prevent a slaughter by indicating [to the enemy] the red crosses on my arms?' The question was mercifully never put to the test. 'There was a sudden fusillade of shots outside, some loud explosions and then silence. The German infantrymen had retreated when their two supporting tanks were knocked out.' Tibbs took the opportunity to try to clarify the situation as he saw it. 'I told my orderlies to collect up and hide all weapons. There were grunts of annoyance but I am sure I was right that the wounded stood a better chance if I depended on the red cross to protect them.' That was his hunch, but a hunch was all it was. He had nothing to confirm that his interpretation of military law was correct. 'Oddly, we had been given virtually no instruction on the red cross and the Geneva Convention.'

The ambiguity that always surrounded medics on the battlefield remained. That they were as vulnerable as the next soldier to

1. Eric Harden VC. This was taken in 1940 and sent to his wife inscribed, 'To Darling Maude From Eric xx'

2. Eric Harden's widow Maud and their son Bobby at the Victoria Cross investiture at Buckingham Palace, 9 April 1946

3. The telegram sent to Maud Harden informing her of Eric's death, 29 January 1945

4. Thailand, August 1945. An emaciated British prisoner at the hospital camp at Nakhon Pathom. If the Japanese had not surrendered on 15 August he could have died within days

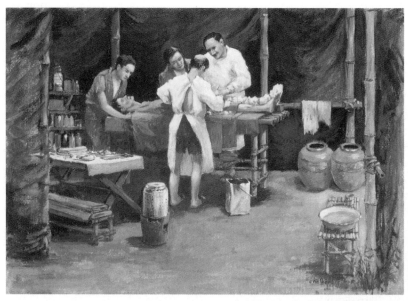

5. Jungle medicine in a bamboo hut lined with mosquito netting. One POW, Jack Chalker, made this drawing as a tribute to two legendary doctors: 'Weary' Dunlop (with moustache) and Jacob Markowitz. They never actually operated together, but they were loved by all their patients

6. Wounded soldiers arriving home from France in summer 1944. The evacuation teams had to make use of whatever transport facilities were available

7. British and Canadian forces help a wounded soldier in a forest clearing in the Nijmegen area, Holland, February 1945

8. Falklands, 1982. Surgeon Commander Rick Jolly during a TV interview with ITN journalist Jeremy Hands at Ajax Bay. Jolly had just told Hands about the unexploded bombs in the field hospital

9. 3 Para medical personnel treating Argentinian wounded at Mount Longdon. Captain John Burgess is on the right at the rear, with Private Kennedy holding the drip

10. Major Roger Nutbeem, who died aboard *Sir Galahad*, and his young daughter Kathryn

11. Kathryn Nutbeem, waiting to sing at the ceremony commemorating the 25th anniversary of the Falklands War in June 2007

12. Survivors of the *Sir Galahad* coming ashore at Fitzroy

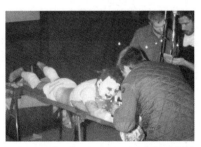

13. A medical assistant at Ajax Bay field hospital applies Flamazine to a burned Welsh Guardsman from *Sir Galahad*

14. RAMC Medic Eleanor Dlugosz, killed by an IED in Iraq, 5 April 2007

15. Sergeant John Jones, killed by an IED in Iraq, 20 November 2005. Holly Percival was one of the first medics on the scene

16. Medics of 4 General Support Regiment provide medical attention to the father of a young Iraqi child, Basra, 2003

17. Colonel Tim Hodgetts briefs the medical team as casualties arrive after an incident in Afghanistan

18. British medics evacuate an injured Iraqi soldier from a forward operating base in southern Iraq, 26 March, 2003

19. RAF fire crews in Afghanistan race to a Chinook helicopter to help unload casualties as ambulances stand by

20. The MERT after an operation in Afghanistan. Flt Lt Damien van Carrapiett is third from left and Sgt Rachel McDonald is far right. The Afghan interpreter's face has been disguised for security

enemy action was underlined the very next day when a mortar bomb hit a tree outside the RAP (regimental aid post). 'The orderly beside me fell to the floor with a large hole punched out of his thigh from the shrapnel. I called to my corporal to hand me a dressing but there was no reply. I turned and saw he was lying silently on the floor. The only mark on him was a small puncture over the heart but it was enough to kill him. He must have died instantly. He was a grievous loss.' Medics were paying a high price for where their duty took them – to the very heart of the battle.

★

By now, the Normandy beachhead had been secured but the way ahead for Allied troops was blocked. The key town of Caen, ten miles inland, was scheduled to be rolled over within a day of the landings, opening up the way for a penetrating advance into the French countryside. But it was heavily defended, and it would take six weeks of an artillery and air bombardment, followed by street-by-street fighting, before it fell.

Bill Helm arrived in France a week after D-Day to join an advanced dressing station five miles from Caen and a mile from the front line. Twenty-five-pound guns were positioned all around and shelling the town ceaselessly. The ground heaved beneath him and the constant concussion made his head ache. As an infantry attack was ordered forward, he was on stand-by for casualties, and then, as the wounded flooded back to him in large numbers, he had to improvise the procedures to deal with them because, despite the training, 'all of us were out of our depth.' A sensible routine took time to emerge, but eventually the orderlies were instructed to deal with the minor injuries – dressing light wounds, giving anti-tetanus injections and handing out sulphonamide tablets – leaving the doctors free to stop haemorrhages, splint fractures and set up transfusions. But they were in danger of being swamped as stretcher jeeps pulled up outside to drop off their loads from the front and numbers piled up in the waiting area, some already dead, some dying, some urgently needing transfusions. Seven hundred casualties passed through the dressing station over the next day and a half, many of them German. Helm recalled badly wounded SS snipers who had been up in trees for days. 'They were a tough and dirty bunch. One young Nazi had a broken jaw and was near death, but before he passed out he rolled his head over and murmured "*Heil* Hitler."'

The British conscripts were nowhere near as battle-hardened as the enemy soldiers. Helm recalled the sight of a group of terrified, disorientated lads, 'exhausted, jittering and yelling in a corner'. No one was immune from terror. Another man, a cook, went into shock when shells fell nearby. The doctor was sympathetic. 'I knew he was a brave lad, and this confirmed for me that battle exhaustion was totally involuntary and had little to do with cowardice.' The horrors were enough to turn any man's mind.

A young tank officer was brought back slung over a tank. 'He had compound fractures of both legs and had lost a foot. He was conscious but very shocked. I tried to transfuse him but his veins had contracted to cords with the shock and I couldn't get a cannula into him. We sent him back to the Casualty Clearing Station but he died.' It was possibly an unnecessary death, brought on by the good intentions but misguided actions of those who had put the man on a tank and brought him in for treatment. Helm recalled his father's advice, gained the hard way in First World War trenches, that it was better to leave a casualty with severe fractures where he lay until medical help could reach him rather than move him back unsplinted. He himself learned another valuable lesson from his very first 'action' – the necessity, as he put it, 'of keeping calm'.

This stood him in good stead as he and his medical team moved up into the front line to set up a CCP, a Casualty Collecting Post. It was initially little more than a hole in the ground in one of the sunken country lanes for which the Normandy battlefield became famous. Positioned between high hedges, with a field of dead, bloated cows on one side, it stank to high heaven. Enemy snipers were just down the track. The main dug-out was big enough to hold six stretcher-cases, and there were other dug-outs to sleep in. Helm's was walled and roofed with planks and blankets, but he had to bend double to crawl inside. It had room for a camp bed and a box, on which he placed a mirror and his shaving kit, but its greatest attribute was that it never leaked, for all the torrential rain that was to pour down on the armies facing each other in Normandy that summer. The doctor took in a small stray dog as a companion and marvelled that he never had to feed it 'because he was never hungry'. He opted not to dwell on what the mutt was clearly doing for food in that village of death and destruction. The job of those at the CCP, the furthest forward of any aid post, was to deal only with dire emergencies. Casualties were picked up by stretcher-bearers and brought in by ambulances, and Helm took a quick look inside and directed them on if he thought they were fit enough for the bumpy four-mile journey to the dressing station. One in ten he could not risk letting go. He had to stop a bleed, splint a fracture or dose them with morphine before it was safe to send them on.

But the dug-out began filling up as the road to the rear was cut off by enemy bombs. 'I had battle exhaustion cases yelling and moaning in one corner, the lightly wounded on blankets in another and the serious cases needing transfusions in another. Some casualties had to stay in the ambulances in which they arrived.' Over the battlefield now hung a heavy fog, and when Helm peered outside all he could see was coloured tracer bullets hurtling too close for comfort. He was anxious. He desperately needed fresh blood supplies, and the weather would slow their arrival. He was worried too about the mental condition of some of his patients, particularly a young lieutenant, lightly wounded, exhausted but in a highly excited manic state and desperate to get back to the fighting. He had taken his objective with the remnant of his platoon – just seven men – and had then been pushed back by lack of support. It took a lot of persuasion to get him to rest for a few hours. He was, Helm concluded, 'a candidate for an award for bravery or a case of acute battle exhaustion. If he survived, that is. He seemed very near his limit.' The doctor himself 'plodded on', as he put it, the fog cleared, the ambulances got away, the blood arrived. 'The CO looked in at 8 a.m. and we must have been a sorry sight. It was raining, I was wearing a German mac and I hadn't slept for thirty-six hours.' This was military medicine in the raw, and no training could ever have prepared him for it.

Not every medic could deal with the stress, and Helm was called on to help out at a regimental aid post where the stretcher-bearers had become very jumpy and were close to battle exhaustion. It was not surprising. They were often out in the open and exposed. They became casualties themselves. One was sitting in his jeep waiting to load stretchers when a mortar bomb dropped through his lap. By an astonishing twist of fate, it did not explode, but the momentum still sheared off his leg above the knee and his hand at the wrist. The doctor braved the gauntlet too as he was driven over to the aid post through a heavy German bombardment on the pillion of a dispatch rider's motorbike. 'We heard the distinctive whine of "moaning Minnie" and "sobbing sister" mortar bombs coming our way and dived for the ditch. This area was like a First World War no-man's land, with many unburied dead soldiers lying around. I landed next to one of our men, who had clearly been dead for several days.'

He found the section of nervy stretcher-bearers frantically digging in and joined them in scratching a shallow depression for himself in the ground. He tried to rally their flagging spirits. 'I reassured them that three quarters of the noise was from our own guns and that they were working themselves into a state of exhaustion by telling each other what hell it was.' In a few weeks, Helm, who in training had been in a funk over the use of live ammunition, had now morphed into a battle-hardened pro who was earning the pips on his shoulders. 'To my surprise,' he noted modestly, 'the presence of even such a young and inexperienced officer as myself was able to provide a degree of reassurance and leadership.' He got the men to act as a team, not just building their own individual scrapes to take cover in but working together to dig a trench big enough to take stretcher-cases. 'This positive work for a purpose other than their own safety seemed to steady them, and all but one came out of his personal trench and set to wholeheartedly, with interruptions when I gave the word to dive for cover.' With the ground prepared, the doctor and his new unit waited for casualties. 'I lay on my back in my dent in the ground, looking up at the firework display of tracer shells and bullets arching up at enemy planes and then curving down towards us. It was a dry and warm night and surprisingly I managed a few hours' sleep.' As the sun rose, he watched RAF Halifaxes and Lancasters pouring cascades of bombs on to the German positions on the outskirts of Caen. Soon after, he and his men abandoned the trenches they had so laboriously dug when under fire and moved on, all that effort for nothing. But that too was the nature of being a medic in a mobile war such as this.

Pressing on, they crossed a minefield, Helm's least favourite activity –'at least with shells and mortar bombs you can hear them coming and run for cover' – and set up in the grounds of a château, where, with the battle deadlocked for a while, they stayed, unusually, for several weeks. Helm constructed a proper dug-out for himself here, digging a deep hole and roofing it with an old bedframe on which he piled clods of earth as protection against airburst shell fragments. Everywhere around was the detritus of war – broken trees, a burnt-out Sherman tank with the driver's blackened skeleton still in his seat, dead horses and dead Germans lying just as they had fallen. Whenever the guns stopped, what struck Helm was the complete, deathly silence. In a field, a little foal was walking in a small circle round its recently killed mother. It had worn a path in the grass and refused to leave her.

The similarity of the scenes around him to the trenches of the First World War was brought home to him when he took a motorbike into the town of Bayeux, where his doctor father, Cyril, had come out of retirement to take command of the tented hospital. Of all people, Dr Helm Snr had an inkling of what his son, who arrived caked in mud, was going through. Thirty years earlier, he had endured the unspeakable as a junior medical officer in northern France. His aid post had taken a direct hit from a shell, and the RAMC orderly he had been standing right next to simply disintegrated. He had lain among half a dozen bodies in a cellar of rubble listening to the shrieks and moans of the dying until he was rescued. At Hill 60 on the Ypres salient, he had toiled for two nights and three days without sleep, and without even lying down, as shells rained on his advanced dressing station and the already wounded were hit all over again. He had treated men choking to death on chlorine gas until he was evacuated sick himself.[17] This new war was different from the trenches, mobile and fast-moving. But the suffering it caused and the heroism it called for, they were unchanged.

The cost – that butcher's bill again – was particularly high at Caen, as attack after attack on German positions was repelled. Medical orderly Len Brown buried seventy-three dead comrades in the soft, fertile earth around his aid post. The fighting was so intense that tanks had to be sent forward to pick up the wounded. It took a massive and merciless air strike by fleets of bombers eventually to dislodge the town's defenders. Brown made his way along the town's shattered streets, holding aloft a red cross flag. As he saw the bloody faces of those who surrendered, 'for the first and only time in my life, I felt pity for the Germans. They were all in.' But Dunkirk, where he had lost numerous friends and very nearly his own life, had been avenged. Another medic, Lance Corporal Eric Harden, who was attached to a Royal Marine commando unit, wrote to his wife back in England, 'Well, darling, we have Caen at last. Perhaps we can get going now.'

And get going the Allied armies duly did, though it was not until mid-August, two months after the invasion began, that the German forces in Normandy finally cracked and fifty thousand of their troops were encircled and surrendered at Falaise. Their physical condition was instructive. Lieutenant Colonel Debenham, a veteran of the fighting in North Africa and Italy, walked into a captured enemy field hospital and turned up his nose at what he saw. 'Three hundred Boches,' he recorded in his diary, 'herded in stables on straw. Lousy. Food scarce. No evacuation facilities. Amputations common. One belly [casualty] had been wounded eight days ago and not operated on. Another, a captain, had abdominal wound, bowels protruded, pushed them back himself, held in with a belt, went on fighting for six hours until he had to pack up due to a second wound.'

It was clear from this that there were brave men on both sides. But there was a huge and significant difference in the medical treatment they had received. In another captured hospital, nearly all of the 1,700 German soldiers were suffering from chronic sepsis, infections of the bone and septic joints. A quarter of them needed urgent blood transfusions. It was like stepping back into the First World War, said one senior British surgeon. He concluded that 'the German standard of war surgery was very much lower than our own.'[18]

German doctors appear not to have been tutored in modern techniques for suturing wounds, had no penicillin to treat gas gangrene and other infections, and transfused blood from man to man rather than drawing on blood banks. In their field hospitals, there was an acute shortage of surgical instruments and sanitary equipment. Scissors sometimes had to be used as scalpels. 'Medicines were scarce too, and there was no attempt to develop antibiotics; auxiliary personnel were also in short supply and poorly trained,' according to one expert.[19] An underlying problem may well have been that the Nazi regime had given low priority to medical care, 'gambling their all on the science of killing, and ignoring or under-estimating the value of preserving their own army in the field,' as a British report put it.[20] It is commonplace among some military historians to suggest that the German war machine was far superior to that of the Allies in the Second World War. Its equipment was better (notably its tanks), its generals more daring and its ranks often more disciplined and better trained. The Wehrmacht lost because the political follies of its Führer left it fighting on too many fronts, until it was finally overwhelmed by sheer weight of numbers. If that analysis is true, then the one notable exception was in military medicine. The skills of Allied doctors and medics far exceeded the enemy's, and the fact that more men in khaki were saved from death and patched up to return to the fray gave the armies of Eisenhower and Montgomery a clear advantage.

★

The advance of the Allied armies into the heart of France meant that one of the RAMC's most unusual doctors could come out of hiding. In the spring of 1944, Major Geoffrey Parker, who had served as a surgeon through the campaigns in North Africa and Italy and was back in London recovering from a bout of jaundice, suddenly found himself pitched into a completely different type of warfare. SOE, the behind-the-lines Special Operations Executive, desperately needed a French-speaking doctor to join a group of Resistance guerrillas operating in the Jura mountains of south-eastern France. The forty-two-year-old Parker, who spoke French fluently, was talent-spotted. At a hush-hush meeting at SOE's headquarters in Baker Street, he was briefed that he would have some two hundred wounded men and women in his care, scattered among remote farmhouses and in hiding places in the forest. 'The local doctors do what they can,' he was told, 'but the risks to them and their families if they are caught treating the *maquis* are frightful. That is why we need to send you.'[21] He would get an extra ten shillings a day on his army pay as danger money.

A few days later, clutching a Colt automatic pistol and an identity card in the name of Henri Martin, a commercial traveller in pharmaceutical products from Brest, he was sitting in the back of a blacked-out Dakota and preparing to parachute into the unknown. A diamond shape of fires flared in the blackness below and he jumped. On the ground to greet 'Parsifal' – his code name – was a cheering mass of a hundred Resistance fighters. 'They were mostly boys,' he recalled, 'with a few skirted figures which could be taken for girls. Every imaginable variety of clothes – layers of them – and all very dirty. Boys and girls alike carried revolvers, loosely stuck in the belt. All had daggers, and a privileged few carried British and German tommy guns. They looked under-fed, and I was to discover later that quite a few were suffering from the effects of under-nourishment and vitamin shortage – sore and bleeding gums and unsteady gait when carrying the lightest of loads.' There was work to do here.

Parker's first job was to set up a field hospital for the *maquis*, and he selected a school building in what was thought to be a safe village. 'The grapevine operated with fantastic speed, and all through the next day pathetic and smelly bundles of half-starved men were coming in by car and cart in twos and threes, without any organization on my part. All of their wounds were infected and fly-infested messes needing to be cleaned up and redressed. Some open compound fractures had to be re-plastered, but nothing could be done about the bad position of some of the fractures, as no anaesthetist was available. There were no abdominal or chest cases; those that had occurred had died of their injuries.'

But then word came that the SS and the Gestapo were making a sweep through the area, killing and arresting as they went, and he had instantly to pack everything and everyone up and head for the hills. With eighty wounded in a handful of steam-lorries, he drove deep into the Jura. Abandoning the lorries, they then set off on foot up rock paths and along forest trails, closely pursued by German forces. Bullets from behind sent him ducking for cover behind a tree. 'It wasn't a very big tree. I pressed hard against it, and wet my pants. I could feel bullets thudding into the other side and others whining past. I don't know how they missed the overlapping bits of my anatomy. I was terrified.' The firing stopped, and he calculated that the enemy soldier who had been shooting at him was out of ammunition. 'I jumped out from behind my tree and there was the poor devil less than fifteen yards from me. He was bending forward to get another magazine from his belt and I shot him in the stomach. He clutched at his middle and pitched forward without a sound. I fired at him again but he didn't move. I had killed him with the first shot.' The remainder of the German patrol retreated, and Parker, shaking, fled to rejoin the rest of his band as they climbed higher and higher.

For weeks they played hide-and-seek in the mountains, always on the move, staying clear of the patrols that kept coming after them, sleeping under the trees and the stars, living off rabbits and berries. One of his companions was a man they called the Executioner, whose job was to deal with anyone suspected of tipping off the enemy of their whereabouts. Parker had to look the other way when a farmer caught telephoning the gendarmes was made to dig his own grave and then dispatched with a bullet in the head.

From their radio operator, they heard the news of the Allied landings in Normandy. 'The effect on morale was enormous,' Parker declared, but the reality was that the fighting was about to intensify. Arms were dropped in by parachute, and the *maquis*, their time come, went on the offensive, harrying German forces wherever and whenever they could. The doctor now took to going out to collect wounded guerrillas hidden in villages and bringing them back to the hospital he had set up in the mountains.

It was also his job to buy desperately needed food – dangerous work, because it took him into towns where the Germans were. In a marketplace early one summer's morning, he was followed. The firm hand of a black-uniformed Gestapo officer was on his shoulder and a brusque voice demanded his identity papers. It was the moment he had dreaded. 'My mind took a few seconds to react to the reality and horror of it.' He knew full well that his name – 'Parsifal' – was on a wanted poster pinned up at the town hall, along with those of four other *maquis* commanders. A reward of a million francs was being offered for their capture, dead or alive. Parker collected his wits, produced his fake papers, told his cover story, refused to panic, kept his cool. 'I could feel the sweat in my hair under my beret, and wondered if it would start to trickle down my face, and show the stark terror that was in my head and heart. If they had made a body search, I would have been a goner. I had my automatic pistol on a string under my shirt.' But his performance was convincing. The German lost interest and sent him on his way. 'Very good, sir,' a relieved Parker grovelled. 'And thank you very much.'

The doctor was now properly set up in a hospital of sorts in the granary of a farm at the top of a steep mountain track. Casualties were bedded down on straw, and when the word got out, more arrived on stretchers every day. There was running water from a nearby stream and a small lake to bathe in. As Parker scrubbed himself clean for the first time in two months, he caught sight of himself in a mirror – with considerable shock. 'My eyes seemed lost and sunk in their sockets, and my cheeks were hollow. In fact I have never been so fit in my life, not in the athletic sense, but in the stringy way necessary to survive this life on the run.' In this more settled environment, Parker was able to carry out something more than basic emergency treatment. He was able to perform 'open sepsis' surgery, leaving wounds to heal in the now accepted RAMC fashion, and improvised a Thomas splint from a bent nail, an old dog collar and some rubber tubing which allowed a man with a gunshot wound to his sciatic nerve to hobble back to his unit and carry on the fight. To his consternation, he was called on to give his medical judgement on a new recruit, a young woman who claimed she wanted to join the Resistance because the Germans had raped her. He was asked to examine her, and could find no bruises or injuries to corroborate her story. The Executioner took her away.

By now, the Germans were on the retreat, and Parker's group increasingly went on the offensive. He joined them on the night-time ambush of a convoy, at which a young fighter named Georges was badly wounded with gunshots to his abdomen – the worst kind. In his hospital in the granary, Parker had had no success at all with these types of injury. He couldn't get the area free enough from germs to risk operating, and his only anaesthetic was a short-term one and unsuitable for lengthy surgery. All his casualties with wounds in the gut had died. Things did not look good for young Georges, even had he been in the granary. Out in the open and at night, his chances were even slimmer. Parker examined the boy. 'Fumbling around in the darkness, I drew up half a grain of morphia from a glass ampoule into my syringe, and took out a small torch which I could hold in my teeth while I slowly gave him an intravenous injection. When it had taken effect, I pulled up his shirt and found three bullet holes in the left lower part of his abdominal wall. Then I gently turned him on to his side and put a finger into his rectum. When I withdrew it, there was blood on my finger, indicating that he had a penetrating injury in the bowel.' Surgically speaking, Parker knew the situation was a simple one. 'Either the boy was going to die from internal haemorrhage, probably within the next half-hour, or he would stop bleeding as the result of a combination of shock, lowered blood-pressure and the morphia injection. If the bleeding stopped, then, given reasonable surgical conditions, I could operate with a fair chance of success, as I had done in North Africa and Italy earlier.' The crucial issue was where to find a suitable operating theatre out here in the wild.

There was a hospital in a town five miles away, but also, a man who had scouted it informed the group, a garrison of thirty soldiers and two SS officers lodged in the town hall. A plan was agreed: they would drive to the town in two lorries. One would take armed men to surround the garrison and stop any Germans leaving, the other would ferry Parker and his patient to the hospital. It was still dark when they descended on the town and the doctor pulled into the hospital courtyard, to be met by two nuns and a night superintendent. 'We have a badly wounded man, and I'm going to operate on him,' Parker explained. 'Oh no you are not,' the superintendent replied. 'I absolutely forbid it. Your presence here will endanger the other patients.' Parker's response was to take out his dagger. 'I went up to him and pointed it at his stomach.' But the man did not flinch, replying that he was going to die whatever he did. 'If I try to stop you coming in, you will kill me, and if you do operate here, then the Germans will certainly kill me when they hear about it in the morning,' he told Parker.

The doctor thought for a moment, then viciously clubbed the man hard in the face. As he lay groaning on the floor, Parker told him, 'I'm very sorry about that, but it is the best I can do for you. I'm going to lock you in your office and, when the Gestapo arrive in the morning, you can tell them you tried to stop me and that is what I did to you. I hope they won't kill you.' The mother superior now led Parker and his men to the operating theatre. The hospital's resident doctor was roused from his sleep and, at gunpoint, invited to be the anaesthetist. 'What if I refuse?' he asked. 'Then you will be killed immediately,' Parker told him, 'and I shall have to manage without you.' 'You've talked me into it,' said the young doctor with a laugh. And so Major Geoffrey Parker

RAMC, alias Parsifal, alias Henri Martin, began the most curious medical procedure of his career, in the dead of night, surrounded by armed guerrillas and assisted by three white-robed nuns.

With a scalpel, he opened up the lower abdomen and found three holes in the intestine. Two were simple perforations and he stitched them easily, but the third bullet had devastated three inches of the large intestine, and destroyed its blood supply. Part of the colon would have to be removed, and the two ends brought outside the body as a temporary colostomy. After an hour, the job was done and Georges was wheeled out of the theatre.

'What are you going to do with him now?' the mother superior asked. 'Take him back to the forest, I suppose,' Parker said, though he knew from experience that transporting a man immediately after abdominal surgery could be fatal. 'He'll just have to take his chance.' 'Would you like to leave him here with us?' the mother superior asked. 'Of course I would,' the doctor replied, 'but he would be murdered in a matter of hours.' But the nun had been busy. 'While you were operating,' she explained, 'we took a bed down to the cellar. Nobody saw us do it, nor is anyone likely to go down there. If the Germans ask, we will say that you took him away with you.'

And that, Parker recorded, 'is what we did'. The Resistance unit pulled out of the town and returned to the mountains, leaving Georges behind. In the back of the lorry, Parker reflected on the insanity of what he had just pulled off. 'I realized it made no sense from a military point of view. If a German motor patrol had come through the town while I was operating, we should have been shot to pieces, and all for the sake of one man.' He had no better explanation for the risk he had taken and the extra lives he had endangered (including his own) than that he felt he had to. The doctor in him, the life-saver, outweighed the soldier. 'I couldn't stand seeing another man die up there in the forest like the other three stomach cases under my care had.' In the end, the Germans left the town a few days later, none the wiser about the operation that had taken place under their noses. As for Georges, with the fighting in France ending, he was taken to a hospital across the border in Switzerland, where his temporarily severed colon was properly closed, 'and he went on his way rejoicing'.

The doctor had one more brave, life-saving act to perform before his own war was over. He was in the city of Lyon in the days immediately after the Liberation and saw a large crowd mobbing two young women whose clothes had been torn off them, their heads shaved down to the scalp and painted with black swastikas. 'They were spattered with mud and barefoot.' They had, he learned, slept with German soldiers in return for extra rations. Now they were going to pay for their collaboration with the enemy. Parker pushed his way through to the girls. 'I told the gang surrounding them that they were a pack of bastards, behaving worse than the Germans, that they were no more civilized than the Boche and should be ashamed of themselves.' Some of his men from the forest were with him and they pulled him away. 'We know and respect you,' they told him, 'and we are proud of you, but most of that crowd have no idea who you are and what you have done. You're lucky they didn't have you swinging from a lamp post. Please don't do anything like that again.' But the truth was that, sometimes in war – as we will see in the next chapter – men, and medics particularly, were too brave for their own good.

*

Geoffrey Parker's war alongside the Resistance fighters in France was unusual in many ways, not least because, as a doctor, he went into it armed, prepared to shoot and to kill, and, on his own admission, did so on more than one occasion. But for most medics on the battlefield, this was an issue about which they were never clear-cut . Airborne medical officer David Tibbs trod this tightrope and unwittingly slipped off. In a battle with dug-in German forces, he crawled forward, waving a red cross flag, to a soldier who had been felled by a sniper but from a distance seemed still to be alive. When the doctor got to him, the man was dead, at which point Tibbs did something stupid. 'Without thinking I stripped off his bandolier of ammunition and flung it back to my guys.' The watching German sniper interpreted this as crossing the line from non-combatant to combatant and did not hesitate. 'There was a tremendous crack,' Tibbs recalled. 'I felt a violent shock, like electricity, in my right arm and found myself lying on the grass.' The bullet had gone through his shoulder and, bleeding profusely, he just managed to squirm away on his side into cover before the sniper could fire again.

Had Tibbs broken the rules? Indeed, were there any rules that would ensure a medic's safety? In the late autumn of 1944, Marine commando Dr John Forfar was part of a Combined Operations assault against heavily defended German strongholds on the Dutch island of Walcheren in the estuary of the River Scheldt. The Marines hit big trouble. Mortars and grenades raked them as they advanced and, in his report afterwards, Forfar recorded that the sand ran red with their blood. The troop commander was missing, and the doctor went forward alone to try to find him. Suddenly, over a sand dune, came a lone German soldier wearing a long greatcoat which flapped at his knees as he walked. Forfar froze. As he wrote later, 'a medical officer in this position is in something of a dilemma. The handgun I carried was for self-defence and I had to decide what constituted self-defence.'[22] There was little time for philosophical ruminating or a rummage through the terms of the Geneva Convention. 'I decided that if it was his intention to take me prisoner I would resist and that if he showed any hostile intent I would shoot.' The doctor's resolve was never tested. As the man drew nearer, Forfar could see something deranged about him. 'He was looking at the ground and muttering to himself and I could now see he wasn't even armed. His mental state was clearly disturbed and I don't think he even saw me as he walked on into the captivity he may have been seeking.' 'Shell shock', that syndrome so redolent of the First World War, was the doctor's diagnosis.

He was glad he had held his fire, but he soon found out that others in this battle were not so merciful. Forfar found his troop commander lying face down in the sand with a bullet through his eye, and with the help of three stretcher-bearers, tried to lug him away. 'As we were lifting him on to the stretcher, five German soldiers appeared over the ridge of a sand dune, opened fire and killed a sergeant who was coming to help us. Then they continued to fire on the stretcher party as we weaved our way among the dunes to the safety of the RAP.' It seemed no quarter would be given, not even to those who went on to the battlefield with the sole intent of saving lives. In this fight to the finish with Nazi Germany, the scene was set for a supreme sacrifice.

7. Bravest of the Brave

'Goodnight, darling, and God bless.' Lance Corporal Eric Harden signed off his almost daily letters home to his wife, Maud, 'Your ever loving Eric, xxxx.'[1] The manager of a butcher's shop in the Thames estuary town of Northfleet, near Gravesend, he was as solid and likeable a fellow as you could hope to meet. He loved his life with his wife and young son, Bobby. There was so much for an energetic person like him to do. He played the violin expertly, but also football for the town and tennis for his local club, swam like a fish, cycled and camped whenever he could get out into the Kent countryside. Son of a stevedore, he was as well rounded and accomplished as any working man could be. He also had a good heart, which was why he enlisted in the St John Ambulance Brigade, went up to London as a volunteer air-raid warden during the Blitz and, eventually – though, as a slaughter-man, he was in a reserved occupation – defied his family's wishes and, in 1942, aged thirty, insisted on joining up.

He did not take instantly to army life. To Maud, his wife, he complained of the bullying NCOs on the training grounds in Devon, and told her how the recruit who slept in the next bunk to him had been worked so hard on a route march that he collapsed. 'The NCO would not attend to him and would not let anyone else do so, so the poor fellow just laid down there and died. That doesn't sound right, does it, Maud? The devils ought to be done for manslaughter.' There were mutterings of mutiny, but these evaporated a few weeks later, after an ecstatically sunny day out on a glorious beach near Plymouth with rocks and rolling seas, 'the best place I have ever seen in my life. I wish you were here with me, duck,' – his favourite term of endearment for Maud. 'After the war we shall have to see if we can't get there ourselves.' His own war took a turn for the better when, after basic training, that St John Ambulance experience came into play and he was transferred from the Royal Artillery to the Royal Army Medical Corps, which for a while took him close to home, to a hospital in Woolwich. But then came a series of postings with his field ambulance unit to remote training camps in Yorkshire, West Wales and Scotland – and more of those letters to Maud.

He told her how he slept on a straw bed and was warm enough with four blankets and his greatcoat on top, 'but gee, sweetheart, I would gladly have your cold feet on me once again. That will be the day, won't it, dear?' His medical training was advancing. 'The MO is going to let me do some injections next week. I pity the first one or two I start on, but somebody has to be the first ones.' He asked her to send him his Home Nursing and St John Ambulance books. From Bournemouth, where he was getting work experience in a doctor's surgery, he was missing her terribly, and made plans for her to come and visit him. He tried to be a good dad as well as a good husband and sent detailed instructions and a diagram showing Maud how to make a catapult for little Bobby.

Then there was a literal change of pace in his life. In September 1943, he was attached as medical orderly to a Royal Marine commando unit and, on a 200-mile route march along the south coast of England, he followed on foot behind the men with his first-aid kit to pick up and treat any drop-outs. 'Who looks after me if I drop out?' he asked plaintively. But that was part of being a medic. It never seemed to occur to anyone that they might get sick or hurt too. They were expected to be invincible. This link-up with the commandos was very much to Harden's liking. He had applied to join the recently formed Parachute Regiment and was disappointed to be turned down. Now he was to get a shot at a permanent transfer to the commandos, and he was in his element, all those initial misgivings about the army dispelled.

The training in the Scottish Highlands in mid-winter was the toughest imaginable, beginning with a seven-mile speed march in full kit, to be completed in an hour. It left him gasping and feeling ancient compared with the rest of the lads, who were in their early twenties. He was also issued with a rifle, which he hadn't had since basic training and, though it felt odd to be armed after so long as a non-combatant, he was soon scoring top marks on the range with a tommy gun. He put himself under the cosh to pass the course, mastering cliff assaults and hand-to-hand fighting and learning survival and demolition skills. There was a notorious 'death slide' to conquer, down a rope over a torrent while under fire with live ammunition. The weather was diabolical. It was so cold that in the morning boots had to be thawed out over candles before they could be put on. 'You have to be made of iron,' he told Maud, and he was. He made the grade, got his precious green commando's beret and was happy. 'I like this life,' he wrote. 'It just suits. Goodnight, sweetheart, God bless.'

But Maud was in despair. She worried that by joining this elite task force he was placing himself in greater danger than he needed to – and she was right. She was pregnant too, as a result of one of his weekend leaves, which made her feel even more anxious for him. But he was supremely optimistic about the future. Maud shouldn't worry about money, he told her. He had savings from his extra pay as a commando and, though there was going to be an extra mouth to feed, 'as long as she grows up to be as good-hearted and lovely natured as you, I won't mind a bit.' He planned to have his photograph taken in his uniform so his little girl could be proud that she was 'a commando's baby'.

On D-Day in June 1944, the men of 45 Commando, Harden's unit, were among the first off the landing craft and on to Sword beach. It was ten days before he had the chance to write home. 'Well, sweetheart, how is the garden looking now?' he asked Maud, as if he himself had been on a picnic. 'I suppose it's full of roses and I suppose the lawn wants cutting.' A week later he let a little light in on what he had been up to.

Eighteen of us were cut off from the rest and bang in the middle of Jerry land. We decided to wait till dark to get out but Jerry opened up on us just before dark so we had to get out quick. I took five chaps with me and led them back to our lines, about five miles cross-country on our bellies. I'm glad we learnt all that field craft now – it came in handy. Only three of us made it, and when we reached our lines our own men opened up on us and wounded one of the chaps. But darling, don't you get worried over this sort of thing. You know me, duck, don't you? I take everything as it comes and it doesn't worry me a great deal.

Maud was not so sanguine, especially since, a fortnight later, she gave birth to daughter Julie. Eric was as proud as Punch at the new arrival. 'I can't keep my mind off her,' he wrote. 'Gee, Maud, you have got your hands full now with the lot of us, haven't you, duck?'

He made it home to their house in Colyer Road, Northfleet, for Christmas 1944, but it wasn't the best of times. The Germans had launched the Battle of the Bulge, their major counter-attack in the Ardennes, and the certainty of an Allied victory in the very near future seemed to be receding. London was hit by Hitler's revenge weapons, the V-2 rockets, and their trajectory to the capital from their launch pads in Holland brought them perilously close to Northfleet. On top of all these worries, the weather was bitterly cold, and there seems to have been some slight disharmony in the Harden household. The garden gate was off its hinges and Maud wanted it mended, but Eric didn't get round to it. Nor had he fixed the washing line in the garden. He apologized to her in a letter on New Year's Day from his base on the Sussex coast, where 45 Commando was preparing for a new mission. 'I just can't get down to odd jobs somehow.' Perhaps he'd be better 'when I'm finished with this lot, eh?'

He knew how hard it was for her coping with his sudden arrivals on leave for a few days and then departing again. 'Poor old duck, you can't get used to me going each time, can you?' This time, he had a feeling he would be away for a long time and, though he had raised her hopes of another weekend at home before he went, this was not possible. 'There it is,' he wrote. 'That's the army all over. I think it will be a very long time before I see you three again. I expect we shall be there until it [the war] is all over. Three months at least, perhaps six.' He promised her he would be careful. 'Don't worry too much, darling. I'll look after myself.'

That letter was dated 12 January 1945. Eleven days later, Lance Corporal Eric Harden was dead. For his heroism, he was awarded the Victoria Cross. No medic had been so honoured with the highest medal for valour since Captain John Fox-Russell in 1917, and none has since.

★

The special mission Harden, medical orderly of A Troop, had embarked on with 45 Commando was to clear a pocket of German resistance on the Dutch–German border. Today, six decades on, a fast, modern motorway from Antwerp to Maastricht sweeps across the River Meuse,[2] through this flat and featureless countryside and away into Germany. Next stop Cologne. But in that harsh winter of 1945, as German troops dug in to defend the borders of the Fatherland, every frozen field was fought over and every village became a miniature Caen. At Christmas, Eric must have given Maud some inkling of where he was going because, in a letter to him after he left, she asked him to let her know in a way that would get round army censorship of the post. 'I wonder if you are where you thought you were going,' she wrote on 14 January. 'When you write, Eric, say, yes you were right if you are the ones who have started the new breakthrough in Holland. On the wireless, they only mention infantry. The commandos don't get any credit, do they?' She missed him. 'I haven't yet got used to the idea of you being gone again.' But she was thinking of him. 'What sort of a landing[3] did you have, dear? I hope it was better and safer than before and hope you won't have to creep through cornfields after not having any sleep for a week. Has the grub improved since the last time?'

Maud's letters, so matter-of-fact and mundane but underlaid with so much anxiety, are filled with the white noise of war. Cutting through the chatter is the interminable hum of human unhappiness and hardship that was the common condition for those left behind to wait and worry. Heroics were not what she wanted, just her man back, her husband and the father of her children. She looked glowingly to the future, when they would all be together again, while struggling with the cares of just getting by in those terrible times. 'Julie [the baby] has lost two ounces in weight,' she wrote, 'but I expect she will be all right now her cold has gone. Bobby is still waiting for his tooth to fall out. His teacher told him she was very pleased with him last week, and today the headmaster did as well. He's one of the best readers in the class. He went for his first lesson on the piano on Monday, and his teacher brought him home and came in to mark the notes on the piano keys. Bobby knows the right hand notes now off by heart, so that's not bad, as it's only Wednesday. He's not a dull child, is he, dear? Even if he won't do as he's told first time. But he'll grow out of that.'

The severe winter weather had exposed problems in the house caused by bomb damage. 'When that snow melted last week it all came through the roof in the bay window where the shell had made the slits.' She was going to keep worrying the authorities to have it fixed. 'While I was sitting here quiet last night, dear, that mouse popped out again and I couldn't help thinking you came down and kept it company on your leave xxx. Wouldn't it be all right if it was that night now? Well, it will come again, and I'll have to look forward to that instead of back.' She signed off, 'Good night, darling, and God be with you, and take all the care you can love. Lots of love and kisses.' There was a domestic PS – 'Do you want your hankies sent on to you, darling?'

A week later she wrote again after a letter arrived from him. She was very thankful to know he was safe and tried to get a hint from him of the degree of danger he was in. 'Is it as stiff [tough] now as it was the first time, love?' she asked. She was optimistic. The papers were full of news of Soviet tanks racing through Poland towards Germany's eastern border. 'The Russians are running away with it again, eh? Perhaps it won't be so long after all before we meet. As long as they don't whip you off to Burma after.' Bobby was doing well at school – 'he's third from top in his class and, as the first and second boys are turned eight, he's doing well, isn't he, love?' He had also just joined the Cubs, and she had to dig in her purse for 9s 10d to buy his jersey and scarf. She had also spent 11s on material for a coat and hat, 'so that's another pound spent. It doesn't take long to go, does it?' The weather had taken a turn for the worse, the streets of Northfleet were ankle-deep in snow and she was worried about bursting water pipes. But the romance had not gone out of her life entirely, for all these problems. She thought of the past. 'There was a lovely moon here last night and it did look pretty on the snow. Like when we were courting and used to sit down in it and declare we were not cold, though we froze to the ground almost.' She thought of the future. She had seen a mate of his, and her husband could have his old position back driving the St John ambulance when the war was over. 'But you won't rejoin directly, will you, dear? Wait a few weeks, then you can, love.' And then she reverted to the present, and her longing for him. 'I freeze at night with two eiderdowns and Bobby to try to warm me, so I bet you are cold there, sweetheart. Do you sleep in slit trenches this time? Sleep, I said, but I meant try to sleep, Eric. And how many blankets do they allow you? Well, darling, keep touching that bit of wood, and then look forward to warming my feet again. Take care, love, great care. Love for ever, Maud.'

Loving wife that she was, she kept worrying about him getting cold wherever he was, so in her next letter, on 26 January, she offered to send him his winter underwear and to knit him some gloves and a woolly hat. 'Whatever you want, it's up to you to ask for.' Julie was talking – well, she had said the word 'Dad', 'as plain as you like, Eric'. And Bobby was getting on with his piano exercises, 'but his fingers are hardly long enough yet. Still he keeps at it.' Maud was taking the opportunity to learn the piano herself but was finding it hard going. 'I can't read the music quick enough yet. Still I'll have a go.' Relations were coming at the weekend as long as the weather wasn't too bad, and she looked forward to the company. 'It gets lonely sometimes, Eric.'

That loneliness was still getting to her after the weekend because, by Monday the twenty-ninth, she was miserable. Bobby was next door with neighbours, the baby was asleep, and she sat down and wrote to Eric how last night she had got a 'silly' notion in her head that it would be so nice 'to go to a dance or something'. Just to get out of the house and feel alive! 'Instead we went to bed and froze and couldn't sleep at all.' But it was him she worried about. 'Shall I send you some long pants and thicker vests, Eric? I expect you can do with them as, gosh, it's cold enough here. All the sinks and bath pipes are frozen this morning. It's about the coldest I've known it. Good luck, darling, and God bless you, Maud.'

The letter was never sent. Before she could pop a one-and-a-halfpenny stamp on the envelope and post it there was a knock at the door – the one every serviceman's wife dreads. Trembling, she pulled open the thin brown envelope that the telegram boy handed to her and read the words that brought her to her knees: 'Deeply regret to inform you 11006144 L/Cpl H E Harden RAMC was killed in action 23 January.'

★

The news had been slow coming from the front. There was not then the instant communication of today's wars, in which relatives know within hours if a loved one is dead or seriously injured. Nor was there a force's welfare officer to break the doleful tidings and, if possible, soften the blow, just a lad from the Post Office on the doorstep, who didn't wait for a reply because, what was there to say? But when the details of Eric's death trickled through – if it was any compensation, and how could it be? – it was clear that he had lost his own life while actively, bravely and selflessly saving those of others. Operation Blackcock, on which he was engaged, had begun on 14 January, aimed at clearing the Germans from the so-called Roer Triangle. It was an essential operation, ahead of an all-out Allied assault on the fortified Siegfried Line, Hitler's 'West Wall'. The advance was slow and difficult, against fierce opposition. Snow, covering the fields and roads, hindered progress. On the morning of 23 January, a Tuesday, the small riverbank town of Maasbracht had finally been cleared of enemy by the men of 6 Commando, and 45 Commando, who had arrived in the area only a few days earlier, came from the rear to march through the line to take up the offensive. Harden – 'Doc', as the men called him – was with the support section bringing up the rear.

Lieutenant Robert Cory was leading A Troop and remembered the townsfolk, exuberant at having been freed from German occupation, rushing out with apples and gifts to thrust into their hands. The troops of 6 Commando had dug in, and cheered their comrades as they 'advanced to contact' at the next objective, the village of Brachterbeek, half a mile down the road. They approached cautiously, expecting resistance. To their relief, the Germans had withdrawn without a fight and, once again, there were effusive greetings from liberated Dutch families, emerging from their houses gleefully but with warnings that German soldiers were still close by. Very close, in fact. The commandos were spread out in open formation and moving down a road towards a railway station on the edge of the village. Dressed in their ordinary brown smocks and green berets, they stood out against the snow like coconuts on a shy. 'We were easy targets,' said Marine John Haville, one of the troop, 'and we were walking into a trap.' Just past a crossroads, the land around them flat and without any significant cover, they suddenly came under heavy and sustained rifle and mortar fire. 'We were completely exposed,' Robert Cory remembered.[4] 'Just to our right were two large potato clumps, some fifty yards apart, and on our left a large electricity pylon with its wires hanging down on the ground. My section dived for cover behind the first of the potato clumps.' From there his men loosed off some rounds at shadowy figures moving in the distance, but to no effect. The Germans were in white winter camouflage suits and could barely be seen against the snow.

Cory decided he had to move his men forward. Not only were they in poor cover, he had every reason to believe A Troop's forward section had reached the station and was already in close-quarter combat with the enemy. They needed help. His men fixed bayonets, 'and on my order we went for it.' With covering fire from a Bren-gunner, they dashed forward across the open ground. Two men, Marine Wales and Marine Wheeler, went down almost immediately, and then Cory himself was knocked over by a bullet in his left arm. 'I picked myself up but was then hit three times in my left leg by a machine-gun burst and went down face first in the snow.' The rest of the section fell back, ducking down behind the nearest potato clump.

The lieutenant was in no-man's land, twenty yards out in the open, his face deep in the snow, and unable to move or even turn himself over because of his injuries. He thought he was going to suffocate, and would have done if his sergeant had not crawled to him under continuing heavy fire, cut away his equipment and turned him on his back. 'He then bound on field dressings which the others threw to him from behind the clump. During this time he was constantly under fire and I kept telling him to get back under cover, which he quietly refused to do until he had done all that he could for me.' But evacuating the stricken Cory from this firestorm was another matter altogether, and he was forced to lie on his back in the bitter cold waiting to be rescued, the blood freezing in his toes and severe frostbite setting in.

Eric Harden was pinned down too. Along with Captain Dudley Coventry and the rest of A Troop's command section, he had pulled back to a brick farm building by the crossroads to set up an aid post. The Germans had a machine-gun post in a windmill nearby and from high up were raking the ground in between. As he peered from behind a hedge, the medic could see the three wounded men in the killing zone ahead of him. It was a hundred-yard dash to them, he calculated, perhaps one hundred and twenty. As smoke from mortar shells drifted along the road, he saw his chance and sprinted across the open space with his medical pack, knelt to treat one of them, then crawled to the second and the third. Cory, the last, remembered his astonishment at finding Harden beside him, jabbing morphine into him as small-arms fire whined overhead and bullets kicked up the snow around them. 'Then he said he was going, but he would be back. I told him that on no account was he to do so.' From the farm, Haville, who was setting up a defensive mortar position, was watching Harden's coolness and dedication in admiration. 'He showed no regard for his own safety.' What was extraordinary was the length of time he was out there, exposed to the enemy's machine guns as he went from one man to the other. Haville didn't look at his watch to check the time, 'but it was a considerable period. And then, to cap it all, he came staggering back carrying Marine Wheeler over his shoulders.'

After zig-zagging his way through the torrent of gunfire, Harden eased the wounded man off his back and on to the ground, made sure he was settled, then turned to go back. He was ordered to stay. The captain was calling up tank support to retrieve the wounded, and for a smokescreen to be laid down. He instructed the medic to wait. Harden fretted. The back-up was slow in coming, and even when it arrived it failed to do the job. A tank went forward to pick up the casualties but was beaten away. The smokescreen simply provoked even more determined firing from the enemy, resulting in more casualties. It was the classic battlefield dilemma, where trying to save lives would only jeopardize others.

Harden refused to be put off. Men were dying out there. He knew that if the wounded were left out in the snow much longer they would die. Quietly but firmly, he urged Haville and another commando, Dick Mason, to come with him as his stretcher-bearers. 'We discarded our equipment and weapons and went with him,' Haville recalled. 'Doc carried the stretcher and was wearing his red cross armband, but that did not stop the Germans, who immediately fired on us with machine guns. As I ran through the snow I could see the bursts of fire kicking up the ground in front of my feet and I wondered what I'd let myself in for. But we continued running, keeping as low as possible till we reached the wounded.'

They strapped Wales on to the stretcher, Harden took the front shafts, with Haville and Mason at the rear, and they ran at a crouch for the farm, as mortar shells exploded beside them and a trail of bullets burst behind their heels. Harden's step never faltered, though he had been hit. When they reached the safety of the aid post, there was a large shrapnel tear and bullet holes in his smock. After a short rest, said Haville, 'we went out again to recover Lieutenant Cory.' The lieutenant, slipping in and out of consciousness, had no idea how long he had been lying in no-man's land, only that he had ordered 'Doc' not to come back for him. But, suddenly, there Harden was beside him again, with a stretcher this time, and Haville and Mason to help him carry it. They lifted him on and, just as before, with Harden at the front and the other two behind, they ran for the farmhouse with their load.

Some forty yards short of safety, Haville heard a click as if something had passed his left ear and saw Harden, ahead of him, stumble and collapse, the stretcher almost falling on top of him. Cory remembered being dropped to the ground and finding the two rear stretcher-bearers down beside him. Haville crawled forward to Harden. 'I saw that a single bullet had entered the back of his head and made its exit by way of a small round hole in the centre of his forehead without shedding a drop of blood. He must have died instantly and without pain. I realized the click I had heard was the bullet passing between Dick and myself.' On being told what had happened, Cory ordered them to leave him and seek cover. They ignored him. 'I told him we would get him back somehow,' Haville recalled, 'though we were in a serious situation. It was obvious that an enemy sniper had his sights on us, and it would have been fatal to stand up and carry the stretcher. Dick eased up the front of the stretcher, I pushed from behind, and we crawled along using it like a sled on the hard snow. It was very strenuous, but we made steady progress. The sergeant major crawled out from behind a hedge and helped us over the last few yards.'

They had made it. So had Cory and Weston (though Marine Wales sadly died from his wounds). But Harden lay dead on the battlefield. As darkness fell, the enemy gunfire slackened off after a tank destroyed the machine-gun nest in the windmill, and the forward sections of the troop returned, bringing with them the Doc's body. He had been 'a very gallant comrade', as Haville put it, 'and a wonderful example of courage and devotion to his fellow men'. He was buried with full honours in a field beside a convent in Maasbracht, along with Marine Wales and other men who died in the battle. His comrades were there to mourn a man many of the younger ones had seen as a father figure, to whom they told their woes. They couldn't believe he had gone. 'We laid him to rest reverently, with our prayers and affection, a cross inscribed with his name, rank, number and unit and the date of his death,' reported the unit chaplain, the Revd Reginald Haw. He had tried to take Harden's wedding ring from his finger to send to his widow but could not slide it off, and it was buried with him.

★

Back in Northfleet, a devastated Maud struggled with the news of his death. 'He was all I lived for,' she told those who came to comfort her. The family future she had constructed in her mind, the dream that had kept her going, was shot to hell. She knew that this war made widows of hundreds of thousands of women just like her, but that knowledge could not ease the pain. 'The poor boy did his bit, and bravely too,' her parents told her, seeking consolation. Be strong for the sake of the children, they urged her, though she knew that well enough. Every night as he lay in bed, little Bobby whispered 'goodnight' to his daddy, and her heart ached. The post brought shoals of letters of sadness and regret, alongside the pro formas from Buckingham Palace and the War Office. The last letters she had posted to Eric – the ones quoted from above – came back through the door, the envelopes over-printed with the cold stamp of officialdom: 'It is regretted that this item could not be delivered because the addressee is reported deceased.' But it soon began to dawn on her that his was no ordinary death. A week after the official notification, Eric's commanding officer, Lieutenant Colonel Gray, wrote from Maasbracht: 'His death has hit us all very hard, for he was trusted, loved and respected by all ranks of the commando. He lost or rather gave his life to save lives of our wounded. Three times he went out to bring in casualties who would have died but for him. I shall always be proud of having had Harden in my unit. He was a very brave and gallant man, and his devotion to duty and his comrades was a fine example to us all. I have recommended him for the Victoria Cross and hope that he will be granted it.'

More tributes arrived. Captain Coventry wrote of Eric's 'heroism and calmness' under fire. 'He was a friend of every man in my troop and of the whole commando. If there were more men like your husband in the world, the war would be over by now, or never have started in the first place.' From her cottage in Dorset, Annette Cory, the wounded lieutenant's wife, penned her deep sympathies and debt of gratitude. 'Your husband was killed bringing my husband in. If it had not been for him, my husband would have died.' Months later, when he was at last on the mend and his arm was out of plaster, Cory himself wrote from his military hospital bed, overcome with emotion. It was impossible 'to convey the gratitude and admiration I feel for your husband. To owe someone your life is to owe them the greatest thing on earth, but not only did he save my life but gave his own in doing it. He was a great man. We were all proud to have him with us. His memory will always be alive and an inspiration to us all.'

Harden's sergeant major and friend, Harry Bennett, was unstinting as he wrote on behalf of 'the lads of A Troop'. 'I was close to him in the action, and his courage was truly magnificent. Mercifully, his death was sudden, with no pain. His face had its usual serene look still, which it always had in life. He was one of the greatest men it has ever been my pleasure to meet. He was my right-hand man. Nothing was too much trouble for him if it would help the chaps, even out of the action. He was always helping with the cooking and rations, apart from his own job. He was always cheerful and full of life.' The troop was on the far side of the Rhine before Bennett had had the chance to write and, as they had battled on after Harden's death, they had missed him terrifically. 'He is always in our thoughts. We are always talking of him. There will never be another "Doc".'

Dick Mason felt he had lost not just a friend but a mentor. 'He was a father to us all. We could talk to him and tell him all our troubles, and he would not say a wrong word about anyone. It is men like him who will make a better world.' Eric's closest chum, a Cornish medic named Sid Gliddon, told Maud how they spent hours together when they were off duty, chatting about their families and thinking about their lives after the war. 'He was coming down to Penzance and I was coming up to see you all. How much we had planned to do!'

All this soothed Maud Harden as she struggled to cope with her husband's death. To Mrs Cory, she wrote with great generosity of spirit that she and the lieutenant must not reproach themselves about Eric's death. 'I find two things to bring slight consolation in the whole sad affair. The first is that your husband's life not only was saved but that he is making progress. I feel Eric did not lose his life in vain. The second is that my husband was killed outright and did not know. He knew how much I dreaded this happening, so I am thankful he was not mortally injured and lying there thinking of us.' His bravery did not surprise her. 'I can easily picture him acting as he did. He must have known what he was doing at the time, and he did it willingly. He died as he lived, a brave, straight, true man.' She poured out her choking mixture of anguish and pride to the Reverend Haw. 'He had everything to live for, yet it counted for nothing when his comrades needed his help. He loved his two children so much, yet, that others might live, he was taken from us. As a son, husband and father as well as a soldier, he was everything good. I thank God for the eight years of our life we spent together.' But, for all her pride in him, there was understandable sadness that he had put his comrades before himself and his family.

The award of the posthumous Victoria Cross for 'her very gallant husband' was gazetted on 8 March 1945. 'His complete contempt for all personal danger and the magnificent example he set of cool courage and determination to continue with his work, whatever the odds, was an inspiration to his comrades,' the citation read. Maud was told in a War Office telegram delivered to her at home.

The decoration nearly didn't happen. Maud showed the original letter from Eric's commanding officer to his sister, who rather foolishly tipped off the press that her brother had been recommended for a VC. The subsequent newspaper reports sent officialdom into a predictable spin. It wasn't just that far more VCs were recommended by COs than were actually awarded and the sifting progress was notoriously rigorous. More damagingly, protocol was being flouted. Charges were levelled of pre-empting the King, who had to approve the award, and there was a period when it looked as if a piqued establishment might deny Eric its highest award for bravery. Maud was mightily embarrassed and pained, especially since, quite unfairly, she was suspected of being the leaker. In the end, good sense prevailed and the VC was confirmed. In the House of Commons, the War Office minister Sir John Grigg used the occasion to pay a tribute. He had seen the account of Harden's courageous actions, 'and I do not remember ever reading anything more heroic'. But he then went beyond the individual to the service he represented as a whole. 'The medical services have been beyond praise in this war. The number of lives and limbs saved by the devotion of doctors is beyond measuring.' It was a moment the forgotten army of medics would cherish, as they cherished Harden's VC. At last, they had been recognized and remembered for a myriad unsung deeds of gallantry and self-sacrifice.

A year later, at Buckingham Palace, George VI pinned the bronze, square-edged cross with its purple ribbon on the jacket lapel of eight-year-old Bobby Harden, standing at attention in his best suit, his hair slicked down, his mother at his side, in a smart hat and with a fox fur over her shoulder. They had come up on the train from Northfleet – in a third-class carriage. Even for a dead hero, rules were rules, and a third-class rail warrant was all the Palace, its courtiers at their most condescending, would offer the widow and her son. The ordinary people of Britain showed themselves more generous. Eric's story captured many imaginations, and a memorial fund in his name raised £10,000, with which Maud bought her house and paid for the education of Bobby and Julie.

To her everlasting regret, Julie, who was six months old when her father was killed, has no memories of him. But his presence filled her life as she strove to find out all she could about him and to make sense of his death. She visited his grave in Holland and followed in his footsteps by joining the St John Ambulance Brigade. Six decades on, she says, 'I am intensely and immensely proud to be my dad's daughter.' She was right to be. He had the heart and soul of a true medic, who heard his comrades' cry for help and could not and would not desert them while there was breath in his body.

★

Would there ever be occasions again for heroes such as Eric Harden? At the end of the Second World War, it looked unlikely, as a new era of warfare began which appeared to change the role of military medics utterly. RAF doctor Aidan MacCarthy, a prisoner of the Japanese, was there to witness the future. He was a slave labourer working in open-cast coal mines on the outskirts of the city of Nagasaki, dealing as best he could with sickness and injury among his fellow PoWs but helpless as their condition deteriorated daily. As American bombers appeared in the sky with increasing regularity, they were switched to digging air-raid shelters and then to carving out a huge pit, which he had no doubt was intended to be a communal grave for the prisoners when their guards massacred them. It was into the shelters he had dug with his own hands that he flung himself on 9 August 1945 when the vapour trails of two B-29s were seen overhead. 'A couple of our men did not bother to go into the shelters, staying on the surface and crouching in the shadow of the barrack huts. One of them shouted to us that three small parachutes were dropping. There then followed a blue flash, accompanied by a very bright mag-nesium-type flare that blinded them. Then came a frighteningly loud explosion, followed by a blast of hot air and then an eerie silence.'

One of the PoWs stuck his head out of the shelter, glanced around and then ducked back in, a look of incredulity on his face. The others rushed to the exits to see for themselves.

Our camp had to all intents and purposes disappeared. The wood had carbonized and turned to ashes. Bodies lay everywhere, some horribly mutilated by falling walls, girders and flying glass. Those people still on their feet ran round in circles, hands pressed to their blinded eyes or holding the flesh that hung in tatters from their faces or arms. We could suddenly see right up the length of the valley, where previously the factories and buildings had formed a screen. Left behind was a crazy forest of discoloured corrugated sheets clinging to twisted girders. Most frightening of all was the lack of sunlight. In contrast to the bright August sunshine a few minutes earlier, there was now a kind of twilight. We all genuinely thought this was the end of the world.[5]

MacCarthy took to his heels and ran for the hills, past an endless stream of burnt, bleeding, flesh-torn, stumbling people. In the first intact village he came to, he stopped running. The doctor inside him reasserted itself, and he set to work, splinting and tying up broken bones. Many injuries were beyond treatment. Melting glass had burnt into bodies and fused with their bones and tissue. A mysterious black rain began to fall, and people who had otherwise escaped the blast began to collapse with sickness. The PoWs were rounded up by the Japanese secret police, marched back into Nagasaki and put to work picking through the carpet of human bodies and laying them out for cremation. A few days later, the prisoners were assembled, to be told that the Emperor had surrendered and the war was over. 'We were all in a state of shock. We cried, hugged each other, shook hands, dropped on our knees and thanked God.'

This new, terrifying weapon, the atom bomb, would fundamentally change the whole nature of warfare between the major international powers. In the post-Second World War years, the burgeoning nuclear arsenals on either side of a divided world seemed to make a nonsense of conventional soldiering. If what MacCarthy had witnessed was the future, then medics would be better training as undertakers for all the good their life-saving skills would do.

8. A Long Way from Home

The Second World War had been a triumph for Britain's military medical services. They were better equipped, better trained and better used than ever before. Their success was exemplified by the tale of nineteen-year-old Trooper Thomas Toughill of the 11th Hussars, whose survival from devastating injuries in 1945 was every bit as astonishing as Sergeant Major Stockton's would be in 2006 (see Chapter 1). Just weeks before the end of the fighting in Germany, Toughill was in the driving seat of a Daimler armoured car on the far side of the Rhine, following the tracks of a German Tiger tank. He reached up to pull down the protective steel visor. 'Suddenly,' he recalled, 'there was a thunderous roar and I was engulfed in flame, along with a terrific impact on my arm and face.'[1] He looked down and saw his broken arm lying in his lap and the middle finger of his left hand, still in the glove, lined up beside it, detached. The ammunition in the armoured car was going to explode any minute, so somehow he levered himself out and knelt, gasping in pain, on the ground. 'Then I saw five Germans looking at me from a hedge ten yards away. They raised their rifles, and I tried to turn away from them. But I felt a burning pain on my leg and another on my hip, followed by a terrific blow in my back and a plopping sound in my chest as the last bullet went clean through me.'

He dragged himself into a ditch and slumped there. Blood was seeping out of him and he was feeling hazy. He was dying. That he didn't was down to a corporal who skidded to a halt in a jeep, picked him up in his arms and carried him to a waiting ambulance. His last memory before blacking out was of being on a table with an orderly cutting off his uniform. He emerged from 'a tunnel, a beautiful tunnel with music being played', three days later, to hear a voice shouting, 'Nurse! Nurse! He is waking.' He was trussed up like the Invisible Man. 'My right arm was in plaster from the shoulder right down to my fingers. My left hand was bandaged like a boxing glove, my chest had heavy padding on it and my face was bandaged where my ear had been severely burnt. I had no voice at all because of a shrapnel wound in my throat.' But, against all expectation, he was alive.

Toughill's wounds were extensive and immense. Thirty years earlier, in the First World War, his death would have been a virtual certainty. He survived because, though he was right up in the front line, an ambulance had managed to get to him, and doctors, who could easily have given him up for dead, persisted in doing their job against the odds. Transfusions had put the lost blood back into his body. Ample supplies of penicillin kept infection at bay. A year of hospital lay ahead. His arm wouldn't mend properly and was a prime candidate for amputation. In 1916, there would have been no question of saving it. Now, the doctors put him in traction to straighten the broken bones and did so. Then came months of painful skin-grafting. A sliver of steel was pulled from Toughill's eye, and it was 1948 before the last piece of shrapnel was removed from his calf.

Toughill was living proof of the medical triumphs of the Second World War. Afterwards, with high-level compliments heaped on the service in the House of Commons, there was a certain amount of back-slapping and self-congratulation. 'Our present-day army is not one of foot-slogging cannon fodder, obeying without thinking, but of skilled and experienced technicians used to controlling and repairing complicated machines, including the human body,' declared one report proudly in 1946.[2] Much had been learned medically in the war – about controlling pain and infection, about the correct treatment of traumatic wounds, about blood trans-fusions, burns, general health and hygiene – and it added enor-mously to the fund of knowledge bequeathed to the newly created National Health Service. Civilian medicine was a huge beneficiary of the war. But military medicine now rested on its laurels. The learning seemed to stop, and little thought was given to updating medical techniques. When British forces parachuted into Suez in the fiasco invasion of Egypt in 1956, most of the glass bottles of blood they carried smashed on landing. New experimental transfusion bags sent from the United States, made from polyethylene and shatterproof, had been left behind in the RAMC storeroom because the brigadier they were delivered to had no idea what they were.

The logistical lessons of the Second World War were quickly forgotten. Air evacuation of casualties, though limited in scope, had been a great success in the last months of the conflict in 1945. At an airfield in Brussels, the lines of Dakotas were an inspiring sight as they arrived every few minutes to fly wounded servicemen home. So impressed was Lieutenant General Sir Neil Cantlie, Director General of the Army Medical Services, that he had no hesitation in predicting that 'ambulance planes' would be essential for future wars. They had been repeatedly requested in the war that had just finished, but turned down because of shortage of resources. This same 'hoary' argument, he said, had been made to deny special hospital ships for the Crimean War and road ambulances for the Boer War, until public opinion clamoured for them and their provision became standard practice. The same would apply to ambulance aircraft. Cantlie was backed by Field Marshal Sir William Slim, whose jungle army had depended on air evacuation of casualties when fighting the Japanese in Burma. The army's adjutant general had made a similar point during the war after witnessing events in North Africa,[3] and the self-same lesson came over loud and clear from the Italian campaign – the medical services needed their own fleet of aircraft. The pleas all went unheeded. There would be no dedicated air ambulances. (Shamefully, sixty-five years on from the end of the Second World War, there still aren't, and the debate goes on over battlefield helicopters exclusively for medical use.)

In fact, the whole process of medical evacuation, one of the war's great organizational successes, went into reverse when the entire flotilla of hospital ships was scrapped and not replaced. This was par for the course. In the new world of the nuclear Cold War, no one could see any point in them. As the implications of arsenals of Armageddon weapons took a hold on military thinking, planning for a conventional war was pushed aside. Even the long-drawn-out and bloody conflicts of Korea and Vietnam were perceived as essentially side issues against the very real possibility of a global nuclear conflagration. For the British military establishment, battlefield medicine had become largely an irrelevance and an anachronism, a dead speciality, killed off by doomsday weapons. Who needed it, or would ever have reason to make use of it again?

It was no coincidence that, in this period, medics even became a source of black comedy, a good laugh. 'Attention! Attention! Choppers incoming. Wounded incoming,' rang out the tinny loudspeaker announcement, sending ultra-cool, wise-cracking, khaki-clad doctors and nubile nurses racing from whatever they had been getting up to in their tents to scrub up and prepare to operate on badly injured men on their way from the battlefront. This was *M*A*S*H*,[4] Hollywood's anarchic take on life in a field hospital. The parched hills the ambulance helicopters scooted around to land their casualties were supposed to be those of Korea in the 1950s during the war with the communist forces of China, in which more than 35,000 American servicemen and 1,000 British soldiers died. In fact, they were filmed in California in the 1970s, and the hard graft inside the operating tent was accompanied by hard drinking and perpetual partying outside.

For civilians on both sides of the Atlantic, director Robert Altman's 1970 feature film, and then the long-running TV series, with more than 250 episodes, which aired from 1972[5] to 1983, would become an enduring – and utterly misleading – image of how the military medical services went about their work. Its macho surgeons and willing nurses were a mockery, but slick and funny for all that. The generation that had fought in the Second World War was not much amused, but the show's irreverence appealed to the new wave of hippies, cynics and peaceniks. It was anti-authoritarian in tone and anti-war in the message it gave out. It was a satire on the perceived lunacies of military life and a subversive assault on the unpopular war in Vietnam, where the helicopters were then flying for real, not just for the movie cameras, and nearly

60,000 young Americans died and 300,000 were wounded. When the Vietnam conflict ended in humiliating military defeat for the US in 1975, the zaniness of *M*A*S*H* underlined the commonly held view that wars like this were history. Then, for the people of Britain, out of the blue, something happened that changed this popular pacifist perception. And it was definitely not funny.

*

Corporal Johnnie Geddes had just arrived with his wife and children at his mother-in-law's home in Newcastle in April 1982 when a one-word telegram dropped through the letterbox. 'Normandy,' it read.[6] History and tradition are the glues that bind fighting men to past glories in the hope of inspiring them to future success, so the secret codeword that summoned him and the other men of the Parachute Regiment to their most difficult post-war expedition to date was an apt one. He got straight back into the car and drove the length of England through the night to report to barracks. As with the Normandy landings of 1944, this was to be another venture across the sea to the beaches of a foreign land, but there the similarities with the invasion of France ended. This time those hostile shores were more than 7,500 miles away, on the other side of the world.

The recovery of the Falkland Islands, British territories in the remote South Atlantic Ocean, which had been seized at gunpoint by the military dictatorship running Argentina, was to be like no other operation of its age. Modern British forces were trained to fight either a global (and, swiftly, nuclear) war, against the Soviet Union, or a localized one, as on the streets and in the border lanes of Northern Ireland. A long-distance conflict of the sort now demanded by the prime minister, Margaret Thatcher, had not been on anyone's radar. It popped up from the history books like some Redcoat adventure in Britain's imperialist past – in South Africa or India or the Crimea, say – but happening, by some extraordinary quirk, in the last quarter of the twentieth century. Unlike the 1944 D-Day landings, it was also hurriedly conceived, woefully under-resourced and, some said, over-ambitious to the point of folly. But national pride demanded it, and the consensus across all political parties supported it. RAMC medic Mick Jennings expressed the thoughts of civilians and soldiers alike when he recalled: 'I was pleased when Maggie said, right, we're going to go and sort this out.'[7] Not that he knew anything about the Falklands. 'I couldn't point to them on a map – I had no idea where they were. My first thought was that they were in the Hebrides, off Scotland. A lot of people did.' Nonetheless, there was an absolute determination that the Malvinas, as the Spanish-speaking Argentinians insisted on calling the windswept, snow-chilled outcrops of rock, moorland and peat bog 400 miles from the mainland of South America, would be wrested back from the usurper, their original name[8] restored and their three thousand inhabitants returned to British rule.

As the Task Force troops assembled at Southampton and set off in a fleet of hurriedly commandeered ships for the six-week voyage south, few believed they would actually go into action. This was the nuclear age. Gunboat diplomacy was a thing of the past. It seemed a safe bet that the politicians would posture for a while and then there would be a negotiated settlement. The Task Force would turn round, hopefully not too far short of the equator, so the lads could get in a spot of sunbathing before heading home. Normal service would then be resumed. Except that it wasn't, and the story told by those on board this armada was of the slowly dropping realization that there would be no turning back. They were going to war, and some of them, perhaps many of them, would not be making the return journey in one piece, or at all.

As mile after mile of the Atlantic slipped beneath the keels and the water turned from summer blue to winter grey, the vastness of the ocean and the increasing distance from home seemed to underscore the puniness of this force in the face of the daunting task ahead. For those among the men with a sense of history, the campaigns that came increasingly to mind were not the victorious landings of D-Day but the disasters of Gallipoli in 1915 and Norway in 1940. The medics on board were among the first to realize they had to prepare for the worst. More to the point, they had to prepare a gung-ho gang of men and boys for the terrible realities of something they had never really envisaged – a face-to-face, bullet-and-bayonet war.

The first mountain the medics had to climb – and there would be many in the weeks ahead – was not Tumbledown, or Two Sisters, or any of the other landmarks on the maps of these little-known islands stretched out on ward-room floors and pored over by the military planners. The initial hurdle was getting the men to take seriously the prospect of being wounded and that their lives might come to depend on what the medics could contribute.

Captain Steven Hughes, recently recruited as regimental medical officer of 2 Para, felt himself to be every inch a paratrooper. The stories of bravery at Arnhem were what had seduced him into this hard-nut regiment. But he was well aware that the fighting men of his battalion paid scant regard to people like him. The macho culture of the Paras derided not only 'crap hats' – their dismissive term for soldiers from other regiments, ones not entitled to the maroon beret of the airborne elite – but also those within the regiment who were not front-line troops. Bandsmen, cooks, medics – even doctors – were a lower form of life. 'Other than for in-growing toenails or a blister or two on exercise, the Toms [slang term for Para squaddies] thought they didn't have much use for us.'[9] When he arrived at the battalion nine months earlier, he had found that several companies did not possess a single medic with the most basic knowledge of first aid, and officers were reluctant to release any of their men for him to train. 'They didn't really see the need.' He had to work hard to win them round, and he still had a long way to go.

Too often he had run-ins with what another soldier, commando Captain Hugh McManners, described as 'G snobs', the operations staff, whose snootiness about the contributions of medics could verge on scorn. They could be as dismissive in their attitudes as the cavalry officers in the Crimea who, 125 years earlier, cantered off with the horses that were intended to pull field ambulances. To McManners, there was an unhealthy paradox in the way the army generally considered the men tasked not to take lives but to save them. 'Few soldiers volunteer to become medics,' he observed. 'The best become NCOs, and those unable to make it as combat soldiers are entrusted with the lives of others, required to be able to resuscitate, maintain airways, staunch bleeding, administer pain relief and splint limbs while leaving the "real" soldiers free for the fighting.'[10]

In the burst of activity before the Task Force left, Hughes ordered 25,000 sea-sickness pills and stocked up with crate-loads of extra dressings and drips. Amid all the flag-waving 'off to war' euphoria around him, and despite his own belief at this time that they were setting out on a wild goose chase, he dug out and scrutinized the statistics of past expeditions and made a sober – and chilling – assessment of potential casualties. What could he do to minimize the death count? He knew the crucial factor would be getting casualties off the battlefield as swiftly as possible for treat-ment. But this was not something they had trained for. In their peace-time exercises in the Welsh hills and Scottish highlands, they played tough and rough, simulating battle tactics and testing their endurance to the full. But when 'casualties' were designated by the exercise umpire, they were merely ordered to report to the regimental aid post, several miles away, on foot. This was laughable. In a real battle with real injuries, that would be impossible. In the Falklands, the absence of a properly rehearsed drill for dealing with casualties could be disastrous.

Over at 3 Para, which was also heading for the Falklands, Colour Sergeant Brian Faulkner was putting his mind to the same problem. A thirty-five-year-old veteran, he had been the battalion's assistant air adjutant liaising with the RAF on airborne operations. Now he was assigned to devise plans for evacuating the wounded. 'I don't think anybody within the fighting battalions had thought about how to do this,' he recalled, 'other than, we've got a doctor, a colour sergeant and some medics with aspirins and bandages in Bergen rucksacks on their backs! Medical services hadn't really been taken too seriously before. But they were once the shooting started. You should hear them shout "Medic" then!'[11]

Faulkner was starting from scratch, having to make it up as he went along – largely from film footage of American forces in Vietnam pulling their boys out of the jungle by helicopter. There were no training manuals for this, no real experience to draw on, particularly given the uncertain topography of the Falklands. About all he knew for sure was that, where they were going, there would be nothing like the paddy fields of south-east Asia. Nor would there be the profusion of rescue helicopters the US had had in Vietnam which had enabled the Americans to get wounded men to a doctor in an incredible average of twenty-two minutes.[12] Geography and logistics meant things were going to be different in the Falklands. So too did the military strategy thought necessary to win back the islands. It had been decided that an action would not be halted if casualties were taken, as had been the practice for the British Army in Northern Ireland. The wounded would be of secondary concern until the objective of any attack had been secured.

With this in mind, medical officer Hughes realized that, in the limited time he had on the journey, he would have to teach the troops to treat themselves as best they could. As the flotilla ploughed its way south, he set up an intensive training scheme to put in place at least one combat medic (and preferably two) with first-aid knowledge in every ten-man patrol. He taught them rudimentary anatomy and physiology, but the emphasis was on the basics – checking breathing and stemming blood flow. They would be the first call in the front line, stabilizing the wounded, saving their lives before they were shipped first to a company or regimental aid post staffed by doctors and specialist medics and then to a field hospital, where surgeons would be waiting.

He gave regular briefings to the Toms on what they could do to help each other. As the weeks progressed, he noticed the numbers in attendance – and their concentration on the advice he was dishing out – creeping up. Reality was sinking in. Men who had been drilling in soft gym shoes to avoid marking the wooden decks of the *Norland*, the converted North Sea car ferry on which they were travelling, were now in heavy combat boots. An air of seriousness replaced the party atmosphere in which they had set out from England. 'If you are hit,' Hughes instructed them, 'you put your own finger in the hole, then drag yourself behind a rock and start your own treatment while your mate secures the ground to make it safe for evacuation. There's no point in stopping to bandage a casualty if you can't move him anywhere. And you're more likely to lose the ground if, for every man injured, another one has to stop to look after him.' The men of action listened intently. Hughes could see a new respect for him and his medics. 'We were no longer considered "idle knackers".'

He coaxed the Toms to open up about their fears – not easy. When he managed to get them to talk, he noticed their relief at discovering they all had the same deep-seated (and often misin-formed) concerns – about pain, about dying slowly but inevitably from abdominal wounds, or how it would be if they ended up with ruptured intestines and a colostomy bag. He told them that 70 per cent of all wounds were to limbs, not heads or guts, 'which came as a great relief to them. If they were shot in the guts and were still alive, they were going to stay alive, because they'd be treated properly. I told them that most colostomies can eventually be joined back up again.' Even if their bellies were split open and their intestines fell out, they shouldn't panic. Guts could be shoved back in and sewn up.

He warned them to go easy on administering morphine, how-ever great the temptation to ease a mate's pain, however much he begged for it. 'If a guy is screaming and shouting, then he'll be happier being alive at the end than if you'd filled him full of morphine and he quietly succumbed.' Screaming, he told them, was good. 'It keeps a man's airway open, and the adrenalin running round his system keeps him alive.' Hughes didn't pull any punches about the crucial issue of getting them off the battlefield, the key to survival. It was going to be difficult. There weren't nearly enough stretcher-bearers. It would be down to company com-manders to get their wounded back to the aid posts in any way they could, which was not ideal but was the truth of it.

In his search for life-saving procedures, he alighted on the Israeli Army's practice of issuing each soldier with his own supply of intravenous Hartmann's saline fluid to carry into battle, rather than these all being kept by the medics. It made sense, and that became the order of the day, despite some opposition. One officer complained bitterly that his already overburdened men were being asked to carry the MO's supplies, and the MO should damned well carry them himself! Hughes had the last laugh. 'The same officer learnt the hard way, after nearly losing his life at Goose Green[13] to a shrapnel fragment in his liver.'

If they were to carry their own bags of fluid, then it was also sensible that they should all know how to administer it rather than have to wait for specialist medics to do the job. Some Toms leapt at the idea of being able to stick needles into each other. But finding a suitable vein and inserting an intravenous drip was a skill that not everyone could master on a well-lit hospital ward, let alone at night on a battlefield. But there was another way of getting liquid into the bloodstream quickly – thrust up the backside like an enema. Rectal infusion, as it was properly called, was not a proven technique (and it was subsequently discredited as being largely ineffective), but Hughes considered it worth having a go. It wasn't going to be harmful, and it might be better than nothing. The Toms were affronted by the very idea. Geddes and his mates reckoned they would rather bleed to death than drop their trousers and have a tube rammed up them in the freezing Falklands wind. The practice sessions were riotous. Major Philip Neame recalled 'everyone running around the deck shoving drips up any bare backsides that happened to be around.' He made sure he went everywhere with his back to the bulkhead 'so no one could have a crack at me'.[14]

That apart, however, the Paras lapped up everything that 'Arsey' Hughes – now, inevitably, his nickname – had to teach them, as he handed out what he called their 'puncture repair outfits' of field dressings. Geddes remembered the instruction to slap one on the bullet entry wound, one on the exit wound, then tie them in place with an elasticated crepe bandage. They were assured that this would 'keep it all nice and tight until help arrives'.

Across on the *Canberra*, the requisitioned P&O luxury liner that was now the main troop ship, Surgeon Commander Rick Jolly of the Royal Navy, a senior medical officer attached to the Royal Marines, was handing out the same sort of advice to the green berets of his command, though it felt bizarre to be doing so. He was acutely conscious, embarrassed even, that his shipmates were his potential customers. The shadow of death and pain hung over the men he was working and joking with. What lay ahead would be no laughing matter. He came up against the same sort of 'G snob' bluster as Hughes was experiencing on the *Norland*: an officer refused to release his men for medical training because they would be the first ashore on the Falklands and needed to concentrate on weapons training and fitness rather than worrying about what to do if they were wounded.

At a heated briefing, he made it clear he had no time for 'bloody medics'. Jolly calmly asked the obstreperous officer to spell out his surname, ostentatiously wrote it down and then explained that he would have it posted in the emergency unit with a tag beside it stating 'Not to be resuscitated'. The bluff worked. 'Quite suddenly he conceded the point,' Jolly noted in his diary.[15] Like Hughes, he spent much of his time on board instructing his fellow Marines on the injuries to expect and how to deal with them. His colour slide-show of graphic and gory gunshot wounds turned many a stomach, and one sergeant major tried to stop his company being shown 'Doc Jolly's Horror Show' on the grounds that it might put the blokes off and undermine their willingness to go into battle. The doctor persisted, convinced that knowledge was better than ignorance, and reality – a large dose of which was about to hit them – preferable to pretence.

He didn't let on but, underneath the appearance he projected of calm confidence, he was fighting demons, holding down his own fears. 'I realized the enormity of what we were embarking on, and I expected a large number of casualties. I might even be one of them myself. There was a very real chance I might never see my family again.' But what worried him every bit as much as dying was whether he would find the inner strength to meet the challenges. Would he be able to cope, or would he crumble? He recognized that, militarily, he was a bit of a dud. 'My talents in organizing fire positions and patrols were what you'd expect from an obstetrician, albeit a commando-trained one.' But he needed to be strong, and that was where he doubted himself. 'I remembered being on the last leg of the commando course, and the final endurance test was incredibly tough. I couldn't hack it, and I began to slow down and fall back. Eventually I stopped. I just didn't have the strength to go on. One of the younger recruits came running back to help me. "Sir," he said, "if you don't get to that finish line with us, we are all going to have to do this bastard thing again tomorrow. Please don't let us down."' That incident lurked at the back of his mind. 'My fear was always that I would let somebody down.'

For Tom Onions of 3 Para, the approach of war meant a new job, a dangerous one he felt ill-prepared for. He was an army cook, like his father before him, had joined the Catering Corps at sixteen and then, instead of being attached to a cushy berth on a missile base in Germany, had been posted to the Paras. He was, he freely admitted,[16] treated with disdain, hate even, because he didn't have his wings and wasn't 'one of them'. But now he would get the chance, whether he wanted it or not, to prove them wrong, to show that he was every bit as tough as the Toms. Along with other chefs, mess staff, bandsmen and Pay Corps clerks, he would go ashore in the Falklands as a stretcher-bearer. On the *Canberra*, he went through a crash course in field first aid. 'To be honest, I was scared stiff. I never expected to go to war, not in a million years. As a chef, my military training had been very basic. I'd only occasionally got into greens to do range work. But now we were actually going to war and people were going to die.' He was philosophical. 'That's what the future held for me. That's the way it was going to be.'

One of the many lessons to loom out of the fog of war was that the disdain that front-line soldiers were prone to heap on those they considered non-combatants was utterly undeserved. Many would come to realize that those whose job was to carry the wounded to safety – summoned to where the fighting was fiercest, in the thick of every action, exposed to murderous fire while others were able to keep their heads down – had to be the toughest of all, both physically and mentally.

The sense of going into the unknown settled over everyone. In the *Canberra*'s first-class section, Captain John Burgess, 3 Para's medical officer, swapped ideas and cases with all the other doctors on board and realized that, between them, they had virtually no experience of operational warfare. 'I'd been in hospitals, I'd put up drips, I'd seen people die, but that had been in a hospital setting. I'd done a bit in Northern Ireland, but I had no concept of what we were facing. I certainly didn't visualize losing colleagues and friends, which was what happened.'[17]

Anxiety levels increased as they steamed closer and closer to their destination and there was still no prospect of a settlement, for all the frantic talks at the United Nations. The likelihood of a peaceful outcome diminished further when a British submarine sank the Argentine battleship *Belgrano* with the loss of 323 lives. 'No more Mr Nice Guy,' Rick Jolly noted. 'Game on!' But whatever 'Gotcha' joy there was over that military success, it lasted less than forty-eight hours. The destroyer HMS *Sheffield* was out ahead of the flotilla on picket duty protecting the aircraft carriers *Hermes* and *Invincible* when an Exocet missile from an Argentine jet tore a gash in her side and set her ablaze. Twenty-one sailors died in the flames and twenty-four were badly wounded. With these first casualties, all pretence was over. One senior officer wrote home to his wife: 'There are two envelopes in the drawers of my desk addressed to you. They tell you how much money you get if I fail to return. Thought I had better mention it!'[18]

The fate of the *Belgrano* and the *Sheffield* – the deaths of 'real people' –made everyone sombre. This was going to be a bloody business. A silence settled over the messes and living quarters as men struggled to overcome their feelings and fears, and the padre was suddenly the most popular figure on board. In the chapel on the *Canberra*, Burgess joined in the singing of 'For Those in Peril on the Sea' with added vigour. The shift in atmosphere, the rise in tension, was palpable. 'Things had changed. We could be fighting –

and dying – soon.' How soon, he was able to calculate when he was given orders to top up the blood bank. Donors were called for, and a thousand pints of 'high-quality red stuff', as Jolly called it, were taken. The timing was crucial. The blood had to be as fresh as possible, but the donors had to be given time to recover their full strength. That meant they must be just days away from going ashore.

Now there were regular air-raid drills, sirens sounding and everyone dashing to their emergency stations. At night, portholes were blacked out and the lights inside dimmed. Overhead, Argentine planes were seeking out the flotilla, and their presence sent the crews to their guns and the troops to seek cover in case of attack. In their cramped quarters, Lance Corporal Mick Jennings and fellow medic Jim Pearson sat playing chess on the bunk they shared. It wasn't the safest place to be. 'We were below the water line, and we knew that if the ship was hit we would be totally stuffed.' He remembered telling himself he would be all right, that he was bullet proof. Others were not so sure and were writing wills and their last letters home.

There was a noticeable gloom when news filtered from man to man that a Sea King helicopter had plunged into the sea while ferrying SAS troopers from the aircraft carrier *Hermes* to the assault ship *Intrepid*. The troopers were an advance party, who had already been on the Falklands to neutralize an enemy air strip. They had been preparing to go in again, to set up observation and sniper positions and create diversions for the main landing. Eighteen of them were dead. An albatross, that traditional fateful omen of the sea, was the cause, rather than the Argentinians. The bird had crashed into the helicopter, bringing it down.

It was a sign of how stretched this whole operation was in these remote waters, and how flimsy the prospect of success or even survival. 'How many more of us might end up lying in some unknown, unmarked grave?' Rick Jolly asked himself. 3 Para private Mark Eyles-Thomas, with some basic training in first aid, was detailed to help with survivors. Some had been in the freezing water for fifteen minutes, and he bathed one of them, semi-conscious, blue with cold and shivering uncontrollably, in warm water to revive him. It was a testing baptism. But what most shocked the 3 Para private – at seventeen, one of the youngest in the Task Force – was the sight of those beyond help, their bodies laid out on tables in the ship's galley.[19]

On the night before the islands came into view, the general apprehension was such that even the non-believers turned up for evening prayers on the *Norland*. 'Welcome, Corporal,' the padre greeted John Geddes. 'Nice to see you. Come to collect some insurance, have you?' Geddes and his mates nodded. At times like this, a man would take whatever comfort was going. Soon, live ammunition was being doled out to the troops, and Steven Hughes issued them with their half-litres of intravenous fluid. Each man also got a syrette of morphine, taped to the inside of his helmet so it wouldn't be smashed, or to the identity 'dog tag' around his neck. D-Day had come – 21 May 1982.

*

They came off the ships in the dark, down into the flat-bottomed landing craft that pitched in the stormy waters of the Sound, the ten-mile-wide passage splitting the islands of West Falkland and East Falkland that would soon earn the nickname 'Bomb Alley'. The fog that had masked the armada's entrance into the Sound twenty-four hours earlier had lifted, and the southern cross glittered, brightest of all, in the starry sky above. Faces were blacked up with camouflage cream, rifles cocked, grenades primed.

Mick Jennings, packed in with his mates, side by side and standing upright like penguins, had newsreel visions of the Normandy landings going through his mind. Would he be wading through water to get on to the beaches? Would they be mined? Would he be running into a hail of bullets? Medical officer Steven Hughes fully expected to have 'customers' immediately. But the landings on the beaches at San Carlos Bay went unopposed, which was both a surprise and a blessing. Stretcher-bearer Tom Onions was weighed down with so much kit he could barely move. 'I had all my medical stuff, a stretcher, 600 rounds of ammunition for the machine guns and two mortar rounds. When the ramp went down, there was none of this Iwo Jima stuff running on to the beach in light order. If there'd been resistance, we'd have been cut to pieces. We were struggling.'

But, though ashore in one piece, many of the men were wet. Hughes's craft beached on a sandbar ten yards from the shore and the men had to wade through the icy water of the South Atlantic to get to dry land. They were soaked through before they had even begun.

This was the start of a major and long-term problem. Many would never get their feet properly dry again. In the coming weeks, 'trench foot', that debilitating ailment of water-logged First World War trenches, would cripple more soldiers than bullets or bombs did. Awash with streams and bogs, the island's terrain gave almost no respite from the damp, and standard Army-issue boots were no help, because they let the water in and, once soaked, were almost impossible to dry out. Soggy skin wrinkled, cracked and festered. It was agony to walk[20] – which made what these men were about to achieve in conquering the Falklands on foot even more spectacular.

Hughes marched off the beach at the rear of his battalion, ready to scoop up any casualties left by the column snaking out ahead of him into the countryside. He found his first – a young Para who stumbled in the dark and knocked himself out on the Blowpipe surface-to-air missile he was carrying. The soldier was unconscious, and had to be carried the rest of the way to safe ground. From the start, Hughes could see the conditions take a terrible toll on even the Paras' fit young bodies. Everything – weapons, ammunition, food, stores – had to be manhandled across pitted, impossible terrain. On that first exhausting march, he lost count of the number of times he tumbled into the peat and then, helpless as a sheep on its back with the weight he was carrying, had to be dragged back up to plod on. Packs were too heavy, the loads too great. A fully loaded Bergen rucksack alone weighed in at 50lbs, a single Blowpipe missile at 48lbs. Festoons of machine-gun belts dragged down necks and backs.

Some men were toting more than 140lbs in all, almost their

own bodyweight. The pace slowed, and the schedules worked out by the planners were already meaningless. 'Knackered barely does justice to the way we felt,' Hughes recalled. As the sun rose on that first morning, he heard the dawn chorus of hundreds of weary men muttering, 'Fuck! Fuck! Fuck!', the air as blue as their bruised shins. It was to prove most people's favourite word for the entire campaign, he reckoned, 'and we meant it every time we said it!'

With the morning too came the first Mirage and Skyhawk jets, screaming overhead and letting fly with rockets and cannon. The men went down on their knees for what, after cross-country marching with heavy equipment (or 'yomping' and 'tabbing', as this was called),[21] would be the second most frequent Falklands activity – namely, digging in. As the Toms scraped away at the mud and shale, the doctor set up his regimental aid post behind a large rock, forming a lean-to shelter from three stretchers and nylon camouflage sheets. He piled blocks of peat around it for protection. As he surveyed his new, damp and draughty domain, it was hard to believe how recently he had been a warm, dry surgical locum moonlighting in an overheated NHS hospital in London.

John Burgess, MO of 3 Para, at least had a proper roof over his head as he and his medical team bedded in at the handful of sea-front houses that comprised the San Carlos Settlement. He had been scared coming ashore, especially since he came in a later wave and it was already light as they crossed the water. As he waded on to the beach, Pucaras, twin-prop Argentine fighter planes, came screaming in, strafing the invading troops.

The Argentine occupiers of the settlement had fled, but not before shooting down two Gazelle helicopters from 3 Commando, which had been escorting a Sea King as it ferried supplies inland in an under-slung cargo net. One of the Gazelles lay on a hillside with its back broken and its tail boom bent back on itself. The contents of the cockpit were strewn over the grass, along with the bodies of the pilot and the air gunner, their flying suits stained with blood. The second Gazelle had landed in the sea and its pilot had survived the crash, only for the Argentine defenders to machine-gun him to death as he tried to swim to shore. The manner of his death shocked the Toms. How dirty was this war going to get? Onions was marching towards the settlement when a Land Rover, with an islander at the wheel, stopped beside him. Lying in the back underneath a blanket was the body of the Gazelle pilot shot in the water. He shuddered at the sight. It was the first dead person the cook-turned-stretcher-bearer had ever seen. 'I thought, "Fuck, this is real."'

The medical team at San Carlos had hardly had time to settle in when they were faced with a major incident. Out in the countryside, eight Paras were badly injured, two of them with gunshot wounds to the head. Burgess climbed aboard a Sea King to fly to the scene. He gazed out through the open door as they travelled fast and low over this sparse, strange landscape, hugging the contours of the hillside to avoid detection. As they crested a hill and spotted the casualties on the ground below, there was an incredible bang from the rear and the helicopter shook violently. The terrified men on board thought an enemy missile had struck them. In fact, the tail had caught the rising ground behind, sending the helicopter into an uncontrollable spin, twisting in the air and tumbling, before smashing into the peat. The soft, springy turf was a life-saver. 'If we'd come down on rock, we'd have been dead,' Burgess recalled.

Shaken, but in one piece, he and the others scrambled from the wreckage and went to work on the casualties they had flown here to treat, his first on the island. This was also the first time he'd ever had to deal with gunshot wounds. Any doubts he had were put aside. 'You just get down and do your job.' In the biting wind, he knelt on the hillside, inserted drips and dressed the most serious head wound, the bullet still deeply embedded, as best he could. Another helicopter flew in, and they were soon back at Port San Carlos. The doctor was surprised by how straightforward his initiation into battlefield military medicine had been. Even the helicopter crash had been a soft landing. But was it always going to be this easy?

Any such hopes were dispelled when it emerged that the Argentinians had had no part at all in this carnage. The incident had been one of so-called 'friendly fire'. Through misreading the map, two Para patrols had strayed into each other's line of fire, and one had shot up the other accidentally. It was a sign of how jumpy everyone was. In that unforgiving landscape, lessons were being learned the hard way, and it was the medics who would have to pick up the pieces when mistakes were made.

★

Those lessons came thick and fast in those first few hours and days of landing on the Falklands. Mick Jennings came ashore at the scenic Ajax Bay, where a warehouse of cavernous proportions – a former whaling station, refrigeration plant and slaughterhouse for sheep – had been designated as the site for the campaign's field hospital. Crews got to work installing a generator, digging defensive trenches outside and setting up operating theatres – in reality, just two collapsible tables – and nursing stations inside. Enemy planes were overhead, being chased off by Rapier missiles and small-arms fire from the ground, and by Harrier fighters winging in from the aircraft carriers out in the Atlantic. He could see the inshore fleet in Bomb Alley come under air attack, deliberately drawing enemy fire away from the troops trying to establish positions on land.

Two Mirages picked out HMS *Antrim* and flew in low together at just below the speed of sound, one on either side, to rake her decks with 40mm cannon. Parallel lines of shells fizzed through the flat water before hitting home. Chief Petty Officer Terry Bullingham threw himself down and curled into a ball, but it was too late. He felt a sickening thud to his face, 'and that was the last I saw – *ever!*'²² Blood streamed from his eye sockets. A piece of shrapnel had taken out his left eyeball, and the concussion of a shell hitting the bulkhead nearby had burst the right. His helmet was pitted with shards of shrapnel. If he hadn't been wearing it, his entire head would have been shredded. As it was, he was blinded. The medics now at his side tried to reassure him. 'I can't see,' he told them, and one said he just had a pair of black eyes. 'But I knew they were lying. They were just wondering how to tell a guy that his eyes had gone.'

The frigate HMS *Ardent* also took a terrible pounding, hit by dozens of bombs and rockets until she was alight from funnel to stern. Bodies littered her deck. The ship's doctor was killed. Casualties were flown in to Ajax Bay, and Jennings lifted a bomb-shattered body on to a stretcher. 'I held his arm, and it was like holding a bag of crisps. All the bones in it were pulverized.'

In the sky above the burning *Ardent*, Rick Jolly had an even closer brush with the horrors of war. In a Wessex helicopter, he had been out collecting casualties, buzzing around the battle as it escalated from small skirmishes to a full-on air attack. He had picked up the Para in Steven Hughes's outfit who had knocked himself out on the missile he was carrying and brought in the bodies of the downed Gazelle crew. Now, perched on a clifftop to shelter from marauding enemy fighters, he looked out over the thin grey naval picket line in Falkland Sound and the ships of the Landing Force strung out behind. 'I was watching history in the making, but also history repeating itself.' Here was a group of Royal Navy warships protecting troop ships from a well-orchestrated enemy air force – just as the Navy had done to save the British Army that escaped under fire from Crete in 1941. This perspective reassured him. 'I felt very calm – and very proud.'

But those fears of letting people down which had so haunted him on the voyage from England now re-surfaced, as one of the Argentinian planes dodging and weaving around the fleet turned in the direction of his exposed helicopter. 'I could see it getting bigger as it headed towards us; it was a truly terrifying sight.' Far from calm now, his heart was pounding, he could taste the fear in his mouth, 'and I just broke and ran.' Jolly dived out of the cabin and into a ditch, expecting the helicopter to erupt into flames behind him as the enemy pressed home the attack. Nothing happened. The fighter plane went past, ignoring the helicopter and its three-man crew, who had remained strapped onboard. A full quarter of a century later, he would still own up to the enduring shame of that moment. 'Chicken shit, really.'[23] As he sheepishly climbed into the cabin, he was greeted by the pilot. 'Oh, you back with us then, Doc?' The sarcasm was withering, and he wondered if he would ever live it down.

Moments later, word came over the radio about HMS *Ardent*, and they were on their way to help, flying out over the water, through palls of black smoke, until the Wessex was hovering thirty feet above the swell just off *Ardent*'s port bow. Jolly was stunned by what he was seeing. 'I could feel the heat and smell the acrid fumes. Here was a modern warship mortally injured. I'd seen nothing like this before, nor had anything prepared me for such a sight. There were flames, explosions, smoke, people dying. She looked as though someone had torn her deck open with a can-opener and the fires of hell were burning inside.' On the upper deck of the listing ship, sailors in orange survival suits were preparing to scramble down on to the deck of the frigate HMS *Yarmouth*, whose captain had, with tremendous skill, nudged her stern next to *Ardent*'s bows.

But other survivors were in the water and struggling. Dunked in the freezing South Atlantic, they might have only minutes to live. The rescue harness was lowered to one of them but, amid the furious spray whipped up by the rotor blades, he was unable to grab it and, even if he had, he was almost certainly too weak to hold on. Jolly crawled over to the door and stared down in disbelief. Below him was a comrade in arms, and he was drowning. 'I could see the agonized expression on his face as he floundered helplessly. If I didn't do something, then who else could? I had to go and get him. He would die if I didn't.' Perhaps, the doctor remembered thinking, this was his chance to atone for his earlier funk when he ran from the helicopter. There was hurried whispering on their intercoms between the crew as they debated whether to let Jolly go to the rescue. The winchman had his doubts, but the pilot gave the go-ahead. The rescue harness was thrust over the doctor's head and under his arms. 'Seconds later, I was descending towards the surface of the sea.'

There had been no time for the lengthy process of putting on an immersion suit, and the numbing cold went through him the moment he hit the water. The doctor in him recognized dangerous symptoms: his heart was slowing, his peripheral vision dimming, the retinas of his eyes clouding. 'But the desperate look on the man's face, his frantic thrashings and punctured life jacket spurred me on, and a fresh adrenalin surge kicked in.' The helicopter towed him across the water until his outstretched fingers were in touching distance of the man. They grasped hands, Jolly spun the man round and gripped him in a fierce bear hug as the Wessex lifted up slowly, pulling them clear of the water. Then the winch slowly wound them in. The doctor clung on, 'begging my shoulder muscles not to weaken in this moment of crisis'. He was in pain, the tendons in his arms screaming. He was already exhausted and drained. 'But I knew that if I let go he would die. I just kept telling myself not to give up, to keep going. I used every ounce of my strength and will in those few moments.'

Finally, they were up at the level of the helicopter and being hauled into the cabin. 'The blood flowed back into my arms and shoulders as I collapsed beside the survivor on the floor.' The doctor leaned over and pummelled the man's chest, and a stream of sea water erupted from his mouth. His eyes opened. He would live. Jolly grinned. The helicopter winchman grinned back, then pointed down. There was another man in the water. The doctor would have to do it all over again. Jolly remembered feeling despair. He had no strength left. Even if he got to the man, would he be able to cling on to him? Should he even try? Hadn't he done enough? And that was when Jolly learned the hardest lesson of military medicine – there is no such thing as enough when a life is at stake. 'I looked into my soul and I realized that I was prepared to risk my own life for another human being. I prayed for inspiration to be able to do it.'

He dropped into the sea again, but with a dangerous plan in mind. He knew he wouldn't be able to hang on to the man while they were winched up together, so he would take off the harness and put it round the drowning man for him to be pulled to safety first. Jolly would then tread ice-cold water until the man was in the helicopter and the line could be sent back down for him. The odds, he knew, were not great. There was a very real chance he himself could now collapse from exhaustion and cold, and drown. But if he didn't take this gamble with his own life, the man in the water would have no chance at all. And, as he could see as he hit the water, that man was in considerable distress, bobbing in the swell, arms outstretched, blood oozing from amputated fingers and a head wound. 'He was watching me with uncomprehending eyes. He later told me that he could not see the winch wire I was suspended from and he thought I was the Archangel Gabriel coming to collect him!'

Heaven could wait. Floundering in the waves, the doctor suddenly realized he need not take off his harness and hand it over after all. Instead, he hooked the end of the line on to the sailor's life jacket, which meant they could be hauled up in tandem without the fast-weakening Jolly having to take the strain of holding on to him. 'It shouldn't have worked, but it did, and together we were lifted up to the safety of the helicopter's cabin, my jaw rattling with cold.' As they headed for the *Canberra*, the pilot nodded in Jolly's direction. 'Well done, Doc,' he said. 'Bloody marvellous.' Jolly would later receive an OBE for his work in the Falklands, but the respect he earned that day from his comrades on the helicopter meant more than any medal. The medic had won his spurs.

★

It was now time for Jolly to go onshore himself, to take charge of the bare-bones field hospital shaping up in the cold and dusty hangar of a building at Ajax Bay. Sheep droppings had to be cleared from the floor, which was ankle-deep in rusting rubbish and tie-on meat labels from the days when the building had been used to package joints of Falkland Island lamb. The 'Red and Green Life Machine', as it came to be called – red for the berets of the Paras and green for the Marine commandos, whose medics shared the use of it – was in business. Air raids were remorseless, and frightening in the extreme, even for combat veterans. Few had experienced, let alone been on the receiving end of, the speed and awesome destructive power of modern war planes. The Spitfires and Stukas of the Second World War were as much relics of history as medieval knights with lances. Rockets, wire-guided missiles and rapid-fire cannon were in a new league of lethality.

Lookouts posted around the hospital would spot the Mirage jets and nifty Pucaras coming low out of the hills, and six blasts on a whistle would send the medical teams racing for cover. Not everyone went. If they had patients on the table, the surgeons and theatre staff continued to operate, though sense and survival might have prompted them to seek shelter. But Jolly realized their courage had risks attached to it. He had to ensure that some medical expertise remained, even if the whole of Ajax Bay were blown apart. So he instituted a routine whereby, when the alarm whistle blew, half would work on and half would hide. The decision of who stayed and who ran for cover was his, and he took to standing at the main entrance of the Life Machine peering out through the massive double doors, big enough to take a whale carcase, for signs of trouble.

From there he saw across the bay to where HMS *Antelope* was anchored, her communication mast leaning at an angle and a gaping hole in her side. Below decks, disposal experts were huddled round an Argentinian bomb which had failed to explode. Suddenly, it blew. 'The fire took hold and, gradually, like some dreadful cancer eating into the heart of the ship, the flames spread along her hull. She burned down towards the waterline and then, in a huge shower of sparks, the aft missile magazine exploded. We watched in silence. Seeing a ship die like this was agony.' One of the bomb-disposal squad was helicoptered in and was on the table. A steel hatch had flown through the air and severed his left arm. Jolly put a hospital apron on over his regulation Navy shirt and took up his scalpel to complete the amputation.

The next day he had his first patient from the other side. Lieutenant Ricardo Lucero's Skyhawk was downed by a Rapier missile, and Jolly, watching from the door, saw him eject and his parachute open just yards from the water. The pilot's left knee was shattered, the cap shifted four inches from its customary spot. Now he lay in great pain in the Ajax Bay triage area, the orange silk of his Buenos Aires squadron still knotted at his neck. 'My boys crowded around him, trying to get their first look at the enemy, before I shooed them away.' The doctor assured the Argentinian that he would be looked after, but the terrified look on the man's face indicated he did not believe this. At the very least, he must have thought they were going to hack off his injured leg. Not until he came round from the surgery, reached down and found that the limb was not only intact but repaired did he relax.

While the enemy pilot was under the knife, his squadron was in the air and had sunk HMS *Coventry*, survivors of which were even now arriving at Ajax Bay in a clatter of helicopter blades. The speed with which *Coventry* was destroyed was astonishing. Her captain's last recollection was of directing operations from his command centre, when the banks of consoles and screens around him disintegrated in front of his face. 'My headset and microphone had disappeared – burnt off me without a trace. So too had my anti-flash hood and gloves. I saw a sheet of orange flame envelop a man as he attempted to get away. He had nearly reached the top of the ladder, and someone stretched towards him and tried to catch his hand, but the fire consumed him, and he fell back with a despairing cry. Through the thick black smoke, I saw the dim shapes of people with their clothes alight, human torches. One of my officers was beating out the flames on his own head where his headset melted into his scalp.'[24]

Some of those who had been pulled out of the sea were brought into the hospital, soaked, flash-burned and shivering with cold and pain. Gentle hands cut off their clothes, their burns were smothered with a pain-killing antiseptic cream, and they were laid down on cool white sheets. One of them, a young stoker, whose red-raw hands were swaddled in protective plastic bags, spotted the sleeping Argentinian pilot and became aggressive. 'The fire that had burned his hands,' Jolly later wrote in his diary, 'now burned in his soul, and he simply could not understand our respect and friendliness for this colleague of the two pilots who killed his ship.' The doctor's Hippocratic principles were vindicated when the pilot woke up and saw the smashed bodies around him. He took off the blankets covering him and, with tears in his eyes, passed them to the wounded Britons around him.

Outside, the noise of battle was still thundering, and Mick

Jennings made the mistake of going outside to look and listen. He could hear the crump of bombs, the half-muffled blast of compressed air, in the distance. San Carlos, a couple of miles away, was getting it, he thought. 'Just then, small arms started going off, and I knew, I just knew, that there was a plane behind me and it was coming straight for me.' He heard the howl of a jet on his shoulder and threw himself into a drainage drift on his left. Another man piled in on top of him. Everywhere, people were diving for cover.

A massive explosion rocked the base as a bomb struck ammunition and fuel dumps. Debris, dirt and stones cascaded down from a mushroom-shaped cloud of smoke billowing upwards into the sky. Phosphorous shells exploded, drenching the whole area in a bright white light. Jennings half-expected to see Argentinian troops come marching through the smoke in a follow-up attack. The danger passed, the dust settled, the fires were put out, but there were casualties, including two dead in a trench. The medics went back to work, although there was an unexploded bomb lying in the back of the building, embedded in ancient pipework. Just a room and two walls separated this 800lb monster from the operating tables.

The medics carried on regardless, despite being urged by the ordnance experts to evacuate the entire area. Jolly refused to move. He gave the order to sandbag the bomb and shore up the walls around it. But he did this not out of bravado or foolhardiness. It might be dangerous to stay, but there was an even greater risk in leaving and attempting to set up shop elsewhere in a hurry. He was privy to top-secret information: the next day, 2 Para were to move out from the hillside above the landing beaches and advance across the wildest of country to take the strategic hamlet of Goose Green. It was bound to be bloody. 'Even if the Paras were both tactically clever and really lucky, there would be a butcher's bill to pay.' He and his cutters and stitchers had serious work to do, on which many lives would depend, and he was not going to let the small matter of a UXB get in their way.

9. Battle Stations

As he advanced behind his battalion along a muddy, pitted track towards the tiny hamlet of Goose Green, enemy mortar shells exploding around him, 2 Para medical officer Captain Steven Hughes desperately wanted to be on some other enterprise. 'Beam me up, Scotty,' he muttered into the constant cold drizzle, recoiling as a round from a sniper's rifle whistled over his head. Phosphorous artillery shells stabbed the darkness of the night. 'Take me back to the NHS and I will work 24 hours a day, 365 days a year,' he pledged, 'because this is not what I spent all those years at medical school for.'[1] Action like this, however, *was* why, as a military doctor, he had chosen to join the Paras rather than any other regiment – though the intensity of the brutal ground war they were now embroiled in was giving him second thoughts. He and his medical team were right up in the killing zone. Theoretically, they should have been coming in behind the fighting and picking up casualties left by the side of the track. But the advance had stalled, a firefight was in full swing and the medics were caught in the middle. To Lance Corporal Bill 'Basher' Bentley, a medic working under Hughes, incoming artillery shells sounded like express trains flying overhead.

Hughes hung back, knowing he had to let his medics be the ones who went forward. With his expertise, he couldn't take as many risks as they did. If he was killed or wounded, not only would the guys on the ground be left without a doctor but the entire Task Force medical team would be impaired. In this long-distance campaign, flying in replacements swiftly from the UK was not an option. 'I had to think of myself as an *asset*.' In his aid post, he listened in to the battle on the radio net and heard the first, urgent call for a medic. Two soldiers were down, and Hughes instantly ignored his advice to himself to stay out of trouble. He scampered forward in the dark, taking cover as best he could, and examined them as they lay on the peat with not even a poncho underneath to protect them from the damp. The rain was ceaseless, like sharp needles in their faces. One had what looked like a fractured pelvis, the other a bullet lodged in his navel. It had ripped into the webbing of his uniform and through his belt before coming to rest, miraculously without causing any damage, except to the young lad's nerves. Hughes made the two of them as comfortable as he could, until they could be lifted out by helicopter at first light. Then, stumbling forward again, he came on his first fatalities, lying by the side of the track. A shaken Bill Bentley had brought one of them back from the battlefield. 'He was a good friend of mine, and his brains had been blown out. As I carried him, his head kept banging against my knee and giving off a hollow sound.'[2] It was something he would never be able to forget. The two dead soldiers had been yards from an enemy machine gun when the first was hit. The other was kneeling down putting a dressing on him when they were both riddled with bullets from close range. 'God knows how many rounds went through them,' said Bentley. 'When I tried to pick one of them up, his arm came off.'

Hughes also knew them both and, like Bentley, he felt gutted, the objectivity that doctors are supposed to bring to their work deserting him. Detachment might be possible in a hospital back home but, here on the peat, looking at a dead man who was a mate, it was hard to be clinical and objective. One of them, he knew, had just become a father. The child was now orphaned. 'You try and suppress those feelings, but it wasn't always possible.' There was no time for reverie and regret, however, as more shells came crashing in. Too close for comfort and, though they missed him, he was acutely aware of the narrow gap that separated living from dying. 'I don't understand people who say they were not afraid,' he reflected later. 'Courage is all about the fear and then still doing what you have to do despite it.'

Just ahead of him, the fighting was remarkably fierce, and the enemy were having the better of it. No one had ever expected the recapture of the islands to be a walkover, but the degree of resistance the British troops were encountering was a surprise. The Paras had advanced in the dark in eight-man sections, over-running enemy trenches and foxholes, taking casualties but pressing on as ordered. But then the steam-roller had stopped. For hours, withering fire from well-dug-in machine-gun and sniper nests in the hilly, open ground ahead pinned them down. The supporting naval bombardment from out in the Sound had ceased. Harrier strike planes intended to take out the enemy position were grounded by fog. The troops were on their own, and running out of mortars, their only hope of dislodging the Argentinians. Things looked sticky, Hughes recalled, the men huddling in gullies and scrapes in the featureless terrain, and casualties mounting by the minute.

He set up his aid post in a gully at a place known as Coronation Point, though there was nothing remotely regal about it. Smoke billowed over it from burning gorse, and with that and the incessant rain it seemed as dark and primitive a place as some ancient field of slaughter where Roman legions slugged it out with barbarian tribes in the mists of Germania. But on this moorland there was no shelter, not a single tree and scarcely a bush. Hughes sent his medics to forage the captured Argentinian trenches for corrugated-iron sheeting, and blankets and parkas to put over the casualties. The only certain way to warm up those chilled to the marrow was to cuddle them, man to man passing on body heat and restoring life. Hughes, scissors dangling on a cord around his neck, cut away bandages and clothes to get to wounds and took cannulas from the pencil pocket on the arm of his smock to insert drips. 'We were all covered with blood – on our hands, our clothes, boots and equipment, and on the ground. We didn't have enough water to drink, let alone to wash anything, so we were completely filthy. Blood-stained dressings lay everywhere.' Discarded packaging and empty cartons of medical supplies littered the floor. The smell of cordite was acrid in the air.

To an uninformed observer, the aid post would have looked like a bunch of blokes just standing out in the rain, but there was method amid the madness. One man was the triage medic, sorting out the seriously wounded from those with minor injuries. The rest worked in two teams, with Hughes moving between them, dressing injuries and administering fluids, morphine and antibiotics. There wasn't much screaming or shouting. 'Everyone was pretty calm, although we were under artillery fire constantly, with shells landing in the peat at the top of the gully or sailing over and exploding behind. There was a lot of firing about a hundred metres ahead where the battle was being fought.'

Bentley, medical pack on his back and Sterling sub-machine gun slung on his shoulder, was pressing forward into the heart of this battle, looking for more casualties to bring back. 'I was already absolutely knackered, but you're driven on by the thought that your mates are out there, dying and injured.' He sought cover in a trench, leapt in and felt something, some*one,* beneath a tarpaulin under his feet, 'as if I had jumped on to a water bed with lumps in it'. The soldier in him outweighed the medic – this was no time to be careless. Instinctively, his finger tightened on the trigger of the Sterling, and he fired a burst of bullets into the bundle. Then, in another trench, he came upon a dying Argentinian soldier. Though the man was unconscious, Bentley knew he could not risk going forward again to treat battalion casualties, leaving an enemy soldier, who could wake at any minute, behind him. He didn't want to use his rifle again, for fear of drawing attention to his presence, 'so I finished this poor soul off with my bayonet'.

The next person he came across was Argentinian too, a youngster shot through the leg and in deep shock. 'I approached him cautiously and as he made no aggressive gestures I was not aggressive either. The better side of me, or my training, took over. I hoisted him up over my shoulder in a classical fireman's lift and carried him back to our own lines.' Only later did he stop to consider the danger he had put himself in. 'Dangling over my back, that young soldier would have been looking straight at my bayonet, still bloody from the comrade of his I had just killed. It would have been simple for him to reach down, draw it and stab me.'

Amid this slaughter, it was heartening for Hughes that the lessons he had drummed into the troops on the ship coming south were proving their worth. He was as reassuring a presence now as he had been then, with his frankness about what to expect if they were wounded and how they would be treated. On the ship, he had regaled them with one story about an elderly man in his care in a civilian hospital in Ely whose stitches had burst after major abdominal surgery, spilling his intestines into his lap. 'There was no great drama,' he'd told them. 'We wrapped his gut in sterile towels, took him to theatre and shoved it all back in again, and he was up and eating breakfast the next morning.' Now a young soldier was sitting in the RAP in a similar predicament, clutching folds of his small bowel to him after being shot in the stomach. 'He was horrified and very frightened but I was able to remind him of that story. You're like that old boy, and you'll be fine too.'

As Hughes had also stressed to them, the most important factor was getting the wounded off the battlefield as quickly as possible. As he predicted, this was proving a slow process, and he cheered 'the magnificent sight' of the first helicopters, four of them, chopping their way through the pall of smoke to 'casevac' the casualties away. It was his decision who to send. He pointed at the urgent cases, gave his orders, and there was a rush as two or three stretchers were bundled across to the landing site and their occupants stashed unceremoniously on board.

The crews didn't hang around. It wasn't just that they wanted to be out of mortar and missile range as soon as possible. They also knew that speed was of the essence for their beaten-up passengers. As they lifted off, the pilots barely glanced at the blood and gore accumulating in the cabin behind them and concentrated on the ten-minute hop back to Ajax Bay. Then they would unload, refuel and be back for more. Whenever helicopters came in to the aid post, they became a specific target for the Argentinian gunners – and a legitimate one. The helicopters had a dual purpose. They came to evacuate the wounded but brought ammunition and supplies with them. The stretchers on which casualties were carried to the helicopter were then loaded with ammo boxes to go back to the fighting men. These were circumstances in which the distinction between medical and military activities blurred.

Then, over the radio, came a message that stunned everyone. The Boss – codename 'Sunray' – was down. The impetuous and impatient Lieutenant Colonel 'H' Jones, the 2 Para CO, with a tight schedule to keep to, had left his command post and come to the front of the action to try to break the deadlock. He had led a charge up the hill and was cut down, along with his adjutant, David Wood, and another officer, Chris Dent. Hughes was devastated by the deaths and had to stop himself from crying out in anger, fear and frustration. These losses were personal. 'David was a real friend who'd helped me a great deal since I joined the battalion. He was my mentor. I felt as if I'd been hit by a truck – first, sudden numbing shock and then sadness. I wanted to stop and grieve for three of my friends, but I knew I didn't have that luxury. The medics were looking at me hard, seeing how I would take it, and I realized that if I went to pieces, there was a likelihood we'd all go to pieces. This is the burden of leadership. I made a conscious decision to block out my emotions.' It was the right thing to do at the time, but later in his life he would pay psychologically for the coldness he adopted that day. 'It was a turning point for me.'

He was not the only one whose emotions needed to be controlled. Bentley remembered vividly how bad things looked at this stage of the battle. 'The row of dead bodies was growing, and when they brought in the remains of another good friend of mine, I confess that I broke down and cried. We were all exhausted and hungry and resorting to eating biscuits from the pockets of the dead, friend and foe alike. The ammunition was running out, we were not getting any useful medical re-supplies, their artillery had us pinpointed, the colonel was dead. Things were looking pretty desperate.'

★

At the hospital in the old lamb-packing warehouse at Ajax Bay, as the helicopters poured in and dropped off their human cargoes, Rick Jolly and the Red and Green Life Machine were mired in blood, bullet holes and blast injuries. An image was seared on Jolly's memory of lines of pale, silent paratroopers in blood-soaked and torn combat clothing. Their faces were grimed with dirt, and there was a bluish tinge to their lips and fingernails from shock and loss of blood. As he took up his scalpel, making snap decisions and working fast, he felt a connection to a tradition of field surgery going back to the Second World War, to Korea and to Vietnam. In his gore-stained apron, he could easily have been a below-decks surgeon in Nelson's navy or a bone-cutter in a tent at Balaclava.

Each casualty seemed to spawn another. An unarmed Scout helicopter sent to pick up the wounded 'H' was set on by a pair of Pucara attack aircraft, whose cannon shells ripped through its fuselage. The crewman, Bill Belcher, preparing to take in casualties, was kneeling in the back rather than strapped in the front. He looked down at the remains of his right leg – 'a soggy end with a few bits holding my foot on'.[3] He was ripping open the first-aid kit to try to treat himself when the Pucara banked and, under-wing machine guns blazing, came back for the kill. The helicopter bounced, turned over and then hit the ground. Belcher, who would have been killed for sure if he had been wearing his seat belt, was thrown clear of the wreck. A 'terrible, bloodied mess', he was now back in Ajax Bay after being rescued by another helicopter. The surgeons got to work, amputating his right leg mid-thigh.

Out on the hillside, the wounded were accumulating in the effort, redoubled by the colonel's death, to take out the enemy positions stopping the advance. Hughes knelt over the rapidly cooling body of a soldier with multiple cannon fragments in his side and neck, and air leaking through punctures in his throat. The remnants of his shredded battle dress were like blotting paper, soaking up his own blood. The aid post was overflowing, and deciding priorities was becoming dangerously difficult. Every case was urgent. One soldier was on his side with a gunshot wound in his back, another, a platoon medic, was half hidden under a sheet of corrugated metal with part of his brain hanging out. He was still conscious and, surprisingly, the least of Hughes's worries. This one could wait. 'He'd been there a while already and, if he'd survived this long, I knew he wasn't in any immediate danger. I also knew there wasn't a brain specialist at Ajax Bay, and the surgeons there would be better operating on someone with, say, a stomach wound.' The doctor's reasoning was sound, but some of his medics misunderstood. Bentley, for one, had caught sight of the exposed brain, 'like toothpaste squeezed out of a tube', thought there was no chance and concluded that the doctor had put the soldier to one side to die. A medic was preparing to fill him up with morphine to kill him off when Hughes intervened. Eventually, the man got his place on a helicopter. He survived.

Not everyone even made it to the aid post for Hughes and his medics to work on. Some of the wounded lay out in the open for hours on end with only the basic skills of their mates keeping them alive. Private Nick Taylor was flat on his stomach about to fire a Milan missile at enemy positions in the distance when an artillery shell struck. He blacked out and awoke in searing pain as his mates were gripping his wrists and dragging him into cover. They reassured him he was all right. His balls were still there, they told him, which was what really mattered, and the pain in his leg was the muscles cramping with shock. He believed them, though later he was to discover they were 'lying through their teeth' – he had thirteen pieces of shrapnel in his arm, back and legs. Shots of morphine helped to ease his panic a little but didn't do a lot for the pain. 'It hurt like hell, and I couldn't feel my hands. I kept asking my mate Blackie to squeeze them and, because I couldn't feel him, I kept asking him if he was doing it. I kept blacking out, and he was slapping my face and telling me not to fall asleep, that the helicopter would be here soon.'

It was a long time coming. There was no quick ambulance ride to Casualty for him. He and several others lay in a shell-scrape for twenty-six hours until a rescue party could get to them. 'I felt very helpless, vulnerable and scared, and the time dragged very slowly. The bloke opposite me had his jaw all shot away, and I kept looking at him and thinking, he's worse off than me. There were several dead Argies across the way too, and I kept looking at them

as well. There were times I thought I'd never get out of there.'⁴ It
would be the next morning before a helicopter could get to him
and fly him out. His leg wounds were so severe it would be a year
before he could run again.

The most daring rescue, from right under the enemy's nose,
was that of Private Dave 'Chopsey' Gray, who was bleeding to
death after a mortar shell landed beside him, tore off his right leg,
shattered the other and filled him with shrapnel. Bob Cole, one of
his mates, distraught and in tears, came to Hughes's aid post to beg
help for him. 'The doc looked at me,' medic Bill Bentley recalled,
'and I heard myself saying, "No problem, I'll go."' He ducked
down and followed Cole a hundred yards up the hill to a ridge
and through a gap in a stone wall. 'Bob opened fire on two enemy
soldiers and I did the same. By the time I reached him he was
thrusting his bayonet into one of them.' They could now see
Chopsey twenty-five yards away down the other side of the slope,
lying in a shallow crater in a pool of his own blood and fully
exposed to the enemy's guns. Bentley crept down to him.

Para legend has it that when Gray was hit, he shouted out, 'I've
lost me fucking leg!', to which the cool reply came from one of
his mates behind a nearby tussock of grass, 'No you haven't,
Chopsey, it's landed over here.' In fact, it was still attached to the
rest of him at this stage, though not by much. Arriving at his side,
Bentley took in the desperateness of the situation, calling for
desperate measures. 'It was obvious I would not be able to deal
with all his injuries on the spot, but I would have to amputate
what was left of his right leg.' He took out the Swiss Army knife
he always carried, one blade of which he kept razor sharp for
emergencies such as this. By now, the Argentinian defenders had
spotted what was going on, and bullets began to thud into the soft
ground around the medic as, lying flat, he sliced away the flesh
and sinew, all that was keeping the leg on. Gray, he recalled, 'just
cringed' at this amputation without anaesthetic; his state of shock
must have gone some way to dulling the pain. The medic was
putting a tourniquet on the stump when he saw a stretcher party
heading across the open hillside towards them. The enemy fire

intensified. More bullets peppered into the peat. 'It felt like the whole Argentinian army was opening up at us. The hill seemed to be exploding.'

The rescue team threw Gray on to a stretcher and, not forgetting the severed leg, which Bentley laid across the end, were quickly off back up the hill, chased by a line of bullets detonating in the dirt like crackerjacks. The medic lagged behind as he gathered up his kit, too precious to abandon. Machine guns pinned him down, and he flung himself into the shallow scrape that Gray had only just been taken from. He lay there, playing dead, until the incoming fire finally faded away, and he ran for it, back up the hill and down the other side to the aid post.

There, Hughes was fighting desperately to save the wounded soldier, who had by now lost so much blood that the doctor could not find a vein in his deathly-white skin. He had to cut away with a scalpel to make an opening for fluids. Fortunately, Gray was too far gone to feel anything. At that moment a helicopter came in, and Hughes shoved the wounded man to the top of the queue for immediate evacuation, 'but I didn't hold out too much for his survival'.[5] Bentley arrived back just in time to help lift the man he had risked his life to save into a casualty pod on the side of the chopper. The sawn-off remnant of his leg went too, as evidence of what, under fire and under duress, the medic had done and why. 'I'd hacked a leg off, and that's a pretty major thing for a medic to do.' Once the heat of battle had cooled, he didn't want some busybody to rule that he shouldn't have done so. The sight of his own leg detached and lying beside him was a shock for Gray. 'I don't think it was until that moment that he realized exactly what had happened,' Bentley said. 'He just looked at it, and I hugged him and gave him a kiss, and said, you'll be all right. Then I closed the top of the pod and they flew him out.'

Gray was conscious when he was brought into casualty reception at Ajax Bay, breathing hard as if he had just run a marathon and talking nonsense at top speed between gulps of air. But he had no discernible pulse and no blood pressure. When the tourniquet was removed, the stump of his leg was dry, which was a bad sign. No blood was getting through. He needed an immediate transfusion. A medic grabbed some blood from the store – it was 'refrigerated' outside in the cold, wrapped in wet hessian– and warmed the bags under his armpits to take the chill off the blood before it was poured into veins that were already beginning to collapse and close up. Three litres later, on the sixth bag, the leg wound began to ooze blood again. There was colour in Chopsey's cheeks, life back in him. He was going to make it.

Night was now falling at the end of an epic, dreadful day and, out at Goose Green, the battle slowed and halted. But helicopters were still in the air carrying in casualties, being guided on to the hospital landing site by hand-held torches flashed from the ground, the only lights now visible on the pitch-black island. With no landmarks to go by, the pilots needed all their skill and daring to find their bearings and home in on the thin shafts of torchlight. The last man they brought in was a 2 Para captain with a bullet hole in his side. He was shocked and shivering. His eyes were wide and staring. A transfusion technician was warming bags of blood with his body heat, just as he had done for Chopsey. Surgeon Bill McGregor cut into the abdomen, then probed inside with his fingers for the source of the severe haemorrhaging. He found a gouge in the liver from a bullet, and delicately sewed up the hole with catgut. But the bleeding didn't stop. One wound was concealing another, and beneath the liver, a major artery had been nicked and was leaking. To fix this required advanced surgery, 'major league stuff', as Jolly put it. Feeling his way with hands as poised and precise as those of a pianist, McGregor slowly and painstakingly repaired this laceration too. When the stitching was done, the suture tied in a surgical knot and the stomach incision closed up, a sigh of relief and satisfaction went round the table.

Jolly called for tots of rum all round, a naval expression of appreciation for an arduous job well done. He glanced around him at the lines of patients, the orderlies moving quietly from stretcher to stretcher in the dim light, checking on those sleeping, giving words of assurance to those awake. He tried not to think of the unexploded Argentinian bomb nestling behind sandbags in a wall just yards away. He had taken a chance that it would not explode. The number of casualties his team had treated was proof that he had been right not to try to evacuate the hospital. He totted up the figures – eighty men brought in, forty-seven operated on under general anaesthetic, and every one of them still alive. Now it was time for his medics to scrub out the two operating theatres, their last chore of the day, and then roll out their bedding around the tables. Sleep now, for tomorrow could be every bit as bad.

Out on the darkened hillside, Hughes was doing his sums too. His records showed he had treated thirty-four Paras, plus dozens of Argentinian casualties. But stretched out in a gully behind a gorse bush were the dead, looking, he thought, like still-life dummies, except for the bullet hole in the middle of one forehead. 'It felt unreal. A few hours ago I had spoken to these people, and now they were gone.' Bentley was still out on the battlefield, searching for a friend he had heard was missing, presumed dead. 'He had been a really funny guy and a great favourite of me and my mates. I dearly wanted to see him, one more time, even if it was just his body.' Snow was falling heavily and the night was drawing in as he made his faltering way through the peat. It was a foolish thing to do, he knew. The area could well be mined, and in the darkness he would most probably walk past the body anyway and not see it. He found nothing and had to give up. Back at the aid post, he saw the dead laid out, wrapped in their ponchos, and he went down the row, pulling back the covers one by one and looking at their faces. 'In the darkness and with their wounds, I could not identify my friend. So I gave each of them a kiss and a hug, wrapped them up again and went off to find a place to sleep.'

Hughes was already tucked up beneath a plastic space blanket, trying to sleep but troubled by the pictures of the battle replaying in his mind, accompanied by a soundtrack of crackling gunfire and blazing gorse. 'When I awoke, it was dawn. I was cold. I couldn't feel my feet at first.' The totally unexpected Argentine surrender warmed him up. Major Chris Keble, 'H' Jones's number two, had taken command and, by a mixture of threats and inducements, persuaded the enemy, still holding the high ground and still with vastly superior numbers, that they were beaten. They came out with their hands in the air and laid down their weapons.

With the Battle of Goose Green over, Hughes now did what he could for the Argentine wounded, moving along the lines of defeated men and examining their injuries, though the enemy soldiers were mystified by his compassion. 'Why you treat me?' one asked in faltering English as the doctor put him on a drip. 'God knows what they'd been told about us,' he thought. At close quarters, the enemy could be seen for what it was – a conscript army, bullied, starved and low on both skills and resolve. The medics dug into their pockets and handed over their rations of glucose sweets and biscuits. They felt sorry for the beaten soldiers. They pulled out all the stops to save the last Argentinian casualty found alive. He had lain out on the battlefield for a day and a half before he was discovered by chance, at the bottom of a pile of corpses in a water-logged trench. He had a bullet in one eye; one of his hands and a leg were broken. He was rigid with cold but also running a fever. He should have been dead, from the gangrene that was already eating into him if from nothing else. Except that, in some strange symbiosis of the sort that can never be predicted – serendipity, some would call it – the cold had paralysed the infection and the fever had kept him from freezing. With his body temperature a chilly 32C, he first had to be warmed up with hot-water bottles and then given fresh blood. In the operation to mend his wounds, the anaesthetist sitting by his head had to ventilate him by hand for two hours, squeezing the life back into him breath by breath. He survived and went home, though one-eyed and one-legged.

The issue of giving succour to an enemy was not always so happily resolved. Out on the peat, Hughes had encountered heli-copter pilots who turned away Argentinian wounded, particularly after losing some of their own men in action. 'No Argies, no Argies,' they would shout as they landed to pick up casualties. The doctor was appalled. 'The Geneva Conventions are very clear that all wounded are to be treated equally, regardless of whether friend or enemy. I worked on the basis of the most serious first, regardless of nationality.' One lad, sixteen years old with a gunshot wound in the arm, was refused twice and kept slipping to the back of the queue. He died in the night, still waiting to be taken to hospital. 'I felt I'd failed him,' Hughes recalled, haunted by the thought that he should have ordered the pilots to comply, at pistol-point if necessary.

Corporal Tom Howard, a medical assistant at Ajax Bay, had more success in pressing the humanitarian case. In his care he had an Argentine sergeant peppered with gunshot wounds, including one in his groin. A bullet was actually lodged beside his testicles. 'He was babbling in Spanish, which one of the guys translated. He had a little three-year-old son back at home and didn't want to die without seeing him again.' Howard was deeply moved. He had a child of his own. 'I wanted to do everything in my power to get him to see his son again – because I wanted to get back to see my little girl.' The man got through surgery but, afterwards, his condition deteriorated. His lungs filled with fluid and he couldn't breathe. A doctor examined him and told Howard to get the padre to give the sergeant the last rites. The English corporal was furious. 'I knew this guy could be saved, so I got a different doctor, who told me to give him a broncho-dilator drug and a diuretic to remove the blood leaking into his lungs. He was cold, and all the hot-water bottles were in use with other patients, so I filled my canteen with hot water, wrapped it in a towel, placed it on his stomach and covered him with a sleeping bag.'

Howard went to grab some sleep – he'd been on duty for sixteen hours – but was warned that the Argentinian would almost certainly be dead by morning. 'I was gutted, feeling that I'd failed.' But the next day, when he returned to the ward, the man was propped up on his elbow, smoking a cigarette and talking to his mate in Spanish. 'I couldn't believe it. I went over to him and clapped him on the shoulder saying something like, "God, you fucking gave me some problems yesterday," and laughed and smiled. He stopped talking, stared at me and just said, "*Que?*" I didn't mind. I was just happy he was going to make it back to his son.'[6]

★

The day after the surrender of Goose Green, a Wessex helicopter touched down at Ajax Bay with a special cargo – the Para dead, limbs frozen in rigor mortis, a poncho pulled over each face. Jolly organized the unloading, and watched, sombre and silent, as eleven stretchers were lined up side by side on a concrete strip. It was a grim, sad business as their clothes were cut away and their personal possessions bagged to be returned to relatives. Not everything would be sent home – some maroon berets were too soaked in the blood of the men who had worn them for loved ones to see. It fell to the doctor to examine each body, pronounce on cause of death and complete a field death certificate. He crouched down as he went from man to man and called out his conclusions to a clerk, who scribbled them down – gunshot wounds to the heart, multiple wounds to chest and abdomen, blast injury. On Colonel 'H''s face, Jolly saw a quizzical smile. His eyes were still open, but he looked peaceful. A single bullet had killed the CO, entering just above his right collarbone, travelling downwards at an angle and exiting through his stomach. 'When I had finished, we stood for a moment in silence, while I remembered my last conversation with him. Then I kneeled down beside his body, closed his eyes very gently, and whispered: "We didn't let you down, Colonel. We really were good enough, and so were you." Then we lifted him up carefully, and placed his body into a plastic shroud and then into a body bag.'

Jolly kept his emotions in check for the colonel and was pleased to have done what he could to treat the dead of his battalion with the dignity their sacrifice deserved. But he fell apart, unashamedly and unreservedly, when another body was brought in, a helicopter pilot who was a family friend. He had been dreading this moment since he had heard of the young man's death. Now, faced with the body, a compulsion came over him. 'I felt I had to find out if he had died before the crash of his helicopter, and not because of it. It took a few minutes of gentle probing, but I found what I was, in a way, hoping to find. There was a circular hole in the right cheekbone. A ricocheting bullet had penetrated his skull and, an instant later, his brain. This knowledge that he had not suffered helped me to adjust. For all that, I felt very weary, and really sad. As I walked away I crumpled, my body racked with silent, almost convulsive tears.'

The next day, a tired-looking Steven Hughes, his face grey with fatigue, flew into Ajax Bay for the funerals. He avoided Jolly's eyes, which surprised the navy surgeon. He knew and liked his 2 Para counterpart, and had heard nothing but praise for their MO from the casualties he had treated in the hospital. Jolly opened his mouth to speak but was silenced by an outburst from Hughes, apologizing, absurdly, for not having done enough at Goose Green and for sending back so many casualties in poor condition. Jolly interrupted this flow of desperate remorse. His colleague had nothing to blame himself for. Every one of the wounded paratroopers ferried from Goose Green to the hospital was alive, he explained. Hughes looked incredulous. All the way in on the Wessex, he had been dreading discovering how many more of his men had died from their injuries. It had to be so. He was certain of it. The only question was how many.

Jolly gripped his arms and, almost shouting to get home his point, declared, 'No, Steve, no! They are all still alive.' The Para MO shook his head. It couldn't be so. He pulled out his field notebook and picked a name. 'What about this one? Private Gray . . . ?' Jolly jumped in: 'Do you mean Chopsey? He's fine. I looked after him myself. Virtually ex-sanguinated when he got here, with no recordable pulse or blood pressure. After two pints of blood, the torn femoral artery started to leak. After another three pints he was fit for theatre.' Hughes stared in amazement as the truth sank in. Then the colour returned to his cheeks, just as it had to Chopsey's. He was transfused with relief and joy, literally flushed with the success he now realized he had helped achieve. All those battered young bodies he had administered to on the edge of a raging battle, patched up as best he could and then sent back down the line, were ALIVE!

Jolly would have taken Hughes to see Chopsey if he had still been on the island. But he, like all the wounded from Goose Green, had been helicoptered offshore, to a hospital ship. The

Uganda, a hastily converted educational-cruise liner, was floating in an internationally agreed Red Cross safe zone fifty miles from the Falklands. By the rules of the Geneva Convention, once there, the wounded were out of the war and could not be returned to the fight. It was a haven of peace, with carpet on the floor and medical staff in crisp white uniforms, unlike the sawdust and khaki order of the field hospital. There were clean, starched sheets on the beds and even a few female nurses. The doctors on board were busy, not least because most of the casualties arriving had open wounds.

This was deliberate. As we have seen, during the Second World War, British military surgeons changed the accepted procedure of centuries and adopted the Trueta method[7] of treating wounds caused by modern high-velocity bullets. The doctors on the *Uganda* carefully chopped out every last bit of dead tissue and then left the wound open 'to breathe', thereby killing off dangerous anaerobic bacteria that only thrive in the absence of oxygen. The dangers of doing otherwise were now all too apparent in some of the Argentinian soldiers who were arriving at Ajax Bay with complications, having been patched up by their own doctors in the old-fashioned way. Their injuries had been sutured straightaway, locking in infection. Gas gangrene, curse of the First World War, and tetanus were often the result. But not for the British wounded, despite all the contaminating bacterial horrors that lurked in the sheep-soiled island earth and were fired deep into flesh on the tips of bullets and shards of shrapnel. The practice known as Delayed Primary Closure – not finally stitching up the wound until a week or more after the original injury – doubled the workload, because every wound had to be worked on twice at least under general anaesthetic, but there is no doubt that it was a life-saver in the Falklands. Men recovered who, in most earlier wars, would have died.

For a brief moment now, the needs of the living were put to one side and the dead took centre stage. At Ajax Bay, the final batch of bodies had arrived from Goose Green, bringing the toll to seventeen, and a grim parade lined up to escort them all to a trench scratched out of the peat and earth on a hill above the bay.

The procession passed a hastily erected barbed-wire enclosure, filling with Argentinian prisoners of war. Around the mass grave stood two hundred men of the Task Force. Jolly looked up at a perfectly blue sky and at the snow on the mountain peaks in the distance. Out in the Sound, helicopters were buzzing between the ships in the fleet and the only sound on that silent hillside was the far-away whirl of their rotors. The first body bag, draped in a union flag, was passed into the ground, then another, 'and by the time you got to seventeen,' Hughes recalled, 'the effect on everyone was devastating. I was crying. So were many others.' A Marine played a lament on a fiddle, an aching melody. 'Ashes to ashes, dust unto dust,' intoned the padre, as the Regimental Sergeant Major marched forward to throw handfuls of earth on the body bags. The sound of the clods on the plastic 'echoed like thunder', remembered Jolly. 'Then we all saluted and slowly turned away.' As ever, once the mourning was over, there were lives to be saved.

However, the events of the past seventy-two hours could not be easily forgotten. 'We had been through an experience none of us had ever expected,' Hughes would recall. 'For three or four days everyone was just ticking over, lights on but nobody much at home.' He felt himself shutting down inside, blanking out the awful pictures of suffering that threatened to overwhelm him. 'I couldn't afford to take anything more on board. I detached myself from what was happening. I felt as if somebody else was doing the job, and I was watching from a distance. I was outwardly functioning in the same way, but I was an automaton. This is a common psychiatric defence mechanism.' He was learning what few soldiers realized – that medics are steeped in the horrors of war in a way that no one else ever can be. All the carnage comes funnelling through them. They cannot look the other way or go charging ahead and relieve their aggression and frustration in the next firefight with the enemy. Other soldiers may see a few mates wounded or be injured themselves. But only the medics see the whole picture, the non-stop pain and misery of war. They run their eye over the entire butcher's bill and, in Steven Hughes's case, there would eventually be a large price to pay.

10. Fire Down Below

At the Goose Green settlement in the Falklands, now under the British flag again, medical officer Steven Hughes set up his aid post in the mess hall of a sheep-shearing station, a proper roof over his head at last. A sorry procession of complaining soldiers, the adrenalin of the fight gone out of them, came by, with gippy tummies and loose bowels, bruises, trench foot. After the inferno of battle, it was back to the slow burn of routine medical work. But not for long. The mail had arrived from home, and Hughes was just sitting down to open a letter when there was a huge explosion outside, rattling the windows. A group of Argentinian prisoners of war had been detailed to clear up a pile of ammunition jettisoned by retreating comrades and move it to a safer position. Maybe they were careless, or perhaps it had been booby-trapped but, either way, the dump blew up. Two PoWs died instantly, and seven others were badly injured. Bullets were exploding in the fireball and flying off in all directions. There was the constant crump of more charges detonating in the heat. One man was dragged clear, and Hughes slammed a morphine line into the twitching body. Both legs had been blown off, one above the knee, the other below. The flesh had been stripped and bones were sticking out. An arm was missing and there was a massive chest wound. The whole body was charred and smouldering and the gagging smell of burnt human flesh choked the air.

Another victim could not be reached. Corporal John Geddes saw him running from the flames, blazing from head to foot, his body turning charcoal-black. The Argentinian lost his way, stumbled and, instead of escaping to safety, turned back into the fire. Geddes instinctively darted to pull him away, but his friends restrained him. It would be madness to try to get to him, and the man was so far gone that saving his life might not be a blessing anyway. But dying this way was an abomination. Someone shouted, 'Fucking do something *somebody*!',[1] and an RAMC sergeant, who had already pulled one PoW from the flames, grabbed a rifle and put two rounds into the writhing, screaming figure, ending his misery.

David Cooper, the 2 Para chaplain who witnessed this, considered it 'the best thing to have done in the circumstances'.[2] The killing was judged merciful by those who saw it, but not by others. There was a complaint from the Red Cross and questions asked in Parliament in London. To Steven Hughes's disgust, 'people without the faintest idea judged him and found him guilty.' The sergeant was even investigated for a possible murder charge, though he was exonerated.

Afterwards, Hughes thought long and hard about the ethical issues. Was it wrong for a medic to shoot somebody to put him out of his misery? It was an impossible conundrum for those whose commitment was to the saving of life but also to the relieving of agony. He concluded that the sergeant's action had been not only humane but brave. He doubted he would have had the courage to do it himself. Many who knew the horrors of war as intimately as he did wished that, in similar circumstances, someone would do as much for them.

Flames hold a particular dread for those who fight wars. Bomber crews of the Second World War, going into battle sitting on tankfuls of highly inflammable kerosene while being shot at with incendiary shells, lived in fear of a fiery death or – worse still, as some of them saw it – of disfigurement. Sailors had nightmare visions of being adrift in burning oil. Every one of these primal fears would explode into awful reality in the next stage of the war, with scenes of destruction and suffering that would be the most searing of the entire Falklands campaign.

Reinforcements – contingents of Welsh Guards and Scots Guards, plus a new medical team, the RAMC's 16 Field Ambulance – had now arrived from the UK in a second flotilla, to bolster the ranks for the final phase of the assault, the advance on Port Stanley, the Argentinian-held island capital.

The irrepressible and affable second-in-command of 16 Field

Ambulance, Major Roger Nutbeem, set his men to work at the Ajax Bay hospital. In a moment of leisure he sat and picked out a folk tune on the battered guitar he carried with him everywhere. Then he reached for a pen and wrote to his wife, Patricia, hoping she and the children were coping in his absence. 'I'm expecting to move forward in the next few days. Wish us luck. I miss you all more than I can say and will be very happy to get back. It shouldn't be too long now.'[3]

To avoid the newly arrived guards having to tab an exhausting eighty miles across the island interior, which some say they were not up to anyway, they were taken by sea to be dropped off in Bluff Cove, a bay just a day's march away from Port Stanley. The medics of 16 Field Ambulance, as the major had predicted, went too. Steven Hughes was already ahead of them. He had been helicoptered to the settlement at Fitzroy, above Bluff Cove, to set up an aid post in the tin-hut village hall there. Now Goose Green was behind him, his principal concern was trench foot, which was hobbling a good half of many platoons. He was worried. He had thirty cases resting in makeshift beds, with bundles of kit on top to keep them warm and their bare swollen feet poking out and raised up to let them recover naturally. The alternative was to evacuate them to the *Uganda* for treatment, but in that case they would be out of the war for good – and it looked as though every last man would be needed to defeat the Argentinians.

At least there were more able bodies arriving. Down in the bay, Hughes could see the landing ships *Sir Galahad* and *Sir Tristram* at anchor, fully laden with Welsh Guardsmen. The only problem with this otherwise cheering sight was that no one seemed in a hurry to get the men off, even though it was broad daylight. Those watching began taking increasingly anxious bets on how long it would before the ships were bombed. As if on cue, two Skyhawks and two Mirages roared over at mast level and a 1,000- pounder plunged into the belly of the *Galahad* and exploded. Hundreds of men waiting below for orders to disembark were caught in the inferno. To the watching doctor, the seriousness of the situation was instantly obvious. He tipped out all the trench-foot cases from the aid post. 'Eff off back to your companies,' he told them. They would have to fend for themselves. An avalanche of emergencies would be on the way any minute.

Welsh Guards officer Captain Hilarian Roberts had been below in the *Galahad* with his men, breaking the dispiriting news to his platoon sergeant that the vessel's rear ramp was jammed and getting off was going to take a long time. The sergeant heard planes, yelled, 'Get down!', and the captain hit the deck. 'There was this enveloping thud, and a huge flame that was billowing straight at me and then over me. I experienced an extraordinary slow-motion feeling of being burnt. I watched my hands go the colour of sickly white-grey washing-up gloves. The skin peeled off like talons of wax. My hair was on fire, and I tried to beat it out with those now useless hands of mine.'[4] He had no doubt he was a dead man. 'Well, that's it, it's finished, its all over,' he thought to himself as a cloud of black smoke descended. His last physical sensation, he realized, would be the smell of his own flesh burning. But the instinct to survive kicked in. The main impact of the blast had gone over him, not through him, and it was this that saved him. 'I'd have been dead if I hadn't been flat on the ground.' Bizarrely, he was covered in feathers, the remains of someone's sleeping bag.

He stood up and began to feel his way to the stairs, though the pain in his skinned hands made each touch agony. He could sense people around him in the same state – shocked, hands dripping, faces beginning to blacken all over. There was a logjam on the stairs but, through the darkness, he heard the steady voice of a senior NCO: 'Keep calm ... one at a time.' Roberts found it reassuring and so took up the cry himself: 'Keep calm ... one at a time.' It seemed to work in suppressing the panic that could have engulfed them all and made escape even harder. 'Eventually, we came staggering out on to the deck, and then I suppose the adrenalin, the immediate instinct to get out, began to wear off, and I felt as sick as a dog.' He clawed his way down a rope ladder and was lifted into a rescue boat. In the water around, patches of oil were blazing. Above, strong winds fanned the flames and *Galahad*'s fuel tanks and ammunition stores exploded.

Sergeant Peter 'Pierre' Naya of the RAMC was down in the *Galahad*'s hold, also preparing for the long and slow process of disembarking, when the planes struck and a massive orange fireball erupted around him. A twenty-year army veteran, he had never experienced anything like this. 'It burnt blokes, it killed blokes. Everywhere there was the screaming of men in agony, pain, shock, fear, panic.'[5] His own backpack was in flames and burning the back of his head. 'I couldn't see a thing; all I could smell was burning metal and flesh and acrid smoke. The heat was scorching my lungs.' Some were lucky. On the mess deck, another medic, Andy Poole, had slipped away from his quarters without permission and was waiting to get lunch when the ship's Tannoy blurted out the call of 'Action stations!' He barely had time to heed it before he was blown to the floor, the lights went out, electric cables sparked and flickered overhead and smoke and flames filled the area. 'I saw one of the Chinese cooks just flying through the air towards me, on fire.'[6] Instinctively, Poole's hand went to his groin, 'to make sure I still had my bits'. He was intact there, and so was the rest of him – but the man sitting next to him was a wreck. 'He was really badly burnt by the flash. I have no idea why him and not me. Just the vagaries of war, I suppose. Somebody up there was looking after me.'

He began to do the job he was trained for. He shook the bodies around him for a response, quickly felt for their pulses, then, when he got nothing, moved on to the next one.

I crawled over bodies of the dead and made my way out into smoke-filled corridors. There were horrors at every turn. I passed the ablutions, where there was a guy on the toilet, except he had no legs. He must have been sitting there when the explosion caught him. He was dead. Then the hold door flew open and a blast of flames and intense heat, plus exploding ammunition, came at me. A figure stumbled out, on fire from head to foot. We couldn't get near him because of the heat. If I had had my rifle with me, I would have shot him, as there was no way he could have survived. But he dropped lifeless to the floor anyway.

Those who could were groping their way upwards, towards daylight at the top of the stairs. Naya grabbed an injured guardsman by the belt and yanked him up, rung by rung. 'He was in agony, but I knew I had to get him up on deck. He kept screaming, "Mind my leg!", but I could see he'd already lost it.' Out on deck, he put his arm round the soldier and half carried him away from the smoke, the injured man trailing a line of blood as the shattered stump dragged across the deck. Everywhere Naya turned, there were terrible sights. Where lads had grabbed hold of red-hot handrails, the skin of their palms had peeled off like kid gloves and bunched in folds over their fingers. Areas of the body exposed at the moment of the flash suffered most – the face, neck, ears, hair and hands. 'Some were completely burnt from the neck up – no hair, no eyebrows, skins black and swollen. Many would carry the scars all their life.' But those covered up weren't unaffected either. Terrible burns were caused by the plastic all-weather clothing many of them were wearing to keep out the cold and wet of the Falklands. They literally fried as the fabric caught light, melted and stuck to their skin. 'It was pitiful to watch men running and rolling around and trying to tear off their clothes, in such pain, such terrible pain.'

Naya's every instinct shrieked at him to get off the *Galahad*, but his sudden thought was that he could be the only trained medic left on the scene. All the doctors had gone ashore before the attack. He looked around and couldn't see any other medics at work. He couldn't just run. Lives depended on him. 'So I got stuck in with what medical kit I had to hand – a single pair of scissors! Everything else had gone, blown to pieces.' Down on his knees on the blistering-hot deck, the flames just feet away and explosion after explosion still rocking the air, he started to cut away at the badly burnt clothes of a casualty. Others were drawn towards him. 'I became a focus for people. They knew someone was there to help.' NCOs were beginning to get a grip on the situation, calming the distressed and organizing lines of injured men for him to see. Naya needed splints for broken limbs and smashed his boot down on a wooden pallet lying on deck to make some. Guardsmen who had managed to avoid injury pitched in with the dressings and intravenous drips from their own packs. 'Everyone rallied round.' He issued orders – 'Grab this, do that.' A drip in here, a splint on there. Do what you can then move to the next one. As he went from casualty to casualty, he didn't even have time to look up. 'I remember trying to put a figure-of-eight bandage round some poor bugger's legs and a field dressing over a fellow's stumps. I used some webbing straps as a tourniquet and a bayonet to tighten it. Then I looked up at the poor devil and saw his face was swollen to twice its size, like a pumpkin, and was completely black with the flash burn.'

He worked at a frantic pace, utterly absorbed in what he was doing. 'It was decisions, decisions. Could I leave this one? What were the chances of saving that one? Who's next for the helicopter? *How much time have I got?*' Over everything hung the fear of another attack from the air or the ship blowing up beneath him. Evacuating everyone was urgent. A navy 'three-ringer' – a commander – offered his services to the sergeant, and together they tried to strap a lad who'd lost a leg into a harness dangling from a helicopter. It wouldn't work, so they lashed him to a pallet and wrapped the harness round that, but when the helicopter began to lift him he rolled off in agony. They got him up and away in the end, but Naya could never quite recall precisely how.

Andy Poole had also made it on deck now, and the vision of hell he saw was hard for a nineteen-year-old to deal with. 'The smell of burnt flesh was terrible, and the screams of the badly wounded made you shudder. Cries of "Medic!" could be heard everywhere. Others were jumping over the side into rafts and landing craft that came alongside, but I had a job to do. There were men still on fire, men with legs missing, men dying. Someone came up to me and said, "You're a medic, do what you can," and filled my hands with syrettes of morphine.' He got stuck in.

Outside, in the sea and on land, a massive rescue operation was underway. Helicopter pilots cut blindly through the smoke and hovered feet from the fires as their crewmen were winched down into the inferno to snatch men from death. Hilarian Roberts's life raft was one of several that began to drift back towards the fire, but a helicopter came low and used its down-draught to push them away from danger. This was not a case of 'every man for himself'. On the contrary, those who had swum or rowed to safe waters turned back to help those still in danger. From the shore, scores of soldiers and sailors, all drawn to the scene by an unspoken compulsion to help comrades in distress, waded out into the freezing bay to grab the injured and carry them on their shoulders to land.

On the beach, Steven Hughes set up an emergency RAP for the flood of casualties coming in on helicopters and staggering from landing craft and life rafts. 'There were guys with burns who would have been stretcher casualties, had there been any stretchers. They were walking up the beach and collapsing. Bodies in bright orange survival suits were lying everywhere. Out in the bay plumes of smoke were rising from the burning ships. It was a horrific scene.'

While his team got to work, he jumped into one of the now-empty landing craft lined up on the beach and told the bosun to take him out to the *Galahad*. He stuck his last remaining cigar between his teeth and drew on it nervously as they neared the inferno. 'I was aware she was a potential time bomb.' They sailed in alongside the stricken vessel, and one of his men tried to heave himself on board but was beaten back by the flames. By then, most of the casualties had been lifted off and so Hughes's craft pulled clear and began rounding up life rafts and ushering them to the shore.

Bill Bentley was with a group of medics who positioned themselves on a cliff above the cove and waved with their stretchers to alert the helicopter pilots to bring some of the casualties to them for treatment. It was the shortest flying route, and the choppers could unload their wounded and go straight back to the ship for more. The injuries were horrific, he recalled – terrible burns, limbs blown off, people burnt black all over. One guardsman had lost a leg, but it was another wound that was puzzling – his throat was ripped wide open. Bentley discovered that the explosion had hurled the young soldier through the wall of the ship into the sea, blown off his leg and set him on fire. Suffocating in the smoke and in terrible agony, he was sure he was going to die and had pulled out his multi-purpose pocket knife to end it all quickly by cutting his own throat. But, instead of the sharp blade, which would have done the job, he had mistakenly been hacking away at himself with the tin opener. A helicopter got to him in time, blew out the flames with its down-draught and put a blast of fresh air in his face before picking him up and carrying him to shore.

On the blazing hulk of the *Galahad*, Naya had been working flat out and was thankfully now tending to the last few survivors. One of the last to get away was a young soldier in great pain from his burns. The medic could do nothing for him but resort to the traditional soldier's standby in an emergency. 'I lit a cigarette and put it in his mouth.' A grin of pleasure creased across the youngster's bewildered, exhausted face. 'He stood holding his blackened and bleeding hands in the air and puffing merrily away.' He wasn't the only one in need of a smoke that day. Hughes, for one, had his cigar. It was said, too, that the moment they hit the beach, some survivors had a cigarette for the first time in their lives, to calm the adrenalin pumping through them.

Naya, who was awarded a Military Medal for his devotion to duty at the risk of his own life, reserved his greatest praise for the helicopter pilots who kept on coming to haul away the wounded. 'They performed miracles. They were unbelievably brave. They saved over three hundred lives that day.' Finally, after he'd been kneeling on that deck for more than an hour, it was his time to get away. Everyone else had gone, but so had all the life boats. 'For the first time, I looked over the side of the ship and, for the first time, I saw how far we were from the land. It would be a long swim. I'd survived the fire and now it looked as if I was going to drown. I knew I'd last no more than five minutes in the icy water. If I jump, I've had it, I thought.' But if he stayed on board he was going to be a dead man anyway. There were more explosions from the decks below. Bullets from the ammunition stores were whizzing around, and he had no helmet – it had been lost in the original blast – to protect him. He began to remove his boots and take a chance, a slim one, in the water.

Suddenly a naval officer came out of the smoke and gesticulated to me. A chopper was coming. I have never been more grateful to see a pilot in my life, and as I was pulled on board I put the sign of the cross on his visor. He just smiled – he was so young. As we veered away from the ship I began to tremble and shake like a leaf. I'd survived, I'd got my hands, my legs, and I was in one piece. I was almost the last one off the *Galahad*. When I got ashore, the first person I saw was our RSM. I was so pleased I gave him a hug and a kiss, and all the other boys too. He shouted something at me but I could barely make it out. I didn't realize until then that I'd gone deaf out there.

Poole was also among the last to be taken off the floating inferno. The medics of 16 Field Ambulance had had a literal baptism of fire. Not all had come through. When roll call was taken, three were missing, presumed dead.

One of them was his best mate, Kenny Preston, a bubbly Lanca-shire lad, a drinking companion and 'a good laugh'. Before they left the UK, Preston had said he didn't think he'd be coming back, and now that premonition had come true. 'I'd seen him on *Galahad* a couple of hours before the attack,' Poole remembered. 'We chatted, and then I said, "See you on land." But I never saw him again. This was my mate I'd been chatting to only a few hours ago. I was stunned, as most of us were. But I thought to myself that, had I stayed below decks where I should have been instead of sneaking up to the mess hall, that could have been me. And now there was still a job to be getting on with. There would be more wounded to deal with. We had to press on. Our lost comrades would have expected no less.'

*

Hughes, reassured that the last man was off the *Galahad*, was also back on land and had returned to his main aid post at the Fitzroy village hall. The more serious casualties had been brought here, and he dispensed shots of penicillin into the backsides of a long line of Welsh Guardsmen before dispatching them to the hospital at Ajax Bay. Here news of the attack had come like a thunderbolt. There was talk of fifty or sixty men dead and many hundreds injured.

Rick Jolly and his teams prepared for a tidal wave to hit them. The helicopters began to clatter in, and every possible hand was at the landing site to bring the stretchers inside. Each new patient seemed to be in a worse state than the last. There was no let-up – the numbers rose incessantly, passing the hundred mark, then nudging towards a hundred and fifty. No one could tell how many more were on the way. What was technically classed as a 'mass casualty situation' was developing rapidly. The real danger was that it would swamp and then submerge the Ajax Bay facilities. Jolly arranged for as many as possible of the walking wounded to be shipped out straight away to be treated in the sick bays of navy vessels in the Sound.

The sickest could not be moved and, about them, difficult decisions had to be made. Priority would have to go not to the most serious cases but to the ones with the best chance of survival. 'We had to do the best we could for the largest number, and recognize that some were so badly injured they would take up too much time and resources to treat and thereby reduce the chances of many others.' To Jolly fell the task of playing God, making those awesome life-and-death choices. He turned away half of those who arrived at the hospital doors. They had flash burns over 10 per cent or less of their bodies – they would have to wait. 'I expected some ranting and raving, perhaps even accusations of betrayal or flint-heartedness. However, the young Welsh Guards-men were stoical and even cheery as we broke the news to them. They stood near the doorway, blowing on their tattered and painful hands to keep them cool. Strips of skin hung from their fingers like thin, wet muslin, and their faces were blistered and raw, the hair singed short. By God, they were brave.'

Their selflessness touched him deeply. 'Each man seemed to know of someone else more seriously injured than himself and wanted him treated first. "Don't worry about me, sir," they would say. "What about Evans (or Williams or Jones)? He's the one that needs you, not me . . ."' In the end, seventy had to be turned away from getting immediate aid. They faced being loaded back into a landing craft and ferried to ships in the Sound, being taken out to sea again when their minds were still full of the maritime horror they had only just escaped. The bumpy crossing over the waves would be physically as well as mentally agonizing. Only afterwards would they get something to soothe their pain, some balm for their burnt extremities. 'I watched them as they marched away into the night,' Jolly remembered, guilty still about the decisions he had to make on other men's lives, 'still blowing on their hands as they went, still maintaining good order and discipline, and with not a single word or gesture of dissent'.[7]

Jolly now had his casualty list down to manageable proportions. The frenzied flow from *Galahad* and *Tristram* (which had also been hit, but nowhere near as badly as *Galahad*) had eased. He was left with ninety or so to treat. Even so, he needed everyone on the base, from cooks to navy divers, to chip in and help with ward chores while the medics put their expertise to use. 'At times like this we worked for thirty hours non-stop. The conditions were filthy dirty, and we were cold and wet. Our number-one priority was hot, sweet tea. That came top of the list, just after keeping surgical instruments clean.'

The brews kept coming and sleep went by the board as they began to work on the Bluff Cove survivors. Those patients with the worst burns needed to be rehydrated, with massive intravenous infusions. Slowly, the life dripped back into blackened bodies, while morphine took the edge off indescribable pain. Surgeons moved from bed to bed slitting bloated fingers to drain away fluid. Flamazine, a cooling white cream of silver and sulpha, was applied. Hands were enclosed in sterile plastic bags to avoid the chafing of bandages. Jolly remembered the concrete floor of the one-time whaling station being ankle-deep in torn packets and cellophane wrapping from the hundreds of dressings used that day and night. The Flamazine ran out on the very last patient.

The survivor in the worst state, according to the doctor, was Guardsman Simon Weston, whose disfigured face and indomitable courage would become, for many, the enduring emblem of the

Falklands conflict. The islands were regained and honour restored, but the cost, counted in scars both physical and mental, was immense. Jolly is frank – the sight of Weston when he was brought into Ajax Bay was terrifying. His swollen face and scalp were red and blistered. His hair was charred. Nerve endings were exposed and the pain so severe that morphine had little effect. He pleaded to be put out of his misery, not for the first time. 'When the bomb exploded, I watched, transfixed with horror, as my hands melted, the skin bubbling on the bone. I was suffocating in the smoke and I was on fire. I begged someone for a rifle so I could shoot myself.'[8] He had got away only by running over the blackened bodies of dead and dying comrades. Most were gonners – only eight of his platoon of thirty survived that day. His wish to join them, for his suffering to end, was ignored by Jolly's team. Instead, he was treated with a radical technique, an anaesthetic that relaxed him into a pain-free trance. Eventually, he recovered (though it would take some seventy-five operations and skin grafts) and, though life had changed for ever for the self-confessed rugby-playing, beer-swilling, woman-chasing Welshman, he still had a life. He was, said Jolly, a shining example of how extraordinary 'ordinary' people can be and of the powerful resources deep within humans that can be tapped in extremis.

That night after *Galahad* and *Tristram* were hit, resources, both physical and mental, were stretched to the limit. There were stretchers side by side, wall to wall, at Ajax Bay. 'We couldn't actually stand on the floor,' medic Mick Jennings recalled. 'We had to walk on the stretchers.' There was a lot of fear among the burns victims. 'Am I going to look like Niki Lauda?'[9] one kept asking plaintively. What could anyone say to comfort him? The sadness of these blighted young lives left Jennings feeling wrecked. Nor was there any consoling thought that this was as bad as things could get. Over all this dedicated life-saving hung an air of menace. The Argentinian airforce had caused all this havoc with just a couple of bombs. Their tails were up. It was inconceivable that they would not try again. As stillness finally settled over the rows of semi-naked men in makeshift cots and stretcher racks in every corner of the hospital and weary medics stood down for a while from their duties, it seemed inevitable that, at first light, another aerial attack would be launched against one British position or another. Perhaps the over-flowing Ajax Bay would be the next target. Jolly feared the worst. He had come through the testing *Sir Galahad* experience by the skin of his teeth, but could he cope with any more casualties?

'I looked at the ghostly, Flamazine-covered faces of the young Welsh Guardsmen, hair and eyebrows singed, fingers like sausages, swollen and damaged. My eyes met theirs, and cracked and blistered lips parted in vain attempts to smile. I knew that somehow I had to get them out of here before the next air raid and away to the cool comfort, the clean sea air and the devoted nursing of our hospital ship.' But it would need a massive airlift to get them all out to the *Uganda*, and when he asked for helicopters, he was told they were all earmarked for the next phase in the advance to Stanley. He was torn, the medical man and the soldier at odds within him. 'I shook my head in disbelief, aware of the need to get this war finished quickly but also of the more immediate needs of these tough and courageous young Welsh Guardsmen who were my charges.'

While the brass hats deliberated and dithered (and eventually said no to diverting any aircraft for this purpose), Jolly was rescued from his predicament by the crew of a navy helicopter. They had been elsewhere on East Falkland when the *Galahad* was hit and now flew into Ajax Bay to be briefed on what had happened. The doctor piled on the emotional pressure as he escorted the pilot round the rows of casualties. One glimpse was enough for the airman to make up his mind. He pulled his gloves out of the pocket of his flying suit. There was work to do, he said, and the sooner he started the better.

His first job was to locate the *Uganda*, which for some reason was out of radio contact. Then he began the evacuation, beginning with Simon Weston. The medic escorting him had a note in his pocket from Jolly for the ship's medical director – stand by for another 167![10] It was going to be a slow process, back and forward, with just one helicopter, but then, out of the blue-grey sky, another pitched up. The cheery pilot – 'I hear you have a problem, sir' – offered to take a load of casualties to the *Uganda* in between his designated duties. The word was clearly out, and soon more and more helicopters were overhead and buzzing in, loading up and lifting off with human cargoes to deliver into the safe hands of the hospital-ship nurses. Within a few hours, the job was done. Every one of the wounded was away, safe between clean sheets and secure from marauding Argentinian fighters. When a military liaison officer arrived to tell Jolly that the generals and brigadiers had decided that he couldn't have any helicopters after all, not a single patient was left. He was greeted by stacks of empty stretchers – and a look of deep satisfaction on Rick Jolly's face.

Meanwhile, the magnitude of all that had happened was forcing its way into the consciousness of Sergeant Naya – and leaving him troubled. His exhaustion was overwhelming, and he certainly deserved the sleep of the righteous as he lay down in his billet in an empty Falkland islander's house at Fitzroy. He, of all people, had absolutely nothing to reproach himself for. His conduct had been exemplary. But this did not stop his mind racing, refusing him the rest he so desperately needed. 'What had happened? What had gone wrong? How were my mates, some of whom I still hadn't seen and didn't know if they were alive or dead? *Did I do enough?*' It was hard getting the sense of death out of his system. In the twilight the next evening, he stood on the cliffs above Bluff Cove and stared, mesmerized, at the eerie red glow coming from what remained of the *Galahad*. Tears rolled down his face. 'She burnt there for days. We all expected her to go up in one almighty explosion, break in half and sink, but she never did.' The entire bridge had caved in and the topside was black and charred, except in patches where the paint had peeled off and the metal underneath was shining in the last rays of the sun. Naya was overwhelmed with sadness. Pride in what he had done that day would come later. He wasn't a hero, he maintained. 'I just did my job. Yes, I could certainly have got off the *Galahad* straight away, but it never crossed my mind to do so. These men were my mates, my family, they were hurting and looking to me as a medic for help. I did it without thinking.'

His thoughts now turned to his real family, his wife and four children back home in Britain. The attack on the *Galahad* and the number of dead and wounded would probably be front-page news already. He wanted to reassure them that he was OK, but there would be no means to do so for a while. 'It wasn't until we got to Stanley that I was able to sneak off to the Cable and Wireless office and send a telegram. Just a few words, "I'm safe and well – Love, P." It cost me every penny I had, but it was worth it.'

For other wives and children, however, the tidings were the worst they could be. Patricia Nutbeem, wife of RAMC major Roger Nutbeem, was in the kitchen getting her two children ready for school when she glanced out of the window and saw the padre and an officer approaching her door. 'Every soldier's wife knows immediately what that means,' she recalled. Her husband had been one of the first of the forty-eight to die, caught out on the open deck when the attack planes came, and cut down by shrapnel. She was all the more shocked by his death because she had never thought that, as a medic, he would be in the front line.

Five-year-old Kathryn remembered being bundled off to school that morning without explanation. 'My granny collected me in the afternoon and brought me home. My mother sat me down and told me what had happened. She was crying. Then, apparently, I wanted to get out pictures of my dad and go through the family photo albums. I must have been told I wasn't going to see him again, so I wanted to look at his picture.'[11] Her life would never be the same again. The *Galahad* had taken her hero, her own special knight in shining armour. Finding him and fixing him in her memory would be a quest she took into her adult years. Such are the perpetual scars of war.

11. Gaining the High Ground

'A soldier goes out and fetches in a comrade under fire and he gets a medal for bravery. But we are always under shellfire and can't dump our stretchers and run for it to a safe spot. We have to plod on, slipping and sliding, shells bursting above and in the earth around us. It's God's mercy that we get through. But we have the patient to think of. Our quickness probably means his life.' So recalled a private in the RAMC who was a stretcher-bearer in the trenches in the Great War.[1] He spoke a great truth. In war, there is nothing more noble than putting your life at risk to save another's. Yet that was the daily – hourly! – stock in trade of the medic. Sixty-five years on from that private's impassioned job description, on a battlefield a long, long way from the Somme, but similar in terms of the cold, the wet and the danger, stretcher-bearers were once again showing their mettle. They were a derided bunch, carved from the ranks of cooks, bandsmen, barmen, store clerks and the like, whom fighting soldiers were prone to look down on. Lying on a stretcher, being hauled to safety, the wounded got a different perspective: they were the ones looking up now, in admiration.

The final battles of the Falklands campaign had much in common with those of the First World War, a thought that went through the mind of 3 Para's Private Mark Eyles-Thomas as he fixed his bayonet, stood up and began to advance towards Mount Longdon, one of a chain of 500-foot-high rocky ridges that surrounded and shielded the islands' capital, Port Stanley. The terrain might be different, but the technique was the same. 'I could see men to my left and to my right advancing in a continuous straight line. It seemed ironic that, despite all our modern technology and weaponry, in the end it all came down to men fighting each other, face to face, hand to hand, yard by yard.'[2] This had been planned as a surprise attack, which was why there was no artillery bombardment to precede it. The men of 3 Para had tabbed many miles, over hostile terrain, at top speed, to get to this point in the north of the island where they could penetrate the Argentinian lines. Longdon was believed to be lightly defended. Stormed in the dark without warning, it should easily fall.

Sergeant Major John Weeks had his doubts about this. Before they set out he had warned the men in his company that some of them would not be coming off the hill. 'It's going to be hand-to-hand fighting,' he told them bluntly. 'You're going to have live stuff exploding all around you. If you believe in Christ, now's the time to have a little talk to Him. I'm certainly going to say a little prayer myself.'[3]

They marched towards the mountain for more than an hour, beneath a rising moon, no talking, the only sound a rhythmic swishing as their boots cut through the grass. In the swirling wind there were flecks of snow. The Falklands winter was kicking in. Then they came to the lower slopes of the mountain and began the uphill slog, still in silence. But what had not been put into the pre-battle calculations was the extent to which the area had been mined. Suddenly, there was a flash and a bang, and a violent scream echoed around the crags and rock runs. At the front of his platoon, Corporal Brian Milne had stood on a mine. Longdon erupted. From well-hidden, well-placed, stone-walled bunkers, the alerted enemy – in battalion-strength, not just a company, as had been expected – poured out mortar and bullets, the empty night suddenly bursting with flares and bright green tracer. It mingled with the red tracer of the fire now being furiously returned by the Paras. It was just like Guy Fawkes Night, according to Weeks.

He was thankful that most of the Argentinians had been asleep when the mine went off. 'What came at us was bad enough, so if they'd all been awake, they would have wiped us off the face of the mountain.' Some platoons had made it to the heart of the Argentinian defensive line before their presence was revealed, and instantly the fighting was close up and personal. Eyles-Thomas lay flat on the ground, aware the mine that had downed Milne was certainly not the only one out there. He could hear the groans of the injured corporal ahead of him. His pal, Jas Burt, crawled forward to help the injured man, and Eyles-Thomas followed. Jas took the corporal's morphine syrette from around his neck and jabbed it into him, but the painkiller was having little effect, so he injected his own into Milne as well. It was a remarkably selfless thing to do. He might need morphine for himself if he was hit . . . *when* he was hit. But, for now, they had to leave the wounded man. Their priority was to maintain the momentum of the attack. Shouting out for a 'Medic!' they pushed on up the hill.

Brian Faulkner, the colour sergeant in charge of 3 Para's aid post, already had his men just yards behind the action. In the long slog to the start line of the operation, they had been donkeys, carrying supplies of arms and ammunition on their backs in their other battlefield role. Now they reverted to being medics. He was conscious of how nervous his band of co-opted cooks, REME (Royal Electrical and Mechanical Engineers) fitters and pay clerks was feeling as they waited with him in the rear. 'We knew this was going to be the big battle, the major occasion.'[4] The noise of the first mine and Milne's scream of agony shattered their anxious contemplation of what lay ahead. The radio crackled into life: 'Starlight, Starlight' – the aid post's call sign – 'move up the mountain . . . !' Faulkner and his men rushed forward, hearts pumping, adrenalin surging, running, as they later realized, through mines. But they were more concerned with what was going on over their heads than at their feet. 'We came under intense fire. It was just like being on a machine-gun firing range, except that we were the targets. We could see the lads going down ahead, blokes being killed, losing limbs and having their intestines blown out. Oh my God, this is real, I was thinking. I had never experienced anything like it before.'

Medic Phil Probets was the first to reach the wounded Milne. 'He was yelling his head off, and I knew I had to stop him, because the enemy were homing in on where the noise was coming from. The mine had blown his lower calf off and most of his heel. The cold was keeping him alive, because it had contracted the blood vessels and slowed the bleeding. I packed the gaping hole as best I could, then put on an inflatable splint to keep everything in place.'[5] As he worked away the thought struck him that he was indeed in a minefield. 'Brilliant,' he remembered thinking. 'How am I going to get out of this?'

That wasn't his only problem. As he examined the wounded corporal, he had to put his torch on to see what he was doing, and the light was a lure for snipers up in the rocks. 'It didn't make me very popular with the Toms, but I had no alternative.' As for those worries about how to get safely out of the minefield, they were resolved for him in time-honoured military fashion. Having stabilized Milne, he was ordered forward to deal with more casualties. He crossed his fingers and 'got my arse out of there'. But the risk he took was demonstrated when, hours later, a Snowcat trundled in on its all-terrain tracks to pick up the corporal, the driver jumped out, detonated a mine and lost his leg.

In those first few hours of the ten-hour battle for Mount Longdon, the casualties were of an order the British army had not sustained or experienced for decades. It was not just the weight of numbers but the intensity that was new. There was no stopping when a man was down, as there had been, for example, in Northern Ireland. The toll was relentless. Faulkner and 2 Para medical officer Captain John Burgess set up the regimental aid post in a sheltered gully beneath a rockface on the western side of the mountain. From here the stretcher-bearers were sent out to bring back the wounded. With constant calls for help coming in over the radio, Faulkner directed his five teams of stretcher-bearers to where they lay. 'Go left, go centre, go right, go as far forward as you can and start picking them up.' They went without hesitation, he recalled, filled with pride at their bravery under the most intense fire. Leave the dead, he told them. Get the ones who still have a chance. One bearer was blown up more than once bringing in the same casualty, hit by the blast from a shell, picking himself up, making it a few more yards and then being blown away again. And once he had made it, he had a quick swallow of tea to shake the ringing out of his ears and steady his nerves and then went straight back up the hill again. 'They all had to,' said Faulkner. 'The guys up front were fighting hand to hand and couldn't bring the wounded back. They were relying on us.'

The pressure was relentless. Tom Onions, converted from army chef to stretcher-bearer and seeing action for the first time, went back and forward across open ground on autopilot. 'The stream of casualties was endless. Go up, pick up the guys, come down with them, then back up there again through the firing and the explosions. Parachute flares going up and flickering. Yelling and screaming all around you. I was scared all right, but it was what we had to do.' Around him he saw scenes from a horror film – a phosphorus grenade exploding in an enemy bunker and an Argentinian sniper running out blazing from head to foot, before a Para finished him off with a rifle volley. A quarter of a century later, the image of that killing, the first he ever witnessed, was still stuck in his head like a bad dream.

Among the first casualties the bearers brought back was medic Mark Dodsworth, one of their own. He had been going forward to the wounded when rifle fire caught him in the pelvis and legs. He was dragged in on a poncho. 'He was conscious and talking to us,' Burgess recalled.[6] He was given pain relief, put on a drip and then taken in the Snowcat to the helicopter landing site to be evacuated. He didn't make it. His death was a hideous initiation for the medical teams, a clear indication of the dangers each and every one of them faced.

They were also becoming acutely aware of how under-equipped they were. In the tab to the mountain, arms and ammunition had been the priority, and only the simplest and lightest of medical supplies had been brought – dressings, drips, painkillers, antibiotics, bandages and the like. 'We were short of supplies,' Faulkner admitted. They would just have to cope with the little they had. But conditions were against them, and even some of the limited medical supplies they had were proving useless. 'I was about to put a saline drip into a severely wounded lad when I realized the fluid was ice-cold and would go through his heart and kill him. So we couldn't give them any drips.' Then a sniper got a bead on the aid post, 'and began picking us off. It was bloody frightening because we had nowhere to hide, but thank God he was taken out.'

Yard by painful yard, the Paras were progressing up Longdon, slowly getting on top of a determined enemy, whose unexpected bravery and defiance they were the first to acknowledge. But the cost was huge. Half of one platoon was down, five men dead and eight wounded. A corporal was hit and lay out in the open while a sniper took pot shots at various parts of his body. As each bullet thudded in, to his thigh, his arm and his head, he kept up a running commentary. His mates could hear him dying but were pinned down and could not get to him. Finally, one could stand his friend's agony no more and – as the sniper had wanted – dashed out to try to rescue him. Three bullets in the chest killed him instantly.

Faulkner moved forward from the aid post, finding scores of casualties, a personal tragedy at every turn. 'The bastards have blown my leg off,' screamed one soldier in anger and pain after stepping on a mine. 'I'm only twenty-one, and the bastards have blown my leg off!' The heroism was immense. A lance corporal was shot in the head while carrying a wounded comrade off the field but refused to stop for treatment. 'He wrapped a field dressing round his head and carried on,' said Faulkner. 'He stayed on that dirty, treacherous hill and kept on going up and down with the wounded, non-stop.'

As well as those brought in on stretchers, walking wounded struggled to the aid post under their own steam. They stumbled in, arms wrapped around each other, bandaged and bloody, like the wounded returning from no-man's land on the Somme. It was a hazardous journey. At least one casualty and the man supporting him were killed on the way down. Those who made it often had injuries so severe they would have left most other men helpless and beyond hope. A corporal arrived with half his intestines hanging out. With typical Para black humour even at times like this, he was instantly nicknamed 'No Guts'.

Once they had reached the aid post, however, casualties were far from being out of danger and able to relax. The position was

under constant artillery fire. Wounded men had lain out on the
mountain fighting to stay alive for hours, then made it to what
should have been a safe haven for treatment, only to find that the
war they had been rescued from was still pursuing them. Howitzer
shells hit the rocks around the aid post and sent shards of shrapnel
in all directions. Having been hit once was no guarantee of not
being hit again. Lightning did indeed strike twice. Faulkner was
up on a rock at the edge of the RAP directing the stretcher-bearers,
pointing to where they should go next, when a shell landed a
dozen yards away. 'It completely blew me away, and I was out
cold for about fifteen minutes.' It was hours before he was on his
feet and back in action. He had been careless to get caught like
this but, by this stage of the battle, as he admitted later, he was so
drained he was beyond caring. 'I must have come pretty close to
death at that point. Another time, a hot splinter from a shell curled
round the back of my neck before landing in the soft peat nearby.'

To Captain Burgess fell the critical decisions of who should be
evacuated first, and how. The only helicopters that could get in
were tiny Scouts and Gazelles, which could take just two casualties
at a time, one lying on a stretcher, the other sitting. For the rest,
there was a six-hour journey over rough terrain to the nearest
surgical field hospital. Like other battlefield doctors before him,
Burgess sometimes had to make the difficult diagnosis that a man's
condition was so bad and his prospect of survival so slim that he
was put at the back of the queue rather than the front so priority
could be given to those with a chance of recovery. Just yards from
where the living were being treated, the dead were stacking up,
wrapped in groundsheets, their smocks pulled over their heads.
Faulkner worried about the effect this sight might have on the
morale of the wounded, but there was nothing he could do. The
body count that night and day of 11 and 12 June was ticking up
like points on a rugby score board. By the end it would be
twenty-three, making Longdon the bloodiest single fight of the
entire campaign.

★

The principal hero of the battle of Mount Longdon was Sergeant Ian McKay, who was awarded a posthumous Victoria Cross for single-handedly clearing an Argentinian machine-gun position that was holding up the advance. Faulkner had spoken to him just a few hours earlier, as they approached the mountain. 'I'll see you in Stanley,' McKay had said, but he never would. Phil Probets, now just twenty yards behind the slowly advancing front line, found the sergeant's body and verified that he was dead. 'He'd been shot in the head, and part of his face had gone.' Others were dead too, men he knew, had spent nights in the pub with. But this was no time to linger or lament over losses. The area was littered with casualties who could yet be saved. Probets set up his own temporary aid post among some rocks, out of sight of the snipers, he hoped. Then he crawled on his belt out into the open to get to the fallen and drag them to cover. He had ten of them lying around him at one point, all needing to be stabilized before the stretcher-bearers arrived to carry them away.

The teenage Mark Eyles-Thomas was in McKay's platoon and had seen his sergeant go up the hill and not come back. He was ordered forward. Around him were Scrivs, Jas and Grose, his three best mates, lads of the same age who'd joined as boy soldiers at sixteen – 'crows' in Para-speak – and, less than two years later, before they were old enough to vote or drink a beer in a pub, were putting their lives on the line for their country. He charged ahead, firing as he went, hearing rounds pinging into the rocks around him and catching in his nostrils the sharp smell of metal on flint. He went to ground just in front of an enemy trench. Through the darkness, he called out for his friends, and heard Ian 'Scrivs' Scrivens reply: 'I'm over here . . . I'm with [Neil] Grose, but he's been shot. He's in a bad way.'[7] There was no word from Jas, and Eyles-Thomas crawled back to look for him. 'I spotted him lying face down, and I called to him but he didn''t answer. Grabbing his smock, I turned him over. His body slumped towards me. A round from a .50 cal machine-gun had penetrated his head and killed him instantly.' He was beyond needing the dose of morphine he had selflessly given to Corporal Milne in the first moments of the battle.

The shocked Eyles-Thomas went looking for Grose next, and found him lying on his back with Scrivs examining him, probing his chest for an exit wound but not finding it. Bad news – it meant the bullet must still be in him. Grose was in terrible pain and struggling to breathe. They tried to turn him on his side to stop his lungs filling with blood and, as they were holding him, a shot rang out. 'Scrivs fell across my lap,' Eyles-Thomas recalled, 'and fluid splattered on my face. He lay motionless in a limp, crumpled heap. He was dead. I sat there not believing what had happened. One minute I was talking to him, with my hand on his shoulder, the next, zap, he was gone. A shudder went up my spine. Everywhere I looked, soldiers lay wounded, murmuring, some screaming. Grose groaned. "You'll be all right, mate. I'll look after you, I won't leave you," I said. "Where's my helicopter?" he asked. "They promised us, if we were wounded, we'd be on the hospital ship in twenty minutes." "It's coming, Grose," I lied. "It's coming. Just stay with me."'

Eyles-Thomas knew that, if he didn't move Grose to cover, the sniper who had dropped Scrivs would get them too. It was only a matter of time. It was a struggle to get the wounded young soldier over the rocks to Phil Probets' makeshift aid post, a distance of just fifty yards but a marathon effort under the mercilessly accurate sniper fire. Another soldier collapsed, shot. Cries of distress could be heard everywhere. They struggled on and, when they finally made it to the aid post, Eyles-Thomas lay down beside his friend, whispering encouragement. 'He knew his condition was deteriorating but fought against it all the time. I checked and rechecked his dressing so he could feel my touch and know I was constantly with him.' They talked about their families. 'I never allowed him to doubt that he would see his again.' In the bleak mid-hours of the early morning, when the body is at its lowest ebb, Grose began to slip into unconsciousness. 'He said he wanted to sleep. I told him if he did he'd miss the chopper. He looked at me and said, "It's all right, I know the helicopters aren't coming." I looked into his eyes and could see that he had resigned himself to not getting off the mountain. He wanted an end to his pain.'

Eyles-Thomas looked around for a medic and saw Probets, head in hands, totally exhausted. 'I could see he was mentally and physically shattered. In those last few hours his eyes had seen so much pain, grief and mutilation. Everyone around him wanted and expected him to perform miracles – myself included. "I've got nothing left," he said. "No bandages, no drips, no morphine. Nothing. Everything has gone!"' The medic ran his eye over Grose, cleared blood from his mouth, but indicated there was nothing more he could do for him. 'For that single moment, and incorrectly,' Eyles-Thomas wrote later, 'I hated him more than I hated the enemy.' The seventeen-year-old sat by his friend's side. 'I cradled him for a moment like a brother. "Don't leave me, Grose," I whispered. He fidgeted in a last desperate attempt to fight against his injury before releasing his final breath.' It was Grose's eighteenth birthday that very day. He had come of age just in time to die.

Eyles-Thomas wept uncontrollably. 'I cried for him, I cried for his family, I cried that he was too nice a lad to have died in such a way, and I cried for not being able to save him. Then I pulled his head to mine, kissed my friend on the cheek and said goodbye.' Probets was devastated too. 'I felt so helpless. He was drowning in his own blood, and we hadn't been issued with chest drains. His injuries, the length of time of his injury and my lack of equipment meant there was nothing I could do for him. He was asking where the chopper was – he was asking for his mum – then he slipped away.'

*

As day began to break on Longdon, 3 Para had made it on to the last ridge. The enemy, having fought hard and well, withdrew. The intense hand-to-hand scrapping stopped, though the long-distance shelling from Argentinian artillery went on, as did rifle fire from a few bedded-in snipers. For the British medics, the lull was a chance to scour the battlefield for casualties who had been missed. Tom Onions was in a stretcher party lugging a corporal with a leg badly busted by gunshot down the mountainside. It was hard work over the rocks and across the steep gullies. Tony,[8] a medic friend of his, a popular figure in the battalion, was with them, and they stopped in a narrow gully between the crags for him to treat the casualty. There, Phil Probets, who had left the aid post and was also coming down the mountain, ran into them. It was one of those post-battle reunions of old friends, grateful to have survived and know their mates had too. 'It was good to see him again, and we had a bit of the usual banter,' Probets recalled. 'He asked me to pass him a dressing for the casualty he was treating, I bent down to get one out of my Bergen, and there was a massive blast and explosion as a shell crashed in a few yards away.' Onions had heard the whoosh of the shell coming through the air a split second earlier, and hurled himself on top of the casualty on the stretcher to shield him. The explosion threw up stones and dirt that then came raining back down on everyone. Through the falling debris, Onions caught sight of his friend, slumped on the other side of the stretcher. 'I shook him, but he didn't move. I undid the chin strap of his helmet, and the top of his head came off. Blood and brains were dripping down his cheeks. It was obvious there was nothing we could do for him. He was dead.'

Onions was mortified. 'He was a really nice bloke. He wasn't as standoffish to a cook like me as some Paras were. We used to chat a lot.' Probets was devastated too. The blast of the shell had blown him down into a dip and, though concussed, he managed to haul himself back up, to see Tony lying on his back, 'steam coming out from under his helmet'.

Back in the aid post after delivering the casualty he had been carrying to the doctor, Onions sat back against a rock and began to cry. Faulkner saw him and was about to order him, none too politely, to get back up the hill to pick up more casualties, when he was told what had happened. The colour sergeant was shocked. The dead man had been his friend too. 'He'd been one of my corporals in Germany and in Northern Ireland. Just an hour earlier we'd been chatting about how to evacuate casualties from the battlefield. Now he'd been brought back dead. It hit me very hard. He was only twenty-four. What a waste.' All he could do now was help the living, and the one most in need at that moment was the distraught Tom Onions.

Faulkner ordered a brew-up for everyone, and they sat and drank, chewed on hard-tack biscuits and shared their thoughts, all the while with shells still falling around them. Then he gently sent the stretcher team up the hill again to search for more casualties. Onions appreciated this. 'If he'd screamed at me to get up there, I don't think I'd have gone, but because of the caring way he did it I just jumped up as if nothing had happened. We had a job to do and we carried on with it.' It was a while before that job was done, and then Onions and the other bearers were able, at last, to sleep. They had no sleeping bags and so, to keep warm, wrapped themselves in the blankets from their stretchers, ignoring the blood, skin and brains that clung to them.

The aid post sprang to life. Over the radio net, Faulkner heard that a force of enemy helicopters had been spotted coming round the mountain in their direction. Was this a counter-attack getting underway? A cry of 'Argentinians! Take cover!' went up. The colour sergeant stood his ground. 'That was it for me. I'd had enough, I'd seen enough and wasn't going to take any more. They weren't going to kill or maim any more of my blokes.' If the enemy wanted to overrun his aid post, they would have to go through him first. Angry now, he yelled out his orders, forming the medics and stretcher-bearers into a defensive perimeter, circled like a wagon train protecting those on it from Indians.

'I armed everyone from the heap of weapons taken off the dead and wounded, and gave them all their positions and their arcs of fire. I picked up a rifle for myself, though I hadn't fired one in anger in all my eighteen years in the army. After all we'd been through, I felt a sense of satisfaction at the thought of fighting. It was the part of a medic's job we usually didn't do.' He took up a position on a ridge of rocks and saw a platoon of twenty or thirty Argentinians heading towards him, firing as they came. A nervous Onions lay beside him, the stock of a Sterling sub-machine gun rammed into his armpit. He felt exposed and underpowered against the advancing enemy. 'I can probably spit further than this gun

I'm pointing,' he thought to himself. But then Faulkner gave the order to open fire, and the band of medical brothers let loose with everything they had. To Onions, it was a matter of survival – kill or be killed – and he was on to his third magazine before the sergeant told them to cease. Faulkner never discovered how many of the Argentinians died, 'but none of them were left standing when we'd finished'. Then, as if to underline the ambiguity of the situation every medic found himself in, he returned to the aid post and resumed work with the casualties under his care, calmly organizing their evacuation to the field hospitals at Teal Inlet and Ajax Bay.

For Onions, still reeling from the death of Tony as well as his role of machine-gunner in defending the aid post, there was one more hardship to bear. It would be the worst imaginable for him, the most devastating of his whole war.

His closest mate in the Falklands was Steve,[9] an engineer attached to 3 Para. They had spent a lot of time together on the *Canberra* on the journey down but hadn't seen each other since the landings three weeks earlier. Steve came through the aid post, helicoptered in from headquarters and on his way to fix a broken mortar stand in the front line. They had no time to catch up properly. Swapping experiences would have to wait. 'Pop in for a brew when you come back down,' Onions called out as his friend headed up the hill. 'A few moments later I heard a shell hit, followed by screams and a shout for stretcher-bearers. When I got there I found Steve sitting in a crevice in the rock. He'd been hit by shrapnel in the thigh, his artery was split open and blood was pissing out.'

Reliving this moment twenty-five years later, Onions was in despair still, incredulous at the loss, still hurting in places that no living soul could reach. '*He died on my lap*,' he kept repeating, the horror of it spooling through his mind again like a film in which he was once again the callow nineteen-year-old he had been in 1982.

I had my knees and thighs under his head. He was screaming and I gave him morphine, but it was pumping straight out through his leg. He was looking up at me, straight into my eyes. I was telling him, 'You'll be fine, you'll be fine, we'll get through this,' but he was just screaming. And then he calmed down, I stroked his forehead, and he tried to say something, which I couldn't make out. Then, looking to the skies, eyes wide open . . . *he just died on my lap*. I still think about it. I still see it. The images never leave me. It was the fact that we were friends, the fact that I picked him up and the fact that I couldn't stop the bleeding.

Just to the side of the aid post, the padre had begun the sad task of searching through the body bags for the personal effects of the dead.

Onions watched. 'He had done two bags and was physically shaking and crying. I asked if he wanted a hand. I needed to be doing something rather than sitting and thinking about all that had happened. Together, we opened the rest of the bags, and they were not pretty sights. A lot of the bodies were mushed up pretty bad. Some had lost heads, lost limbs, bodies blown apart. In one was a young lad I knew, but what I saw was just a waxy white body. There was nothing left of the person. It wasn't him any more.'

Brian Faulkner came to help out too. 'You look at them,' he recalled of this thankless duty, 'and think, oh God, there's so-and-so, I know his wife, I know his family, his children go to school with my children. You take their wedding rings, watches, photographs, everything. Here is the sad reality of war, thrust right in your face.' Just as with Tom Onions, the images of Mount Longdon would never leave the colour sergeant's mind. 'I still see dead eyes looking at me.' But they don't haunt him – they make him proud. 'It was a tough battle, but we won. Our guys got in there with fist and bayonet, sometimes two lads taking on eight Argentinians. I was proud of them.'

*

The taking of Mount Longdon was the beginning of the end for the Argentinian garrison on the Falklands. The other strategic ridges around Port Stanley were conquered at the same time or over the next three days, and names such as Mount Harriet and Wireless Ridge were added to the battle honours of the Royal Marines, the Scots Guards, the Gurkhas and the Paras. Hundreds of Argentinian soldiers surrendered without a fight, but others resisted to the end. The victory was not easily won.

On Tumbledown, the stretcher-bearers excelled themselves, to the surprise – and then the admiration – of Scots Guard company commander Major John Kiszely. He had, he admitted, gone into the battle with a low opinion of the gaggle of mess barmen and quartermaster's clerks attached to his elite company. A middle-aged lance corporal in the stores attracted his particular fury: the man was certain to be a hindrance rather than a help. 'Then I saw him going forward to pick up casualties. He was standing right out in the open and people were screaming at him to get down. But there was a sergeant he knew out there dying, and nothing was going to stop him getting to him. When I saw how brave he was I felt ashamed. He was a quiet, self-effacing man. He earned his Mention in Dispatches many times over.'[10] More than that, this stretcher-bearer was an inspiration to others. 'Fear is infectious. When the bullets are flying around and everybody is looking to see what the next bloke is doing, if people are hiding or running then that becomes the thing to do. But courage is also infectious. Someone you might have expected to be lying behind the rocks was seen to be doing his duty, and others followed his lead. His bravery was catching.'

Among the most courageous were the helicopter crews who coaxed their machines into the tightest spots to bring out wounded soldiers. Captain Sam Drennan was an Army Air Corps pilot who, along with his co-pilot, Corporal Jay Rigg, had been on plenty of supply and scouting missions around the island but hadn't been near the front line. At their base at Fitzroy, they were now briefed to fly to Tumbledown to pick up casualties. They could see the fireworks erupting on the mountain fifteen miles away. They weren't *ordered* in. Nothing so uncouth. 'The squadron commander simply said that things were not terribly healthy up there,' Drennan recalled, 'the baddies were resisting fiercely, but would we like to *give it a go*? He was wearing his worried face!'[11] It was pitch black, with no moon, and they weren't equipped with night-sights. As they stepped out to their Scout, Drennan thought, 'This is going to be an interesting night!'

Their objective was Goat Ridge, where a Gurkha mortar platoon was dug in. A navy helicopter had already tried to get in, come under fire and retreated. The much smaller Scout would have a better chance going into this cauldron, though it would mean getting further forward on Tumbledown than any helicopter had been so far. As if to underline the point, a missile hurtled past their tail. Drennan skirted down a rocky slope at a snail's pace of 50mph, searching the ground for the casualty they had come to collect. He had it in his mind that he would drop the chopper on to the hillside if another missile locked on to them. 'I'd decided I'd rather break the aircraft by dumping it than have the missile impact blow us to a thousand bits.' He closed his mind to the near-miss shells bursting all around.

They found their landing site, dropped in, and Gurkhas came forward under the rotor blade to put their wounded colleague into the pod on the side. Rigg went outside to supervise the loading. Drennan sat at his controls, fascinated by the puffs of exploding shells getting closer and closer. They lifted off and headed for a nearby ridge, where an injured Scots Guardsman was waiting to be picked up too. Rigg crouched out on the skid as they made the hop through the air, poised to jump off and haul the man aboard the moment they touched down. His life was in the balance. They were dropping into mines and, if they landed on one, then Drennan, the pilot, with armour plating between him and the blast, had a chance, but his co-pilot, out on a limb, would be a dead man. They were lucky, picked up their man, Drennan piled on the power and they scooted for home at top speed. 'As we zoomed over the crest of the mountain, we both gave out a great cheer because we were safe! It was our first time under fire and we were elated: we had broken the duck, lost our virginity! We'd managed to get in and get out again without getting killed.'

And then they turned round after dropping their casualties and went back for more. They felt they had no choice. 'Suppose it was us out there,' Rigg said, 'bleeding to a death on a mountainside, and people were saying they wouldn't come and get us. No, that wouldn't do.' Drennan agreed. 'Some had been lying wounded out there for hours. Some had died, some were dying. What moral alternative did we have? These soldiers, and their families, were relying on us.' He had an extra reason. He was a former Guardsman, and it was his old regiment, the Scots Guards, who were out there on Tumbledown taking a pasting.

Soon the two airmen were back in where the fighting was toughest, on the topmost ridge, with the enemy waiting on the other side. From the ground came warnings to stay away, which they ignored. 'We landed, and Jay jumped off, doing his Audie Murphy bit. We were both high on adrenalin by then. The wounded were being carried to us by big hairy soldiers whose tenderness in looking after their comrades brought a lump to my throat. All the time the bullets were cracking over the top.'

Among those they rescued was Lieutenant Bob Lawrence, who had been felled by a bullet to the head. His medical orderly had wrapped him in bandages to staunch the massive loss of blood and lain on top of him to keep him warm in the bitter cold of that midwinter night. They knew if he drifted into a coma he would probably never wake. He had been waiting for more than two hours to be evacuated and had thought the helicopter would never come. It only did so, he later guessed, 'because Sam Drennan disobeyed orders. He used to be a colour sergeant in the Scots Guards and he'd heard that a number of us had been wounded and that an officer was dying.'

The eight-minute flight to the aid post in the community hall at Fitzroy was a nightmare for the lieutenant. In the hurry to get him on the Scout, he was placed awkwardly in the cabin and, as they took off, his wounded head was exposed to the cold air. Rigg put his own furry hat on him, but it blew away. If he wasn't to freeze to death, they had to move fast. 'We didn't bother with stealth,' Drennan recalled. 'We dived over the side and sank down the mountain as fast as the Scout would go.' They handed Lawrence over and then returned in the Scout to the mountain, nipping from spot to spot between the rocks, picking up whatever casualties they could find. It was, in Drennan's phrase, 'a "bring out your dead" situation, except that our Tumbledown tumbril was for those still living'.

One man had been lost on the mountain for hours and was almost on his last gasp.

We got him on board, and he was just lying there, like a rag doll covered in gore, looking up at Jay with big, frightened, staring eyes. He was in a terrible state. Although it was freezing cold, Jay took off his gloves and held his hand really tight. This poor lad was really holding on – as if he was clinging on to his life. I kept looking back at him and thinking, 'Jesus Christ – I hope he makes it!' Then his eyes went into a look of death, and I thought we'd lose him. But I took a short cut and the Scout flew faster than she'd ever done before. When a man's life is ebbing out of him, every second is vital until the doctors get a needle into him. That probably saved his life.

But willpower played a part too. Indelibly printed on Drennan's mind was the image of his co-pilot holding this dying lad's hand. 'He was willing his strength to go from him into the other guy.' Rigg was twenty-one, the same age as the soldier. 'He had so much life left in him,' the airman explained, 'I couldn't let him die.' And he didn't. He survived. There was never a better explanation for the bravery of all those involved in saving lives in that conflict in the South Atlantic.

★

The surrender of Port Stanley was a relief. As the Argentinian forces laid down their arms and white flags fluttered in the snow, the genuine fear by all concerned that there would be one last – and very bloody – battle for the town ended. Medic Mick Jennings heard the news while treating a casualty in the field hospital at Fitzroy. 'I couldn't help but cheer. Then I looked down at this guy who'd lost a leg to a mine and I thought, "You don't feel like that though, do you?" I put my hand on his shoulder and said to him, "It's because of you that we won this, well done." But it was hardly much consolation to him.'

Para medical officer Steven Hughes was on a ridge looking down on the Falklands capital when news came over the radio that it was all over. He walked away to be on his own and sobbed. 'All the pent-up frustration and suppressed grief was uncapped.'[12] Then a sense of elation took over, his tiredness was gone and he sauntered down the road and into the town, which was now British again.

Then came the cleaning up – and the accounting. Rick Jolly packed up his equipment at Ajax Bay and took one last tour of the rickety old building where hundreds of lives had been saved. Stars shone through the ruined roof. The unexploded bomb that fell there on the third day of the landings – and could have wrecked the entire medical plan before it was even underway – was still in place, embedded in some old pipes. 'The greenish cylinder still looked threatening and evil in the dim light of my torch beam.'

The war to retake the islands cost the lives of 255 British servicemen; a further 777 had been wounded.[13] The death toll could so easily have been many more if it had not been for the brilliant job done by the medics.

The Task Force returned to a jubilant United Kingdom but, among the men who got down in the dirt and the gore to secure victory, there was a more sober and sombre sense of occasion. The horrors they had seen would haunt many of them for a long, long time. More than a quarter of a century later, there are, as medic Phil Probets put it, 'some guys who are still on that mountain'. The war goes on still in the head of stretcher-bearer Tom Onions. 'It's very raw. I haven't come to terms with it. I have nightmares and flashbacks. I cry if I see something about the Falklands and the names of guys I knew are mentioned.' Nothing can wipe away these terrible memories. Whenever he took a bath, Bill Bentley would imagine he was back at Bluff Cove. 'But instead of actually helping the guys who were brought off the *Sir Galahad*, there was a kind of smoke through which I couldn't reach anyone. I was just standing there watching it, incapable of helping.' It hadn't been like that, but the unkind and unforgiving fog of war would cloud many minds in the years ahead.

The medics had seen sights that were an affront to the senses. Andy Poole's worst casualty was a soldier who had lost both his legs to a mine. 'The rest of his body, basically just his torso, was a mess too. We really tried for him, but we lost him. The stretcher he came in on was so badly soaked in his blood that we had to burn it.' Another death had a particularly scarring effect on Ajax Bay medical assistant Tom Howard.

When he was brought in I couldn't believe what I was seeing. He was a handsome, fit young man, and both his legs had been blown off from above the knee joint. The tib and fib were completely stripped of flesh, and the bones splayed outwards. I held his hand, and the only thing I could think to say was, 'Don't worry, we're going to repair the damage, and then you'll be going home.' As we were wheeling him into theatre he called out, 'I want my mother, get my mother.' He was brought out a few minutes later, a blanket pulled over his face. His heart had arrested twice on the table, I was told, and twice he was brought back, but the third time it couldn't be re-started. The doctors found a large fragment of metal that had gone up inside his groin and ripped through all his intestines, liver, and ruptured his right kidney. He was literally blown apart inside. I couldn't believe that people could be so brutal as to have sat down and designed the mine that had done such a thing to this boy. I changed from the fully committed soldier I had been before that to someone who is anti-war. I will never serve again, not even in the reserve.[14]

His pacifism was an understandable reaction to such close-up exposure to war's horrors. But it is only one side of the coin. The eternal enigma of armed conflict is that it brings out the worst in mankind, but also the best. The human spirit is indomitable, the will to live more powerful than the desire to kill, as survivors such as Bob Lawrence would testify. He was the Scots Guard lieutenant lifted off from Tumbledown dying from a bullet wound in his head. When Drennan and Rigg's helicopter dropped him at the Fitzroy field hospital, he was *not* rushed into surgery. He was deemed not to be saveable, and others with a better chance were put ahead of him in the queue for treatment. 'I was there, fully conscious, for three and a half hours,' he remembered, 'because they thought I was going to die and there was no point in working on me. I was awake for all of that. My brain was hanging out and I lost about five and a half pints of blood. I couldn't believe the pain I was in. Had someone said, "If we cut off your arm, your head will stop hurting," I would have let them. But I kept sitting up and talking. People say how brave I was, staying awake and enduring all that pain, but the fact is that I was more frightened of dying, and if I had gone to sleep, I probably would have died.'[15] He did recover, and for that unexpected gift of life he was grateful. 'I lost the use of my left arm, and my left leg is bad, but I'm able to get about. The brain surgery causes me periods of black depression. My biggest disappointment was that I was so badly hurt I would never be a soldier again. But at least I''m alive.'

Such resolve and will to live put added responsibility on medics. In modern warfare, it was becoming less and less acceptable to give up on someone, to let a wounded man slip away, however bad his injuries. The Falklands War was pivotal in this change. The Second World War had been fought with conscript armies amid a consensus that the cause of victory was greater than the survival of any individual. Among the western Allies, human life was not considered as inhumanely cheap as in the Soviet Union's Red Army, where 10 million were consumed on the battlefield, a staggering thirteen times as many as the combined losses of Britain and the USA. But, even so, for the western armies, that war was fought on the assumption of mass casualties. One man's survival was important, but not the priority. By the 1980s, such thinking was no longer appropriate. The modern army was a tight band of professionals, not cannon fodder. Volunteers to a man, they would not fight without the assurance that they would be given *every* chance of getting home in one piece and, if wounded, *every* chance of making a recovery. The priority given to a well-trained, finely honed medical service was the emblem of that guarantee. The Falklands, those far-distant islands that few people in Britain had ever heard of, put medics firmly on the military map. Their vital role in the conflict gave them an esteem they had never been afforded before.

But only those who fought in the Falklands and felt on their faces the chill winds of its battlefields were truly aware of what a close call the conflict had been. It wasn't a case of victory snatched from the jaws of defeat – nothing so simple or melodramatic. Rather, there was so little margin for error in such a long-distance war that defeat was always a distinct possibility, for all the outward bravado of Britain's political and military leaders. As he journeyed home, 3 Para's medical officer John Burgess was conscious that he had with him just half of the eight-man team of medics he had left the UK with. Four were wounded or dead. 'But if circumstances had been slightly different, it could have been an awful lot worse,' he conceded. When, years later, he looked back at the crude conditions they had endured, the war seemed to belong to a different era, one of 'fixed bayonets and two aspirins and a shell dressing'. The replacement medical kit he expected never arrived, they ran out of food and almost out of ammunition. By the time they took Stanley, half the battalion was down with diarrhoea and vomiting.

On the twenty-fifth anniversary of the conflict, surgeon Jim Ryan was shocked to recall how austere and primitive the conditions under which he and all the other medics worked had been, not that different in essence and style, he reckoned, from the Boer War and the First World War. Equipment was limited – Burgess's jest about two aspirins and a shell dressing was uncomfortably close to the truth. There wasn't even an intensive-care unit. 'This was the age before field ventilators and oxygen generators,' Ryan recalled.[16] 'We used paper towels in the absence of any linen and worked with a bare minimum of instruments. The lighting over the operating tables was appalling, sometimes just bare bulbs.' There was no imaging from X-ray machines and body scanners, and laboratory support was confined to typing blood groups. The majority of surgeons were, technically, trainees – not novices, by any means, but yet to complete the nine years of hospital work required in those days to qualify fully in the scalpel trade. Nor had they received much targeted instruction on the arcane requirements of war surgery, apart from the odd secondment to the military wing of Musgrave Park Hospital in Belfast, where army casualties in Northern Ireland were sent. Ryan was not alone in stuffing a well-thumbed copy of Kirby and Blackburn's *Field Surgery Handbook* – 'the military surgeon's bible' – into his tunic pocket and referring to it for guidance when in doubt. Anaesthetists, trained by necessity in foolproof, safety-first procedures in civilian hospitals, had to learn quickly to be less cautious and more open to improvisation than they were used to.

Under the circumstances, they had all done brilliantly. It was the justifiably proud boast of the Ajax Bay medics that they did not lose a single soldier or Marine who arrived at the field hospital alive. Their achievement was all the greater, given that the hospital's role had been intended to be much more of a transitory one. The original plan was that the hospital ship *Uganda* and the sick bay on *Canberra* would be where the bulk of the serious surgery was done. In the event, a shortage of helicopters – largely because a dozen were lost when the container ship *Atlantic Conveyor* was hit by Argentinian Exocets – meant there was no swift and certain evacuation of casualties off the island. Ajax Bay had to double up as both an accident and emergency department and a surgical centre. In all, it handled 722 patients, nearly half of them Argentinians, and carried out more than 200 operations under general anaesthetic.

However, the fact that everyone who reached the hospital survived begged an important question. One hundred and seven British servicemen died in the land battles. Could some of them have been saved if they had arrived on the operating table sooner? The truth was, as Hugh McManners recalled, that 'the marginal cases had already died in the extreme cold and wet while waiting hours (and sometimes days) for evacuation.'[17] A 'buddy care' approach to battlefield casualties, allied to 'scoop and run' evacuation, meant that often those who were first on the scene – such as stretcher-bearers, of whom there were precious few anyway – did not have the medical skills to save the lives of the seriously wounded. In civilian life, ambulance drivers were morphing from chauffeurs with flashing blue lights and a siren into paramedics experienced in dealing with life-threatening emergencies. Clearly, the same development had to happen in the military. The suspicion had to be, too, that those with life-saving surgical skills needed to be closer to the action, if not at the very heart of it, if they were to be more effective.

In the reassessment that followed the conflict, it was clear to some that a new sense of purpose was needed in the whole field of military medicine. McManners was of the controversial opinion that the rethink did not go anywhere near as far as it should have done and that the British infantryman was in fact short-changed in what followed. 'The British army made a number of unfortunate deductions from the Falklands,' he wrote. 'In Vietnam, the US achieved excellent levels of survival through having thoroughly trained medics forward with the fighting troops and getting heli-copters in quickly to evacuate men to surgical hospitals. The British military establishment decided that it could not afford to deploy enough high-grade medics forward with the fighting troops and that, because of the vulnerability of helicopters to ground fire, flying up to the front line to collect casualties was too dangerous. In the Falklands it seemed that the men's own first-aid skills had been enough. It was decided that the high levels of medical aid provided for US troops would not be given to British troops.' Besides, the main theatre of operations, as far as the generals and the politicians were concerned, was still on the plains of northern Germany, where, if the Cold War ever went hot, the first battles with the Soviet Union would be fought. The Falklands had come out of left field and been dealt with, and no one envisaged an out-of-area operation like that happening again in a hurry. Now the army and air force could get back to the front line that really mattered. For the medics, normal service was resumed, treating in-growing toenails in sick bays in Osnabrück and Fallingbostel and, on the surface, everything returned to the way it had been before the successful foray down in the South Atlantic.

Some in the field of military medicine, however, reflecting on what had and what had not been achieved on the long haul to Port Stanley, felt a wind of positive change from the experience, blowing away the cobwebs on accepted practice. 'The Falklands War was a watershed,' declared Ryan. 'Never again would surgical teams operate in disused factories dressed in khaki flannel shirts with no gowns or theatre linen.' Recruitment and training were upgraded. The service went on to a more prized and more professional footing – even if some key questions, such as the easy availability of rescue helicopters, the use of tourniquets[18] and where precisely it was best to locate the 'front-line' surgeons, remained (and remain) matters for continuing debate. Men fighting decades later in Iraq and Afghanistan would benefit more than they would ever know from the tough lessons learned at Goose Green, Bluff Cove and Mount Longdon.

12. Bitter Pills

For army medic Mick Jennings, the lesson of the Falklands was not one of inspiration but of disillusionment. The charred, disfigured bodies of the *Galahad* casualties were imprinted on his mind. 'I hated the way that the war had affected all those young lives. All the way back home to England, I was determined to leave the army.' His plan was to study computer science at night school and build an entirely different career for himself. But, in the end, he couldn't face losing the military camaraderie that had been the centre of his existence since leaving school. He realized how much he would miss 'the lads and the crack', and so he stayed.

In 1990, as a thirty-five-year-old sergeant major, he found himself preparing for war again, for what was billed as 'the Mother of all Battles'. This was going to be as different from the South Atlantic campaign as it was possible to imagine. The battleground was closer by some five thousand miles, hotter by a hundred degrees, and the risk of catching anthrax or tetanus came not from dead sheep but from deadly weapons the enemy were believed to possess. At least British forces were not alone this time. They were part of an international, US-led coalition to seize back the city-state of Kuwait, which the soldiers of the Iraqi dictator Saddam Hussein had overrun, in defiance of the United Nations. A force of hundreds of thousands assembled in the desert to take back what he had stolen.

Saddam's army, it was feared, would not be easy to dislodge. His elite Republican Guards had a reputation for ruthless efficiency, but the biggest danger was that the Iraqi leader would fight back with weapons which the world had dangerously flirted with during the First World War but never dared to exploit fully – chemical and biological ones. If that happened, the coalition forces might have to resort to their own doomsday arsenal of tactical nuclear missiles

– 'dropping a bucket of sunshine' on Saddam, as the squaddies put it. Either way, it seemed a near-certainty that casualties could well be unprecedented in scale and in type. The British medics prepared themselves for a war ranging over long distances – reminiscent of the Desert Rat days in North Africa half a century earlier – involving close fighting on a large scale with the Iraqi army. Armoured field ambulances would go forward to assist the surgical teams attached to each armoured brigade. Casualties would be ferried back as quickly as possible to massive field hospitals in the rear, in Saudi Arabia or on its borders.

For Jennings, the Falklands seemed a puny affair by comparison, its primitive field hospitals and tiny surgical teams old-fashioned and dwarfed by the massive medical operation now swinging into action in safe areas far away from the front line. The make-and-mend days of Ajax Bay were gone. A system as extensive and layered as any civilian hospital trust was in place and, with his rank, Jennings found himself more of an administrator than a medic. The only casualties he ended up actually treating were troops with burns from over-enthusiastic sunbathing. But over the whole enterprise hung an air of menace – the possibility of attacks spreading choking, blistering phosgene gas or, worse still, disease-laden bugs. The fear was very real, Jennings recalled. 'It wasn't a game. When the Scud missiles were flying, we really did expect to be hit by this stuff and to be dealing with mass casualties.' Medics – including, for the first time in a front-line position, women – were busy sticking needles containing cocktails of prophylactic drugs into arms and thighs. Everyone drilled in cumbersome NBC (nuclear, biological and chemical) protective suits and respirators. They were issued with syringes of anti-nerve-gas serum to inject themselves with in the event of a chemical attack.

The size of the medical teams deployed was an indication of how seriously the threat was being taken. Reservists were called up. Hundreds of musicians, including the RAF's renowned dance band, the Squadronaires, stowed away their trombones and clarinets and switched to stretcher-bearing. Along with Puma helicopters, they would be a vital link in the evacuation chain from front-line dressing stations to a base in Saudi Arabia and then back to the UK. The system was geared up to shift 1,600 casualties a day if necessary, with non-stop streams of helicopters and Hercules transporters. For RAF nurse Frank Mincher, who joined up after the Falklands, the nearest he had expected to come to front-line action was when he was posted to the Greenham Common air base, which was under siege by women camped at its edge in a prolonged protest against cruise missiles. The first Gulf War changed that. 'We expected mass casualties. I heard a worst-case figure of thirty thousand.'

If it came to this, then Andy Smith, another post-Falklands medical recruit to the RAF, would be better prepared than most. As part of the 'crash and smash' team called to the scene of aircraft accidents to, literally, pick up the pieces, he was intimately aware of the gruesome side of the business. Down on his hands and knees, combing through scattered wreckage for human remains, was a hard and hardening experience for a nineteen-year-old. 'High-speed crashes make an awful mess of bodies. The biggest thing you're likely to find is half a femur or half a skull. We had to pick up as much as we could before the birds got them, and lay them out on a tarpaulin.'[1] Sometimes the bodies were those of people he'd known. 'Perhaps you'd done their aircrew medical a few days before and chatted to them, and now you were picking up tennis-ball-size bits of their body. I once found a glove with the hand still inside. It wasn't nice. You learn very quickly about the fragility of life.' Here was a side of a medic's duties few realized, a world away from the relative glamour of saving lives.

Smith had moved on to more advanced work by the time the Gulf crisis blew up and was fully trained for medical emergencies. Lying in his tent reading one day, a massive explosion seemed to be the start of all he feared. 'I thought it was a mortar attack or an IED [improvised explosive device – a bomb]. I grabbed my medical snatch bag and ran towards the sound of screaming.' In the kitchen, a pressure cooker had blown apart, and one of the chefs was badly hurt. 'His arm was hanging off, held on by two inches of skin at the elbow. I put a line in and got some fluids into him.

He also had bits of metal in his leg.' To Smith, it seemed like a dress rehearsal. Much worse lay ahead, surely? Everyone was on edge with expectation.

In the early hours of a January morning in 1991, the first planes took off into the dark desert sky and headed for Baghdad. 'It' was on, and nobody could be sure what had just been unleashed. One pilot remembered sitting in his cockpit, the engines firing, and wondering whether he was about to initiate World War III.[2] At the RAF hospital in Bahrain, the commander calmed his young team of WRAF medics, but the prayers of the chaplain put the fear of God into some of them. Air-raid warnings sounded, and they took cover in sand-bagged shelters wearing protective suits, rubber gloves, respirators, boots and helmets. The charcoal in the suits turned their skin as black as coalminers'; the claustrophobia turned their stomachs.

Five weeks of air bombardment paved the way for the ground attack, a massive onslaught in which thousands of vehicles sped across the desert, meeting very little resistance. Experienced Territorial Army surgeon David Rew, ex-SAS and ex-Para reservist, boarded a Bedford field ambulance and took his place towards the front of the column as part of the unfortunately acronymed Forward Advanced Resuscitation Team – FART for short, though the name was quickly changed. 'Our role was not to get into anything complex with casualties but to stop bleeding, clear airways, all the basics so they could be transported back to the field hospitals.'[3] He didn't feel he was doing anything radically new. Surgeons, he knew, had operated this far forward in the desert battles in North Africa in the Second World War. 'The instruments don't change, nor does the anatomy and the physiology. Back in the 1940s they were in Austin trucks, whereas we were in Bedfords, and they had glass bottles for blood transfusions rather than plastic bags, and wooden stretchers instead of gurneys. Everything else was pretty much the same.'

There was some truth in this when applied to far-ranging desert warfare and special operations, as the adventures of RAMC doctor Lieutenant Malcolm Pleydell behind the German lines in Libya in

1942 showed.[4] But the battlefield order in the Second World War had generally placed the most experienced doctors well to the rear. It was from the Falklands that the lesson had been learned that quick access to the best medical care was the key to saving lives. Now it was deemed right for someone of Rew's seniority to be pushed well forward. This, however, didn't apply to more than a handful of doctors. It was still considered prudent to concentrate the bulk of the surgical resources well behind the lines, in hospitals geared up to receive large numbers of casualties. But Rew's FART, out rounding up casualties rather than waiting for them to be delivered, was the blueprint for the MERT (Medical Emergency Response Teams) of the future.

In reality, they had little to do in that first Gulf war, which quickly turned into a rout of Saddam's reluctant-to-fight soldiers. Coalition casualties were few and mainly came from booby traps left in deserted Iraqi bunkers. They were generally helicopptered straight to hospital, before Rew's team, chasing to catch up with the fast-moving attack force, got anywhere near them. For all the drama of being close to the front line – and on one occasion even straying ahead of it into the enemy's line of fire – Rew had little to do. 'I saw lots of desert, lots of tents, lots of burnt-out tanks and lots of Iraqis surrendering,' he recalled. 'But the only surgery we did in the whole of the four-day ground war was a single Iraqi soldier with multiple fragment wounds in his legs. There was no helicopter immediately available to evacuate him, so we parked three ambulances around to form a little amphitheatre, laid out a stretcher table, put the chap to sleep, debrided his wounds and cleaned up his legs.'

It fell to Andy Smith to see the full horrors of that war. As the Iraqi army abandoned Kuwait and retreated back across the desert to its own borders, it was pounded from the air. The road to Basra became a highway of destruction and death, littered with bodies and wrecked vehicles. Burnt and twisted corpses leaned out of the turrets of armoured cars in macabre poses. Smith was in a team following behind this trail of devastation when he saw an Iraqi running towards him. 'I pulled out my pistol and cocked it. I was a second away from shooting him when I realized that he was trying to give us a present. He was trying to trade his video recorder for his life. I calmed him and handed him over to the Military Police at a checkpoint down the road. I suppose you could say I actually captured an Iraqi – not what you'd expect when you're a medic, is it?'

The experience disturbed him. 'I'd always wanted to be in a battle, ever since I joined up, but coming that close to actually killing somebody really scared me. I still think about that now, seventeen years later, and I'm glad I didn't shoot him. Of course, I could have been wrong. If he'd been carrying a bomb or a weapon, I could have been dead.' It was a life-or-death decision that, in the years ahead, many British soldiers would face as they battled phantom armies of guerrillas and insurgents who were indistinguishable from the civilian populations they emerged out of and melted back into. In the wars of the future, the humanitarian streak that ran through medics such as Andy Smith and was the basis of their calling would be severely put to the test.

*

Tim Hodgetts did not make the cut for the Gulf war. A junior doctor in the RAMC, he had to remain behind in the UK, stuck in a dreary posting in Northern Ireland while the vast majority of his colleagues were shipped to the Middle East. Yet it was in cold, murky Belfast rather than the hotspot of Arabia that he would be inspired to begin the process of transforming the army's medical services, fitting them for the wars of the twenty-first century.

He was sitting in the officers' mess of the military wing at Musgrave Park Hospital in Belfast in November 1991 watching the rugby world cup final between England and Australia on television when a Semtex bomb planted by the IRA in a service tunnel exploded, devastating the staff social club. The ground floor collapsed into the basement. Not only were casualties trapped in the rubble amid fire and smoke, but the facilities to treat them, namely the emergency and resuscitation departments, had been wiped out. Hodgetts, though junior in rank, was the most senior clinician present. He took charge, commandeering equipment and rooms in the adjacent civilian wards and treating casualties on the spot because of fears that evacuating them might lead them into more danger from booby traps or snipers.

For five hours he directed operations, working out what he had to do as he went along, because, as he rapidly discovered, there was no emergency plan in the event of the hospital's own facilities being out of action. Though two soldiers were killed and eleven other people injured, he did a good job. But, as he saw it, not good enough. His mind was made up: firstly, he wanted to specialize in emergency medicine; and, secondly, he wanted to set up comprehensive procedures and train others how to deal with similar extreme situations. Musgrave Park had become, in essence, a battleground that day. The lessons from the bombing could carry over into casualty treatment anywhere. Emergency medicine as a separate discipline for military doctors was soon to become a priority. No longer would the assumption be that general surgeons and physicians could just turn their hands and their skills to dealing with battlefield injuries when necessary. Military medicine not only needed a distinct training all of its own but a set-up with its own specialist casualty department to respond to emergencies.

It was a philosophy that, to begin with, was at odds with prevailing military thinking. Military medicine was going through one of its all-too-frequent periods of retrenchment. With Saddam supposedly back in his box, this was seen as a time to adjust to the post-Cold War world that had emerged from the collapse of the Soviet empire, to cash in the so-called 'peace dividend'. Defence needs were reviewed, spending slashed, regiments merged, redundancies demanded. Just as they had been in the aftermath of the First World War three quarters of a century earlier, and then again after the Second World War, the medical services took a major hit. Among the casualties were the specialist military hospitals, all of which were phased out, and hundreds of medics, who were made redundant or relegated to the reserve list. It was a short-sighted policy that would have a disastrous effect on the all-embracing nature of the military medical services for years to come.

The shortcomings of this policy of wholesale axing and down-grading of military medicine were soon exposed. Events in the Balkans revealed that 'history' had not ended – as some over-optimistic western political philosophers argued[5] – and nor had war. War was not over but changing from being played out on a world stage to a localized one. Conflicts would be smaller but, given the historic enmities involved, more vicious and more bloody than ever, and laid-off medics were wanted again to deal with the suffering. Not only that but the nature of these conflicts demanded focussed medical services. The time was right for Hodgett's radically reorganized casualty system.

It swung into action with the NATO military intervention in Kosovo in 1999, a peace and policing action to curb Serb-inspired ethnic cleansing. The countryside was mountainous, rugged and remote and, as a consequence, evacuation slow and unreliable. For the first time, armoured field ambulances going out to casualties, whether military or civilian, were tooled up to the same high standard as those on the streets of Britain. In the back, instead of just bare racks for stretchers and a few bandages, were defibrillators, suction equipment, splints, drugs, monitoring machines, plus the paramedics trained up to use them. The field hospital had its own casualty unit, with triage area and specialist resuscitation rooms. Its first patient was a local man with broken legs and a smashed chest who had been beaten up with an iron bar and left by the road to die. Friends brought him in, and he lived.

Over the next few months, more than a thousand cases were treated and two hundred and fifty operations performed, more than half of them on civilians. Military doctors and nurses found themselves dealing with injuries unseen by British medics for almost a generation – not since the Falklands, in fact. There were gunshot and stab wounds to deal with, as well as the horrendous consequences of mines, grenades and cluster bombs. A fourteen-year-old boy lost a hand and a leg after picking up a cluster bomb. A six-year-old threw a stone at a mine, which exploded and hurled shrapnel into his legs and abdomen. A farmer trod on a mine when crossing his own field. All these were the rotten fruits of war. But there was routine work to do as well, such as injuries from road accidents. Unusual for a military hospital was a servicewoman's acute ectopic pregnancy.

The doctors learned to improvise. When a local teenager needed an emergency operation to amputate both his legs, it was discovered that one surgical saw had broken on the previous patient and the only other one the unit possessed was blunt. A carpenter's hacksaw, suitably sterilized, did the job. Then, when a heavy weight was required to put a pelvic fracture in traction, a dumbbell was lifted from the soldiers' gym.[6]

Decision-making was speedy because, as a matter of policy, the casualty department was manned by surgeons and anaesthetists of consultant status rather than by junior doctors. The result was that seriously injured patients could be on the operating table within fifteen minutes of coming through the hospital door, something that was almost unheard of in civilian hospitals, where the ranking consultant is generally at the end of the chain, not at its start. For Hodgetts, the lesson was clear and a new model established – 'seniority saves lives.'

The knowledge gained from all this activity was invaluable. This hard disk of experience – the 'institutional military medical memory', to use Hodgett's phrase – would be there to draw on in bloodier conflicts in other regions in the years ahead. What saved lives in the backstreets of Pristina, the Kosovo capital, would in the future be replicated in Iraqi villages and on the barren plains of Afghanistan. Hodgetts could see that, at the very end of the twentieth century, the nature of conflict was changing, and medics would have to adapt to these new realities. For one thing, their basic brief would be wider than ever before. In the Falklands, almost all the casualties the doctors dealt with were military personnel from either side; the same applied to the first Gulf war. But, in Kosovo, it was civilians, particularly children and old people, who were increasingly in the firing line, and not accidentally, as the result of being caught in crossfire, but as the deliberate targets of attacks and genocidal mass killings. Injuries were rarely minor. A common terror tactic was to throw a grenade into a house full of people, and the result of such unconscionable violence in a confined space was that the wounds of the few who survived were likely to be extreme.

The deaths of youngsters could be horrible to witness, even for the likes of Private Peter Keegan, a combat medical technician with a Territorial Army unit of the Royal Green Jackets. He was an experienced medic who'd served in a crash team in the Balkans before and had seen his share of horrors. Life's hardships were second nature to him – he had decided to make a career in medicine when, aged thirteen, he had found his father nearly dead from a whisky and pills overdose. But what he now witnessed would shake him to the core.

Within hours of arriving in Pristina for a six-month tour, he and his ambulance crew were called to an area of waste ground where two children, a brother and sister, the boy nine, the girl twelve, had been killed by a mine. The details of the scene were disturbingly unforgettable. 'Her hair was curly, his brown and in need of a trim. The mine had exploded between them, and each had one side of their body blown off, from head to foot. The curious thing was that the remaining half looked normal. The little girl was wearing jeans and a little summer top, the boy a T-shirt and trainers. It was a bizarre scene. I expected to see body parts scattered around, but there was nothing there.'[7] As he bagged the remains of these two children, Keegan felt saddened by the sheer pointlessness of it all. 'I tried not to let it affect me personally, but these are the realities you face as a medic.' He took them to the overflowing mortuary in a local hospital. 'There were so many bodies. The fridges weren't working because there was no electricity, and the stench of rotting meat was beyond imagination. It was a real eye-opener for my first day in Kosovo, but worse was to follow.'

When he got back to his company headquarters, a fellow soldier took him down into the cellar. The building had previously been occupied by Serbian police and had an underground torture chamber. 'There were shackles and chains on the walls, blood all over the floor and human heads stacked in a corner, half a dozen of them, all of young men. We found a sword and handed it over to the United Nations police.'

More than half a century earlier, British medics had had to confront the unspeakable horrors of the Belsen concentration camp in Nazi Germany when they were called in to nurse the survivors after its liberation. Now, one of their successors was facing sickening evidence of yet more genocidal atrocities in the very heart of a now supposedly civilized Europe.

*

A dozen years after his thrilling 1991 dash towards the Iraqi border, David Rew found himself back in the same place, suffering inside a suffocating NBC 'Noddy' protection suit. A second Gulf war was about to explode. Like the rest of the world, Rew had watched on television the terror attack on the Twin Towers in New York in 2001, and he had known then that there would be an accounting to come. In the civilian hospital where he worked, he expressed his instinctive view that another war was on the cards. 'People looked at me very strangely,' he recalled.

The direction the American-led retaliation took did surprise him, however. Afghanistan, home to Al Qaeda and the Taliban, was an understandable first target. But then the Bush administration turned its big guns on the old enemy, Saddam Hussein, once more. The opinion Rew had formed of the Iraqi dictator back in 1991 was that he was a paper tiger whose only concern was personal survival. He was sceptical about claims that Saddam was about to unleash weapons of mass destruction. Nonetheless, in 2003, here he was back at a field hospital in northern Kuwait, hurriedly throwing on his IPE (Individual Protection Equipment) kit, pulling on the mask, checking the colour of the chemical-detection paper stitched to the outside – and hoping not to collapse from heatstroke. 'We were in and out of the gear regularly, and had it on for a full five hours on one particular alert. I had to treat thirty-two people for heat exhaustion. In many ways, the equipment was worse than the threat!'

The signal for an incoming Scud missile was the rhythmic

sounding of a car horn, and the camp was so nervy that, more than once, the warning beep from a reversing lorry sent everyone into a panic. 'Gas! Gas! Gas!' went up the cry, and they would all rush to mask up. Bob Steer, one of the many Territorial Army medics called up, was told in pre-deployment training that twenty minutes was the maximum period a body could stand being in a full NBC kit. 'But on our very first day I sat in a trench with mine on for something like six or seven hours. Scuds were supposed to be on their way. We were told one had hit another camp and a yellow mist had exploded out of it.'

But there were lighter moments too. At Camp Coyote in Kuwait, where a two-hundred-bed tented hospital was set up, Philip Rosell, an army surgeon, was out jogging, wearing ski goggles to keep the dust out of his eyes. From a billet he passed came the wonderful jazz strains of a Blue Brothers number, but it was not a record that was washing out and over him but the real thing – live music. Military bandsmen had arrived to take up their fighting role as stretcher-bearers and medical orderlies but were keeping their hand in with a jamming session. The insane incongruity of it all tickled him. 'I was getting my very own blues concert while running in ski goggles in a war zone – such a strange sensation.' He felt as if he had dropped into a scene of madness and mayhem from *M*A*S*H*.

The medical set-up for this second bite at Saddam Hussein embodied all the advances and alterations in approach that had been proposed and debated over the past decade. The consensus was that the vast majority of soldiers who died in combat would do so within ten minutes or so of being injured, their wounds so severe they were unsaveable. For the rest, there was generally a window of two to three hours in which they could be treated – for the bullet to be removed or the haemorrhaging lesion to be stitched. So surgeons from a wide array of disciplines were ordered into forward positions, and the first field intensive care units were set up under canvas so that even complex cases could be handled close to the battlefield and not only at some remote hospital far behind the lines. Each forward surgery team had a dozen light lorries and could pack up and move on to a new location at great speed. The first Gulf war had shown that it was perfectly feasible for the battlefront to advance sixty miles or more in a day, and the medics had to keep up. They also had to be flexible in their approach. If casualties could easily be evacuated, then their job might simply be to clamp an artery or bandage an abdominal wound and leave it to the surgeons at the main field hospital to do the complex work. But if they were in remote areas and sandstorms grounded the casevac helicopters, they had to be prepared to handle difficult cases, for days on end if necessary.

For David Rew, the developments were historic. 'We were taking a quantum leap. The old-style field hospitals were designed for quick and dirty surgery. Now we had forward positioning of very high levels of skill and equipment to give the guys with major wounds the best chance of survival.' It was the proper response to a new type of warfare. Until the late nineteenth century, wars had usually been fought out like board games between opposing sets of combatants on a small battlefield. The twentieth century saw total war between nations, with the full engagement of large armies and civilian populations. Post-Cold War modern warfare, however, tended towards small, geographically precise engagements and policing actions, complex in structure, often with more than two opposing sides and including irregular militias and small groups of insurgents.

For medical planners, this was a new world. 'You no longer get a whole battalion wiped out from an artillery strike, as you did in the First World War, or twenty thousand casualties in a day on the Somme. Or even a mass attack such as D-Day. Today's battlefields are widely dispersed, with relatively few individuals in any one place and generally taking injuries in small numbers.' But the greatly enhanced power of modern weapons, particularly in deliberately targeted anti-personnel explosives such as mines, IEDs and suicide bombs, meant the wounds were likely to be serious. 'So, whereas, before, we as medics had to do the minimum for the most,' Rew explained, 'now it was a case of doing the maximum for the few. If a vehicle is blown up, there are three or four bad casualties, who need instant, intensive treatment. We're taking incredible expertise into the field now, and the expertise is not any one individual surgeon but multiple surgeons with different skills, A & E specialists and anaesthetists.'

Among those who found themselves moving further to the front than they had ever expected was RAF Flight Sergeant Frank Mincher, a trained casualty nurse. He took his place on a rescue helicopter with a new-fangled Immediate Response Team. It meant completely rethinking how he did his job. Procedures usually carried out in the calm sanctuary of a hospital ward would have to be done in the cabin of a fast-moving Puma. In the air, he put a drain into the chest of a badly hurt Iraqi. He, like most other medics in the second Gulf war, cut his teeth on injured and sick civilians, because there were so few military casualties. The American advance was rapid, the resistance slight. Baghdad fell in little more than a fortnight.

The British contingent's role was to secure the southern section of the country around the city of Basra, and Tim Hodgetts, now an RAMC colonel, was in the back of a blacked-out ambulance following the troops across the border into Iraq. They were better equipped for the job than any medics before them had ever been, but he still felt exposed. Though he had access to a mobile X-ray machine and an ultrasound scanner, the nearest CT scanner capable of giving the best picture of internal injuries was hundreds of miles away, and he had no neurosurgeon or burns specialist. As for his two surgical teams, they could easily be swamped by a run of casualties. He remembered feelings of frustration and apprehension. Just staying alive was an effort in the desert, with the heat, the restriction on water, and food out of army-issue packets, but he and his men had to be able to perform to the highest standard, however austere the conditions.

In the event, just as with the first Gulf war twelve years earlier, the fighting never reached the intensity that had been feared. There were notable acts of bravery, however. Trooper Chris Finney of the Blues and Royals, just eighteen and a soldier for less than a year, was driving a Scimitar armoured car in action against enemy armour when it was mistakenly attacked by coalition fighter planes. He escaped, but then turned to see that his gunner was trapped in the turret. Finney went back through flames, smoke and exploding ammunition to rescue his wounded friend and to get him away, as the planes roared in, spraying cannon shot at him for a second time. He also tried to save the driver of another armoured car, despite now being wounded himself. Another soldier was saved by his Kevlar helmet. His Land Rover turned over and fell in such a way that only his helmet stopped it crushing him. Incredibly, it took the weight of the vehicle as he lay underneath for nearly an hour waiting to be rescued.

And there were deaths. Kosovo veteran Peter Keegan, with experience of handling the dead, was given the job of mortuary technician and received his first body shortly after the invasion began. 'I unzipped the bag, and the whole of his body was burned beyond recognition. But then I saw a tattoo on his leg and I recognized him as a mate I served with in Kosovo. It was a shock, but this is what you see when you are a medic.' Andy Poole, who had served in the Falklands, was another mortuary worker, and recalled the sight of burnt and headless bodies from the fighting. Amputated legs and arms were also brought to him to be tagged and bagged.

The conquest of Basra and the surrounding region was relatively trouble-free, though not without moments of dread. One ambulance driver remembered approaching Basra airport, where serious opposition was expected, in the dead of night. In the back of his mind was the thought that his 'wagon' wouldn't stand a chance if it was hit by a rocket, and nor would he. Certainly, the red crosses painted prominently on the sides and roof were going to offer no protection. Frank Mincher was helicoptered into the scene of a 'friendly fire' incident and, though an experienced A & E nurse, shuddered at the awfulness of the injuries he saw that day. 'I'd seen nothing on that scale before.'

Generally, the most harrowing task for the medics was dealing with the terrible injuries sustained by children. Keegan transferred to hospital work and was moved by the plight of a little Iraqi girl, with lovely dark skin and beautiful big brown eyes, who had stood on a mine. 'She had lost her left leg below the knee and was in a lot of pain. I talked to her as I changed her dressing, and a little smile of gratitude came on to her face. I found that very rewarding. It made my work as a medic worthwhile.' A corporal driving back to the hospital found his way blocked by a group of distressed local people around a car. He got out and saw the limp figure of an eight-year-old boy on the bonnet, with gunshot wounds in his stomach. His father called frantically to the medic: 'Help my son, please help him.' It took half an hour to reach the hospital but, to the soldier, sitting with the boy in the back of the blisteringly hot ambulance, and watching as this little life slipped away, time was achingly slow. 'His father kept asking me, "Is he dead? Is he dead?"'[8] But there was nothing more the soldier could do.

TA medic Staff Sergeant Bob Steer opened the rear doors of an ambulance that had just arrived at the hospital to find an entire Iraqi family, 'a lad, a baby, a mum and dad', inside. Their house had been hit in a bombing raid. 'The baby was burnt to a cinder, dead. The boy had had his arm blown off. It was my first real experience of major trauma and, though I had trained for situations like this, it knocked the stuffing out of me. I can still see the image of that family.'

Lieutenant Colonel Paul Parker, a surgeon in one of the close-support operating teams, treated two small boys, brothers, both with terrible, suppurating leg injuries. Their distraught father did not want his five-year-old son's leg amputated. 'That was very emotional,' Parker recalled, 'especially when you have kids of your own, as I did. But I knew I had to amputate. If I didn't he would die of infection. These are tough decisions, because you have to make them pretty much on your own. You are out in the field, miles from anywhere and you just have to get on and do it.' This burden of responsibility was why he believed front-line doctors had to be experienced. A war zone, where decisions came thick and fast and the price of dithering could be an unnecessary death, was no place for juniors with L-plates.

Parker felt the hand of history on his shoulder, linking him to an illustrious past, when, near Basra, in a cemetery by the River Tigris, he discovered the grave of a pioneering and reforming military doctor, Sir Victor Horsley. A major in the RAMC in the First World War, he did important work at Gallipoli, and then in Mesopotamia. He had been years ahead of his time, declaring his wish to get as near to the front line in any conflict as he could, because 'there is no doubt that one can be of most use the nearer to the firing line, as the worst cases are the most difficult.'[9]

That Parker was even able to make this journey into the Iraqi countryside to honour a long-dead medical hero was significant. It meant that in the immediate aftermath of the successful invasion of Iraq and the downfall of Saddam, there was a semblance of peace. One soldier recalled the joy of being welcomed as liberators by the local population. 'Children lined the streets waving and hoping for ration packs of sweets and biscuits that we tossed to them.' Parker felt safe enough to put on his lycra shorts and go jogging outside the camp, exposed and unprotected apart from sunblock. The locals waved, and he would wave back. The smiles, though, would not last.

*

Though Baghdad had fallen, Saddam was in hiding, and the then US president George W. Bush had declared the war was over, medic Bob Steer was taking no chances. He was in a convoy motoring from Basra – where the British forces were now digging in – to the town of Al-Amarah to pick up a nurse and escort her back to base. This being his first time out on patrol, he decided to wear body armour, much to the amusement of the driver of his soft-skinned Snatch Land Rover, a laid-back Liverpool lad who, in the intense heat, preferred the ease of a thin T-shirt. As they drove through the desert, Steer sweltered 'like a stuck pig', but was still reluctant to chill out. He jammed his helmet tightly on his head and clung on to the rifle he had just been issued with. He had the last laugh. 'We were in the middle of nowhere and passing an old burnt-out tank when somebody opened up with a Kalashnikov. Bullets whizzed over the top of us.' The driver hurled himself down into the well beneath the dashboard, and the vehicle swerved from side to side as he tried to steer, unseen and unseeing, from the floor, with just one hand above his head on the wheel. Steer tried to crawl into the back to return fire but was stopped short by the bulkiness of his body armour. By the time he freed himself, they were past the danger point. The ambush, brief and, on this occasion, bloodless, was over. But it was a sign of a changing situation.

A new and deadly war was beginning. The conquest of Iraq had been pretty much a free ride for the coalition. The cost of hanging on in there to stabilize this benighted country and perhaps help it towards democracy would be enormous.

13. Under Siege

For British troops in their fortified camps in the southern Iraq provinces of Maysan and Basra in the summer of 2003, each day's dawn was signalled by ritual recitations from the Koran amplified from the minaret of a nearby mosque, followed by the rapid crackle of AK47s. In the early days of the British occupation, the guns were fired into the air by local men as a daily demonstration of joy at the demise of Saddam Hussein, long hated in this region of marshland, waterways and oil wells two hundred miles from Baghdad. The soldiers were irritated at being woken from their sleep in this way, but also concerned. The indiscriminate loosing off of volley after volley indicated that the local population had no shortage of either guns or ammunition. The question was: how much longer would they be content to aim them harmlessly over their own heads?

The truth was that, very quickly, the British presence came to be resented. The people in this area had a fierce tradition of independence. They had been unusual in defying Saddam over the years, and had been persecuted by him as a result. They had thrown out his ruling Ba'athist party in the very first days of the invasion, and chased away his soldiers days before the British even arrived. They were not grateful for being liberated, because – as they saw it – they had liberated themselves. And now – as they saw it – they were under occupation. All too soon the early-morning fusillades began to represent anger, not joy. However, it would take some serious casualties before the politicians calling the shots on the coalition side grasped that the mood had changed and that the isolated, under-strength and under-equipped British contingent was facing a growing insurgency.

What began with graffiti and stone-throwing turned into gun-slinging and full-scale fighting in a frighteningly short space of time. It was the way in this part of the world. Iraq, as historian Richard Holmes explained, was not only dangerous and unpredictable, but 'its stark, shocking violence is binary, full on or full off, often with little warning that the switch has flicked.'[1] Six military policemen, soft red berets on their heads rather than hard hats, and only lightly armed, for a friendly, hearts-and-minds visit to the civilian police chief in the town of Majar al-Kabir, were caught out by the mood swing. A mob turned on them and butchered them in cold blood. A platoon of paratroopers on a separate mission in the town was outgunned in a fierce firefight and barely managed to escape. A Chinook helicopter sent into the town on a rescue mission was forced away by rocket grenades, narrowly missing crashing into overhead electricity lines as the pilot piled on the power and pulled away from trouble. A hundred bullet holes shredded its armourless skin, and seven of the twenty-man quick-reaction force on board were hit. Back at base, a bullet was found just inches from the gearbox. If the aircraft had been brought down, there would have been little chance of survivors.

Territorial Army medic Bob Steer was waiting at the helipad with four ambulances when the Chinook arrived back. His job was to guide it smoothly in. 'I could see it way out in the distance, then it came straight on and did what I can only describe as a handbrake turn on to the landing site. The pilot ignored my signals and just got her down fast.' This was an emergency. 'The ramp went down, and the loadmaster frantically signalled us forward. Inside was complete carnage, with Paras yelling and screaming, and blood and guts everywhere.' All the casualties he had received until now had come in ones and twos, and generally been stabilized and sedated by the time they reached him. But this was a job lot of frightened boys with fresh wounds, suffering badly. The half-mile drive to the base hospital was nightmarish, and remembered by him as testing in the extreme. The casualties were handed over to the A&E trauma team, and Steer stayed to help, putting up drips and taking blood pressures. 'I was glad to be doing my job, being part of a team.'[2]

The Majar al-Kabir incident in June 2003 was glossed over. To the anger of the squaddies (and the families of the dead men), the murder of the six Red Caps went unpunished, subsumed by the political imperative of trying to remain at peace with the local populace. But it was a pointer for the future. The days of relaxed patrolling were over. Helmets went back on heads, body armour was routinely donned, and rifles were cocked as the British forces increasingly became an army under siege. Deaths and injuries would rise inexorably in the coming years and, by the time the British garrison withdrew in the spring of 2009, a total of 179 troops had come home in body bags and more than 400 suffered serious battle wounds.

Sergeant Major Dave Falconer of the 1st battalion of the Princess of Wales's Royal Regiment – who were dispatched to Iraq in 2004 – gave a solemn, and deeply important, promise to his men that, if they were wounded, he would personally come and rescue them. At the end of every pre-battle briefing session, like an old-fashioned police sergeant sending his officers out on the beat with a cheery 'And be careful out there . . .', he reassured them with his pledge: 'I will get you out.' He converted a Warrior tracked troop carrier into his own ambulance, with stretchers, oxygen, intravenous fluids, chest seals, dressings, morphine and painkillers, plus a medic in the back to administer them. Whenever the call came that one of his men was down, he would race to the scene in minutes. 'The soldiers needed to know that, when things went wrong, I would be there, through thick and thin,' he explained, 'that I was going to get them off the ground and back down the chain.'[3] It was this assurance that sent them into battle with the confidence to give of their best.

But being in a Warrior was no guarantee of safety, as Sergeant Adam Llewellyn was to discover. By now, a full-scale insurrection had taken hold, orchestrated by the so-called Mahdi army of Shia militiamen which had collected around a militant ayatollah, once an opponent of the Sunni Saddam, now an implacable enemy of the *kafirs* (non-Muslims) occupying what he saw as his holy land. Virtually every patrol that went out was being ambushed. What the military theorists were describing as asymmetric warfare, between forces of totally different sizes, with no fixed lines and an irregular enemy concealing itself among a host population, was being enacted in every town and along every highway. Its weapons were not those of mass destruction but small, precisely targeted and very effective.

Majar al-Kabir, where the Red Caps had died, had become a complete no-go area. In Al-Amarah, the provincial capital of Maysan, the soldiers were tasked to take back the streets and reassert the authority of the tottering coalition-backed civilian authorities. They set out from the aptly named Camp Cherokee into Indian country. In his Warrior, Llewellyn was standing in his turret, the last but one in a line of vehicles driving slowly through the town, when a small boy, no more than ten years old, he reckoned, darted from cover and hurled a petrol bomb. It smashed on the front of the troop carrier, and the flaming fuel exploded around the sergeant. His screams pierced the air, and he jumped to the ground, rolling around, on fire and panic-stricken.

The sight was terrifying. The rest of the patrol ran to help him, doused the flames and, mindful of the possibility of follow-up sniper fire, bundled him into the back cabin of his Warrior. His mate, Sergeant Chris Broome, tried to ease his burns with water, but the inside of the Warrior was so hot that the scalding liquid just burned his skin even more. 'I gave him morphine, but it didn't seem to work. His screams were going right through me. His shirt was completely burnt from his arms, and the skin was hanging off in a terrible mess. His hands were just raw flesh.' Above them, the turret was still blazing, and the flames were beginning to lick towards the Warrior's ammunition locker. Broome broke off to put out the fire with an extinguisher and then returned to his badly injured mate, comforting him as best he could before they were taken to safety. It would be many painful skin grafts later before Llewellyn was anywhere close to recovery. His hands and arms were unusable for a long time.

The fact that a child had been responsible for such devastating injuries angered the troops. Major James Coote had to calm first himself, then his men. 'We had been stoned by kids before, seen gunmen using women and children as human shields and as weapons carriers, but this was the first time someone had sent a child to physically attack us. My initial reaction was to go back in and hand out some retribution, but that would have undermined what we were there to do. After a few difficult talks to my soldiers, we went back into the area as peacefully as we could.'⁴

Their restraint was commendable, but still the security situation deteriorated. Three months later, during a hot encounter in Basra, Major David Bradley was directing operations from a Warrior turret, trying to pinpoint an enemy firing position in a nearby building, when an RPG struck. It hit the rifle he was carrying, and the blast knocked him aside. He remembered a voice (his own) in his head saying, 'This is bad, very, very bad.'⁵ He lifted up his right hand and saw it was cut in two. His body armour was burning. Just then, his driver leaned up from his seat below, grabbed him by the belt and tried to haul him down inside. But that was not the direction in which the major wanted to go. His instinct was to get out, and he began climbing from the turret until he was slumped on top of it. 'The noise was incredible. Bullets ricocheted off the vehicle, and the crackle of high-velocity rounds intensified as the Mahdi militia tried to shoot me off.' Somehow he slid himself back inside the turret, and the Warrior drove at high speed through the streets back to base, the gunner alternately firing his chain gun at anyone who looked threatening and poking the major in the ribs to stop him falling into a coma.

When they got to Camp Cherokee, medics from the Royal Horse Artillery took charge of Bradley and found that shrapnel, including fragments from his own rifle, had blown clean through his body armour and deep into his chest. There was also metal in his right eye and a large cut on his face. His teeth and jaw were intact, which was a relief. 'The prospect of facial reconstruction and eating through a straw for months was very unappealing,' he later recalled. Also intact were what a sergeant demurely referred to as his 'family jewels'. Bradley was grateful for this information. 'Every soldier is concerned about his manhood at times like this.'

He was helicoptered to the calm and air-conditioned field

hospital at Shaiba, the airfield south of Basra which was the main base for British forces in Iraq, and hurried into the operating theatre. Just before the anaesthetic took effect, he told the surgeon to 'sort me out so that I can go back and kill those fucking bastards!' The doctor opened his chest and removed the shrapnel, some of which had penetrated perilously close to his heart. A massive bleed almost got out of control, and he arrested. Twice the monitor registering his heartbeat flat-lined, but the crash team went to work and pulled him back. All this he learned later. His first recollection after being given the pre-op anaesthetic was waking up in hospital in Birmingham four days later, hooked up to electronic monitors, his face and body swollen and covered in blood – but alive.

His wife Lara was by his side. She had been at his bed for two days, waiting for him to come round. The fight to survive was over, but the battle to get better was only just beginning. There would be dozens more operations, large and small. His damaged hand was grafted to his stomach for three weeks to let replacement skin grow over the area destroyed by the RPG. One finger was amputated, and the bones recycled to repair the others. Slowly, he came back to life, coming off the feeding tubes in his throat and eating normally again. Physios worked on his limbs and lungs. Two months after that crushing strike in a Basra street, he was well enough to leave hospital and go home.

*

Just a week before Major Bradley left Iraq in a coma, on a stretcher and badly burnt, part-time medic Bob Steer had returned to duty. It was a year since the Territorial staff sergeant's last posting there and, as he took his place on the trauma team, he could see instantly that the situation had massively deteriorated. 'Same place [Basra], same hospital [Shaiba],' but the wounds he was dealing with were of a different order altogether. Victims of road accidents and small children who had toyed unwisely with scatter bombs and mines had previously been the A&E's staple diet. Now, there was a flood of military casualties from roadside bombs (IEDs) and shootings. The tension had gone up several notches and, with it, the caseload.

'People were coming in with arms and legs missing and their bodies ripped apart by bomb blasts.' On his very first shift in the hospital, a British soldier died on the operating table after an IED strike. 'He was covered in blood and had lost a leg. I'd seen death before, but this was different. He was in our care, and it was hard to see him alive one minute and dead the next, you know, finished, final, all over. He was only in his early twenties. It brought home to me that what I was doing was for real. I had to ask myself whether it was worth it – not politically, but in a personal sense.'

There was always plenty of routine medical work to do, and days went by with a run of minor injuries to deal with – cuts and bruises, a bad case of sunstroke. But over everyone hung the fear of a major incident. It became a reality one hot, sunny Sunday. A roadside bomb exploded underneath a Toyota pick-up crammed with Iraqi policemen. An American convoy coming in the opposite direction saw what happened, stopped, and not wishing to hang around in case of a second attack, hurriedly stashed all the bodies in a Humvee armoured car and drove straight to the hospital. Steer remembered them arriving without warning, 'cars screeching to a halt, doors slamming and then these casualties being hauled in. There were ten of them, all Iraqi police apart from a detainee, and he was dead from head injuries.' It was like a hospital in the UK being hit with a massive motorway pile-up or a train crash. 'They all had fragment injuries and were screaming and shouting. There were broken arms and legs, and head injuries.'

Such incidents would become the norm for Steer when he transferred from Shaiba, going up country and up tempo, to a base in the middle of the desert thirty miles to the south of Baghdad. Camp Dogwood was a sprawling complex that housed all the logistical and support services for the US forces in Iraq. It was a target of constant attacks in an area dubbed, with good reason, the Triangle of Death. But the core of its fighting force had been shipped out to join a major anti-insurgency drive in the key rebellious city of Fallujah, forty miles away. On the instructions of then prime minister Tony Blair and defence secretary Geoff Hoon, a battalion of the Black Watch was sent to man Dogwood while they were away. They were short of medics for this potentially dangerous work, and Steer volunteered to leave behind the relative comfort of Shaiba and go. 'It sounded exciting. I wanted to be out there, doing the job I was trained for.'

Donning full body armour and getting on board a Chinook for the hop from Baghdad airport to Dogwood brought home to him that he was about to get all the excitement he could ever want. 'A Navy Seal, a US special forces guy, briefed us that we were flying into a hot landing zone at two o'clock in the morning and not to be surprised if bullets were flying. What he said really put the wind up me. To be honest, I was shit scared.' In place of Shaiba's extensive facilities and hundred-strong staff, he found himself one of just a dozen medics setting up a temporary regimental aid post in the rubble of an old, run-down Iraqi warehouse. The ten-bed unit was enclosed in a large tent they erected inside the building, while Steer's sleeping quarters, which he shared with three other sergeants, were in a disused toilet, 'and the hole was under my bed'.

Dogwood was soon under attack, regularly hit by mortars and rockets fired from villages out in the desert at any time of the day or night. 'Because it was so quiet out there, you could actually hear the mortars leaving the tube, and then there was an awful gap while you waited for the impact.' He went through hell inside his head at these times, thinking death – *his* death – was just seconds away. That almost every shot missed did little to ease the anxiety. The fact that he was in the middle of an increasingly nasty cat-and-mouse war was inescapable.

Not long after their arrival at Dogwood, the Black Watch mounted an operation to root out those mortar-bombers and to block off possible supply and escape routes for the insurgents battling with American forces at Fallujah. Two Warrior troop carriers headed out of the camp and on to a long, dusty road leading to a village where the insurgents were believed to be hiding. Without warning, a roadside bomb detonated beside the lead Warrior, ripping off its front four wheels. When the second vehicle moved in to help, it too came under mortar attack and careered off the road. Eight men were down and under fire – but they were not the real target. They were the bait. Other vehicles raced out from Dogwood to the rescue, and one, with three soldiers and a local interpreter inside, set up a perimeter roadblock nearby to control access. A suicide bomber – the first time the British contingent had ever encountered one and a frightening development in the enemy's armoury – blew it up, killing all four occupants.

The bodies were brought to Steer's aid post. 'They came in the back of a Warrior, and they were a mess, blood everywhere, body parts missing. Then the insurgents mortared us, so it was complete bedlam for a while. There was nothing we could do for these guys apart from treating them with the respect they deserved. I was very conscious that this was somebody's son, somebody's brother. The images are still with me.'

A week later, another Black Watch soldier died when his Warrior went over a mine. 'He was killed instantly,' Steer recalled, 'but his mates couldn't get the body out. They needed to get out of the area quickly, so they put chains around the Warrior and dragged it back to camp.' The medic went inside the hatch to get him out.

At first he looked all right, with just a bit of blood on his face. But then I saw that his whole bottom half had virtually gone. It was a shock. Dealing with the dead is the worst part about being a medic. Saving lives makes you feel good. You get a buzz when somebody comes off the table alive and you know that you've helped save them. That's what you are trained to do and what you want to do. But the converse is when you are dealing with the dead, and you know that somebody's going to have to take the awful message to his loved ones.

*

By the time RAF casualty nurse Frank Mincher returned to Iraq in 2005, the political situation had worsened still further. His postings there before had been benign; almost nothing had happened. But now the country was a cauldron. This time he would earn his keep. 'Al-Amarah in particular had turned into the OK

Corral. One of my first jobs was to fly into the football stadium there to bring out two bodies with gunshot wounds.'

The increasing problem was roadside bombs, which produced hideous wounds. Mincher was called to treat the victim of one, a civilian who was working in Iraq as a diplomatic bodyguard. His 4x4 was blown apart by a device made from three mines wired together on top of each other, which blasted the vehicle clean across the central reservation of the dual carriageway he was driving along and down a bank on the other side. Three other occupants, also bodyguards, were killed outright, but he was still alive and had been taken by ambulance to the British base at the Shatt al-Arab Hotel, where Mincher came by helicopter to collect him. 'If I say he had two hundred wounds, that would be no exaggeration,' the medic recalled. 'Every part of his torso, body, legs and arms had shrapnel damage to it. He was bleeding out and was as white as a sheet.'

On the way to Shaiba in the back of a Sea King, the casualty's heart stopped beating because of that loss of blood, 'and we were jumping around trying to resuscitate him'. Alongside Mincher that day was Territorial rifleman Private Chris Grant, a member of the armed protection squad that went with the medics on emergency calls. He watched in awe as they worked on the casualty in the narrow space in the back of the helicopter, crashing his chest heavily to try to keep his heart beating. Grant had never seen real-life drama like it. Thirty chest compressions . . . two deep breaths into the mouth. Voices counting out the process were lost in the din of the helicopter's engines and the rush of the slipstream outside. Thirty more compressions . . . two breaths, and so on, again and again, never giving up. To the medics, it was a well-drilled routine. To Grant, it was heroic. 'They were hitting his chest so hard I thought they would break his ribs, but I suppose that's what you have to do if you're going to save someone's life. I was so impressed with the job they were doing.'

They were just about keeping the wounded man alive as the helicopter wound down towards the hospital landing site, but then disaster struck. There was an ear-splitting bang as the eight-ton machine clipped the ground and lurched back into the air, its tail rotor a mangled mess. The helicopter went into a spin, bits of blade flying off in every direction, 'and we're trying to perform cardiac massage,' Mincher said. The aircraft turned through several circles, hit the ground again, bounced up, and then crashed back drunkenly, nearly tipping on its side. 'Get out!' Mincher yelled, and they all piled off with the stretcher and began pounding the man's chest on the ground. Even when he was on a trolley and being sprinted into the A&E room, they were still pumping away. 'It impressed all of us,' Grant said. 'We had just crash-landed, and it was all the rest of us could do to stumble out of the helicopter. But the medics just kept on going with their treatment and hardly even seemed to blink.' If the helicopter had toppled over, as it very nearly did on landing, there would have been many casualties. The young rifleman's legs went to jelly beneath him as he realized what a close shave he had just had, but the medics, he recalled in admiration, never for one moment lost their composure. 'Frank came out from A&E after a while, and he was as cool as a cucumber.'

But Frank Mincher was not as sanguine as Grant imagined. He and his team had delivered their patient to the doctors still alive, but there was to be no good ending to this story. The civilian died, and Mincher followed that time-honoured but pointless medic's tradition of beating himself up, of wondering if he had done enough. It was the flipside of being a life-saver. 'You start to wonder if he'd have had a better chance if we'd got to him earlier or made different decisions. I felt disappointed and down.'

He found solace in his mates. The emergency medical response team he headed was a close-knit and sociable bunch who trained together in the gym and played volleyball when not working. Much of their time on duty was spent waiting around for a shout. One day, after word came in about an incident in Basra, they were on standby and in a high state of readiness. They often hung around like this, armed and in body armour, anxious for the command either to go or to stand down. Mincher was thinking about home. He had been on base for two months now and was rostered to begin a fortnight's leave the next day. He was going home to see his wife and children back in England. But tomorrow was another day because, suddenly, it was a 'go', and there was work to do. A rescue beacon had gone off in the city. Two SAS troopers working undercover were missing, snatched from their car. No one was sure if the Iraqi police had arrested them, or if they had been kidnapped. Given the uncertain loyalties of the police, many of whom secretly (or sometimes openly) supported the Mahdi army, the difference might well be academic.

The medical rescue team piled into the Sea King, which swooped backwards and forwards at low level over the city, beating out a systematic search pattern while eyes in the cockpit looked for any signs of the lost pair. In the back, Mincher and his team sat in silence. More waiting and worrying. Then a car was spotted below, abandoned, its doors wide open, and the helicopter dived in for a closer look. There was no sign of the missing men, and the search now shifted to an area around the Al Jameat police station and jail. The Sea King dropped down again, and this time landed. Mincher, a doctor and a medic exited behind their four-man close-support detail, their personal-protection unit. The blazing heat hit them as they stood on the street, watching the helicopter immediately lift off and disappear into the distance. The choppers never hung around. They were too tempting a target for insurgents. Sixty seconds, ninety at the most, was their preferred limit for being on the ground.

A welcoming party of British soldiers, all on high alert, their eyes glancing in every direction for signs of trouble, hurried the medics along. 'We sprinted through deserted backstreets,' which, reflecting later, Mincher realized did not bode well. At the time, however, he was unconcerned by the absence of people. On the contrary, everything seemed fairly routine. They were embarked on a simple snatch-and-run operation, no more. No danger. But, outside the police station, an argument was going on between British troops and Iraqis, and a threatening crowd of locals had gathered and was swelling all the time. That's where everyone had gone. A serious situation was developing on this baking Basra street.

Major James Woodham, a cool and experienced officer of the Royal Anglian Regiment, was negotiating to get the SAS men back, but the temperature of the encounter was rising by the minute. There were machine guns pointing in his direction from the roof of the police station. Behind him, the troops had thrown up a cordon to stop the two captives being spirited away. More troops were on their way, more hostile Iraqi militia too, pitching up in pick-up trucks, bristling with machine guns, aimed in ever-increasing numbers at the British troops in their khaki desert fatigues. This was shaping up into a full-scale confrontation, one that could trigger the sort of violence which would destroy what little remained of the trust and goodwill the British forces had been trying to build in Basra.

Mincher walked towards the front door of the police station, bold as brass. He had a job to do. There were men being held inside whose medical condition he needed to check. An Iraqi policeman stood in his way and pushed him back. The RAF nurse heard the unmistakable rapid rattle of weapons being cocked. 'I looked up and saw the machine guns on the roof.' He was tempted to push back, 'being a stroppy Jock', but this was a situation for discretion, not impetuous valour. He and his medical team pulled back, and took cover behind a line of yellow school buses. 'But then the Iraqi policeman I'd already had my run-in with had the buses moved, and we were left once again exposed to the machine guns.'

Mincher moved into cover once more, this time behind a Warrior armoured vehicle, and watched as the gunner lined up his sights on the more aggressive sections of the gathering crowd. 'My heart was beating very fast,' he remembered, and faster still when he turned and saw gangs of youths advancing across an open patch of waste ground behind him. 'I started to get worried. We were being surrounded. The hairs on the back of my neck were standing up, as they do if you walk into a pub back home on a Saturday night and see a big crowd of yobs hanging around and trying to intimidate everyone.' He heard his protection team quietly talking to each other, assessing the situation and plotting escape routes in case things turned really nasty.

Woodham was now inside the police station, having persuaded the reluctant and volatile Iraqis to let him in, and he had confirmed that the two hostages were there and had even managed to see them. They had been beaten up and were sporting cuts and bruises, but were otherwise OK. Negotiations for their release were complicated, turning on legal niceties and clearly going to take a while. He was aware that time was running out – the scene outside was growing more aggressive and unpredictable by the minute. He knew full well the pressure on the soldiers trying to hold the line and keep their cool. 'You're young and perhaps on your first operational tour,' he wrote later, 'and you have a seething mass of people moving towards you, chanting in a language you can't understand, waving their fists, looking very angry. At any moment, someone with an AK47 might appear from the crowd and fire at you. The noise is such that you can't hear instructions on the radio. It's very hot and your adrenalin is up. You're nervous and probably frightened.'[6]

Outside, Mincher was summoned from his safe haven behind a Warrior to treat a casualty. A British interpreter, a Navy man, had gone inside the police station with Woodham to help with the negotiations, but was overcome by heat exhaustion. He was in a bad way when he was brought out, needing urgently to be re-hydrated on a drip and cooled down in an air-conditioned hospital ward. Immediate evacuation was imperative, or he could easily collapse and die. Mincher radioed for help, then put the sick man into the back of an army ambulance and drove to an open space, a waste tip a mile away just about big enough for one of the smaller army helicopters – a Lynx – to get in. The Lynx appeared overhead and touched down in a flurry of dirt and rubbish from the tip. It was not designed to carry casualties, but they loaded in the stretcher anyway, crossways, with the casualty's head and feet sticking out of the sides. His condition had by now visibly worsened, and the doctor in Mincher's team decided he must go with him.

Around the impromptu landing site, another large crowd was gathering and, the moment the Lynx had gone, they hurled themselves at the soldiers, lobbing petrol bombs and stones. Bottles smashed in the dust and burst into flame. The startled British soldiers, caught on the back foot by this fierce onslaught, realized they were in real trouble. 'Some Special Forces troops were with us, and they shot over the heads of the crowd to try and hold them back. It didn't have much effect. As we climbed into the ambulance to escape, the crowd was already surging around us and we couldn't get the doors closed.'

The mob now numbered several hundred, all angry and shouting and throwing missiles. The same fate as the Red Caps suffered at Majar al-Kabir became a distinct and frightening possibility. Mincher had no doubt that his life and the lives of his team, bodyguards and all, were seriously at risk. As demonstrators lunged at the vehicle and tried to grab him, he pulled out his pistol, his last line of defence. His greatest fear was that they would be overpowered and kidnapped.

Through his mind flashed pictures of a notorious incident in Northern Ireland in 1988 when two plain-clothes corporals on undercover duties fell into the hands of a mob in the Republican stronghold of Andersonstown and were lynched, their capture and desperate efforts to escape caught on camera. It had been chilling to watch. Now, he was facing a similar ordeal, and he steeled himself to fight for his life in a way he, as a medic, could never have expected to do. The fact that he was supposed to be going on leave the next day somehow added to his consternation. Instead of embarking on a fortnight of rest and recreation back in Blighty, he thought to himself, he might be a prisoner or, worse still, dead. 'I told myself that I wasn't going down without a bloody fight. I wasn't going to surrender meekly and let them take me away.' His only concession was to take his air-crew helmet off, thinking it might be making him more of a target. But still stones and other missiles came hurtling through the ambulance doors at them, while in a ring outside, the protection force was on its knees in firing positions in a last-ditch bid to keep the crowd at bay. Petrol bombs shattered around them, and the hail of stones on their heads was non-stop.

They were saved when more British troops rocked up and the

ambulance took its place in a heavily armed convoy of Warriors, forcing its way through the narrow backstreets of Basra, heading for the dual carriageway that would take them to safety. But one armoured vehicle behind was in trouble, halted by a petrol bomb and on fire. A soldier popped out of the turret and was seized by the pursuing mob. Mincher's ambulance halted too, and his protection team raced back into the crowd, rifles and machine guns blazing, to grab the captured soldier by the hair and drag him away. 'He was unconscious from the beating he'd been given. We hauled him in and went to work on him.'

By now, a full-scale battle was in progress. More casualties came to the ambulance for help, injured by bricks or with burns. The medical team spilled out on to the dusty road to treat them. The convoy then started up again, the Warriors surrounding the ambulance, inching its way past buildings from which gunfire was crackling. A crowd, grown to five hundred or more, was in pursuit and clamouring around every time the convoy was forced to a halt. The troops, in full riot gear, were strung out in a defensive line and taking a heavy battering. They concentrated their limited fire on the petrol-bombers, who were becoming increasingly daring, egged on by the baying crowd.

Twenty yards away, a Warrior took a direct hit. Burning petrol seeped inside, and a ball of fire shot up from the turret. The bodies of men came cannoning out through the air, arms frantically beating at the flames enveloping them, their dramatic exit captured in photographs that went round the world, illustrating the chaos into which Iraq was descending. What the cameras did not see that day was that the gunner was still trapped inside and had to be dragged clear. Mincher ran towards him, tugging off his body armour as he went and using it to try to beat out the flames. To his surprise – Iraq was never less than unpredictable – a local man rushed forward with a bucket of water from the canal, broke through the cordon gathered around the casualty and drenched the burning soldier, helping to douse the flames. 'It was bizarre,' said Mincher. 'He was lucky our boys didn't shoot him.'

Inside the ambulance, a full drill was underway to save the

casualty's life. The burns to his face and neck were severe, and he needed morphine and emergency fluids. 'His head was swollen up like a football, he was deteriorating fast, and I was sure he was going to die. As I worked to save him, bricks and petrol bombs were still landing on the roof. I knew that if I didn't get him away quickly, I would need to get a tube into his throat to open up his airways, and that would not have been easy in the circumstances.'

The only chance the soldier had was if a helicopter could get in to evacuate him. The Warriors and troops fanned out to secure a big enough square for a single-rotor and extra-manoeuvrable Merlin, a recent addition to the air fleet, to land. It came in under fire, and half a dozen casualties were bundled on board. Mincher found himself pulled inside too. As the Merlin took off, a wave of relief flowed over him. After dropping off his patients, 'I was shaking and soaked with sweat, but also very thirsty. And very, very tired after six hours out there, constantly on the move, in very hot conditions and in full body armour.'

Meanwhile, the confrontation he had managed to get away from with his life was still unresolved. Back at the police station, a beleaguered Woodham was losing the battle to keep the lid on the pressure cooker. Local people had been hurt in the ruckus outside, and their friends, mullahs and militia among them, invaded the building to exact revenge. Dozens crammed into the small room where he was trying to work out a deal with a judge, and the major found himself at the wrong end of an AK47 held by a screaming Iraqi, his finger twitching on the trigger. 'There was nothing I could do if he chose to shoot,' he recalled. 'For some reason he chose not to.' But the stand-off went on for hours until, as night fell, the troublemakers seemed to lose interest and drift away. The switch that historian Richard Holmes spoke of in relation to Iraqi violence had clicked off. The next day, British tanks made a frontal assault on the police station, but the hostages had by then been smuggled out. They were found in a house a mile away and released. The incident was over, though it was not without repercussions. Relations between the British and the people of Basra plummeted, never fully to recover.

At Shaiba, however, Mincher reflected on his good fortune. 'We had done our bit and come away relatively unscathed.' He was even back in time to go on the leave he had been so concerned about missing. When he boarded the transporter plane the next day to go home, the Warrior soldier he had rescued was there too, sedated, hooked up to a ventilator and looking 'terrible'. But he was alive. He had been kept breathing and hydrated in the vital period between going up in flames and reaching the hospital. The efforts of the medics had saved him from certain death. In fact, there were, surprisingly, no British fatalities from that explosive encounter at the police station. And Mincher was happy to have played his part. 'We treated nineteen casualties that day [19 September 2005], and nobody died, which in a very bad, deteriorating situation, with rocks, small arms, petrol bombs, lots of flames and vehicles going up, was a pretty good result!'

He was not untouched by the experience, however. The enormity of what he had been through hit him once he was home. 'My wife had watched the burning Warrior on television, but she had no idea I was there. She knew that, as a medic, my work involved helicopters and evacuation, but not that I actually went out on the ground. When I looked back, I realized it was probably the worst day of my career and also the best, the most frightening day but the most satisfying.' He was rightly proud of what he had done. 'You really learn things about yourself. You always wonder how you're going to react under fire and, when it happens, there is a horrendous level of fear going on, but that's what drives you along.'

He was proud too at being in the vanguard of military medicine as it changed and adapted to the new circumstances of twenty-first-century warfare. The job medics did was taking on a fresh urgency and importance. 'Our soldiers at the front deserve the best care and treatment, and we should be continually pushing the borders to get better and more expert care to them. I think we can be very proud of our medical services, really proud.'

That sense of achievement stretched to the way the medics handled the hardest part of their job – death. The troops, who had stood their ground outside the police station and refused to be intimidated by a mob urged on by Mahdi army militants, now felt the backlash of that encounter. With relations between occupying army and the occupied hopelessly soured, the number of bombings, booby traps and sniper attacks shot up to new levels.

Major John Mayhead, company commander in the 1st battalion, whose beat covered the northern half of Basra, began ticking up one serious incident a day. The killing of a popular sergeant, Chris Hickey, whom he had known for fourteen years, was a hard blow, not least because it happened on the very day the battalion's tour was ending and they were due to hand over to an incoming regiment. Some of the pain was eased by the dignified behaviour of the medical staff at Shaiba. It fell to Mayhead and his company sergeant major to identify the body. 'We were met by the padre and the commander of the field hospital. They were superb. They talked about Sergeant Hickey as a person and reassured us that nothing more could have been done to save him. They prepared us for his injuries before we were taken to where Chris lay. We bowed our heads in prayer, then quietly left. It wasn't clinical at all, but very calm and respectful.'

Later, Mayhead returned to retrieve the body and was 'amazed and humbled' as the entire medical team turned out to honour the sergeant as he was brought out to begin his last journey back to his home in Yorkshire. They lined the path from the entrance of the hospital to a waiting helicopter. A piper played a lament as the coffin, draped in a union flag and flanked by six doctors, was slow-marched with great dignity and solemnity, as if they were on parade at the Cenotaph in London. 'I hand to your care the body of your brave comrade, Sergeant Chris Hickey,' the hospital commander declared, and saluted. Mayhead was overwhelmed by the simple grace of the occasion. 'There was not one dry eye out there,' he recollected. 'I was incredibly moved by the entire experience, and I know that it meant a great deal to my men to see their dead comrade treated with such respect.'[7] He said as much to the doctor, whose response still rings in his ears. 'He told me forcefully, "Any soldier in this hospital, alive or dead, comes under my command. They deserve the greatest of respect, and I will make absolutely sure they are given it.'''

The ceremony, Mayhead discovered, was held for every soldier who died at Shaiba and, though the parades were voluntary for hospital staff, attendance was always 100 per cent. 'It is easy to assume that in such a place as a field hospital, in the middle of a conflict, the medical services could become hardened and matter-of-fact about the issue of death,' he said later. 'The compassion and respect shown to Sergeant Hickey showed that they under-stood one of the most important tenets of military power – the moral component. As soldiers, risking our lives every day, we need to know that someone appreciates our sacrifice, especially when lives are lost. And in that dusty, arid piece of desert just outside of Basra, we realized that people did care, and cared a great deal.'

14. A Woman's Place

Who would ever have thought that something resembling powdered soup or gravy granules would be a battlefield life-saver? But that was precisely what a revolutionary product called Quik-Clot became as science came to the aid of military medicine in the twenty-first century, just as it had done in the past with chloroform, morphine and penicillin. Derived from high-absorbent volcanic ash, QuikClot did just what the name on the sachet said. It accelerated the clotting process by soaking up water in the blood, activating crucial cells known as platelets and concentrating the bio-chemical elements that cause coagulation. To treat a deep wound in an emergency, one medic would hold apart the ruptured flesh while another ripped open the package, poured in the contents and then carefully added water. The powder fizzed like sherbet or liver salts as it went to work under a hastily applied bandage, and gave off considerable heat in the process, painful for those treated with it and occasionally causing burns. The discomfort was, however, slight against the benefits of shutting off a bleed, particularly given that those to whom it was administered were likely to be badly wounded and suffering anyway. The side effects were a small price to pay for the gain in survival prospects. 'Bleeding marvellous' was the verdict of the army magazine *Soldier*[1] on this important development and it became a standard piece of kit in the Bergens of British medics in Iraq. They also carried Hemcon, a new dressing impregnated with a substance derived from crushed shrimp shells that formed an instant sterile seal over open wounds.

QuikClot and Hemcon were American in origin, as were a number of other innovations that emergency-medicine specialist Colonel Tim Hodgetts and his RAMC colleagues were now assembling. Knowledge in this area had come a long way since the

Falklands, pushed along in no small part by the contribution of the fiercely professional Israeli army, whose experience of hard-hitting military operations (along with the extra incentive to preserve lives that comes from being a small nation with limited manpower) was second to none. They were long-term exponents of the very sort of asymmetric war that the coalition forces were learning on their feet to fight in Iraq.

From the US special forces came a new and faster field tourniquet. It was a wide nylon band with a Velcro fastening, a friction buckle and a tightening rod that could be twisted with one hand. A man could apply it to himself, unlike the traditional pencil-thin rubber piping and crude weighted metal clasp, a garrotte-like device that had changed little in a hundred years and which tended to cause additional problems by slicing into the skin. The new tourniquet got an immediate thumbs-up from medics and casualties alike.

All these innovations were a response to the growing realization that the biggest threat to life on the battlefield was not breathing difficulties but catastrophic bleeding. A man could 'bleed out' in a matter of minutes. Now, the process could be slowed and even halted.

At the Centre for Defence Medicine at Birmingham University, his British research base, Tim Hodgetts encouraged feedback from the front line to establish what worked and what didn't at the sharp end. When medics complained that the regulation field dressings, still based on a Second World War model, were fiddly and wasteful, he had them re-designed. Training was stepped up, and the new role of 'team medic' was created. One in four soldiers going into action, whether on an offensive operation or a routine patrol, was trained to give advanced first aid within seconds of someone being wounded. In the Falklands, doctor Steven Hughes had done his best to get just one in ten of his Paras to this level.

Full-time medics, too, were now much better equipped. In the pouches of the specially packed rucksacks on their backs, they had every possible device to deal with a traumatic haemorrhage, including spare tourniquets and dressings, a pump to suck out

21. Falklands, 1982 – the 2 Para Regimental Aid Post during the battle for Goose Green. The smoke is caused by burning gorse set alight during the attack

22. Afghanistan, 2006 – 3 Para doctor Captain Harvey Pynn treats the 'wheelbarrow' casualty during the battle at Now Zad

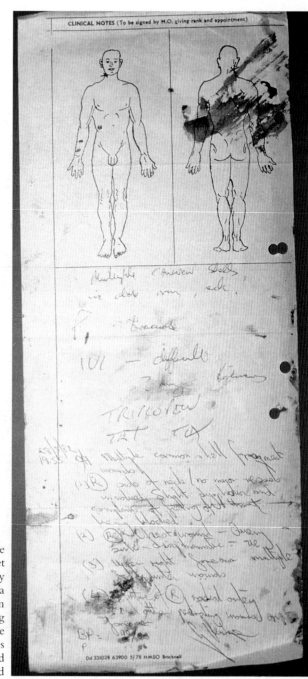

23. Falklands – the medical notes sheet from a casualty treated by 2 Para doctor Steven Hughes during the battle at Goose Green. The notes are clearly stained with blood

24. RAF Sergeant Rachel McDonald aboard the MERT helicopter in Afghanistan. Rachel was awarded the 'Paramedic of the Year – 2007' award for her courage during a mission to evacuate mass casualties from FOB Robinson

25. Private Holly Percival during her tour in Afghanistan, 2009. Holly was part of the medical team sent to the IED incident in Basra, November 2005, where Sergeant John Jones was killed

26. Iraq, March 2003 – an RAF medic tends to two British marines from 42 Commando after they were injured during the conflict. The Puma helicopter crewman keeps a constant vigil, checking for threats from the ground

27. Iraq, September 2005 – a soldier escapes from a burning Warrior during the incident at a Basra police station where two undercover SAS soldiers were being held captive

28. RAF Flight Sergeant Frank Mincher, *far right*, treating other casualties in an ambulance during the same incident in Basra

29. Troops under attack at the police station in Basra

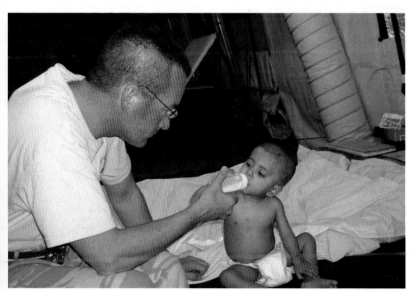

30. Surgeon, Lieutenant Colonel Paul Parker attends to the 'smallest casualty' of his time in Afghanistan. Parker also operated on Sergeant Major Andy Stockton

31. Flight Lieutenant Andy Smith after an emergency evacuation mission in Afghanistan, 2009. Medical kit is positioned for easy access on his body armour

32. Andy Smith and the MERT in action in Afghanistan – this casualty was a Royal Marine with serious leg injuries

33. Sergeant Major Andy Stockton three days before the incident where he lost his arm in a firefight with insurgents in Afghanistan, 2006

34. Andy Stockton with his partner, Emma, following a parade where Afghanistan campaign medals were presented at the Royal School of Artillery, Larkhill

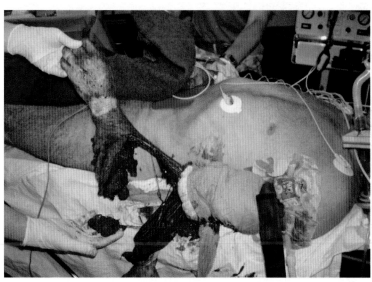

35. Lieutenant Colonel Paul Parker examines the remnants of Sergeant Major Andy Stockton's arm after his evacuation from the battlefield

36. Corporal Stuart Hale with his sniper rifle before the mine strike at the Kajaki Dam, Afghanistan, 2006

37. Corporal Stuart Hale and Sergeant Stuart Pearson – both were injured in the Kajaki minefield incident

38. The Queen presents Corporal Paul 'Tug' Hartley with his George Medal. This was awarded for 'his courage and complete disregard for his personal safety' during the Kajaki Dam minefield incident

vomit and blood from the mouth, and special seals with a release valve to go over a chest wound. Ultimately, though, it was better to prevent soldiers being wounded in the first place. Hodgetts saw it as part of his job description to harry the Ministry of Defence to improve personal body armour and, above all, to do something to strengthen the thin-skinned Snatch Land Rovers used as patrol vehicles and ambulances, absurdly (and almost criminally, in the view of coroners at inquests on some victims) under-protected from IED attack.

The clearest sign of the upgraded, new-look medical services, however, could be seen by glancing along the lines of medics as they prepared to go into action. The ranks were no longer all men. For the first time, women had been cleared to go into the front line. Equality of opportunity had not stretched to giving them aggressive infantry tasks as such, but they were welcomed in a medical role at every level, as paramedics, nurses and doctors. There was an added benefit. Treating civilians as well as soldiers had become a major part of the job, and it was noticeable that local women and children felt more at ease with a female medic than with a man, particularly in Islamic lands. In every other respect, however, the changing nature of war meant there was almost no difference between what they and the men were expected to do. Old, clear-cut distinctions between active and support roles no longer applied. The girls went into battle armed, armoured and ready for action alongside the blokes.

Private Holly Percival was one. Like many a medic, she had a personal reason for her choice of career, one tinged with great sadness. 'I was twelve when my brother was killed in a car crash. A few months later, my mother killed herself. My mum was a paramedic. From a young age my ambition was to be a paramedic like her.'[2] Some children hit by such a double tragedy might have shied away from anything to do with hospitals and accidents. But, far from being repelled, Holly was drawn towards the fascinating subject of medical trauma. Aged eighteen, she was thinking about taking a degree course in paramedical science.

The second Gulf war in 2003 altered her university plans. 'I'd always been a fan of the military. At home, we loved watching Trooping the Colour, and all the old war films. I grew up with that sort of thing. So I looked into the idea of a medical career in the army. When Iraq happened, I wanted to get out there and do the job for real.' She joined the RAMC to train as a combat medical technician and, in late 2005, she was posted to Basra. Aged twenty, she said goodbye to her father, a London taxi driver, and sister, and went to war. They must have been terrified for her. Surely two premature deaths in one small family was enough? 'But they didn't show it. My dad was quietly confident about how I'd get on.'

Her first month on call at the waterside Shatt al-Arab Hotel in Basra, which doubled as an army base, was quiet. She was on standby to go out in the back of an emergency ambulance, but nothing happened apart from routine sick parades. Lulled into a false sense of security, she was checking equipment and drugs one afternoon when there was a loud boom in the distance. On a quiet backstreet, a routine patrol from the Royal Regiment of Fusiliers had been hit by a roadside bomb. 'Si' – Corporal Simon Proctor, her crew commander – 'rushed from the ops room to say we'd been crashed out.' Holly dashed to put on her body armour, helmet and webbing, grabbed her med bag of kit and equipment and then raced for the ambulance. 'Scouse, our radio operator, yelled at me to get my rifle. I'd forgotten it. I'd been so busy concentrating on my medical pack it hadn't occurred to me I'd need it. I ran back and picked it up and then climbed into the ambulance.'

As the vehicle hared out on to the Basra streets, she was told to 'prep' for casualties. 'All we'd been told was that there were two casualties, but no one knew how serious their injuries were.' She turned on the oxygen regulators, put on her gloves and clipped a pen to her watch strap so it would be easy to get at to write up her notes. 'I was really excited, because it was my first call-out in a combat situation. But I was nervous.'

She had every reason to be. Later, fingers of suspicion would point at the Iraqi police for having lured the fusiliers into a trap. A policeman was seen using his mobile phone at the time the bomb went off, possibly detonating it from a distance. It was an indication of the dangerous and unpredictable complexity of the type of warfare the British forces were engaged in, where unknown enemies lurked around every corner. The ambulance in which Holly rode might itself be heading into another ambush. A double hit was par for the course. As the ambulance bounced and rattled along, she bent down and peered through the hatch into the driver's cabin. In the windscreen ahead she could see nothing but a thick fog of dust and sand. She had no idea how the driver was managing to find his way.

Poor visibility was the least of their problems. Their arrival at the scene was greeted by a hail of rocks, hurled by Iraqi youths and thudding against the side of the ambulance. Holly put on her rucksack, undid the steps at the back and readied herself to leap out into this mayhem. 'Then Si opened the rear doors and I jumped.'

It was like stepping into a newsreel. On one side of the dirt road a Snatch Land Rover, its flimsy armour no protection against the exploding IED, lay crashed and crushed against a wall under a dazzling and baking sun. On the other, on a high grassy bank, sat groups of local people, just watching. Beneath them were the stone-throwers. The quick reaction force was already setting up perimeters, the first five yards from the incident, the second at twenty yards, and checking for any more devices.

Two bodies lay by the wreck of the Land Rover. The thought that went through Holly's mind was how closely this resembled the training exercises she had been on before deployment. But the 'casualties' on the training ground in Aldershot had spurted stage blood and moaned in fake agony, play-acting for effect. The sounds of distress that filled the air here were all too real, the blood hot and freshly spilt. The shock on the faces of the other members of the patrol was also the genuine article, as was the change in that look to one of relief when they caught sight of the red cross on her arm. Their belief in her scared her. 'I was a young, inexperienced medic, and everyone was looking at me and Si for help.

They weren't to know this was my first time in action.' It was her first experience of that daunting weight of expectation soldiers place on medics. 'They look to you as the expert. Their mates were lying on the ground terribly injured, and they put all their faith in us, in *me*. It's a huge responsibility.' She couldn't help wondering if they were disappointed that it was her. 'The medics are all they have left to pin their hopes on, and then this young girl pitches up! I'm sure they'd rather have seen a strapping man coming towards them!'

But she would have to do. She jumped across a ditch and ran to the Land Rover, where the casualties lay covered in blood and with flies already collecting on them. One of them, a corporal, had managed to stagger out on his own, but the other, Sergeant John 'Jonah' Jones, had had to be pulled from the wreckage. Holly knelt beside the corporal. 'I could see that one arm was completely off and the other one was at an unnatural angle. It had been bandaged with field dressings, and whoever did it had done a good job, because the bleeding seemed to be under control.' He was awake and alert and making his feelings evident. As Si ran over to Jones, he accidentally kicked the corporal. 'Watch my fucking arms, you fucking clown!' the wounded man yelled, his annoyance a positive sign. The sergeant, on the other hand, was as quiet and still as the grave. He had a faint pulse but was not breathing. Si slipped an OPA (oral pharyngeal airway) plastic tube into his throat and began resuscitation.

As Si fought to save the sergeant's life, Holly focussed on the corporal with an intensity that astonished her. 'I remember the adrenalin pumping through me, but I also felt numb and distant, as if someone else was doing all this, not me.' A stretcher was brought, the casualty was lifted on, and Holly and three soldiers took a corner each to walk him to the ambulance, clambering up and down the ditch as they went and trying not to drop him. 'We put him into the back of the ambulance, taking care not to bump his arms.' Sergeant Jones was slid in next to him, and Holly, on her knees in the narrow aisle between them, quickly fitted an instrument to measure his oxygen intake. Time, she knew, was running out. By now his pulse had disappeared, and she gripped his wrist and probed under his chin, trying, hoping, to find it. There was nothing.

As the clumsy, top-heavy ambulance lumbered over cracks and pot holes and cranked up to full speed, she looked up from the stretcher where Jones lay and saw that the other man's stump had started to bleed again. This was every medic's big fear – two casualties at the same time, both needing urgent and exclusive attention. She called for help, and Si, who was in the front seat, clambered back through the hatch, both of them now working frantically away in a tiny space that rolled and rocked constantly as the vehicle lurched along the desert road. Their medical Bergens had upended as they grabbed for equipment, and the contents were strewn over the floor.

The mayhem in the cramped back of the ambulance was a memory that would always stay with her. 'There were two of us with two Priority 1s [with urgent life-threatening injuries], and as we were being tossed about we kept knocking into the remains of the corporal's arm hanging limply down by his side.' But the bigger problem was the sergeant, who was not breathing. Si struggled to clear an airway but all efforts to ventilate the dying man simply produced more blood. The medic shouted at him to try and jolt him and bring him back, but he seemed beyond help now, in another place. Si kept trying nonetheless, hoping beyond hope, refusing to give up the fight to keep a comrade alive.

All of a sudden the ambulance braked hard and swerved, throwing Holly over Si's back and on to the head of one of the patients. Outside, an Iraqi car had tried to cut up the ambulance. Other locals were hurling rocks at it and, in the driving seat, Jay was crashing the wheel from side to side to avoid them. 'We had Warriors escorting us in the front and back,' Holly recalled, 'but it was a pretty hostile situation. In the back we were being thrown around, slipping on blood, clinging on as best we could while still trying to treat our patients.'

She tried to get another tourniquet on the corporal to stop the bleeding from the stump of his arm. 'He screamed out in agony and asked me for something for the pain.' He had already had a morphine jab, so she reached for the Entonox gas-and-air machine and handed him the mask to put over his face. She wasn't thinking straight. Both his arms were out of action, and he couldn't take it from her. She had to hold it in place for him. He spat it away, complaining that nothing was coming through the tube. She soothed him, telling him the cylinder was cold and the gas would soon kick in as it warmed up. In truth, she knew his wounds were so severe that Entonox was unlikely to make much difference. She rolled him on to his side to ease his pain and stop him screaming. 'There wasn't anything more I could do for him.'

After what seemed like hours but in reality was minutes, they arrived at the Shatt al-Arab Hotel, and medics were tugging at the doors to get at the casualties. Sergeant Jones's stretcher was hauled out first, Si still at his side, leaning over and trying to respirate him. A doctor examined him for vital signs. There were none. After a few minutes, he called it – dead on arrival. The priority shifted to the corporal, who was very much alive, alert and chatty, though incoherent from the amount of pain relief he had had. With his arms a complete mess, a line was put into a vein in his foot, and Holly held up the bag as life-saving fluid drained into him. Another medic finally fixed on the tourniquet she had been unable to manage in the ambulance. The wounded soldier huddled under a blanket, but Holly could tell he would make it.

Next to him, though, lay the lifeless body of his platoon commander. The sergeant's mouth was open after all the work that had been done on his airways, but his eyes were closed. Holly watched as his dog tags were removed from around his neck. 'I was in a state of shock, numbed,' she remembered. She looked at him, registering his face in full for the first time. He had been a keen amateur boxer, an Aston Villa supporter, father of a five-year-old boy he had hoped one day to take to see his favourite football team play. He was funny, energetic and liked and respected by his colleagues. Holly discovered all this about him later. He was unforgettable to her in a different way. 'In my mind I can still see him. I'd seen dead people before, a mate who was killed in a car crash, but this was different. It was a sad image – the reality of death, I suppose. Here was someone who'd been full of life, but now the life had gone. That's what I saw in his face. The reality of what we were doing struck home. I felt a huge sadness, and a let-down at losing him after everything we had been through.'

The loss was intensely personal to her, her feelings towards this dead man she had never known strangely possessive. She was changing, taking off her bloodstained trousers and body armour, which would be kept as forensic evidence of what had happened, and stowing them in a plastic bag, when she saw some soldiers sauntering past the resuscitation room where his body lay beneath a blanket. They glanced in, and she quickly jumped up and shut the door to protect his privacy.

Later that evening, a helicopter came to ferry the body to Shaiba, and the men of his regiment lined up for that sad – and increasingly frequent – ceremony of escorting the fallen to the landing site. Jonah Jones was the ninety-eighth British soldier to die in the Iraq conflict in the two and a half years since the invasion of March 2003. The toll would climb into three figures soon enough. The padre walked ahead of the ambulance, the sergeant's comrades at his side. 'They were all friends of his, and I could see the pain on their faces,' Holly recalled. 'It was awful.' A piper stood by, but his last lament was lost, drowned out by the noise of the helicopter, its motors kept running for fear of attack. It was paramount that one death should not be the cause of more slaughter.

For weeks afterwards, the events of that traumatic day would run through Holly's head when she tried to sleep. Her troubled thoughts would not leave her alone, until she took the padre's advice and wrote them down in meticulous detail. This laid the ghost, and she began sleeping again, her mind at rest. But the events were never forgotten. She had, as she later acknowledged, grown up that day. 'I took my job as medic and soldier a lot more seriously afterwards.'

★

A little over six months later, nineteen-year-old Michelle Norris, a private in the RAMC, did *her* growing up in the back of a Warrior armoured vehicle in the town of Al-Amarah as British forces in Iraq engaged in a rare pitched battle. A night-time operation to seek out and destroy stockpiles of weapons turned into a full-on confrontation with the Mahdi army, as hundreds of fighters surrounded the patrol. It was more than enough action even for a rugby-playing tomboy who had always been mad about the military. 'I remember sitting on my dad's knee watching old war films. We'd have *Battle of Britain* on and knew it so well we'd say the words before the actors did. And the next morning I would wake up thinking, "I want to be a soldier, I want to do all that."' She had first planned to join the Royal Artillery but, with both parents working in a hospital and her brother in the St John Ambulance, she had a natural interest in medical matters. 'I suppose it was inevitable that I'd choose the RAMC,' she said.[3] She volunteered for Iraq as soon as she could. 'I joined the army to see and do things I wouldn't otherwise get the chance to experience for myself.'

She was a medic with C company of the Princess of Wales's Royal Regiment when they went into Al-Amarah on the night of 11 June 2006 in response to a spate of recent attacks. Sitting nervously inside a Warrior alongside the combat troops, all tooled up, fired up and waiting for the order to dismount, she could hear the reports flooding in over the radio net as contact after contact was joined in the town. The thought of what a rocket-propelled grenade or a bomb might do to them was difficult to get out of her mind as they kept watch through the long, dark night, 'wondering when you're going to get hit'. Outside, the guns of two hundred insurgents cracked non-stop. But then, just as it was getting light, they were ordered to go to the aid of another Warrior, which was bogged down in a ditch. A hostile crowd was surrounding it and edging closer every minute. As Michelle's team arrived on the scene, they were hit by a stream of bullets. Rounds 'pinged and dinged' off the metal sides, and the turret was taking a pasting. Inside it, the vehicle commander, Sergeant Ian Page, very much

Michelle's mentor and a father figure she confided in, was hit in the face. He had been standing with his head out of the turret and his rifle up, scanning round for targets. An incoming bullet struck his rifle and ricocheted into his cheek.

She shouted up to find out if he was OK, but there was no reply. She tried to get to him and tugged at the door of the internal cage that separates the cabin from the bottom of the turret and allows it to revolve freely. It wouldn't open. She tried again, desperate now to get up to the wounded sergeant. But the door stayed jammed. 'I realized the only way I could reach Ian was to get out of the vehicle and up on to the top of it.' She yelled to the driver to stop, then pushed her way past the other soldiers inside the Warrior, opened the back door and jumped. 'Be careful!' a voice called out to her, but she was already gone, out into the heart of a raging battle, rockets and grenades exploding all around her. The enemy sniper who had picked off Page spotted her immediately, and she came under fire straight away. Others joined in, four more gunmen targeting the slight, girlish figure now clambering up the side of the Warrior and over its roof towards the commander's hatch. She got to the top of the turret and peered down. 'Pagey was looking up at me, with this massive hole in his face. There was blood everywhere, and he was in a lot of pain. I could see the fright in his eyes.' What she couldn't see was an exit wound for the bullet and, though it had in fact gone all the way through him and out the other side, she had to assume for now that it was still inside his head – 'another complication', as she put it mildly later. It might be in the back of his throat and obstructing his airway, or in his brain. 'I just didn't know.'

She realized there was nothing much she could do from the top of the vehicle. She also realized, for the first time, that she herself was in mortal danger, that the bullets cracking around her head were meant for her. Time had stood still. She had been out in the open for three, maybe four, minutes, but to her it had seemed like seconds. Now, real time resumed with a jolt as a bullet smashed into the radio mounting a few inches from her. Then the gunner's hand came out of the turret and dragged her inside, next to the bleeding Page. She remembered thinking, 'What do I do *now*?', and she must have said it out loud, because the sergeant, who had spoken not a word so far, mumbled through teeth gritted in pain, 'Traverse the turret.' The gunner swung the turret, which unjammed the cage door, and the soldiers in the back pulled them through into the rear cabin. Now she had a little bit of room to get to work.

The Warrior took off, aiming for the nearest helicopter landing site. Crouching in the back, Michelle applied a field dressing to Page to try to staunch the blood. 'I knew I couldn't give him morphine for the pain because it's not allowed with a head wound. It affects breathing and blood pressure and can make things worse. So I checked his vital signs, his pulse, his respiration, his pupil dilation, the colour of his skin.' This wasn't easy. 'There's not a lot of light in the back of a Warrior. It's usually pitch black, but some was coming in from one of the top-cover hatches. There was also a glow from a small red light.' She peered at the patient, and he looked OK, 'considering'. But it was hard for her to tell. He was her first real casualty, and her first gunshot wound, 'so I had nothing to compare it with'. She talked to him to keep him awake and told him she needed to get fluids in him to make up for the loss of blood. 'He pulled away and grimaced. He made it clear he didn't fancy a line being put into him. But the important thing was that he'd understood me.' His response convinced her that, if nothing else went wrong, he was going to make it.

By now, they were at the landing site, and the evacuation helicopter was arriving. The sergeant was on a stretcher and away in minutes. Michelle briefed the medic taking over and stood back as the chopper lifted off. Then she climbed back into the Warrior and, as the citation for the Military Cross she was subsequently awarded put it, 'immediately and without hesitation returned to the battle'. She remembered sitting in the back of the Warrior as it continued on its patrol through the streets of Al-Amarah and worrying if she could and should have done more. 'I got myself quite worked up, with all sorts of stuff going through my head. What if he dies? What about his poor wife and parents?'

This was still in her mind when the action finally wound down and she returned to camp. It was the medic's job to wash out the blood and gore in the Warrior, but a kindly sergeant major, realizing what she had been through, stood her down. Some of the men were ordered to do it instead. But she insisted on doing her bit. 'The lads tried to stop me, but I wanted to do it. I couldn't just sit around. At that stage I didn't know whether Pagey would survive, and I knew I'd just break down if I had nothing to do. So we cleaned it out.' The citation for her award also recognized her mental toughness – something not always fully appreciated in medics – for carrying out 'this psychologically difficult task, even on being told that someone else would do it'.

It was a while before she heard that Page had come through an operation and was fine and making good progress. The doctor who brought her this news had no doubt that she had saved his life. 'If it wasn't for you getting to him when you did and doing what you did, he would have died,' he told her. Michelle broke down and cried. To her embarrassment, she was the hero of the hour. 'People kept coming up to me and shaking my hand. But I was only doing my job.' She was a hero back home too, as the first woman ever to be awarded the MC, which was presented to her by the Queen. 'Her total disregard for her own personal safety to save the life of a comrade showed incredible bravery, particularly for a soldier so young and inexperienced,' read the citation. 'The bravest girl in the army' was how one newspaper described her.' She was 'gobsmacked'. 'Lots of people did far braver things and didn't get medals. Look at Pagey. He had exposed himself by standing up in his turret and letting them shoot at him. How brave is that?'

The greater reward came when she returned from Iraq to Germany and was queuing at the barracks to hand back her body armour to the stores. 'I heard someone say, "Cheers, Pagey," and I realized he was working there in the Quartermaster's office. I walked in, and he dropped his book and said, "Private Norris!", and he walked over and gave me a big hug and a kiss and said, "Thank you." I had tears in my eyes.'

★

As the military demands in Iraq increased and the dangers grew, so more and more young people were rapidly trained up as combat medics. A few months behind Michelle Norris in the intensive pre-deployment course at the military medical training centre at Keogh Barracks in Hampshire was the vivacious Eleanor Dlugosz, a nineteen-year-old of unusual talents and high spirits. Known as Ella or 'DZ', she was a long-haired blonde who loved bubble baths and ball gowns – and action, plenty of it. As an energetic schoolgirl growing up in the English countryside, she rode horses, fished and went shooting. She was feisty and demanding – but not naughty enough to make the final selection for *Brat Camp*, the Channel 4 reality-TV programme that puts out-of-control kids through the rigours of wilderness training in America. She had applied because she wanted to be on the television, and begged her mother to exaggerate her faults – 'I promise I'll be good if you tell them I'm really really bad!' – to give her a chance. She got as far as the final twenty.

Her grandfather, Lionel Veck, remembered her out hunting on Exmoor, always up with the pack on her grey mare and in the river up to her neck in pursuit of a stag.[4] Her love of adventure and the outdoor life was why she had joined the army. On training camps, though just five feet two inches in height, wearing tiny size-four army boots and looking 'drop-dead gorgeous', she proved her toughness, never hanging back, being the first to jump into a freezing lake or to cut off the head of a chicken for the supper pot. The sergeant used to goad the big and brawny boys in her platoon: 'You wusses! Are you going to be beaten by a girl?!'[5]

Though she longed to drive a tank, as a woman soldier she was denied a posting to a cavalry or an infantry regiment, so she opted instead to be a medic, because that guaranteed she would get to the front line. Her mother, Sally, proudly watched her graduation at Keogh, 'so smart in her uniform, and all those young faces with her, eager and keen and ready to go'. Both of them knew the risks, though there was a tacit agreement between them not to mention the danger she faced.

Eleanor had one stint in the British hospital in Iraq and then returned to the UK for an upgrading course, taking her from a

Class Two to a Class One medic. From basic first aid, cleaning up and scrubbing out, she graduated to more advanced work, the sort that saves lives. She learned how to make an incision through the skin and the cricothyroid membrane of the larynx to open up a patient's airway. She could drain a lung and give resuscitation. At home, she drank sherry with her mother and, together, they sang along to the soundtrack of *Grease* and Gilbert and Sullivan's *Mikado*, but her heart was elsewhere. She told her mother she was longing to get back to Iraq once the course was over.

She was deployed back to Basra at the beginning of March 2007. Major Phil Carter, officer commanding 24 Close Support Medical Squadron, remembered her return. A girl he had thought of as rather quiet and reserved in carrying out her hospital-based duties burst back on the scene with her Class One qualification, a changed person, confident and with renewed vigour. She was fully operational for front-line duties. He watched her setting out on patrol, climbing into a Warrior, chatting away to the infantry guys, and clearly valued and respected by them in return. They loved her obvious zest for life and the permanent smile on her face. It cheered them up on difficult days.

She had been back in Iraq less than a month when she went on a reconnaissance patrol with the Duke of Lancaster's Regiment, to which she was now attached. With her was another RAMC medic, Corporal Kris O'Neill, and they were sharing a Warrior with Second Lieutenant Joanna Yorke Dyer, an Intelligence Corps officer, Kingsman[6] Adam Smith and a civilian interpreter. They had been on a night-time mission to raid an arms cache and arrest an Iraqi whom Intel had identified as a key insurgent leader. They were returning to base when a massive roadside bomb detonated beneath the vehicle, tore through its unprotected underside and killed them all instantly. The one survivor, a military policeman, remembered hearing a big bang, 'and the next thing I was looking up at the moon'.[7] The blast made a crater three feet deep, and the following morning local children were seen dancing round the wreckage and waving a battered soldier's helmet.

Phil Carter and his team were devastated by the deaths of two of their medical colleagues. 'They were ours, and it hurt us,' he recalled.[8] The bespectacled twenty-seven-year-old O'Neill was a mature and unflappable medic to whom the others looked for guidance, DZ the bright young thing who trailed laughter in her wake. The terrible irony for their RAMC colleagues was that they had not even had the glimmer of a chance to try to save them. The two had been declared dead at the scene, and all the skill and determination of dozens of medics and doctors counted for nothing. 'People dealt with the shock and the grief differently. Some took out their feelings in the gym, some talked quietly in groups, some kept their thoughts to themselves,' Carter remembered. 'I threw myself into work.'

He formally identified the bodies when they were brought back to the hospital later that day. Trained as a GP, he had seen death before, 'but not on a personal level'. The bodies were laid out on separate trolleys in a tented area, and he lifted the sheets covering them to see their faces and confirm their names. 'Strangely, it wasn't shocking, just very quiet, and so desperately sad. The sergeant major was with me, but we didn't speak to each other. No words were necessary. We tried not to show any emotion at the time, but we both found it hard afterwards. We took solace from the fact that we had done the right thing. In civilian life, a family member would normally identify a body, but on military operations that's not possible. We are their family, and we performed that duty on behalf of their own loved ones.'

He then had to sit down and compose letters to those loved ones. 'That was truly difficult.' He could no longer bite back his feelings. The ramrod military shoulders drooped a little and cracks appeared in the doctor's professional detachment. He was overtaken by a desperate desire to talk to his wife. 'I couldn't stop thinking about my family and my kids. When you go off on operations, you always have that bravado that "It'll never happen to me." But as I wrote those letters, I knew that it could.' He struggled with the thought that it might have been his own family who were on the receiving end of words just like the ones he was struggling to compose.

In the household in England that was soon to receive Carter's tribute to his colleague DZ, there was a numb air of bewilderment. Two officers in civilian clothes had come to the door of her grandfather Lionel Veck's home in Swanmore in Hampshire looking for Sally, Eleanor's mother. They would speak to no one else. A retired fireman whose working life had made him no stranger to sudden death, he guessed their purpose. 'I'd heard on the midday news that there had been an incident and four people had been killed in a Warrior. There was no detail, no mention that two were medics, but if you've got somebody serving in that part of the world and there's been an incident, you think, oh God I hope it's not . . . That happens every single time the news comes on.' It was why Sally wouldn't have a television in the house and never listened to the news. 'I knew that, if there was something I needed to be told, then somebody would come and let me know – *and they did*.'

Sally, who was asleep after her nightshift as a hotel receptionist, was woken up and came downstairs to confront her worst nightmare. 'They said that there'd been an incident and Eleanor had been travelling in a Warrior and unfortunately she'd died. There was nothing else they could say. They stayed about an hour, saying who was going to come and see me the next day and where I could ring. But it didn't sink in. It was a blur, and I can't really remember much. I was in a state of instant shock.' In the garden was a shed, and she took to hiding there in the following days and weeks, not wanting to see any of the friends who came to offer words of comfort. There was no comfort for her. 'I shut the shed door and just sat there in a chair, holding photographs of her and weeping. The dogs would come and sit with me. Dogs know. They can sense hurt.'

Hundreds of letters of condolence arrived, and great swathes of flowers. Two of the envelopes in the huge postbag had unmistakable handwriting – Eleanor's. She had sent them before setting off on that night sortie in Basra. They were as chatty and bubbly as ever, telling her mother what she had been up to with her mates, but there was an undercurrent of reality about them that seemed uncanny in the light of what had happened. Some of her friends had been injured, she wrote, and she had treated them. She was worried that one of them was not going to make it.

Her funeral was a massive affair, with hundreds packing the medieval St Peter's church in the small Saxon town of Bishop's Waltham, near Winchester, and spilling out into the churchyard, where the service was relayed on loudspeakers. It was a spring day in a green and lush place, England in all her April finery, as far removed as one could imagine from the dust-strewn Middle East street where she died. Her coffin, draped in the union flag, was brought on a horse-drawn carriage, and eight RAMC colleagues carried it inside. On top perched her distinctive high-brimmed army cap, a woman soldier's formal headwear. That two women had died in this one incident seemed especially shocking and sparked unusual media interest. Fresh debate began in some circles about whether it was right, even in these enlightened and egalitarian times, for women to be on the front line and exposed to such danger. The ever-cheerful DZ would have laughed away such an idea. 'She loved the army,' her mother said, her voice cracking with pain and pride. 'It was what she wanted to do, the life she wanted to lead. I couldn't have stopped her, even if I had wanted to.'

Eleanor's death had a profound effect on Michelle Norris, for, between them, they encapsulated the lottery of war. Both were medics, both were nineteen, both went to Iraq. One returned with a top medal for conspicuous gallantry, the first Military Cross ever awarded to a woman soldier, while the other came home in a coffin, the youngest woman soldier to die in combat. One lived. One died.

'Ella was in a Warrior, doing exactly the same job as me,' said Michelle, nervous at the parallel, 'and she was blown up.' It could, she knew, just as easily have been the other way round. 'You try and forget about the risks you're taking and the danger you're in, but there are certain moments when you can't. You have to sit down and have a think, or a cry, or talk to someone. But there has never been a moment when I've regretted joining up.' The late and much lamented Eleanor Duglosz would have said 'amen' to that thought.

For her grandfather, there was some solace in the widespread impact her death made. 'It focussed public opinion on the reality of war. And the various ceremonies and services in Eleanor's honour all help to keep that in the public eye. It would be so neat and tidy politically for what happened in Iraq to be lost in the smoke and forgotten, but for her sake I hope it never is.' He was speaking a year after her death, by which time British involvement in Iraq was winding down, the troops withdrawing to an enclave at Basra airport and leaving the city and the countryside, theoretically, to the Iraqi army and police but, in reality, to the Shia militiamen who had been their enemies, the killers of Kris O'Neill and Eleanor Duglosz and the scores of other British dead. It was the debacle, verging on defeat, that many critical of the Iraq war had always dreaded.

It is hard to think of another foreign venture that British forces entered into with so little public support at home. Iraq was a politician's war – Tony Blair's, on the coat tails of the United States – every bit as much as the Falklands was Margaret Thatcher's. But instead of a quick, clean kill, as in the South Atlantic, there was a long-drawn-out occupation that cost lives, sapped morale and missed many of its objectives. From the start, millions of ordinary people had doubts that the war was wise or winnable, but the politicians prevailed, through a dubious drive of anti-Saddam scaremongering. When, after the initial victorious invasion, no weapons of mass destruction were found, the case was unsustainable. But, by then, British forces were in place and could not be withdrawn without loss of face.

They stayed to implement an ill-conceived plan of reconstruction, while in the eyes of the Iraqi people they turned from liberators to a force of occupation, to be fought and resisted at every turn. Piggies in the middle of this absurd political muddle, British troops performed with exceptional bravery, skill and dedication, despite being undermanned and under-equipped. In December 2008, to everyone's relief, the prime minister Gordon

Brown announced an end – the remaining four thousand British troops would leave Iraq by the summer of 2009, which they duly did. By then, however, a not-dissimilar war every bit as bitter and bloody had been going on for several years a thousand miles away, against the Taliban insurgents of Afghanistan, and in the battle for that country of high mountains and dry deserts, there was no end in sight. It was less of a hole-in-the-corner conflict than Iraq and, to begin with at least, it was fought much more out in the open against a skilled and organized enemy. It was fierce and fast-moving, the quintessence of modern warfare. For medics, saving lives under these conditions would be hugely testing.

15. On Afghanistan's Plains . . .

Corporal Stu Giles never knew for sure whether the first life he saved on the battlefield was that of an ally or an enemy. The man in the baggy *shalwar kameez*[1] who was brought to him on a wheelbarrow with his leg smashed apart by a bullet could have been an innocent, a young Afghan farmer caught in the middle of this battle raging under a fierce summer sun in June 2006. More probably, though, he was a Taliban guerrilla, who, just moments before incurring his atrocious wound, had been trying to kill any khaki-clad Para he could line up along the barrel of his AK47 rifle. Giles was a company medic with the 3rd battalion of the Parachute Regiment, who were among the earliest batch of British troops to fly into Afghanistan that year in what was intended as a policing mission, to bolster the democratically elected government there in its struggle to contain Islamic extremists. This police work – taken on, to the horror of the military, while Iraq was still an unresolved mess eating up manpower and resources (as well as costing lives) – soon escalated into bloody war. At Now Zad, one of a number of hostile townships in the desert where the troops were tasked to make their presence felt, came the first major head-to-head.

For the Paras, this began with what to them was a routine 'search and cordon' mission of the type they had often mounted in Northern Ireland. Intelligence reports identified a mud-walled compound on the edge of the town as a bomb factory and a Taliban safe house. A force of around a hundred dropped in to seize and neutralize it. 'We were being fired on before we'd even managed to get off the Chinook,' Giles recalled. He never liked being in a helicopter, crammed in alongside his mates as if they were pilchards rather than Paras. The noise of the engines reverberated like an express train in your head while your mind tried not to think too much about what lay ahead when the ramp went down. For all its size and horsepower, it was a potential death trap. As he saw it, 'you're inside a great big tin with a couple of big engines strapped on. I couldn't wait to get down on the ground and back on my two black taxis, my own feet. At least then you have some say over your own destiny.'[2]

The Chinook travelled low across country and came in fast, the pilot cutting his speed at the last minute to dump the aircraft down and disgorge its contents of fighting men on to the hot sand. As they raced off the ramp and fanned out, looking for cover, bullets came spitting from wadis nearby, and the sound of gunfire cracked through the air. An advance party of Gurkhas had set up a perimeter and was already engaging the enemy, who were putting up fiercer resistance than anyone had expected. Green tracer flashed backwards and forwards. A full-scale battle was shaping up, of a sort that the Paras, as a regiment, had not experienced since their glory days in the chilly wastes of the Falklands.

Giles, though medically trained, was first and foremost a fighting soldier, and he threw himself down alongside the machine-gunners, who had a bead on Taliban positions in an orchard a few hundred yards away and were returning fire. It felt good to be with his mates. They gave each other confidence. 'Camaraderie is what Paras thrive on. It's almost as important as your weapon.'

The fighting intensified. Masked and black-turbaned gunmen ran out from behind the shelter of a long mud wall, sun-baked and as hard as concrete, and stood to fire rapid volleys before ducking out of sight again, only to reappear, guns blazing once more, at a different point. Others lurked in the doorways of the compound, shooting furiously, then dodging away. There were eighty or more of them in all, circling like hyenas in packs of a dozen, one soldier reckoned, and popping up from every direction to bite and snarl and then run off.

Handfuls of civilians scuttled around and added to the chaos and the uncertainty. Women and children huddled in sheltered spots, terrified, adult hands curled over small heads as if they could ward off the storm of bullets. The Paras were being halted – pushed back, even, in places – until Apache gunships arrived in the sky overhead to rake the Taliban positions and break the deadlock. The troops moved in to secure the compound while, outside, running battles continued for the next four hours.

Giles was spreadeagled in the dust of a dried-up riverbed when he got a call on the radio – a casualty inside the compound needed urgent medical attention. 'I ran into the courtyard and was presented with this Afghan guy on a wheelbarrow.' The medic ducked as bullets smacked into a wall behind him. 'I had no idea who he was. He could have been in the local police or army and therefore, technically, one of us. Or he might have been a civilian in the wrong place at the wrong time. Or a Taliban fighter. I just didn't know. It wasn't like the Second World War out there. We weren't fighting an enemy in a recognizable uniform.'

The wounded man's allegiance was, in any case, immaterial. 'If you're a medic, what you see is a human being in need of help, and your job is to give the same care to friend and enemy alike.' This was something Giles had thought through and felt strongly about. 'Isn't that what we signed up to in the Geneva Convention? He's a casualty. Somebody else can make the decision later about whose side he's on. Of course, the enemy don't think that way. But then, as my dear old mother used to say, "Treat people as you'd like to be treated yourself."' Which, as guns continued to blaze around him, he did.

He knelt down in the dust to examine the man slumped in the barrow, his limbs, tipping over the sides, a mess of blood and mangled flesh. The Afghan's tibula and fibula were totally smashed. 'The bone was snapped in half, and his foot was closer to his knee than it was to the floor. By rights he should have been screaming in agony, but he was very calm and quiet.' Giles found himself admiring the man's stoicism. 'Before I could splint him I had to untwist his foot and straighten his leg, but he hardly flinched.' This was clearly an enemy to be reckoned with.

His immediate job done, Giles handed the man over to the boss, Captain Harvey Pynn, the A company doctor, who had just made his way through the vicious fighting outside and into the compound. The thirty-two-year-old Pynn was, like Corporal Giles, seeing action for the first time, though he had a long pedigree of military service to draw on. His grandfather had been a Para sergeant major who fought in North Africa and Italy in the Second World War. His father was an RAF pilot. A cousin was on the *Sir Galahad* when she was bombed in the Falklands. 'He was burnt, but not badly. I remember it well. I was eight at the time.'[3]

Arriving at Camp Bastion, the main British base in Afghanistan, from England, had been a shock – the barrenness, the dust that invaded every nook and cranny, the energy-sapping heat that made even the lightest of exercise a struggle to breathe. The training 3 Para had undergone back in England was an indication that it was no picnic they were embarking upon. 'Suddenly, the doctor and the medics are everyone's best friend,' Pynn recalled. 'I didn't need to encourage the guys to come to medical training. They asked for it.' He taught them how to deal with catastrophic haemorrhage and airway control and schooled them in the use of the new and faster field tourniquet and QuikClot, the powder that stopped bleeding. Even those men who picked up the smallest knowledge of first aid might learn enough to gain the seconds and minutes vital to saving a comrade's life, or their own, on the battlefield.

Pynn's mood, as dark as the wind-blown dirt tornadoes that whipped along the bleak ground at Bastion, had lifted when he joined a platoon of Toms on a foot patrol in the desert town of Gereshk and they tabbed through streets where the smells of fresh baking and barbecued meat from market stalls mingled with that unmistakable Third World stench of rotting faeces and detritus. Inquisitive locals smiled and waved. 'We stopped cars and motorbikes and checked them without complaint.' There was no obvious sign of the Taliban. He felt confident. The winning of hearts and minds seemed a real possibility. 'That was supposedly why we were there – to reconstruct the country, not to blow it up. The Americans had been doing *that* for ages.'

The next day he came up against a harsher reality, when an Afghan Army convoy was hit by a roadside bomb, and casualties were brought into the British camp. Three bodies lay in the back of a pick-up truck, 'blown to smithereens, all severely mangled, with femurs shattered, intestines hanging out, decapitated. It was obvious they were dead, but to double check, I opened the airway of one of them, and his head nearly came away in my hand.' The doctor was stunned. 'I'd never seen anything like this before, not even in a textbook on traumatic injuries. All this damage and destruction from what was a fairly small bomb.' The danger sank in. 'The enemy are not selective. Doctor, padre, infantry soldier, we are all equally at risk. This could happen to any of us.' His fourth viewing of *Black Hawk Down*, in the mess tent, reinforced the message.

And now here he was in the middle of his first firefight – that moment professional soldiers long for and dread in equal measure, wondering how they will stand up to the test. 'It was hairy stuff, but this was what I'd joined for – to go on operations with the battalion. And here I was with 3 Para on the most aggressive op since the Falklands. I was very conscious of my own vulnerability but I don't remember being scared.' He didn't have time.

The rotors of the Chinook screamed as they ripped up the leaves from nearby trees and it slammed on to the landing site. As he raced off down the ramp, Pynn was glad in that instance that he had opted not to wear the latest full body armour. When he had tried it on, it was as restrictive as a suit of armour and felt as if it weighed a ton. He knew he would need to be as nimble as possible on his feet, and he had ditched it in favour of a slip-on chest protector. Now, he was running, keeping as low as possible, heading for cover. 'Outside the compound, I threw myself into a muddy ditch – probably the urinal cum shitter cum used-needle depository.' Above his head the Apaches circled, their chain guns chattering as they dumped round after round into the Taliban positions. He was astonished by the enemy's persistence. 'They seemed willing to take us on, no matter what firepower we hit them with.' They even blazed away at the helicopters two thousand feet in the air, and one was forced to wheel away, a bullet in the tail.

It was in a lull in the skirmishes that two men were seen pushing that wheelbarrow with its bloodstained, badly injured human cargo towards the compound. They were searched for booby traps before being ushered through to the courtyard, where Stu Giles straightened the Afghan's broken leg and then handed him over to Pynn, who by now had climbed out of the stinking ditch in which he had taken cover and made it inside the walls. The doctor had no doubt whose side this man was on. 'He was blatantly Taliban, though he adamantly denied it. Nonetheless, I treated him to the best of my ability.' With gunfire crackling around him, he was putting his own life in danger for an enemy combatant, but this was a not uncommon occurrence in this strange conflict. A paramedic, RAF Sergeant Rachel McDonald, had at one point found herself treating a Taliban fighter with gunshot wounds and discovered clear evidence of explosives on him. She put the incriminating package in her pocket to hand over to the Intel boys later and went on treating the man. The incongruity made her laugh. 'In one hand I've got my first-aid kit to try and save his life and in the other traces of the explosives that he could have killed us with. It was a mad feeling.'

In the insanity of Pynn's particular situation, what worried the doctor most was the logistics (not to mention the personal danger) of getting his enemy casualty to hospital for surgery. To save the man's life, he would have to transport him to a rescue helicopter, which would mean crossing open ground to the landing site with the man on a stretcher or on his back. How was he going to get there without being mown down by other members of the man's guerrilla unit? In the end, Pynn decided that it simply had to be done, and the quicker the better. He bundled the wounded Afghan back into the barrow, put his own head down and trundled as fast as he could the quarter-mile to the helicopter, risking a sniper's bullet every step of the way. It was a selfless and thankless act in difficult circumstances and over rough terrain, but they made it to the helicopter in one piece and the Afghan was hoisted on board.

Pynn climbed in after him. The man's condition had noticeably deteriorated, and the doctor made the difficult decision to go with him, though it meant leaving behind his own men in an as yet unfinished action. On the flight to Bastion he put in a line, pumped fluids into his patient to keep him going and radioed ahead for a crash team to be ready to operate the moment they touched down. At the hospital, the medics were shocked less by the casualty and more by the sight of Pynn. He was covered in blood and gore from the wounded man. In their pristine smocks and having had little but routine cases to deal with so far, they were suddenly made aware of the stark realities of military medicine. There was a war out there, and it was not going to be pleasant or easy.

But the Paras were exultant that night. Their mission had ended with eighteen Taliban gunmen dead, and others captured. 'The guys had fought hard and used lethal force when necessary, but showed admirable restraint when civilians were in the area,' Pynn noted. Better still, 3 Para had returned to base intact. The nearest they had come to taking a casualty was when a bullet thudded into the chest of one of them, but, by some miracle, the spare magazine he was carrying in his webbing took the full impact. They had been lucky . . . so far.

★

The euphoria of the battle won at Now Zad lasted only a few days, until news came of the British task force's first death. Captain Jim Phillipson had been killed in a shoot-out at Sangin,[4] and the refrigerated mortuary container at Bastion opened up to receive its first, body-bagged occupant. The mood among the men was gloomy, and the latest sandstorm could not explain away all the red eyes seen around the camp that day. 'It was a stark reminder that we're not here to play games. At breakfast, there was even less conversation than usual,' Pynn recalled. He knew much would rest on his shoulders in the increased fighting that now seemed certain to lie ahead. 'I'd be dealing with serious casualties in the next few months. I had to prepare myself for the worst.'

The thought galvanized him into creative action. The wheel-barrow at Now Zad had made him aware of a flaw in the 'casevac' plans. Flying in helicopters to take out the wounded was all well and good, but what if the only safe landing place was a long way from the action? As well as making himself a target for the gunmen, he had nearly crippled himself pushing the wheelbarrow and its occupant over deep furrows and ditches. 'In the old days, we had armoured ambulances to take casualties off a battlefield, but they were no use out here. But we did have quad bikes with trailers for ferrying ammunition and other supplies around, so I had these adapted by an army metal-smith and fitted with a special frame to take two stretchers side by side. Although not a comfortable ride, this was quicker and safer than trying to run carrying a stretcher.' Here was a modern solution to an ageless problem. The quad bikes were every bit as innovative in getting injured men off the battlefield as the horse-drawn ambulance carts of the American Civil War, or the mule panniers and the field litters of the Franco-Prussian War.

Without realizing it, the men of 3 Para were about to embark on their most dangerous mission. It began with what was intended to be a quick in-and-out insertion into the town of Sangin, on the banks of the Helmand River, to pick up a civilian casualty from the compound of Afghan government offices in its centre. Once there, the casualty was evacuated but they were ordered to remain. Taliban forces were believed to be massing for an attack. Sangin, with its fourteen thousand residents and a farmer's market crucial to the local economy, must not be allowed to fall into their hands.

An epic siege lasting several weeks got underway. The Paras bedded in to their dirty and dusty quarters, building sandbag fortifications (known as sangars) for machine guns on the rooftops of the mud-and-breeze-block compound and in the garden, and strengthening the outer walls. The living conditions were rough – there was no running water, no electricity, no beds and just a handful of plastic garden chairs to sit on. Then again, as one observer noted wryly, no one ever joined the Paras to be comfortable. From the top of a two-storey tower, spotters, their powerful .50 cal machine guns at the ready, had a clear view over the houses and shops of the town and the dead ground between it and their makeshift fort. They were acutely conscious that an attack could come from any one of three sides, and probably from all three at the same time.

At sundown, the Paras prepared themselves by testing their mortars, the sound of their explosions mingling with the cries of the *muezzin* from the town mosque just a few hundred yards away. The atmosphere was eerie. As he laid out his aid post next to what had been designated as the ops room, Pynn's mind drifted back in time to Rorke's Drift, the British outpost besieged by a Zulu army in southern Africa in 1879. Now he knew how the outnumbered garrison of red-coated soldiers there must have felt as they heard the war cries of the enemy warriors camped around them and waited for the inevitable attack. His illustrious predecessor, Surgeon Major James Reynolds, had won a Victoria Cross for his courage in continuing to treat the wounded, despite the waves of assegai-wielding warriors crashing over the outpost's makeshift barricades and clawing their way through mud walls into his aid post. Pynn could only hope he would do as much if the worst happened.

It would mean protecting himself at the same time as treating casualties – being a soldier as well as a doctor. He would also have to prepare himself to carry out real surgery, if lives were to be saved. If a firefight went on for a long time, there would be little chance of rescue helicopters getting in to evacuate the wounded to hospital – in which case he would be left as their only means of treatment. 'In my head I went through lists of possible injuries, checking off that I had the correct equipment to cope with them.' He zipped open his medical pouch, containing twenty kilos of supplies, and went through the contents. With these he could handle several seriously wounded casualties. But what if there were more? His mind raced over the possibilities, and he reckoned that the worst-case scenario would be a Chinook trying to land, being hit and crashing. 'We'd have forty or more casualties to deal with. I had to plan medically what I would be able to do in those circumstances – probably not a lot, but I had to think about it anyway.' He cleaned his rifle and re-checked his supplies. He was nervous. 'I had the basic equipment, and I probably had the skills. But I hadn't got the experience, and I wasn't sure how I was going to cope.'

Pynn's apprehension was matched by increasing truculence in

the town itself. Para foot patrols along the streets were met by sullen looks and the occasional stoning. Radio intercepts picked up chatter suggesting fighters were gathering. Shops in the bazaar closed early, and locals were seen to be leaving. Everything pointed to an imminent attack. It didn't come – not that night, nor the one after. There was sporadic firing, but not an all-out onslaught. The Taliban had the seventy defenders suspended in a state of constant readiness and high anxiety. Pynn was not alone in feeling uncomfortable. 'I had always imagined myself out on assault oper-ations, not stuck in a defensive location like this, the turkey in a turkey shoot. It's more stressful to be in a defensive posture. The pressure on the Toms manning the sangars was immense.'

It was a nail-biting week before the enemy opened up with any seriousness, with a fifteen-minute flurry of heavy gunfire into the compound from a dry riverbed 350 yards away. A rocket-propelled grenade took a chunk out of the front of the main building. Then, after a lull of four days and nights, the Taliban came again, creeping through the dark towards the compound. At 11 p.m., the noise of gunfire startled Pynn out of his sleep. He dived for his helmet and his body armour. Bullets crashed into the walls, and the rounds seemed so close that he had the dreaded thought that the enemy were actually in the compound. After a moment, he came to his senses and realized that couldn't be the case. Three heavily armed sangars stood in their way, and they wouldn't easily get past them, not given the hell of a fight the Paras inside them were putting up with machine gun, cannon, missiles and mortar.

The fact that he thought this possible, even briefly, was an indication of how jumpy he and the whole garrison were becom-ing. Once again, he cleaned his rifle, making sure it was ready. When this particular flurry of fighting finished, as abruptly as it had started, the Paras could see how close the Taliban had come this time. Thermal imagery showed a dozen bodies littering the open ground immediately outside the compound, cut down by the massive fusillade from the sangars. 'The surviving few had disappeared with their tails between their legs,' remembered Pynn, whose work had been confined to treating two minor injuries. 'A

Company, 3 Para had yet again proved a fearsome adversary,' he noted. Perhaps now it was all over. With his three-month posting in Afghanistan approaching its end, he dared to hope he might manage to get through his tour without any serious incident. But he was by no means certain. 'We're right at the sharp end here, so there's no place for complacency or wind-down. I need to stay sharp until I'm actually on that RAF Tristar out of Kabul.'

His caution was justified. Taliban reinforcements were now pouring into Sangin, spurred on by the losses they had just incurred, rather than deterred. The insurgents had lost face and badly needed a victory to demonstrate to the locals that they were as strong as ever. Calls for suicide bombers went out over the radio and were picked up in the Signals listening post in a sangar on the roof of the compound. Pynn chanced a trip into the town with a heavily armed patrol and saw families packing up and leaving. A chemist's shop he had visited before was shut and shuttered. 'It's like the OK Corral here,' he observed laconically. A 'significant contact' – deadpan military lingo for an all-out assault – could be expected any time soon.

The next night, the Taliban attacked with their biggest weapon, a 107mm Chinese-made rocket. It was a powerful but notoriously inaccurate device, which this time found its target, smashing through two concrete walls and demolishing the rooftop Signals sangar with an almighty explosion. 'We've been hit,' a voice from a neighbouring sniper's sangar telephoned down to the ops room. 'Blood is pouring out of my ears and a lot of blokes are screaming.' In his aid post, Pynn broke out the stretchers, while rescuers raced to the roof, which was a shambles of red-hot shrapnel, shattered sandbags and concrete. Signallers lay dying; other soldiers were seriously injured and writhing in pain. Sergeant Major Zac Leong tied a tourniquet around the shoulder of one casualty and pounded his chest to try to draw breath. Those who could get to their feet staggered down three flights of stairs to Pynn's aid post. The doctor got to work on the first two dust-covered figures who fell through his door, bloodied and in agony from shrapnel wounds in their buttocks and thighs.

As he was dressing their wounds, a party of soldiers appeared carrying a limp, bloodstained body that showed no sign of life at all. The man's left arm had been sliced off at the shoulder, leaving just a stump. He wasn't breathing and had no pulse. With no electricity and just a gas lamp to work by, Pynn pumped the soldier's chest to try to re-start his heart, but he knew it was futile. The soldier was dead. There was blood in his mouth and wounds behind both ears, indicating a brain injury that would probably have ruled out survival anyway. 'The first death on my watch,' the doctor noted later. 'I was devastated.' He said a quick prayer before turning his attention to the other casualties, stabilizing them as best he could, because he knew he wouldn't be able to evacuate them until first light at the earliest, seven hours away.

Minutes later, the inert body of another soldier was carried in from the roof, grey and unresponsive, with a large hole in his chest. But one of the stretcher-bearers desperately believed he could detect a pulse, and Pynn thrust his hand inside the gash and felt for the heart to massage it with his fingers. It wasn't even flickering, let alone beating. The life had gone. A local interpreter was also dead, still lying in the wreck of the sangar, his brains dashed against a concrete wall by the force of the blast. The only consolation the doctor could find in all this slaughter was that all three must have died instantly and not have felt a great deal of pain.

He turned his attention from the dead to those he could still help, the living, a dozen of whom were crowded in and around his tiny aid post for treatment. The place was a mess of bodies, blood and stained bandages. Some had small wounds – a slashed thumb, a stone chip in the chin – and could be patched up and sent back into the fray. Others needed more extensive treatment. They were Priority 2s, with serious but not acute injuries, and ideally needed to get to a hospital as soon as possible. That was out of the question. Pynn made them as comfortable as he could while, around him, the battle continued. The thunder of mortars and the echoing clatter of the .50 cals never stopped and seemed to get closer and closer. 'I was scared stiff and sweating profusely in my body armour and helmet. From the ops room I could hear chatter over the radio to expect further assaults, so we cleaned up the RAP and readied ourselves for the next wave of destruction. It went through my mind that we might be overrun by the enemy.' This was his greatest fear. 'I did not want to be taken prisoner . . . be tortured . . . probably beheaded. I would rather have shot myself. I had an escape plan, which was to jump in the fast-flowing canal at the back of the compound and hopefully wind up somewhere safe. I didn't know whether it would work, but . . .'

It never came to that. Apache helicopters and fighter planes flew in to drive off the attackers. But the rest of the night was filled with anxiety, the fear of another assault. Dawn came, 'the most welcome I've ever witnessed. The birds sang, as usual, but there was a grim atmosphere around the blokes. I forced some breakfast down my face through the knot in my stomach.' Pynn knew that, with three dead and seven wounded, he and his medical team had come close to being swamped. If there had been many more casualties, he would have had to prioritize treatment, and to make the agonizing decision of who he could save and who he must let die. 'It had all taken place in the dark as well, the most austere conditions one could imagine for treating the seriously injured. This was a real blooding.'

Nor did it stop there, as the next night the garrison took the initiative and laid down a lethal rain of mortars and automatic fire on anything in the town that moved. 'Groups of Taliban advanced from all directions, and were repelled or vaporized.' Wild foxes scavenged on the bodies strewn everywhere. Aircraft circled overhead, pouring down heavy cannon fire. Pynn lay on the floor of the RAP, deafened by the constant barrage but growing in confidence that the worst might be over. Once again, dawn brought some respite from the battle, and weary soldiers were able to stand down, but it was noticeable that the bravado had gone out of them. They were quiet, thinking their own thoughts, eyes glazed over in what Pynn called 'the thousand-yard stare', as the death of comrades sank in. He thought of Caroline, his wife of less than a year, to whom he regularly spoke on the satellite telephone.

But he couldn't phone her now. After fatalities, there was an immediate lock-down on communications, to stop the names of the dead slipping out until next of kin had been told.

Back in London, Caroline was more aware than other soldiers' wives that something was up. She worked as a news editor on ITN and saw the agency reports coming in of the battle at Sangin and the British deaths.

I didn't know he was in Sangin as such but I knew he was off base [Camp Bastion] and was probably in some pretty dangerous situation. But then everything went quiet, and for a long time all we heard from the Ministry of Defence was that they were trying to contact next of kin. The thought flashed through my mind that they were trying to get in touch with me but couldn't because I hadn't told the army welfare people where I worked and they didn't have my mobile number. That day I chewed my nails down to the quick. I was convinced it was Harvey. I remember being worried about how I was going to be told and how I would react in that moment. That was something I used to dream about all the time he was away. I really worried about that . . . funny, isn't it? That night there were still no names from the MoD when I left work. 'We still can't find the next of kin,' was all they would say, and I thought it had to be me. I remember driving home and, as I turned into our road, I was trembling and hyperventilating. I was convinced there was going to be a car outside waiting for me with two men in it, bearing the worst news.[5]

But it was other families who would be hearing the doleful truth that night. Her doctor husband was alive, though wishing with all his heart that he was somewhere other than hunkered down in the Sangin compound. 'The guys who've been to Iraq say they've never encountered battles like this,' he noted. 'This is by far the toughest deployment that even the most hardened modern-day paratrooper has ever endured.' It was on a par with the legendary fighting 3 Para had done in the Falklands, 'and I'm proud to have been part of it. But I can't wait to get back to the comparative safety of Bastion and then on to England.' Not only was his tour nearing its end, with just a few weeks to run, but he and his men were about to be relieved. Another group of Paras could step up to the mark. A Company had done its bit. But getting home was not going to be quite as easy as Pynn hoped.

*

A Chinook was incoming, arriving with replacements and to take out a batch of tired troops from A Company. They were in high spirits. The fighting had died down, and not only had they just had their first uninterrupted night's sleep for a week, they were also thinking of home comforts. A patrol edged out of the gate of the compound and across a wadi to secure the landing site. This was a quick task, and as routine as any operation at Sangin ever could be, so they hadn't bothered with helmets, just their maroon Para berets. Medic Stu Giles went with them. 'We were a little anxious, but who wouldn't be? We were in one of the most dangerous places on the planet at that time, and you could never be sure what was going to happen. But we had the machine guns on the outer fence at our backs, so we felt pretty safe.'

They fanned out left and right to form a box, 'and then everything kicked off. Rounds came wanging round our heads. We were ambushed.' He threw himself flat on the ground, 'the adrenalin pumping, the heart going, looking to see where the shots were coming from and returning fire'. Instantly, a man was down, and the cry went up for help. Giles and the platoon sergeant, Dan Jarvie, leapt to their feet and ran two hundred yards through the bullets to where Jacko – Private Damien Jackson – lay in a heap in the dust. 'I don't know whether that was brave or stupid,' the medic reflected later. 'But in the Paras the guys are family and so it's shit or bust to help them.' He had braved bullets for a wounded enemy – how much more would he risk for one of his own?

I didn't stop to think. Frankly, you wouldn't make a very good medic if you did at times like that. Dan and I just got up and ran, and it was as if we had blinkers on. All you can see is that one of your mates is hurt and you have to get to him. Dan was the best running companion I could have had. I'd known him my entire army career and I totally trusted him. Only after it was all over did I stop and say to myself: 'Christ, I could have left my wife with no husband and my kids with no dad.' But at the time it didn't enter my mind. We just ran.

They skidded to the ground and crawled the last few yards to Jacko, who had been dragged down into a small depression which gave very little shelter from the enemy snipers. Corporal 'Prig' Poll was lying with him, going through the drills, checking his airways, making sure he had not swallowed his tongue. He couldn't detect breathing. 'Take over,' he urged Giles, though he believed Jacko was dead.[6] Giles set to work. 'There was just enough cover to lie prone, but if you put your head up you were a target. I shielded Jacko with my own body so I could examine him without him being hit again. It was obvious he had serious wounds. A bullet had gone in through the lower part of his stomach and out through his buttock. He had bad internal injuries, was bleeding heavily and was in shock.' There was, as always, an expectation of almost superhuman abilities placed on the medic. 'You're supposed to have all the answers. Everybody looks at you to take control. I got one of the lads to apply direct pressure on to the front wound while I went through the first-aid checks.' Dan Jarvie was frantic. Later, he would recall this as the worst thing he'd seen in his life. 'He was lying back and I was shouting at him, "Jacko, look at me, don't fucking go, stay with me." But he was quiet, really quiet. He had gone white and he was looking up.'[7]

All the time Giles was working away on Jacko, trying to resuscitate him, the Taliban were keeping up a withering hail of fire. A guerrilla could be seen with an RPG launcher; there were machine-gun nests up on the roof of a nearby building. The other Paras in the patrol were shooting back from whatever cover they had been able to find, giving as good as they got. 'Obviously, I was too busy to join in the firing, and I was vulnerable. I was totally reliant on the others. It was like being a passenger in a fast car as opposed to being at the wheel and in control. But, as you get on with your job, you trust your mates with your life.'

Mates – that was one of the Paras' great strengths. But it also put an extra burden on Giles. A mate's life was ebbing away in front of him . . . a *mate*.

You're trying your hardest, and what makes that more difficult is that it's one of your friends. I'd known Jacko for years. He was someone I was used to having a laugh with, sharing a beer, and he was in deep trouble. I controlled his bleeding as best I could, but then I saw he'd stopped breathing. I gave him mouth-to-mouth and got him breathing again, and by then a stretcher party had arrived. I manoeuvred him on to the stretcher and briefed the lads on what I'd done and what to tell the doc when they got him back to the RAP. I didn't go with them. My job was to stay with the patrol in case there were other casualties. I was on the ground another ten to fifteen minutes, though it felt a lot longer, before we were able to head back to the safety of the compound. Then I raced off to the RAP to see how Jacko was. I wanted to help the doc with his treatment.

Inside the compound, Pynn had gone to meet the stretcher as it was hurried through the gate. He knew Jacko well too – the private was one of the team of medics the doctor had schooled in emergency first aid when the battalion first arrived in Afghanistan. Now, one look was enough. He was 'blue and unresponsive', his arm hanging limply down from the stretcher. The doctor knew nothing could save him. 'We couldn't stop his internal haemorrhage. The bullet entry and exit wounds were so small I was unable to probe inside and find the site of the bleed. The speed at which he died suggests that the abdominal aorta had been hit. We tried resuscitating him for half an hour, pumping his lungs and his heart until I was drenched in my sweat and his blood. But it was no use. The luck that 3 Para had been having had run out.'

Pynn was devastated to have lost a comrade.

I sat with my head in my hands as Jacko was put into a body bag and it was sealed up. I stayed inside the RAP for some time because I couldn't bear to look his mates in the eye. I'm the doc, and I felt ultimately responsible for losing him. I struggled to hold back the tears as I finally went into the ops room. Stu Giles was there, and the look on my face told him his patient had died. He broke into floods of tears, blaming himself. Jacko had been breathing when Giles put him on the stretcher, but must have gone into cardiac arrest due to loss of blood on the way back to the compound. A catastrophic haemorrhage in this part of the body was extremely difficult for him to control, especially as he himself was under fire at the time. I tried to reassure him. Even if I had been next to Jacko when he was shot, it is unlikely I'd have managed to save him. It was his bad luck that the round struck a major artery.

But neither captain nor corporal could stop torturing themselves with what might have been. 'The thought goes through your head. What if I'd been with Stu, next to him, could we have done something more? It's not guilt, just that, seeing Jacko's lifeless body, I felt useless. As soon as he came through that gate, the doctor in me knew he was dead. But, as a soldier and a comrade, and with all the effort Corporal Giles and the stretcher-bearers had put in, I had to give it a try, just in case. They were all looking at me with that look in their eyes that says, "Come on, Doc, save him." And I couldn't. I just couldn't.'

Giles will never forget the agonized look of loss on the doctor's face as he emerged from the RAP.

He's a man who normally stands proud, but he looked shattered. He didn't have to say anything for me to know that Jacko hadn't made it. I broke down, and I was inconsolable. I blamed myself – did I give him enough care, could I have done better? I know now that I gave him the absolute best I could at that time but, in the heat of that moment of knowing he was dead, my emotions took over and I questioned my own ability. I'd never lost a patient before. I shouldn't really have broken down in front of the younger blokes. Seeing me so emotional wasn't going to help them. So, straightaway, I had to pick myself back up and try to set an example. But I found that hard, very hard. The really devastating thing was knowing that everyone had done their best, yet it didn't work and Jacko was dead. But you have to get past the sadness and the doubt – for the sake of the next patrol you go out with. You have to get on with your job.

In his heart of hearts, Pynn suspected that he, the doctor, had been in the wrong place. 'The speed at which Jacko died made me realize that, to be of use, I needed to be located as far forward as possible.' He had nothing but admiration for his medics, but their clinical skills were limited. He could do so much more than they could. 'It obviously puts me at risk to go that far forward, but my job is to support the fighting men.' As it was, he had gone further into the front line and exposed himself to more danger than some in authority in the army thought advisable. A dead doc was no good to anyone; other lives might be jeopardized if he was killed. It was his *duty* to stay alive. That was one argument.

But Pynn had made his choice to go up-country with his men, and not out of bravado or misplaced machismo.

I had no wish to see action for its own sake. Firing a rifle doesn't sit comfortably with me; my role is to save lives, not to shoot people. But the days of the doctor being with the quartermaster and the supplies at the back of the battle group are gone. If a guy gets injured, there's no point in me being two hours away by patrol. You need to be there with them. That's the reality of modern warfare. The Medical Emergency Response Team can come in and pick up casualties, but someone has to be on the ground to treat casualties at the point of wounding, and I didn't feel comfortable just leaving my medics to it.

Even so, he still wondered if he could have done more. He was not God, he knew. Life or death was not his choice to make. That decision had been taken out of his hands by the chance bullet that sliced through Jackson's artery. But could he have saved a life if he had been out with the patrol rather than back behind the walls of the Sangin compound? The remotest possibility – and it was no more than that, not even a probability – was a cross he would continue to bear. And the doctor and the medic were not the only ones whose emotions overwhelmed them in the wake of Jackson's death. The dead soldier's platoon came to pay their respects. They were hurting, each in his own way. One placed the dead man's beret – every Para's proudest possession – on the body. Dan Jarvie, fifteen years a paratrooper and hard as nails, wept. Pynn was startled. 'To see the sergeant with the reputation as the toughest man in 3 Para reduced to tears was devastating. I went outside and sat under a tree with a brew. I had to recompose myself to deal with any further casualties that tonight might bring. We were expecting another attack and, if we were contacted, the guys would be hungry for revenge. This mission takes on a new meaning now. This is war. May the soul of Private Jackson rest in peace. I said a prayer for his parents and his girlfriend before putting this whole experience behind me to concentrate on what lay ahead.'

In the sadness and the anger of Jacko's death, the doctor felt a newly intensified sense of camaraderie for 'this band of brothers'. As efforts were now directed to shoring up the defences of their 'fortress', the doctor took his turn filling sandbags for the sangars. 'No job is too menial for anyone. It's one big team, and everyone mucks in together. Some of our guys were on the roof as an RPG whizzed overhead from the bazaar. It missed, but we returned fire with interest, as usual, and the starlit sky glowed with red and orange as mortars and artillery rained in on the bazaar and a few shops burst into flames, but probably long after our enemy had fled.'

It was to be his last encounter with the hostilities for a while. He left the compound that had been his beleaguered home and hospital for eighteen long days and even longer nights. The Chinook climbed up and out over the hills of the Sangin valley, and he hoped he'd never return. Just twenty minutes later, they were back in Bastion – had it really been so close all along? 'It was a relief knowing I was out of immediate danger and that I was going to be able to sleep without the prospect of being attacked. I realized how much weight I'd lost and how pleasant it was to be back on fresh rations. I also realized how angry and pent up with aggression I'd been.'

A memorial service was held for Jacko, with three hundred sombre Paras crammed into the cookhouse to say their farewell.

He would have been twenty today, Pynn remembered thinking. 'Some people may find it curious that these tough guys turn to some sort of God in times of stress. But it's not desperation. It's a clinging to someone or something that may help them. They find it cathartic and comforting. All those hardened Toms were there, praying, because they'd lost a friend.'

Before returning to England, Pynn found himself back in Sangin, with all the sad and terrifying memories that went with that battle-field of a town. 'My heart sank as I crossed the footbridge over the canal and back into the fortress that I hoped I would never see again.' But, apart from a few desultory attacks, the Taliban were quiet. As the RPGs flew in, old sweats like Pynn calmly put on their helmets and sat behind the sandbag walls, while those new to the fort threw themselves down on their belt buckles. 'It's strange how familiarity breeds contempt, even with live fire.' The doctor was even able to do what he and everyone else had osten-sibly come to Afghanistan for – help the locals.

A platoon went on patrol in the town and brought back a ten-year-old boy who apparently lost his mother and father in one of our mortar attacks and who himself suffered shrapnel wounds in the elbow that had signs of infection. He was a chatty little kid, though a little nervous surrounded by all these English soldiers. He wasn't angry and didn't show any signs of hostility towards us – even though we had apparently recently killed his family. Either he was telling lies, or the price of life here is so little that death is just part of daily existence. We cleaned the wound, dressed it and gave him some antibiotic syrup and sent him packing with a pocketful of boiled sweets. He was the first of several takers that came to the front gate asking to see the doctor. It's significant that they feel comfortable approaching the compound. However, we must still be careful. There's an enemy out there, even though they may be 'sleeping' for now. We can't afford to get complacent, but I think we may have turned the corner in Sangin.

Pynn left soon after, but in some ways a piece of him would always remain behind. 'The Sangin experience was one that will shape my military career,' he concluded. 'Not since the Falklands has a regimental medical officer had to deal with such an intensive period of hostile intent and casualty numbers. My time there taught me the value of life and the fact that this is no game we're playing here – it's dangerous. I was thankful to leave in one piece.'

★

The doctor's tour was over, and he was on a plane on his way out of Helmand Province at the very time that, back in Sangin, his medical corporal, Stu Giles, was once again proving his mettle on the battlefield. The desert town was tense again, with the Paras of A Company back in the government compound and determined to maintain their hold over the insurgents. The Taliban were to be hounded, denied access and ease of movement. Vehicles were stopped at checkpoints, and the bazaar was patrolled.

Giles was with a detail tabbing through the streets in the mid-afternoon heat, a show of strength to ram home the message of who was in charge. The medic was taking the back marker with Jarvie, as usual, from where they could keep an eye on what was going on around and ahead. 'We passed kids on the street and ordinary people going about their normal lives, buying and selling and going to the mosque. We were acknowledging them, trying to be as friendly and courteous as possible.' On the surface, the atmosphere seemed far from hostile, but the Paras' nerves were jangling. They were reluctant to stand in one spot for too long and have more than a fleeting conversation with the locals. They were targets, and they knew it. Best to keep on the move.

Suddenly, there was shooting at the front of the patrol. Two gunmen were running along a roof above the street, two more were in a doorway ahead, and others were popping up behind. The Toms, caught in the open, dropped down and fired. Two of the gunmen fell. As the patrol traded bullets with the enemy, Private 'Eddie' Edwards was hit. Once again, Giles found himself running at full pelt alongside Dan Jarvie, bullets kicking up the dust at their feet as they went. 'We were racing along a dry riverbed and into the marketplace, where there were stalls selling fruit.

Eddie's mates had dragged him behind some cover. His leg was a real mess. The whole front of his leg was splayed open, and I was looking at raw meat.' Jarvie took in the deep wound stretching down from thigh to knee, and was sure the young soldier was going to lose his leg. 'Eddie,' he told the young soldier, trying to relax him with a quip, 'there'll be no more fucking tap dancing for you for a couple of months.' Giles pulled out a tourniquet from his Bergen and quickly looped it round the limb. 'This was a massive injury, from which he could bleed to death, especially in such a hot climate, where the heart and the adrenalin are pumping hard, so I needed to act fast. Then I got as much field dressing on as I could. I got Dan to hold Eddie's legs as I splinted them together. "I'm sorry, mate, this is going to hurt," I warned him. "I don't care," he said. "Just do whatever you've got to do." He was in a great deal of pain, but he stayed conscious throughout.'

This was to be no repeat of Jacko. Out there on the ground, Giles stemmed most of the bleeding, paying no heed to the bullets flying around him. Two of the remaining gunmen had been forced to retreat and taken refuge in a hut. Phosphorus grenades smoked them out, and the rest fled, leaving Giles free to supervise the evacuation of his patient back to the RAP. There, he and the doctor, Captain Phil Docherty, Pynn's replacement, poured QuikClot into the wound and put a field dressing tightly on top. 'It got very hot and very uncomfortable for Eddie, but it saved his life.' So had Giles. The professional medical opinion afterwards was that, without his prompt action out there in the Sangin killing zone, the private would have died. As it was, he not only lived but kept that lacerated leg, though the recovery of muscles ripped apart by splinters from his shattered femur took a long time.

Giles was self-effacing as he talked through his exploits in Afghanistan, but his modesty hid extraordinary courage, which was recognized with the award of the Military Cross, the army's third highest medal for valour in the face of the enemy, for his treatment under fire of first Jacko and then Eddie. The citation read: 'Corporal Giles demonstrated the highest standard of medical skill in treating these two casualties, and did so at significant personal risk, with little regard to his own life, in order to save the lives of others. What is remarkable is that he did this on two occasions and was aware fully of the associated dangers of going forward and treating the casualties in exposed positions when under fire. His courageous and exemplary conduct and the contribution to saving life deserves very high public recognition for gallantry in the face of the enemy.'

He received his medal from the Queen herself, at Buckingham Palace, and was thrilled. 'Who'd have thought I'd be talking to her and getting the Military Cross? That's quite a hard thing to top.' He was, though, following a family tradition. His great-grandfather, an infantry officer, won the MC and Bar in the First World War. 'I heard a lot from my nan about his career. It was one of the things that pushed me towards the army.' He hadn't intended to join up. He was eighteen, a mechanic for Ford and had two hours to kill before an interview for a job with BMW.

I passed the recruiting centre in Colchester, and there was a guy outside with leaflets saying, 'Join the army, be the best.' I went in and watched a video on the Paras, and that was it. As a kid, I remember the images from the Falklands, the battles at Goose Green and Mount Longdon and the march into Stanley. They were my heroes then, but I never imagined I could be one. I joined as an infantry soldier and decided to specialize as a medic after my dad had a heart attack. I was about to go to Northern Ireland in 2000 and was home on pre-deployment leave when he collapsed. I already had some basic first-aid skills, and I managed to save him. That was the spur for focussing my career on the medical side. If you can save the most important person in the world to you, your dad, then that's as good a reason as any for getting better at it so you can save others.

The skills to do this can be learned, but the courage to do the job has to be found deep inside, and it did not come easily. 'My role as a medic,' Giles would say, 'is to run into the firefight to help a casualty. But it's something you have to have personal battles with yourself over. It's a conscious decision. Someone is hurt and may be dying. Are you going to go to him or wait until he's brought to you? But seconds save lives – as every medic always says. It could almost be our motto. The quicker a wounded man gets treatment, the better is his chance of survival. Me sitting behind cover and arguing the toss is not going to help him. And it's not going to cut much ice with your mates either. There are guys ahead of you, even if it's only fifty yards ahead, who are advancing into battle, and they've got no choice about it. The least I can do is back them up when they need it.' But rushing in where angels fear to tread could be a problem in itself – particularly if where you're treading turns out to be a minefield.

16. Where Angels Fear to Tread . . .

No post in Afghanistan could ever be described as an easy ride – certainly not Sangin or Musah Qala or Now Zad, or any of the other desert strongholds where the Taliban would hold sway if given half a chance. But there was an extra dose of hardship for those manning and maintaining the positions protecting the Kajaki Dam, a 300-foot-high concrete and rock-filled structure straddling the Helmand River and creating a lake thirty miles long. If the whole objective of the mission was to bring light to a benighted nation, then the dam, with its massive hydroelectric and irrigation potential, was a symbol of what the western powers thought they could achieve. The electricity it generated could power the lighting of schools for evening classes, of hospitals, and of refrigeration plants to store the country's wheat crop, as an alternative to its opium-based economy. Destroying that potential was, equally, a crucial part of Taliban strategy, and the dam came under frequent attack from the insurgents. Its remoteness in mountains sun-scorched during the day and marrow-chilling at night made the outpost at the dam – Forward Operating Base Zeebrugge – and the three observation posts on hills around it, ramshackle remnants of the Soviet occupation of Afghanistan twenty years earlier, an endurance test, even for those acclimatized to this harsh terrain.

It was on one of those bare hills, codenamed 'Normandy' as a nod to regimental history, that after a night sleeping out under the stars, Lance Corporal Stuart Hale, a 3 Para sniper, woke on the morning of 6 September 2006. Far below him, in the crisp light of day, he could see a small town whose occupants were clearly on the move, packing their possessions into cars and, so he thought, heading back to their villages. He read this as a good omen, that the Taliban forces around Kajaki had withdrawn and the locals were feeling safe enough to return to their homes and get on with their lives. 'Great,' he thought. 'The war's over.' He couldn't have been more wrong. 'It turned out those people were moving away from the area permanently because they knew things were going to get a whole lot worse.'[1]

He breakfasted on a bag of bacon and beans from a ration pack and then, as his eyes roamed the arid land below him to the south, he spotted a checkpoint being set up along a road out of the town. Through field glasses, he could make out two figures in the unmistakable black garments and headgear of the Taliban. 'They'd drawn up barriers to create a sort of chicane and were stopping vehicles going through. They had rifles, and they were forcing money out of any locals who came along, intimidating them.' Here was a threat that had to be dealt with, and quickly, before the guerrillas could settle to their task and call in reinforcements. With his platoon commander, Corporal Stuart Pearson, he discussed calling in an air strike on the checkpoint, but they ruled this out: there were houses nearby, children were running around, so civilian casualties would be almost inevitable, 'and I didn't want that on my conscience'. He decided to go in on foot, get within rifle range, 'and take those guys out individually myself'. Two sniper shots from close by would get the job done without endangering anyone else. It would be just another thankless task in an increasingly thankless operation.

Hale, frankly, was wearying of this war. On his last leave, his wife, Shannon, could see in his face how drained he was. At night he tossed and turned, unable to rest, clearly troubled. 'He didn't say much about what they were up against – he wasn't allowed to. But I knew that sometimes they were fighting twenty hours a day and not getting any sleep. There was lack of water, lack of food – they were dug in and living in holes in the ground. Waiting for supplies, nearly running out of ammunition. To me, it sounded like the worst fighting since the Second World War. I just prayed that he would get through it and come back.'[2] Hale had every reason to want to get home in one piece. Shannon was pregnant, and they were both thrilled at the thought of starting a family. Hale was twenty-four and had been in the military since just before his sixteenth birthday. A different future beckoned, if only he could get through this tour.

He set off down the hill, leading the way, close behind him a Fusilier with a Minimi light machine gun to back him up should he get into a firefight and a radio operator who could double up as team medic. 'That's covered all eventualities then,' he calculated. It was 10.30 a.m. when they began their descent, literally in leaps and bounds through the rocks and scree, the lance corporal jumping ahead, then stopping to cover the other two as they followed behind. There was cover, too, from the top of the hill, where another sniper had them in his sights, tracking their every move in case of trouble. Hale reached the bottom first and took a cautious dog-leg jog, first in one direction, then doubling back on himself along flat open ground, keeping a wary eye on a nearby hill in case, as seemed all too likely, the Taliban had set up a position there. He came to a dry riverbed and, instinctively and without pausing, stretched out his right leg to hurdle it. 'Normally, whenever I hop or jump, I land with both feet and knees together. It's what we're taught in parachute training. But I got lazy this time.' Luckily. 'I jumped with just my right foot out, and as it touched down I felt it slip away beneath me. I fell. I didn't hear anything. I didn't see a flash or feel a blast or heat. It was as if I'd stood on a banana skin.' In this matter-of-fact manner, he was maimed.

He didn't realize at first and cursed himself for dropping his rifle, leaving himself defenceless, when at that very moment a Taliban Kalashnikov could be aiming at his head. He scrabbled across the dirt to reach it , 'and it was only when I raised my hand to go to lift it up that I saw the little finger on my right hand was hanging off. Then I looked down and saw the stump.' The bottom of his right leg had been sheared off. Shrapnel had exploded into the meat of his calf. The bone was broken, and his leg was splayed out at an impossible angle. 'Then I knew. I'd stood on a mine.'

*

On 'Athens', one of the other hills overlooking Kajaki, Lance Corporal Paul 'Tug' Hartley of the Royal Army Medical Corps was having a lie-in. Some of the platoon had gone off for a swim in the lake but, that morning, he had chosen not to go with them. 'It was always great going down to have a swim and a wash, but by the time you'd flogged back up the hill, you were sweating all over again and there didn't seem much point. I couldn't be bothered.'³ Hartley was an old Afghanistan hand. He'd been there on his first tour in 2004 and was now six months into his second. He'd been out with Special Forces, been under fire, seen plenty of action, but never been scared, never thought about the chances of dying . . . until the events that were now to unfold.

Corporal Mark Wright, his platoon commander, hauled him from his bed. 'There's been a fucking mine strike. Let's go.' Hartley pulled on his shorts and laced up his boots, grabbed his medical Bergen and followed Wright and the rest of the platoon as they hurtled down Athens, then up Normandy and down the other side. As he ran, he wished he'd been fitter, that he could go faster. But this was tougher than any assault course he had trained on. 'All I could think was that mates of mine were going to die because I couldn't get to them quickly enough.' He was knackered – 'absolutely gopping' – but covered the mile of rugged country to the riverbed in a little over fifteen minutes. As he came down the side of Normandy, he could see Stu Hale propped up on the bank below. He could also see what Hale had failed to notice – the tops of mines protruding from the ground. 'I'd once been in the Royal Engineers, and this was something I always looked out for. But we hadn't known that minefield was there – not until our guys were in the middle of it!' Only later would they discover these were remnants of an old war, sown by soldiers long-departed. This was not a Taliban trap they had stumbled into, but a Red Army minefield from the Soviet occupation.

Stu Hale lay there surveying his stump, 'a pretty gory sight, believe me'. He screamed his head off, more, he later thought, out of anxiety and the fear of pain rather than the pain itself. His radio man, Private 'Jarhead' Harvey, had rushed to his side as soon as he went down and helped to fill him with morphine. 'He'd been a good thirty yards behind me and had come straight to me, without any regard for his own safety – which was contrary to all our drills. Some people say it was quite stupid of him, because he might have triggered another mine himself. But, to my mind, he was just brave. He saw his mucker in danger and he reacted.' Now, as he lay on that sun-scorched riverbed, Hale's concern was that a Taliban attack was about to be launched. He wasn't to know the mine that had felled him was an old one. He naturally assumed it was newly laid and that a coordinated ambush would follow. He fumbled once more for his rifle and called out to Stuart Pearson, now arriving pell-mell down the hill with reinforcements, to stay on alert.

Pearson made his way forward, jumping from solid rock to solid rock to avoid soft earth where more mines could be lurking. Hale was calmer now and quieter, and when Pearson got to his side he swallowed down the pain and managed a joke. Was having one leg going to ruin his chances of being selected for the SAS, his big ambition? he asked, and they both roared with incongruous, tension-easing laughter. 'You'll be fine, Stu, you'll be back on your feet in no time,' said Pearson, and they laughed again. A cigarette was held to Hale's lips, and he took a long drag from it. His mind began to wander, and he started to talk about Shannon and how much he loved her. He wanted the baby she was carrying to be called Alex if it was a boy and Sophia if it was a girl. If he died, he pleaded, would someone, anyone, please make sure this last request of his was fulfilled? A slap across the cheek dragged him back from the coma he was slipping into. 'You can name him yourself, you prick, when you get home,' he was unceremoniously told.

But it was difficult to disguise the agitation of the young soldiers who were clustered round the wounded lance corporal, shocked by what they were witnessing. For some, it was the first time they had seen a casualty close up. One of them had the presence of mind to stem the bleeding by tying on a tourniquet improvised from a piece of cloth. Then 'Tug' Hartley arrived with Mark Wright and the rescue team from Athens, and took over, instantly shouldering the heavy burden of responsibility, seeing the relief in the other men's faces that a medic had arrived and hoping he could conjure up the magic to justify their almost childlike faith in his healing powers. His presence reassured Hale too. 'I was very relieved to see him. I remember him talking to me and putting me at ease.' Exuding confidence was a large part of the medic's armoury – acting swiftly, not panicking.

Hartley took a Combat Application Tourniquet from his pack, wound the band round Hale's leg, above the makeshift bandage already on it, then ratcheted the self-tightening windlass until the flow of blood stopped. Thank heavens for these latest tourniquets, which could be put on with just one hand. He inserted a cannula in Hale's arm and began an intravenous drip of saline solution. The leg was shredded from the knee downwards, the ligaments and tendons dangling like so much offal on a butcher's slab. 'I could see his kneecap and into his thigh. The little finger on his right hand had also been hit by the blast and was partially missing.' Hale was quiet – 'chilled out' – partly from the shock of his catastrophic injury, partly from the ampoule of morphine jabbed into him. The crisis seemed to have passed. Down there in the dust of that dried-up stream, two soldiers held Hale's crumpled leg stable to ease the pain of the fracture, and slightly raised to stop the blood flowing down. Others put their ponchos above his head to shade him from the merciless midday sun.

By now, 'Tug' had some professional help alongside him: his mate and fellow medic, Lance Corporal Alex Craig. Craig had been given a lift up to the top of Normandy by an American soldier in a four-wheel-drive jeep and then come hotfoot down the other side and straight into the minefield to where everyone was gathered around Hale. He knew the risk he was taking. 'I tried to make sure I stood on firm rocks, but in the end you just have to get on with it.'[4] 'Tug' was glad to see him. The last time they'd been together they had been chatting about home and friends, and licking their lips at the prospect of a beer or two together in a good old English pub. Now they were side by side, with a man's life depending on their courage and skill. 'With two of us there, it was better. We helped each other out, bounced ideas off each other, worked methodically as a team. He was my "wing-man" and I was his. And, apart from Stu losing his leg, there was no particular drama at this point, other than to get him out as quickly as possible and to an operating theatre to be sewn up.'

To effect this, the rest of the rescue team were now busily at work plotting a route out of this deadly terrain, to safe and solid ground a dozen or so yards away, to where a helicopter could then be summoned to take Hale away. They picked out the route at great personal risk. With no specialist detection equipment and no time to wait for any to be brought, they lay flat on their belt buckles and inched their way forward, prodding the ground gingerly ahead of them and marking the way with tape and small flags. Fortunately, they were close to the edge of the minefield – or so they thought – and it didn't take them long to mark out a safe exit line. Hale was lifted on to a stretcher and, with four softly treading bearers at each corner, and Hartley at the rear holding aloft the bag of IV fluid attached to his arm, he was ferried along this flag-lined corridor to be settled in comfort to wait for the helicopter. Once they reached this objective, Wright directed the rest of the platoon to follow behind, to withdraw from the riverbed and make their way back up the hill, as far away from this buried barbarism as possible.

But minefields tend not to reveal all their deadly secrets quite so readily. Corporal Stuart Pearson had started out towards the hill, carefully following the footsteps of the stretcher party, when a loud explosion lifted him clean off his feet and sent his body ripping though the air. He sat where he fell, his left leg simply gone. 'Oh shit, not me!' he remembered thinking. 'Why me?'[5] 'Tug' Hartley heard the bang and felt the blast, looked up from the stretcher where he was treating Hale and saw Pearson thirty feet away on the ground, screaming in the agony of what medics would characterize in the dry language of their calling as 'a traumatic amputation'. As Pearson gave vent to unimaginable pain, the rest of the platoon froze in their tracks. They had believed they were on the edge of the minefield but, clearly, they were still in the thick of it. The miracle was that more mines had not been triggered. The bigger miracle would be if they emerged with no more casualties. As it was, they felt as if they were in some sort of horror film, where no one was safe, where one by one they would fall to the mad axe-man.

Craig was already at Pearson's side, and Hartley stood up to go forward and help him. A shout stopped him. 'Don't fucking move,' Craig called out. Hartley did as he was told. The realization hit him that he had, just seconds before, walked along that very stretch of ground while supervising Hale's stretcher party. How had he missed the mine? How had it missed him? Perhaps he had trodden on it but it had not triggered, not then, waiting for the next man, for Stu Pearson. Were there more? Most certainly. Was anywhere safe? Not that he could see – not even the spot where he was standing. The same thought must have struck one of the soldiers in the party, because he began to scream, to panic. It looked as if he was about to run. Hartley barked an order, told him to stop, to sit down, to face the hill, away from the minefield and the terror gripping those men still stuck in it.

Craig was leaning over Pearson and could see straightaway that his right leg had been blasted off below the knee. There were multiple wounds on his body, including to the groin, which seemed to cause the groaning Pearson most distress. 'Typical bloke!' Craig muttered to himself. He worked fast to put a tourniquet on the leg, then assessed the situation. 'So that was two mines that had gone off, but we were coping. We just needed to get these guys out of here as quickly as possible.' While Craig did what he could for the badly wounded Pearson, Wright made his way across the minefield with more morphine. With Pearson down, he assumed command and was directing operations. 'He was so calm,' one soldier recalled, 'like he was on an exercise, as if it was just a drill.'[6]

The reality was that all he or anyone could do was sit tight and wait for the helicopter to come and haul them out. The minutes dragged by, an eternity of tension and a growing sense of isolation. Ears strained for the Chinook, but the best part of an hour passed before they heard the sound of its engines echoing through the mountains. And there it was, hovering noisily overhead, and at last those on the ground dared to think the incident was about to end.

Hartley looked up, saw the loadmaster's thumbs-up from the door and waited for the cable to drop down so he could hook on his casualties and have them winched up to safety. No cable came. Instead, the Chinook picked up speed, flew past and then turned for a second approach, coming lower and lower, trying, the startled men below suddenly realized, to *land*. It was madness! In a minefield! Hartley was furious. 'We'd radioed requesting a small helicopter with a winch, and they sent a huge Chinook without one.' Wright was going ballistic, frantically trying to wave the helicopter away, shouting and swearing into his radio to those back at base to get the effing thing out of there. It was too late. As if in slow motion in some terrible car-crash movie, the helicopter came relentlessly on, the down-draught kicking up dust and sand, disturbing the top soil, threatening to pile pressure on those hair-trigger metal plates, to complete a circuit that would cost more limbs, or even lives.

As its wheels touched the ground, the ramp came down at the back and the loadmaster was there again, waving at Hartley, a hundred yards away, to get his stretcher over there and on board. 'I signalled, "No," and then gave him the letters ATO for "Ammunition Technical Officer", a mine-clearance team. I was holding my hands up above my head in the shape of an A and a T and an O, just like some idiot dancing along to the YMCA song.'

Whether the loadmaster cottoned on, or whether Wright's frantic radio calls had finally got the message through to base is unclear but, either way, those on board changed tack. The Chinook suddenly lifted off, prompting another huge surge of air on the fragile ground below. The platoon huddled against the blanket of dust that now enveloped them. Wright and Craig crouched down over Stu Pearson to shelter him from the wind. There was a bright flash. The intense downwash had churned up the ground, hurling stones into the air, and one had come down and detonated a mine.[7] It exploded against Mark Wright's body, shattering his right arm and peppering his chest and neck with shrapnel.

Alex Craig collapsed too, choking and spluttering, blood draining from deep chest wounds. 'Mark took most of the impact,' he recalled.

It just blew him away. But I was right next to him, and the blast caught me too. It ripped the shirt off my back. The noise and the dust were incredible, and the heat! My right side felt as if it was on fire. I realized immediately from my breathing that one of my lungs had collapsed and was filling with blood. I'd seen this happen to other people and I knew I was in a bad way. But I didn't think I was going to die. I remember lying back and looking at everything unfolding around me and thinking, yeah, that's now the third mine that's gone off. It seemed pretty damn unreal . . . a very unlikely thing to be happening, to be honest.

*

As the dust cloud cleared and the Chinook disappeared out of sight, 'Tug' Hartley could hardly believe what he was seeing. Thirty feet away, Wright was slumped on the ground in a sitting position. And the sound that filled the air now empty of the screech of the helicopter was his scream of agony.

Now there were four casualties, all with devastating injuries. And three of them were still lying where they had fallen, even deeper inside the minefield than he was.

That's when I made my mind up that I had to go across and treat them. There was no one else. I couldn't see Alex – he had just disappeared before my eyes – and I knew it was down to me to do something. But I really didn't want to cross that minefield, and for a split second I thought of picking up a rifle and shooting them, putting them out of their misery. It sounds mad, but I was desperate. I was thinking what would happen if I was the next one to tread on a mine. Then there would be no one to help them at all. Putting the lads, my mates, out of their pain seemed the only solution.

The thought was no sooner in his head than discarded – though the memory of it, of what he contemplated doing, still haunts him. But his mind pulled itself back from the unthinkable. It was a good job it did. Alex Craig had come to and, though by rights he should have stayed where he was, he was being helped out of the riverbed and up the hill by another soldier. Mark Wright, his life-blood oozing away into the dust, was screaming for help, and the soldier nearest to him, Fusilier Andy Barlow, a machine-gunner attached to 3 Para, was trying to give him first aid, although the injuries were beyond anything a bandage could achieve. Hartley shouted out instructions to strap up what remained of the corporal's arm, to try to staunch the loss of blood, but could get little sense out of the confused and shocked trooper. The medic stood there, frustrated amid the chaos, the yelling and the screaming, until he could hold back no longer, however crazy it was to walk into a death trap. 'I thought, "Shit, I'm going to have to go over there." I was the medic, I was the one expected to do something. In my head, I'd expect any soldier, whether a medic or not, to have done the same for me. It was a very conscious decision. They are British soldiers and they are part of my family. I was aware of the danger but I had to do it.'

He stripped off his T-shirt – it was needed to make tourniquets – and picked up his medical Bergen. It had been under Hale's legs, propping them up, but he had a more pressing use for it now. He slung it a yard into the minefield. Then, when it didn't go bang, he jumped on to it, picked it up from under his feet, threw it another yard, jumped again, and so on. 'In retrospect, it wasn't a very safe method of clearing mines! There wasn't much left in the Bergen, and it probably wasn't heavy enough on its own to set off a mine anyway.' But it was effective. He was halfway across to Wright, 'when I looked back to where I'd come from and where I was going, and I realized it was my son's first birthday tomorrow. What was I doing here?! I wanted to go back – but sod's law says, if you try and go back, that's when you're going to get it, so I kept going forward.' He had come ten yards and had another couple to go to reach the corporal when there was another loud explosion. Fusilier Andy Barlow had reached down to pick up a bottle of water, shifted his weight, *boom!* A mine went off beneath him. The already wounded Wright and Pearson were caught in the blast. Another soldier, Dave Prosser, nearby, and cutting up shirts to make tourniquets, was struck in the chest by metal shrapnel and stones. So too was Hartley, perched on his backpack.

'The explosion lifted me off the ground and dumped me back down on my arse. I couldn't breathe. I couldn't hear. All I could see was a cloud of dust, and I couldn't force any breath into my lungs. I believed I was dead. I was bleeding from my shoulder, and I remember thinking very clearly, "This is what it's like to be dead." But, if I was dead, then why did it hurt so much when I tried to breathe? I was thinking to myself, if I can stand up, I'll know I'm not dead, I'm alive.' Hartley pushed himself to his feet and surveyed the scene from hell emerging out of the dust settling around him.

There was all this screaming and shouting going on, and people with limbs blown off. 'Fuck me,' I thought to myself. 'How bad's it going to get?' And then, though I knew I hadn't died, I was sure I was going to, that we all were. None of us were coming back from this, and all I could do was make everyone as comfortable as possible. So I just walked the last few steps to Mark, thinking whatever's going to happen is going to happen and I can't do anything to stop it. I was thinking about my family, but the immediate thing was to see what I could do for the lads in their last minutes, because they're your family too. Thinking I was going to die was calming. It chilled me out, took away all the fear, because I knew it was going to happen.

That peace of mind enabled Hartley to get on with his job, to complete what he firmly believed would be his final mission. He squatted down on the ground to examine Mark Wright's injuries and strapped a CAT tourniquet round the stump of his arm. The left side of his chest was a mess and all he could do was pack it with some bandage. He could see the corporal's knee was shattered too. He then drew his three casualties together into a triangle around him, their heads and feet touching each other. That way he could treat them without moving himself and avoid the risk of detonating another mine. He dosed Barlow and Pearson with

morphine and showed them how to keep each other topped up.
'That also helped me check their responsiveness.' As time moved
on, this became an increasing worry. He could see the light draining out of their eyes. He chatted away to them, trying to keep
them alert – 'I was just being their mum really' – but in his own heart
he believed he was doing little more than delaying the inevitable.
There was no way they were coming out of that riverbed alive, and
there was nothing anybody could do to change that.

He tried to soothe an increasingly distraught Andy Barlow, now
in great pain. The morphine wasn't working (it later transpired he
had an unusually high resistance to the drug and was virtually
immune to it). The more agitated he became, the faster his heart
beat, and the more he bled. Hartley had to shout over the soldier's
screams to explain to him why he needed to stay in control.
Meanwhile, Pearson was slipping in and out of consciousness, and
had to be kept from falling into a sleep that could all too soon be
permanent. 'I told him everything was going to be all right, but
I didn't really believe it myself.'

Wright, more grievously wounded than any of them, with half
his face blown away as well as all his other injuries, nonetheless
managed to keep himself going with a stream of wisecracks and
conversation, telling 'Tug' how he was about to get married but
that the wedding might have to be postponed for now. He joked
about the insurance money they would all be able to get their
hands on. The medic could see the gaping hole in the corporal's
neck. 'He was thirsty and kept asking for something to drink, and
I was pouring water into his mouth and watching it gush out of
the side of his neck.' They stayed in their tight huddle, the medic
and his trio of casualties, in the middle of that minefield, as if in
their own private prison.

On the edge and up the hill, a growing line of would-be
rescuers watched, unable to move forward to help for fear of more
explosions and more mayhem. A helicopter with a winch was
apparently on its way. Fifteen minutes, Hartley was told. When
he asked again, it was still another fifteen minutes, and then another
after that. 'Tell the pilot to look out for a fat bloke in blue shorts,'

Hartley joked to the soldiers outside the minefield. 'That'll be me!' They couldn't miss him, either, because his exposed torso was going a bright and dangerous shade of red in the sun.

Still there was no sound of engines approaching in the sky, and after a while Hartley stopped believing the chopper was ever going to come. That was when he too felt himself slipping away, the pain of his heat-seared lung, sunstroke, dehydration and sheer exhaustion all combining to tell his body to seek release in sleep. Time lost any meaning. He would look at his watch, thinking an eternity had passed, to find that only two minutes had elapsed. He would look again and see that a whole hour had gone by.

They were running out of water, and he called on the soldiers outside the minefield to lob in some bottles in a pouch – a risk, of course, if it landed on another mine, but they were desperate. They'd even drained the last of the intravenous saline solution in Hartley's medical pack, just to moisten their lips. A chance would have to be taken, and the pouch came soaring in. 'Thank God I'd played rugby for the army,' Hartley said, 'and I was able to catch it. That water was fantastic, the best I've ever tasted.'

Still the silent crowd stood and watched, with no idea how this drama in the Afghan desert was ever going to play out. 'It felt strange, us lying there in the open, and them just watching, so near and yet so far. I wasn't angry with them and I didn't think they were chicken or anything for not helping. There was nothing they could do, and I felt sorry for them. I couldn't have stood there as it all unfolded. It must have been fucking dreadful, just looking down at your mates and not being able to do anything.'

Among those helpless spectators was Alex Craig, still not sure how he had made his escape up the hill, and beating himself up about whether he should have stayed in the riverbed to help. The thought that he had let his comrades down still troubled him years later, though with no good reason. He was grievously wounded, more severely than he realized. His life was in danger – a doctor who treated him confirmed as much later.

As it was, he was one less body for the rescuers to worry about. When he finally struggled into the observation post at the top of

Normandy, he knew he urgently had to decompress his chest, to let the air out, otherwise he would suffocate. It meant driving in a needle between the ribs, but he didn't have the strength left to do it to himself. Calmly, he took a cannula from his pack and guided one of the Paras there on how and where to insert it. This was a tricky enough procedure for a seasoned practitioner in a hospital ward; here, with a complete novice, it was battlefield medicine of the most extreme kind. But needs must.

Craig put a mark on his skin where the puncture had to be made, and lay back. The Para, to his credit, did not flinch, and nor, to his credit, did Craig. 'He was definitely going to do it,' Craig recalled. 'Great guy! God bless him!' At the last second, they heard a call from outside that a doctor was on the way, and they paused. A helicopter was landing, the Medical Emergency Reaction Team was piling out, an RAMC colonel came racing in and took over. He made his incision, inserted a drain into Craig's chest and, for one at least of the Kajaki minefield victims, the life-and-death drama of that day was over.

Out in the minefield, there was no such relief. Three hours[8] had gone by since the mine had hit Mark Wright, six and a half since Stu Hale – still waiting to be casevaced out – had first wandered into the minefield. Suddenly, a US Black Hawk was overhead. One had been requested from the Americans by the commanders back in Bastion as soon as the emergency was declared, but none had been immediately available. To his annoyance and frustration, Colonel Stuart Tootal, the 3 Para commander, had his request questioned. Was a helicopter *really* necessary? And when he had insisted that it was, the matter had been referred up to NATO level for approval. The delay in the upper echelons was disastrous for the soldiers down on the ground. But now, at last, in a whirlwind of noise and fuel fumes, the American cavalry had arrived – one of the so-called 'Dust Off' platoon, whose logo painted on the helicopter's side was a raunchy girl bursting out of her blouse under the motto, 'Hanging out there to pick you up.'

'They're here! They're here!' Hartley called to his triangle of casualties, 'and you could see the colour and the hope come back into their faces.' All except Wright. The arrival of what he had been waiting for broke whatever spell of unreality he had been lost in. 'For the first time, he began to talk about dying. If things didn't work out, he wanted me to tell his missus he loved her and to let his mum and dad know he'd been a good soldier. I told him everything was going to be all right, and I promised to see him back at Camp Bastion. I promised. He made me promise . . .'

From out of the hovering helicopter, the American rescue crew fast-roped down into the minefield with a seven-foot-long metal stretcher. Hartley urged them to be careful, 'but they just went to work and were running around, clipping in Stu Hale and then Andy Barlow. I was just scared they were going to set off more mines.' Hale lay there while the crewmen scooped him up, admiring their professionalism and their bravery. 'It may well have been foolhardy, but at some point somebody had to come and get us out. They just got on with it.' The risks were still enormous, and not just from the mines. The US crew must have been aware that, just two months earlier, a fellow helicopter medic, an experienced staff sergeant, died when his line snapped in mid-air and he fell three hundred feet to the ground. Hale knew none of this, and was euphoric and, on his own admission, giggling like a schoolgirl as he was hauled into the air and strapped into the belly of the Black Hawk, relieved to be rescued after so long in distress but also tranquillized by the fresh syringe of morphine that was pumped into him.

They were back in ten minutes for Mark Wright, then again for Pearson and Prosser. All five were landed beyond the minefield and transferred to a waiting Chinook to be flown to the hospital at Camp Bastion. The Black Hawk then returned to the riverbed to pick up Hartley and the stretcher-bearers who'd been with Hale since they first tried to carry him out of the minefield. As he awaited his turn, Hartley, his casualties gone ahead of him, was standing on his own and surveying the now-empty scene of so much destruction and pain. He was still struggling to breathe. Now he had a moment to think, the shrapnel in his chest began to ache. Something caught the corner of his eye a few yards away. It was the emblem of a wing on a green T-shirt. Without thinking where he was and what he was doing, he walked – *walked!* – over and picked it up. The shirt was Alex Craig's, blown from him by the mine that caught him and Mark Wright. It was bloody and torn, but the proud words stencilled on the chest were clearly visible through the grime and gore – 'Airborne Paramedic'. As a memento from a minefield, and of extraordinary heroism, it took some beating.

The cable came down for Hartley, and he clipped on, but he could still barely believe it. 'They winched me up, and all the way I was sure something was still going to go wrong and I was going to die. It was not until my bum was on that bit of metal in the helicopter and one of the blokes gave me a bottle of iced water that I finally grasped that I was safe and on my way out. I looked at the rest of the rescue team who'd been down there on the ground with me, and not one of us said a word. We just looked at each other and sort of hugged each other . . . and that was it.'

At Camp Bastion, as he limped and wheezed his way off the helicopter, Hartley was met by his good mate, Gary Lawrence, the medic who just a few weeks earlier had saved the life of Sergeant Major Andy Stockton (see Chapter One). Lawrence was taken aback by his friend's condition. 'He was pepper-potted with shrapnel, had burns like soot marks to his face and his chest and he couldn't breathe properly. It brought home to me how vulnerable we all were. You think you're invincible, but we're none of us bullet-proof.' But he was alive. One of the minefield casualties, Hartley now discovered, was not.

His first thought was that it was Alex Craig who had not made it, but then he found him lying on a treatment table in the Accident and Emergency tent with a team of doctors around him putting a new drain in his chest. His condition had been deteriorating since that emergency procedure to relieve the pressure in his chest up on the hill. He had been the last of the injured to be air-lifted from the scene, and the MERT helicopter had got him to Bastion none too soon. Hartley pushed his way through the crowd round the bed and handed over the T-shirt he'd found at Kajaki. The two of them wept. 'We were just looking at each other,' Craig remembered, 'and trying to get our heads round what had happened. It all seemed so unbelievable. Tug said, "I've got your T-shirt, I went through a minefield to pick it up," and I told him he was an idiot! It was all a bit emotional. We were both completely drained, but it was a relief to see each other. I was just pleased that he was fine.'

There were more tears when Hartley learned that it was Wright who was dead. The loss of blood had been unsustainable, and in the helicopter on the way to Bastion he had gone into cardiac arrest. Hale had been lying beside him, 'screaming for him to hold on', but Wright had gone. Hartley was mortified. 'I was sick about him dying. He was an awesome bloke, a real pro and the bravest man I ever knew. As I said in my official report on the whole incident, he exercised command and control the whole time, giving outstanding leadership in dire circumstances. His presence contributed significantly to the eventual rescue and survival of those who were injured and prevented others from also becoming casualties.'

'Tug' had one more duty to perform. 'I'd promised him that he'd be OK and that I'd see him again. So, though I was offered the chance to fly straight back to England, I stayed for Mark's farewell ramp parade when his body was repatriated. I went into the ambulance where his coffin was waiting to be slow-marched on to the plane. I had promised him I would see him again, and I did. I just wish it hadn't had to be like that.'

*

Stu Hale had almost no memory of leaving Afghanistan. He had a vague recollection of being in the helicopter on his way back from the minefield and then being in the Bastion operating theatre. But the journey home on an Aeromed C17 cargo plane with the other Kajaki casualties passed him by. It was not until he was in Selly Oak hospital in Birmingham that he began to come out of his coma – a full five days later. But still he suffered. Hooked up to life-support systems and barely conscious, he then endured days of intense paranoid hallucinations as his mind processed and misinterpreted what was happening to his body. These terrors are a common enough phenomenon for patients in intensive care but, afterwards, Hale had something to judge them against. And he reckoned the hell of those nightmares was 'the most awful thing I've ever experienced. I would rather do Kajaki ten times than go through that again.' He was too scared even to press the button for more morphine, thinking he would die if he did, and suffered hours of unnecessary and excruciating pain until he was made to realize he was safe. 'Your brain plays tricks on you – it was a horrific time.'

Shannon, his wife, sat beside him. She had been out in Colchester when she got the news of his injury. They had just sold their house – part of their plans for a new life – and she was on her way to sign the papers when her mobile phone rang. A voice said: 'This is 3 Para Welfare. We need to come and see you.' She stopped in her tracks, as if hit by a hammer. She hadn't heard a word from Stu, not a letter nor a phone call, for five weeks, because he was up-country. 'You think the worst, that he's dead, and I asked but they said, no, he'd been injured. And they wouldn't tell me any more.' At home, two visitors from the battalion filled her in on the details. She was in shock. 'He's a sniper, so perhaps I expected him to have been shot. But when they said he'd walked into a minefield and he'd lost his leg, I went cold, shaking, sobbing, really sobbing. I knew how devastating this would be for him. Unless you're in the military, you can never really understand how awful the loss of a limb is to a fit young career soldier.'

When she peeped into the Selly Oak intensive care unit and saw him, unconscious and wired up to a life-support system, her heart almost broke.

There were all these brave young men in there who'd lost limbs. That's the cream of our youth, all at the peak of their physical fitness and now just broken. It didn't even look like him. They'd all had this mad facial-hair-growing competition while they were out there, and he had a massive moustache coming right down on to his chin. I just broke down when I saw him lying there. And where his leg should have been, there was just a sheet. Nobody knew for sure he was even going to pull through. His other leg was quite badly injured too, and he'd lost a lot of blood. The doctor took me and Stu's mum to one side and said they still didn't know whether they were going to be able to save the other leg, because so much shrapnel had gone into the knee. I think he was millimetres away from losing the tendon that controls your lower leg and, if that had gone; he would have been a double amputee. It was bloody terrifying, horrendous.

Life could have got worse for Hale. It didn't. It got better, as did his shattered body. His child was born, the one who had occupied his thoughts as he had lain wounded in the minefield. It was a girl and, for all his fears that he might not survive, he was at the birth to name her Sophia.

'Having her was a big thing for Stuart,' Shannon recalled. 'When he was lying out there on the hard ground at Kajaki and losing blood for all those hours, the one thing that kept him going was to get back and see this baby being born. She looks just like him, she's got a big smile like him, she's very placid like him. Got all of his best qualities.' Shannon knew too that he needed one other thing to see him through the ordeal of recovery – to be with his mates. Whatever plans they had had for him to change career now went on hold. 'One of the first things I said to him when he came round was, "Right, Stuart, you're not leaving the army. You're staying in, and that's it. Whatever they find for you to do, it's something to belong to and to hold on to."'

His determination to get back to a normal life – 'or as close to it as possible' – astonished even her. He was soon up on a prosthetic leg and getting around with a walking stick. Not long after, he was back in the gym, getting fit again, as a prelude to returning to work. When the last 3 Para contingent came back from Afghanistan, he was there to welcome them. 'Yes, I was in my wheelchair but it was important for me to be there.' The camaraderie of military life would see him through.

With him in Selly Oak was Alex Craig, who found it difficult adjusting to a non-military environment, where there was little comprehension of what those returning wounded from Afghanistan – in increasing numbers – had been through. He reacted badly to the loud crashes of the metal medical bins on the ward, each bang a nerve-racking reminder of that long, long day when explosion after explosion had shredded the silence of the desert. It took him a long while to get his health and his fitness back. His mind, though, still plays tricks. 'I still think about that day – should I have gone back in, could I have done more for Mark? There is a level of self-imposed guilt, and it nags away at me. I expect it always will.'

As for 'Tug' Hartley, he had come out of the Kajaki minefield relatively unscathed, but it was never truly out of him. Back home, he was a changed man. He drank too much and was short-tempered. 'I thought I was coping, but my wife sat me down one day and told me I wasn't. I felt this anger, unbelievable anger. At work I would get frustrated, wound up. I never hit anyone, but I could feel myself wanting to. Loud noises would set me off. Every time I heard a helicopter, it just drove me mad, made me so aggressive.' He had all the classic symptoms of post-traumatic stress disorder but with an edge unique to medics. 'I used to imagine all my friends getting injured and me not having the bottle to go in and help them.' Eventually, he was medically discharged. 'I was told it would be the best thing for me really. In my own mind I was 50/50 about staying, but I knew Afghanistan was going to be around for many years to come, and I never want to be put back in that situation. It's not watching mates dying that was the problem. It was making promises I couldn't keep.'

The award of a George Medal, one of the highest for bravery, was little consolation.

To be honest, I was pissed off by it. There were ten of us who went in as a rescue party and only three of us got awards, and one of them was dead [Mark Wright]. Everyone who went into that minefield acted above and beyond, put their lives at risk, and yet some got no recognition. I would rather have got nothing, or got the same as everybody else. I did what I hope every British soldier would have done for me. I'm not the fittest soldier, I'm not the best soldier, but you know when it's one of your own you've got to do everything you can. You do your best. I feel a bit bad about the way it all happened – not being told there was a minefield there, the helicopters not having winches, but I'm still very loyal.

The Kajaki incident does, however, strain credibility, if not loyalty. It showed members of the British Army and the medics responsible for their welfare in a truly glorious light – if raw bravery and the willingness to risk all for one's comrades are the only measures. But it was also a series of preventable disasters, a dismal catalogue of errors by those who send young men under-equipped to fight a shoestring war whose military objectives are hard to fathom. A board of inquiry was forthright in its findings. The minefield should have been known about in the first place – it was on some maps but not all, and the information had not been relayed to all the soldiers patrolling the area. The Chinooks should have had winches and hoists to extract the casualties.[9] It also transpired that the soldiers had had to turn off their radios because of a shortage of batteries and battery chargers, leaving them without communications at vital times, when a quick message could have stopped the incident escalating. Far from Corporal Wright's injuries being so severe that he was unsaveable (which was the line put out by the Ministry of Defence), the expert care he received on the ground was such that he might have survived had it not taken so long to get him to hospital. The men on the ground that day did their duty. It was others who let them down, who left them, in every terrible sense, without a leg to stand on. The statistics of this sorry incident said it all – one dead, six seriously injured, three lost limbs.

There was one further casualty – the promising career of Colonel Stuart Tootal, the 3 Para commander. He resigned from the army when his tour of Afghanistan was over, reportedly in disgust at equipment shortages and what he considered the poor and shoddy treatment of his troops. 'Resources were stretched to breaking point,' he said. We never had enough helicopters.' The Kajaki minefield was where all those deficiencies were exposed, at a fearful human cost. A civilian coroner who heard the tale unfold at an inquest in Oxford[10] two years afterwards concluded that MoD chiefs should hang their heads in shame for the lack of equipment that had cost Corporal Wright his life. This death, he declared, had been preventable.

17. Shifting Sands

When she hit the town, back home in Swansea, for a Saturday night of partying with her old schoolfriends, Rachel McDonald always wore her 'killer heels'. They gave the petite paramedic a lift. But she needed no boost to her stature as she did her job in Afghanistan. In combat gear, carrying a rifle and in desert boots rather than sling-backs, the RAF sergeant was a towering presence as she dashed between hospital and battlefield in the back of a Chinook. Her presence too was more evidence of the growing part women were taking in the wars of the twenty-first century. In Britain's armed forces – unlike those of the United States – they were still denied an aggressive role as fighting soldiers. In theory, they were kept at a safe distance serving in support units behind the front line. In reality, there was no longer any such thing as a front line. In Afghanistan, as in Iraq, the sands were continually shifting.

Rachel had little idea of what to do when she left school except that she'd had enough of studying and wanted to see something of the world. She had been an army cadet, and was attracted to a military life. She applied for training as an RAF nurse but was persuaded instead to join as a medic. 'I didn't really know what I was letting myself in for. I knew I'd travel and maybe not to the nicest of places all the time. But it never occurred to me that I'd end up quite as close to the front line in a combat zone. I never imagined that I'd be running off the back of a Chinook under fire.'

In the Iraq invasion of 2003, she was based in Kuwait and, though she saw the results of the fighting, she didn't experience the immediacy of battle. 'The casualties had been through many medical points of aid before they got to me.'[1] But, three years later, as she prepared to deploy to Afghanistan, she saw a newspaper report describing Camp Bastion, the place she was heading for, as the deadliest place on the earth. 'I remember being really, really nervous. I talked to my parents about what I was embarking on, but not in any great detail, to be honest, and I didn't tell them how scared I was. My mum was desperately worried. I didn't want her to know too much.'

Flying into Bastion was the first of many eye-popping experiences. The fine, ash-like dust, churned up by hot desert winds and swirling in plumes through the camp, was an immediate shock to the system. 'We stepped off the plane into the middle of a sand-storm. I could just make out some tents in the distance, and that was it. What had I let myself in for?' Apprehension took the edge off her excitement at being on her first operational tour as a full-fledged paramedic, a step up from the medical assistant she had been in Iraq. She knew she would have to shoulder more responsibility – she would be leading a four-man team – but had not reckoned for the degree of human suffering she would encounter. 'If you're a paramedic back home in the UK, you're unlikely to have to deal with gunshot wounds to the head and with someone whose brain is hanging out. Nothing can prepare you for that. The first few incidents were very nerve-racking.' She felt extra pressure being a woman in this aggressively male world. 'There was no way I was going to let anyone think I couldn't do as good a job as the guys. You have to keep up a pretty tough exterior. Underneath, you're as emotional as everyone else. But you can't show it, not in that environment.'

Her first major 'shout' – an alarm call – came from Forward Operating Base Robinson, just outside Sangin, and at Bastion, she and her team raced for the Chinook and threw themselves and their gear into the 'cab'. Then they were on their way, a helter-skelter ride across Helmand, the province's pretty lakes and land-scape (as well as its pulverized villages) flashing past less than a hundred feet below. Conversation was difficult above the din. The combat troops who would pile off first to secure the landing site were crouched around her, rifles at the ready. Nobody knew for sure what they were heading into. They never did. As usual, information was sparse – just that a detachment of Afghan Army and coalition soldiers had been ambushed in a village. Apparently, women were among the attackers, spotted on rooftops directing the fire. So she wasn't the only one of her sex fighting in this war.

The platoon had made it back to FOB Robinson, but this too was now under attack. How many casualties? No one knew. Could be a dozen or more, maybe two. How bad were the injuries? Not sure. Better prepare for the worst, she told herself as the helicopter scooted through the air, getting closer every second to what would be her first major contact. 'Don't think about fear, just think what you are going to do. I go through the procedures in my head, the checks to be made. Just concentrate on the job in hand. Go over those procedures again and again.'

This one was going to be hairy from the start. There was flak coming in, and bullets flashing around the helicopter as it came in to land. 'We'd been told the Chinook could take quite a bit of small-arms fire, but what if someone out there had an RPG? That thought petrified me.' Suddenly they were down on the ground and, without thinking about it, Rachel was on her feet and running off the back. She could see puffs of smoke coming from a nearby bluff – gunfire! The compound was ahead of her, a good half a mile away. She set off towards it with one of the doctors, then turned in her tracks to see the Chinook climbing back into the air. This was a shock. They had been expecting the pilot to wait, but with so much gunfire around, he had decided his aircraft was too tempting a target to sit on the ground. He radioed that he would return in twenty minutes. She would have to have her first batch of evacuees ready by then.

She ran on, and was now breezing into Robinson, veering past its protective Hesco blast walls, into the central compound . . . and into a chaotic scene of hurt and frightened humanity. She had never before seen so many casualties together in one place. 'They were everywhere, moaning and groaning, some leaning against walls with bandages on arms and heads and legs, others on stretchers. I counted more than twenty. How the hell were we going to handle all these?'

The answer to her own question was to start at the beginning of the line and, coolly and calmly, examine them one at a time in order to make a preliminary assessment of their injuries. 'I started at one end and the doctor at the other, and we worked our way along.' Most were from the Afghan Army and didn't speak any English, which made communicating with them an additional problem. But if she felt overwhelmed (and for a split-second she did), she wasn't going to show it. 'You can't just walk away. You're there. You've got to do your best.'

She had twenty seconds to examine each patient and come to a conclusion about his condition; then she had to move on to the next one. 'There was no question of trying to treat them. We just had to establish how bad they were and work out how to get them out of there.' One had chest wounds that were urgent and life-threatening – Priority 1 – five were serious (P2), and eighteen were P3s, with less serious bomb-fragmentation wounds. All were shocked and in pain. 'We knew we had to get them out of there as quickly as possible and on to the helicopter. Only then would we able to start treating them. But first we had to get them to the landing site half a mile away.' From outside, the snap of rifle fire made it clear that the enemy was not going to give them an easy ride.

Two flat-bed trucks were found, and the stretcher-cases were loaded on to them and driven off. There wasn't room to take everyone, and some of the walking wounded had to do just that – walk. They plodded out from behind Robinson's protective walls in single file, trailing blood and bandages. Rachel was on one of the trucks with the most serious cases, moving between her patients as best she could over the rough ground, securing dressings, making sure they weren't too tight or too loose, 'in my own little world, not thinking about what was going on around us, the gunfire or whatever, totally concentrating on the casualties'.

Waiting at the landing site, tucking down behind whatever cover he could find, was RAF nurse Flight Lieutenant Damien van Carrapiett. He had come off the Chinook with Rachel and the doctor but stayed put so he could guide the helicopter in when it returned. He had watched the two of them head off to Robinson but then lost contact with them. His radio signal wouldn't penetrate the Hesco blast walls, and he had no idea what was happening until he saw the convoy of makeshift ambulances and limping men emerging out of the dust and sand in the distance and making their way towards him. 'It was a bit of a shock to see so many of them,' he recalled.

He summoned help and, within minutes, two Chinooks were flying in. Rachel took all the stretcher-cases in the first one. The rest piled into the second helicopter, followed by the Paras of the protection patrol who'd been on picket duty around the landing site. The cab was overflowing, more than forty men in helmets and body armour swaying with every turn, hanging on as best they could on that high-speed, low-level dash back to Bastion. All were crouching, trying to keep their heads down, in case of attack, knowing that in the past, soldiers riding in Chinooks had been shot by bullets from the ground.

Van Carrapiett was one of the strap-hangers in the back. 'You just couldn't move, let alone start treating people. There was a guy with multiple frag wounds in his thigh, another with bullets in his arm. When I joined the RAF in 1999, I never imagined I'd be picking up casualties in conditions like this. What we did in Afghanistan really was very unexpected. It wasn't playing at being soldiers; it was the real deal, believe me.'[2] The age of those he treated always gave him pause for thought and admiration.

I'd done ten years in conventional Accident & Emergency departments, dealing with broken, dying and dead people pretty much on a daily basis. I wasn't a stranger to violent death or the idea that people could inflict violence on each other. But what really got me was how young some of these guys were. You take the casualty's date of birth, and you think, Christ, they're just teenagers, born the year I was doing my O-levels. Yet they are putting their life on the line for Queen and country and, for me, there's the real difference from somebody who's been mashed to bits in a car accident on the M5. It ups the ante. It adds an extra dimension to looking after them.

Despite his familiarity with death and violence, he never under-estimated the effect the sight could have on others. 'Sometimes casualties with bad injuries would be groaning and leaking blood all over the place, and we'd be beside them on the floor trying frantically to save them. And I'd see the looks of horror and disbelief on the faces of the force protection guys and those not so badly wounded, all of whom were watching. It could be harrowing for them to see somebody badly wounded on a stretcher fighting for his life and, perhaps, a dead body lying next to him. That's really tough to get your head round. Even some of the younger medics were shocked.'

Rachel McDonald, at twenty-six, was older and more experi-enced, but even she shuddered at the memory of the British soldier she tended who had been shot clean through the head, an entry wound at the front and an exit one at the back. 'Soft tissue – his brain, in fact – was hanging out, and I was holding it in place and trying to pack it back into his head. The training does kick in, and you do it, but it was still a shock. We picked him up and got him into the helicopter. He was still conscious. I was talking to him, reassuring him.' Another casualty had burns over three-quarters of his body.

His injuries weren't compatible with life, and we didn't think he'd make it. We couldn't even get a cannula into his veins, because they had all shut down, so we couldn't give him blood or fluids. But he did survive. And that's when what we do is really gratifying, when you know you've made a difference. But there is another side of the coin, and I was gutted when a patient died, especially if it was one of our troops. I never got used to that. Medics are humans too; we get emotional, and after a death I always needed time alone. I'd go out of the back of the tent, tell people where I was, but I needed to think, to give way to my grief and to compose myself.

There was one particularly dreadful day, when two soldiers died. The first had taken serious wounds to his stomach and chest, and his heart stopped beating in the back of the helicopter. Rachel resuscitated him and banged at his chest, and she got him back . . . but he later died in theatre. 'His injuries were just too much. Poor lad. He was only twenty-three.' Later that same day, she nursed a young Afghan farmer on the flight back from Sangin, but he died too. Then, in the early hours of the next morning, she held the hand of another British lad on the *via dolorosa* flight back to Bastion. He'd been shot in the neck and, crouching beside him in the dark in the Chinook cab, she cupped her hand and spoke softly into his ear, trying to calm his fears. 'I built quite a rapport with him,' she recalled of their brief encounter, and she was glad to have helped ease his suffering with her calmness and closeness. But as he was lifted from the helicopter and rushed into the bright lights of A&E, with nurses and doctors scrambling around him, she feared the worst. 'I just hoped his brain hadn't been penetrated.'

She willed him to live, to put up a fight. And then she ran four miles round the Bastion perimeter wall as fast as she could, punishing herself, releasing the tension, simply coping with all the emotions of sadness and loss which were never far below the surface and which at times like this threatened to overwhelm her. She trained four days a week – jogged and cycled and did sit-ups by the score. Exercise was an answer of sorts, personal fitness a means of control in a world where so much else was arbitrary and awful and out of her hands. 'I WILL go home a size ten!' she wrote in her diary.

That diary is a fascinating insight into her world, full of girly interests and intimacy, as if she were on a fun spree with her mates in Ibiza, but interwoven with grisly everyday events of staggering solemnity, violence, courage. It is *High School Musical* meets *Apocalypse Now*. 'Very nice welcome,' she wrote on returning to Bastion for her second tour in mid-2007. 'The girls in my tent had already made up my bedspace for me. Wow – even got mattresses here now! Knackered! Good night's sleep. Zzz . . .' But within forty-eight hours she was reporting: 'Four casualties. One a young Afghan girl, approx. 12 years old. Shrapnel wounds on her chest, very distressed. Reassured her, held her hand, but she wouldn't have understood me. Nightmare getting her out of the ambulance.

Rear doors wouldn't open, had to pass her through the front hatch. She deteriorated in hospital – developed haemo-pneumothorax [lungs flooded with blood]. Docs inserted chest drain. Bless her, only a small girl and caught up in this mess. War is ugly.' After twelve hours of non-stop activity, she finished work at 11 p.m. and could think of only one thing. 'Sleep, sleep, sleep!'

There were days when she could relax – 'sunbathed, went to the gym (bike, plus cross trainer), treated myself to chocolate pudding for tea'. She had her eyebrows dyed and her nails mani-cured by a captain named Zoe who, in civilian life, was a qualified beautician. But then the Americans dropped a bomb on a school and she was summoned in early to A&E. 'Fifty casualties, nearly all poor innocent children.' On an emergency flight into the outpost at Sangin, the Chinook circled 'for bloody ages' while an Apache attack helicopter cleared out a nest of Taliban snipers on the ground. 'By the time we got to the casualties it was pitch black, and I was quite nervous of the surrounding threat. We got in and out OK, though; no shooting at us this time.' On that one shift alone she was on three 'shouts', an almost continual cycle of scrambling into the cab, arrowing across the desert, giving first aid, returning with casualties, administering oxygen, morphine and antibiotics, and then, no sooner back at base than going straight out again to repeat the procedure. 'Two very poorly children, one with part leg amputation, the other with gunshot wound to chest and possible penetrating brain injury.' It was hard on the body and the emotions. No wonder that on her Sunday off she 'just chilled'.

When she wasn't flying, she helped in A&E. Choking back her own distress, she comforted a Marine lying in one of the bays. He'd been 'top cover' in an armoured vehicle, standing in the turret, when it was attacked by a rocket, and his armour burst into flames. He had burns on his face, arms and legs. His mate, the driver, was in a worse way. He had been trapped at the wheel and been pulled out, more dead than alive, from the wreck. What was so gutting the first Marine, he told Rachel, his eyes full of tears, was that he should have been the one driving at the time. Guilt and self-recrimination were the flipside of the intense camaraderie that bound the soldiers to one another. Their physical wounds were almost always compounded by the mental anguish of wondering if they could or should have done more.

One of the strangest aspects of the Afghan fighting was that, unlike the military encounters of earlier eras, the 'real' world, the one beyond the confines of the war, was never far away. To those who fought in the foreign wars of the nineteenth and twentieth centuries, in places such as Afghanistan, India and Africa, home and family were a long-distant memory, coupled with the hope that you would see them again one day. But the coalition forces could regularly speak to their families on the satellite telephone. News, and sport in particular, was beamed into televisions in the mess. You could be fighting for your life one moment and the next be sitting down with your mates and watching a live feed of England going out of the World Cup in a penalty shoot-out. On television, Kevin Pietersen was smashing fours and sixes off the Sri Lanka bowlers at Edgbaston while, outside the camp walls, an altogether more serious struggle – for life and death – was under-way. If it felt surrealistic, that was because it was. For Rachel McDonald, the internet (when it wasn't down) was her route to the real world. 'On for a whole hour! Ordered some running shorts from M & M Sports.'

It was a world she was increasingly anxious to return to. When she began her second tour, she found the experiences of the first weighing heavily on her. What she had already seen, far from making her blasé, had made her more alive to danger.

I was much more worried going on that second deployment. The threat levels were so high. But it was also that I had decided I was going to leave the RAF at the end of it, and I couldn't stop wondering if I was tempting fate. Every time I got on board a helicopter, I was aware that this might be my last flight. On my way into a hot spot, in my mind I'd be going over the chat I'd just had with Mum on the phone. I'd think over everything we'd said, and I'd be glad I'd told her I loved her. And it would be going through my head that it might be the last conversation I'd have with her, ever. By then Mum knew the sort of thing I was getting up to. I'd won an award as Paramedic of the Year [given by the Ambulance Service Institute] for that operation at FOB Robinson, and it had made her the proudest mum in the world. But it also meant she found out precisely what had happened and how dangerous it had been. And that made things worse. I would worry about my mum worrying. Strange, you're the one in the firing line; but it's the people back at home you're most anxious about.

Her feelings intensified after the Taliban brought down an American Chinook near the Kajaki Dam. 'Thankfully, we didn't have to fly into the area to assist, not that I didn't want to. But I am left feeling really scared at the thought,' she wrote in her diary. It brought home to her that one lucky shot for them – unlucky for her – was all it would take. 'The bastards have found something that can get us.' The thought nagged away at her. 'It's my last tour, but you always read stories of people getting killed within their final few months of being in the forces. I don't want to be one of them. I've got a whole life ahead of me yet. Felt quite emotional. Mum and all the family must be having kittens at home. Thank God I'm leaving soon. I can't put everyone through all this worry over and over again. Nor me, for that matter!'

Rachel did make it home, back to Swansea, where she could get those 'killer heels' out of the wardrobe, be happy-go-lucky again, the life and soul of every gathering. But she would never be the same girl who first went to war. 'Young Rachel', as she now thinks of herself when she joined up, had matured in a way that set her apart from others who had not seen what she saw. She didn't talk a lot about her experiences, reasoning that her friends 'probably wouldn't want to hear about them and don't need to know. Some of them still don't really believe it. Well, they do, but they find it difficult to believe that it was me who's been in a war zone, in combat, held a man's head together. I'm proud of what I did, and I'd do it all again if I could turn back time. But I think I made the right decision to leave when I did.'

★

For paramedics such as Rachel McDonald, the principal job was to get casualties from the front line to the hospital alive. It fell to them to preserve a life to give the doctors a chance to save it. Lieutenant Colonel Paul Parker, a senior surgeon at Camp Bastion, was careful never to rush to his patients. He would be alerted that the emergency medical team was in the air but, rather than dash to the operating theatre to wait, he preferred to use the time to go to the mess tent for a bacon sandwich – because he knew the odds were that he and his team wouldn't get another chance for many hours. 'I waited until I heard the helicopters returning. I knew it took between seven and ten minutes to get the patients off the Chinooks, into the ambulance and across from the landing site. So you count five minutes, and then you put on your gloves and your apron. It was sensible given what lay ahead. People make the mistake of thinking emergency surgery is a sprint but, in reality, it's a marathon, and that's what you have to prepare for.'[3]

In the Second World War, it was established that there was a limit to how long surgeons could operate before they were so exhausted they needed days to recover. The precise number of hours varied with the individual, but that everyone had a ceiling – or a 'wall', in marathon terms – was indisputable. This was one thing – perhaps the only thing – that had not changed in military medicine since the 1940s. If the men wielding the scalpels didn't pace themselves, they would make mistakes.

As it was, their work demanded extraordinary calmness and maturity. For Parker, this was why surgeons of his seniority had to be as close to the front line as possible. 'The twenty-first-century battlefield moves very quickly, so we need surgical teams to move forward with the battle. And they have to be the most experienced surgeons.' That had not been the case in the Falklands, where the bulk of the surgical team were young men who had yet to complete their formal training. There had been just one surgeon and one anaesthetist of consultant status; the rest were at various stages of experience and qualification.

In Iraq and Afghanistan, this changed, and with good reason. 'The front line is not the place just for junior doctors,' Parker said, 'because sometimes you have to make a decision not to operate, sometimes you have to let people die.' Stark choices were unavoidable. 'If a casualty has a gunshot wound that goes in one side of the head and out of the other and he's unconscious and totally unrousable, mortality is virtually 100 per cent. You could spend a lot of time on the operating table trying to suck out the dead brain and save him, but at the expense of someone with a spleen or a liver wound that is treatable. It's a senior decision to say, right, move this chap to one side, under the care of a padre with some morphine.'

In the end, everything was rationed, even life itself. 'If you've only got twenty or thirty units of blood and you have someone who's been shot through his liver and is almost dead, then you could use up half your supply trying unsuccessfully to save him. That's the decision you have to make sometimes: life or death.'

Playing God was never easy. At the very least, the stress of witnessing life at its rawest and death at its ugliest could become too much for the medics, and even the steadiest and most seasoned of hands was known to lose its grip from time to time. Parker's colleague, Lieutenant Colonel Philip Rosell, an orthopaedic surgeon with a twenty-year career in military medicine, had what he called his 'wobbly' moments. He was making instant clinical judgements that, in civilian hospitals at home, would have involved lengthy discussions between whole teams of specialists – whether or not to amputate a man's arm or leg, for example.

In the tented hospital at Camp Bastion, it was often his call alone whether a limb would be lost or not. 'I was very aware that I was making life-changing decisions. But, yes, I did have to cut off quite a few legs, and I got fed up of doing it at one stage. Every time, you're dealing with a broken body or a shattered life. That gets to you. I was pissed off at seeing young blokes coming in with limbs hanging on by bits of tissue. What was it all for? I just didn't want to see another broken body. I was a long way from home and I'd had enough.'[4] The feeling passed. With a good night's sleep, a quieter shift, the stress of that responsibility – though not the responsibility itself – lifted, and he was back on track, mending those broken boys, doing, as he put it, 'the best job any military surgeon could ever hope to do'.

On the table one day he had a young Special Forces soldier who'd been hit by three high-velocity rounds – one through his pelvis, one through his hip joint and one through each of his legs – and was going down fast. 'By the time he reached us he was already almost clinically dead. We gave him more cardiac massage in the operating theatre, because his heart stopped again. We opened his belly and clamped the aorta to switch off the blood supply. Though that in itself was pretty dangerous, it allowed us to take a few moments to consider what to do next.' Rosell quickly ran an expert eye over this body, with its mass of catastrophic wounds, each one of which could be fatal on its own. Where to start? The abdomen was open, the pelvic vein was punctured, and he reckoned it would take an hour of surgery at least, possibly two, just to stop the bleeding there. Both legs were tourniqueted. The clock was ticking, and a life was ebbing away. A decision had to be made. 'I'm looking at his legs, and they are both perfectly salvageable injuries, but we've got a dying patient. We released the tourniquets, and one leg was bleeding so heavily I had to put the tourniquet back on straightaway. The other one was just oozing a bit, so we could leave that. I said: "*That* leg we'll save; the other one we can't."'

It was a practical response based on a straightforward calculation of time. To have operated immediately on the heavily bleeding leg would have delayed the lifesaving surgery on the soldier's abdomen, and the abdomen wound was the critical one and had to be dealt with first. But that meant it would be several hours before Rosell got to the tourniqueted leg, and the simple clinical fact was, after four hours with its blood supply blocked off, a leg was unlikely ever to work again. After six hours, it would be beyond any surgeon's skills. This, as ever, was the downside of tourniquets, though such difficulties were far outweighed by the benefits. Binding a heavily bleeding limb as tightly as possible on the battlefield bought time, saved a life that might otherwise be lost there and then. The Toms swore by their tourniquets as a first aid, not just a last resort. Some went into action with them already in place, one on each arm and each leg. If they were hit, they needed only to tighten it themselves, without wasting time. The seconds saved could be vital. More to the point, knowing the tourniquets were already in place boosted their morale and encouraged their faith that, however hot the encounter, they had done all they could to up their chances of coming out alive.

Tourniquets were not, however, 'magic bullets'; they could not do the impossible – any more than Rosell with his scalpel could. Faced with this soldier with multiple injuries and time running out, he knew he had to cut his losses. 'It was a really hard decision because, by leaving the leg for now, he would almost certainly lose it. But all we could do was save his life and then see what we were left with.'

Copious amounts of blood were needed for this patient if he was going to have any chance at all, and an emergency call went round the camp for donors. There were two hundred volunteers on permanent standby, already typed and cross-matched for emergencies like this. They stopped whatever they were doing and came at the double to the blood bank to be bled. In the end, the medics tranfused fifty pints into him – more than the total normally held in reserve in some hospitals back in the UK. His entire blood supply was renewed six times, which was an extraordinary achievement. Only in a war would such devastating wounds have to be dealt with, but only in a war were there the concentrations of fit, young and willing people whose plasma could be tapped at any time to provide the means of saving a life. And it worked. The soldier (minus his one leg) survived, thanks to emergency, selfless medicine of the highest order, involving not just doctors and nurses but the entire service community at Bastion.

Rosell knew how incredible this result was. 'He was effectively dead on his second round of cardiac massage, but we used every facility on him and he eventually got through it. It just couldn't have happened a few years ago.' These were people playing at the very top of their game, using all the collective experience gathered in long-distance conflicts going back to the Falklands, to D-Day and Dunkirk, but refined most recently in Iraq.

The Gulf was where, for the first time, a fully fitted intensive care unit (as opposed to an aid post) had operated in the field. Bastion went even further. Rosell reckoned that the emergency care provided in that tented hospital in the middle of a desert, with lights hanging from the canvas roof, plastic sheeting on the wooden floor and barely enough room for the drip stands, was better than in many NHS hospitals. Technology was often[5] the very latest – CT body-scanners and digital X-ray machines that could give an internal image of injuries in seconds. It was a whole world away from the grimy meat-packing warehouse in Ajax Bay, with stretchers on the floor and a tea urn that doubled up as a sterilizer for surgical instruments, where the Falklands casualties had been treated. And things were improving all the time. Paul Parker had needed to wield a hand-saw to amputate Sergeant Major Andy Stockton's arm back in 2006. Now he was performing the same operation with a power tool. The medics boasted, with good reason, that you had a better chance of surviving a gunshot wound or a stabbing in Afghanistan than if you were attacked in the street directly outside a major London teaching hospital.

One reason for this high standard of care, of course, was that everyone, from platoon medic to surgical consultant, was getting a lot of practice. Medic Bob Steer, a veteran of Iraq and the early operations in Afghanistan, returned to Bastion as part of his Territorial Army rotation in 2007, and felt the change. 'Things were far more intense than I'd seen in Iraq. We were really, really busy.' Working with the trauma team, it felt to him as if the flow of casualties through A&E never stopped. It was like being on a production line, he recalled after one suicide bombing resulted in mass casualties. In the corner – at the end of the line, as it were – lay piles of amputated arms and legs. If it hadn't been for the yellow clinical bags they were tied up in, he observed, this could have been a field hospital in any war in the past century. 'In Iraq we went for days, if not weeks, without an incident, but in Afghanistan there was at least one virtually every day. And whereas in Basra the vast amount of casualties we dealt with were locals, here, increasingly, they were our guys, shot or blown up.'

With no sign of a let-up in the violence, roadside and suicide bombs took an ever greater toll of coalition soldiers, and posed new problems for the Bastion surgeons. Bullet wounds were relatively easy to deal with – they were usually a straight, clean line through tissue. But IEDs would cause thirty to forty penetrating injuries, legs blown off, arms blown off, skin, flesh and bone ripped apart and flayed open. Nor were the injuries just plain blood and gore. Because these bombs were usually laid in the open, in ditches and beside roads, lots of dirt immediately got into the wounds. 'These were incredibly complex cases, and they took an awful lot of time and effort to clean and to sort out,' one surgeon recalled.[6]

If they could be sorted at all, that is. In Philip Rosell's diary for the second half of 2007, the ominous initials 'KIA' (Killed In Action) cropped up with depressing regularity. At a Sunday church parade, he and his comrades gave vent to a defiant rendering of 'I Vow to Thee, My Country', knowing that, just forty-eight hours earlier, two British soldiers had been caught in an ambush and made 'the final sacrifice'. The second verse of that hymn, normally omitted in a Britain where congregations are wary of patriotism, seemed particularly relevant:

> I heard my country calling, away across the sea,
> Across the waste of waters she calls and calls to me.
> Her sword is girded at her side, her helmet on her head,
> And round her feet are lying the dying and the dead.

Rosell, his mind filled with thoughts of home and friends, had not long returned to his quarters when he was called back to the hospital to treat three men seriously wounded in a rocket attack. 'Interpreter with head injury came back in full arrest – *unsuccessful resusc.* The second was a soldier with high traumatic amputation hip level, loss of large amounts of buttock tissue. The third had bilateral severe leg injury, traumatic below knee amputation one side, high thigh wound with mush to mid-tibial level on the other side.' The surgeon worked through the night, cutting away the man's left leg at the knee and the right at the upper thigh. One death and a double amputation – these were grim times. On another day he noted, 'three lower-limb amputations and two hand partial amputations before tea time!' Outside, the coming and going of the MERT helicopters bringing in each new crop of broken bodies seemed endless. The rescue teams were now flying as many as ten missions a day.

Some conditions were beyond even the collective expertise at Bastion. The lungs of a soldier caught in a blast up at Kajaki – still as much of a flashpoint as ever – were so badly burned that the only remedy was to fly him back to England to hook him up to a heart-lung machine. It was touch and go. There was every chance that, scarcely able to breathe, he would die before he got there, but it was a risk the doctors had to accept. It was the right call. The man survived. 'Good news to end the day on,' Rosell noted when he heard. He celebrated the saving of a life with a vigorous work-out in the gym. But it was small compensation for the loss of three of the soldier's comrades who had died in the same incident.

A day later, the doctor watched as a large patrol of armoured vehicles assembled inside Bastion to go out on a night mission, and he called out his best wishes to the troops as they headed into the setting sun. 'Hope I don't meet them again in the next few days as casualties,' he thought to himself, full of foreboding. He had the same reaction to a pleasant young Grenadier Guards sub-altern he shared a joke with. 'Seriously do not want to see him as a punter,' he wrote.

In the early hours of one Saturday morning, he was in his accommodation 'pod' and just about to get into bed, when the padre collared him. A major incident was going down at the village of Garmsir: two soldiers were dead and four Priority One casualties were on their way in. The action on the ground had been so intense that the helicopter had been held at bay for several hours before it could land to evacuate the wounded. These men were going to be in a desperate condition. They finally arrived at 4 a.m. One had taken a bullet through the head – 'v. poor prognosis' – one had an eviscerated bowel, another a shoulder wound, and a fourth had a two-inch bullet from an old-fashioned Soviet rifle embedded in the soft tissue of his lower leg. Their patrol had been caught from behind by Taliban forces, and the fighting had been very close and extremely nasty.

The next helicopter brought a fifth casualty, a medic, who had been advancing under fire to care for the man with the head injury when a 500lb bomb collapsed the compound wall on top of him. Like so many others in this situation, he was tormenting himself that he could and should have done more to help his wounded comrades, when in fact he had done all any man could be expected to do. 'Very impressive bloke' was Rosell's verdict. For the next six hours, until, outside, the sun was high in the sky, he fought to save them, cleaning the wounds, removing loose dead bone, repairing and pinning what he could. All five pulled through and, twelve hours later, they were splinted up and on the ambulance-plane heading back to England.

Rosell, as if he hadn't had enough violence that day, relaxed by watching the cult Vietnam war movie *Full Metal Jacket* on a big outdoor screen erected in the camp volleyball court. It was most appropriate. 'Full metal jacket' was US Marine slang for a 7.62 bullet, the very sort he had just dug out of the flesh of one of his patients. He laughed along with the film's snappy dialogue, and the classic military profanities and 'motherfucker' insults of Gunnery Sergeant Hartman. 'Excellent to hear all those lines again,' he commented. One had particular poignancy in the circumstances: 'The dead know only one thing – that it's better to be alive.'

There was still no let-up. A few hours later, he was woken to be told that another batch of casualties was arriving in fifteen minutes. One dead, four minor injuries. They were US Special Forces, whose armoured Humvee had hit a mine. 'Bizarre to have one killed outright with severe blast and lung injury and major burns while the others were almost unhurt.' Sometimes the sheer arbitrariness of war was utterly bewildering.

If he ever doubted that, a suicide bomb at Gereshk the next day confirmed it. Six casualties were flown in. One was a small boy with ball-bearings in his scalp, another had 'a penetrating wound to todger'. The film that night was *A Bridge Too Far*, about the abortive Arnhem operation in 1944. The relevance of its title and its subject matter – an under-prepared, over-ambitious military expedition in which raw courage was simply not enough to ensure success – could not have gone unnoticed.

Working alongside Rosell for a while was Territorial Army captain Ed Clitheroe, a junior doctor from Chester. He was trained in treating trauma, but he had never seen trauma like this. Back in England he had done four months of paediatric surgery as part of his training. His first patient on his new beat was a child, but there the similarities ended. The ten-year-old Afghan boy was brought into Casualty with a knife in his head, pushed in right up to the hilt. He had been in his father's shop when there was a dispute with a customer. The customer pulled out a knife and lunged at the father, the boy got in the way and the blade went down with full force into his head. It was lodged in his brain. Amazingly, the boy was conscious, talking and on his feet – he had *walked* into the hospital with his father.

An X-ray showed the knife resting at an angle behind his eye and penetrating the frontal lobe. Simply to have pulled it out would have killed him or left him brain-dead. The most meticulous and intricate surgery was called for. The newly arrived (and shell-shocked) Clitheroe scrubbed up to assist, and watched in amazement as, over the next few hours, the surgeon in charge delicately probed inside the boy's head until the knife could be removed, all the time aware that one slip could start a massive and fatal bleed. The lad recovered.

Not every outcome was so uplifting, however, and what came to haunt Clitheroe were the victims of suicide bombings, many lacerated by the ball-bearings packed inside the devices and suffering multiple wounds that required teams of surgeons working in tandem to deal with them. 'They were very emotive injuries, especially among the children. The randomness just didn't seem fair. I could never get used to that. And there were times when, no sooner had we cleared one lot and cleaned up than more were arriving.'[7] But when he stood back from all those feelings after returning to the UK, he was proud of the people he had worked with, and proud of himself. 'It was the finest medical job I have ever done. One of my frustrations was that the reporting in the media did not reflect what we were doing and how good the treatment was.'

Little of the work the Bastion surgeons did was ever routine. The removal of bullets and shrapnel from organs and limbs, the repairing of stomachs and bowels and broken bones, the deep scraping-out of wounds and skin-grafting of burns – all this demanded skills across many specialisms. Being a doc of all trades was what mattered.

In civilian life, surgeon David Rew specialized in operating on breast cancer, hernias, gall bladders and thyroids. But as Lieutenant Colonel Rew of the Territorial Army, and taking his tour of duty in Camp Bastion, the niceties of NHS practice had to be left behind. 'In six weeks there I saw more major trauma than in the whole of the rest of my career. I was doing children's neurosurgery, maxillo-facial surgery, abdominal surgery, chest surgery. I was a true old-fashioned general surgeon of a type we rarely see these days.'[8] The expertise required was unparalleled in the history of military medicine. Once a field doctor's job would be to cut off a leg, splint an arm and apply a bandage. Not these days. In the twenty-first century there are nearly forty extra procedures which a surgical trauma team needs to be skilled in, according to Paul Parker.[9]

With demands like these, it also helped if a doctor had an ability to ignore fatigue. Every member of the Bastion surgical teams was acutely conscious that there was no extra manpower to call in beyond those in the camp at any given time, no back-up. If a doctor went sick – and, in that climate, no one was immune – then everyone had to double up. As it was, the hospital was having to treat as many as twenty-four new casualties a day, and it was not unknown for surgeons to work sixteen hours at a stretch. Clitheroe was so exhausted during a marathon session of surgery that, in a lull, he kicked off his boots, climbed on to the temporarily vacated operating table and fell asleep. The job demanded physical fitness and mental toughness. 'You've got to be able not just to withstand the onslaught, not just to survive, but to thrive on it,' said Paul Parker.

Even when a doctor's tour was over, his work wasn't. Rosell was on the flight back home when the condition of a casualty on board, bound for Selly Oak, worsened. The poor man was unable to empty his bladder, and there, on the floor of the Tristar, Rosell inserted a catheter and rigged up a drainage bag. It was as near to a routine procedure as he had ever come, and even then it was at 35,000 feet in the air.

*

At the end of the day, the real achievement of the medics in Afghanistan was measured by the number of men who – as with the Special Forces soldier Rosell had saved – were surviving wounds that, in previous conflicts, would have been fatal, offering no hope of recovery whatsoever.

This process began with the preparation the troops on the ground received before going into battle. They were drilled in what to do if their patrol took casualties, and carried with them into battle a compact pocket booklet that guided them through the correct procedures. The idea was not new – a similar card had been doled out to soldiers in the Second World War (though to what effect is unclear, since it was issued only to corporals and above). The twenty-first-century version was altogether slicker, easy to flip open and follow under the most extreme circumstances – and went to everyone. It was a no-nonsense, question-and-answer, do-this-don't-do-that document to help troops do what was right if a comrade went down. It was printed, helpfully, on plasticized card so blood could be wiped off.

Common sense prevailed in its instructions. If they were under enemy fire, they were told to 'win firefight' first – the military priority always came first. But when they could turn their attention to their wounded, it instructed them on the recovery position ('face down, head to one side'), on opening airways, and pressing fingers and knuckles hard into open wounds to stop the bleeding.

'DO NOT remove embedded foreign objects,' it declared. Give morphine for pain relief – jabbed into the thigh with an auto-injector – but not if the casualty had a head injury or difficulty in breathing.

Rew, who had been in Iraq, noticed a sea change in the skills and awareness of the front-line soldiers. The team medics in each section and platoon – now one for every four soldiers, a ratio previously the preserve of Special Forces – were better too, and not just in numbers. They were better trained than ever before and better equipped. Each wore a special belt with extra quick-action tourniquets, extra dressings, two Hemcon bandages which formed anti-bacterial seals over wounds, and a suction device to suck out vomit and blood. They had gloves, scissors and coloured priority labels – red for 'action now', yellow for 'soon' and green for 'can wait' – to attach to each casualty for the information of the next level of medic who took over from them.

The speed with which most casualties were picked up by the emergency medical teams of doctors and nurses, as well as para-medics, and 'casevaced' to hospital was another reason for greater survivability – though it was never fast enough. It was still taking an average of just over three hours to get the critically wounded to hospital and, as in the Kajaki Dam incident, sometimes significantly longer. Paul Parker took every opportunity to lobby for a dedicated fleet of small helicopters – lightweight Black Hawks rather than chunky Chinooks – for the exclusive 24/7, all-weather use of the medics, rather than always being on call for other purposes, such as ferrying troops or supplies.

Increasingly, too, the issue of whether doctors should expose themselves to the dangers of the front line was being settled in favour of the action men. The driving force came from the top, from RAMC colonel and A&E consultant Tim Hodgetts, who had no doubt that the welfare of his patients came before his. Serving in Afghanistan, Hodgetts felt doctors had no prior claim to survival. 'The life of a consultant in emergency medicine like me is no more important or vital than the life of a private soldier.' He led from the front, much to the surprise of soldiers in the field, who were not used to seeing a full colonel running off the back of a helicopter to treat them as they lay wounded and under fire. Hodgetts recalled dropping down into a poppy field as bullets rattled into the side of the Chinook. A wounded American soldier was carried fireman-style back inside the helicopter. As the Chinook rose into the air, Hodgetts went to work with procedures that would once have had to wait until the casualty was in hospital. 'We can intubate and ventilate. They can have chest tubes and surgical airways put in. Some helicopters have cold boxes to store blood so we can give transfusions. We now have special needles that go directly into bones to get fluids quickly into the body.'

His rank gave him no more control than any other doctor had over the perilous conditions in the back cab of a Chinook hurtling at full tilt back to base. 'It's noisy, it's cold. It's vibrating, it can be pitch black, apart from a couple of torches. We are kneeling on the floor. We are not secured. It is like Alton Towers without the popcorn!' But his calculation was that the benefits to his patients were worth all the extra risk to men and machines.

For all the speed and skills employed, the most crucial development increasing the survival prospects of the fighting men was the Osprey body armour they wore. This was often what saved the 'unexpected survivors', as Hodgetts called them – the men with three-limb amputations, a penetrating brain injury, 75 per cent burns or whose heart went into arrest in the back of the rescue helicopter and who would probably not have made it five years ago. Now, they could, and routinely did. The 'golden hour' that had once seemed the critical limit within which the life of a seriously wounded man could be saved was now reckoned to have shot up to four hours.

Such advances, while saving lives, did, however, pose uncomfortable issues about the quality of the lives being saved. Were men surviving who would have been better off dead, whose injuries and loss of limbs, organs and vitality meant they themselves would have preferred to be dead? These were questions the doctors did not feel qualified to answer. 'When a casualty comes in,' David Rew explained, 'if he or she is alive and saveable, in the general sense of resuscitation and surgical treatment, you do what needs to be done. At that time, you don't know whether they are going to live or die and what their quality of life is going to be. Your job is to save that life and to give them the very best chance of a high-quality life, accepting that it may be as an amputee. Should we keep this guy alive? It's not our job to make that ethical judgement. You have to do your best for them at that moment. It's the only thing you can do.'

Rew never ceased to be amazed by the courage of those he treated, their humour, their stoicism, their superb motivation. 'They come in with multiple injuries, arms and legs missing, and they still crack jokes with the surgical team about being shot or stepping on mines. Some even ask for photos to be taken so they can show friends back home. That's the sort of indomitable spirit they had – and when we saw it, we weren't going to let them die, not if we could help it.' Later, he would see men he had brought back from the brink of death not only surviving but thriving back home in the UK. 'Some are doing extraordinarily well. OK, it's not the life they had imagined for themselves, but a combination of inner drive, support and the fact that the army is trying to offer them ongoing careers means they're not giving up. They still have an incredible lust for life.' He was glad he had not let them die. And, in most cases, so were they.

18. Scars That Will Not Heal

Only Andy Stockton, the sergeant major who lost his left arm to a rocket-propelled grenade in Sangin, could get away with suggesting to his mate at Headley Court, the Defence Medical Rehabilitation Centre in the Surrey countryside, that they should sneak out of the Elizabethan mansion, with its neurological beds, physiotherapy gyms, hydrotherapy pool and prosthetic-limb department, nip down the lane to the pub and get 'legless'. His companion, a bomb-disposal officer whose legs were sheared off when trying to deal with a suicide bomber at Camp Dogwood in Iraq, laughed at the use of the word which so neatly described his condition, drunk or sober. He might have glared at anyone else mouthing it, but not the one-armed Stockton, aka 'Captain Hook', a man who rose above the physical damage he suffered and did his best to help others in a similar situation to do the same.

'Twelve of us would go for a drink,' the sergeant major recalled, 'and we'd joke that we had only eight legs and six arms between us. I believe the banter and black humour were part of the recovery process. You have to keep your mates' spirits up, and they keep up yours in return.' It worked. Another amputee wore a T-shirt with a slogan on the front proclaiming, 'I went to Afghanistan and all I got was this crappy false leg.' Others were planning to go sky-diving and sailing. One had a simpler ambition – 'to be able to stand in a pub with my dad, in a pair of trousers, not leaning on the bar and nobody knowing'.[1]

Stockton was an amazing role model. Within hours of coming round from the operation to amputate his arm at Camp Bastion hospital, he was up on his feet and outside the ward dragging on a cigarette and chatting away as if he'd just had his nails clipped. Within a year, he was skiing, white-water rafting and taking an instructors' diving course. He was driving a specially adapted motorbike, which he bought from his £57,000 compensation payment, a paltry figure compared with the small fortunes often paid out in damages to 'victims' in civilian cases with far less serious injuries, but it did enable him to pay off the mortgage on his house and get on with his life. He has eight different attachments for his prosthetic arm, including a snooker-cue holder, a ski-pole holder and a hook to amuse his children – hence his nickname. Like Admiral Nelson, he was an action man before an enemy shot away his arm, and he was determined to be an action man afterwards. But, unlike Nelson, his injury meant that he left the service. He would not have been returned to the front line, and he couldn't face that. 'I'm a soldier. I want to run around with a gun,' he said. 'I didn't join the army to be stuck behind a desk.'[2]

He quit, as have a significant number of the seriously wounded returning from Iraq and Afghanistan since 2003. A few – the wise ones, perhaps – stayed in the down-graded jobs they were offered, realizing that this was the moment they most needed the comradeship, the protection and the mutual support of service life. Shannon, the wife of paratrooper Stu Hale, disabled in the Kajaki minefield, saw this clearly from the start, and the first thing she impressed on him after he lost his leg was not to leave the army. It was something to belong to and to hold on to, she reminded him. Her husband agreed. 'What's the point in me having a desk job in civvy street when I could just as well have one here with the guys?' he said. He retrained as an intelligence officer and, in that role, ironically, was posted back to Afghanistan. 'It'll be different. I won't be out on the ground and back behind my sniper rifle. But I can still count for something out there, do some good, make a contribution.'

For a lot of other casualties of the front line, the idea of working in the welfare office or the regimental museum – of being, as they saw it, second-class soldiers and an object of pity – was too great an indignity. Sadly, they did what they had never done on the battlefield and crept away to lick their wounds in private, the psychological effects of their condition, their sense of loss, even harder to come to terms with than their physical impairment.

To overcome these feelings takes almost superhuman reserves of guts and determination. Gunner Adam Nixon lost his left leg to a pipe bomb in Basra and, from being a marathon runner, was wheelchair-bound, constantly in pain and haunted by the fear that he might yet lose the badly damaged other leg as well. His life became a never-ending series of flashbacks, panic attacks and insomnia, punctuated by painkillers and anti-depressants. Until, that is, he was persuaded to go on a skiing trip to Colorado with similarly 'wounded warriors' from the US forces. Strapped into a spring-mounted bucket seat on a mono-ski, he hurtled down through the snow with a smile of happiness and achievement on his face. 'This is the most fun I've had in years,' he told an observer. 'Until now I've just stayed at home and festered, but I've had enough of dwelling in the past. I want to get going.'[3] Moving on means somehow becoming philosophical about what has happened to you.

As a serving soldier, Andy Stockton had thought about dying, but not about being wounded. When he was on active service he always made sure his insurance payments were up to date. 'I knew I might come back in a body bag and I wanted to leave something for my family. But it never occurred to me I would come back maimed.' With soldiers, it never seems to. But now it had happened he accepted it as part of the deal. 'If you take the Queen's shilling, you take the chances too.' He 'moved on to new things', as he put it, without a glance over his shoulder at what might have been. No regret and no resentment. But not everyone returning maimed or disfigured from Iraq and Afghanistan can cope with what has happened, and who can blame them?

Gradually, society – though, sadly, not so much the state – has woken up to its responsibility for these young men and women damaged in the service of their country. Active publicity for places like Headley Court has helped. So has the involvement of figure-heads such as fellow-soldiers Prince William and Prince Harry in their cause. But it is noticeable that the burden of after-care and rehabilitation has had to be taken up largely by charities. Once a wounded man or woman leaves the service, the state turns its back.

The skiing trip that put sparkle back into the life of Adam Nixon was organized by BLESMA, the British Limbless Ex-Service Men's Association, which is funded totally from voluntary donations. Long may organizations like this continue. They will have to, because the wounds sustained in the wars in Iraq and Afghanistan will not quickly heal.

When then prime minister Tony Blair took Britain to war with Iraq in 2002, he spoke gravely of the 'blood price' the nation must pay. Those who did the paying in lost limbs and shattered minds and were then cast adrift may wonder whether they were grievously short-changed in this transaction. The reality of learning to live without a limb, possibly two, is harsh, for all the jocularity among mates and the public displays of Bader-like grit and determination in front of visiting princes and dignitaries. On parade, the wheelchairs and crutches are inspiring symbols of courage, but in private they all too often mean broken dreams, disappointment and despair, a mental torture harder to bear than the physical pain. There are no quick fixes. However good and high-tech modern prosthetic limbs may be, adapting to them is an arduous process. 'It's an ongoing drama with the legs,' said Shannon Hale of husband Stu. 'You think, oh, you lose your leg and you get a prosthetic one. But it's not as easy as that. For the first two years, the stump keeps shrinking, which means going back for new fittings all the time. Just when you think he's OK and he's walking really well, the stump has shrunk again, the leg is moving in the wrong way and he has to go back for some more adjustment.'

Ironically, the problems of this growing army of war-wounded are the direct result of the very successes of medics. In Afghanistan, through their bravery under fire and the new discipline of emergency medicine, lives are being saved that, without a doubt, would have been lost just a few years ago. Colonel Tim Hodgett's 'unexpected survivors'[4] are a phenomenon to be proud of. There is an internationally agreed points system for assessing the severity of injuries, and a total of seventy-five used to mean certain death. Not any more. 'We are now getting survivors with injury scores of seventy-five and saving more lives than ever,' said Hodgetts. 'But that, of course, has implications for future care.' The catastrophic need no longer be fatal. The challenge thrown up by the Falklands War to get more men home alive has been met and answered. The new challenge is to make sure those saved lives are worth living.

★

For medics, suppressing their emotions is vital if they are to do their job properly. They cannot give in to anger and aggression, as fighting soldiers often do in battle. They are the calm in the middle of the storm. They cannot move on to the next firefight when someone is hit by a bullet or a bomb, as fighting soldiers do. They must stay and confront the pain and the gore. They are the ones who cradle the frightened and the dying, cursing their own inability to save them, to perform the hoped-for miracles. The horror – for that is what it is – cannot easily be absorbed.

It is no coincidence that a disproportionate and rising number of medics are on the books of charities that help veterans who have problems adjusting back to ordinary life. The stress of dealing with incredibly horrific trauma is having a lasting effect, says Toby Elliott of Combat Stress, the Ex-Services Mental Welfare Society, another voluntary organization having to take the strain of after-care when governments draw the line. All the anger that Gary Lawrence, the medic who rescued Andy Stockton under withering Taliban fire, managed to hold in at the time came flooding out when he got home to England. The adrenalin dried up, leaving a void that was filled by nightmares. 'I couldn't sleep at night. I'd just be fidgeting.'

For another young soldier, the recurring dream was of a small child sliced in two when a British unit fired into a crowd at Basra in Iraq. He would wake in a panic and, though nineteen years old, climb into his parents' bed to find comfort in his mother's hug. It hadn't been his bullet that killed the boy, but he could never get out of his head the picture of the little lad's father sitting on the street and hugging what was left of his son. The soldier's mother would rub his nose, just as she had when he was a baby, and soothe him back to sleep.[5]

For many others, drink eased the anguish, if only for a while. Gary Lawrence would sup with his mates until he could no longer stand their belly-aching about the trivial irritations of army life. As he sank the pints and shots, he remembered clearly how, one morning, he had gulped down tea with a bright young officer and then, later the same day, pulled his ashen-faced corpse, a bullet through his brain, from an ambulance. Among a crowd he would find his mind straying away from the conversation and back to the butchery of the battlefield. The memories were as alive as ever. As he talked about them, he struggled to hold back the tears. He was trying to work these matters out on his own, but he was not too proud or dismissive of 'shrinks' and counsellors to know that, if and when he needed help, he would ask for it.

These days, it is there for the asking. It was heartening that the recruits the authors observed on the training ground at Aldershot[6] had no illusions about the horror they might experience in Afghanistan but were confident they could ask for and get help to deal with it as a matter of course. There was no bravado on display, just an honest appreciation of the damage that war can do to the mind of even the strongest man or woman.

To an extent they are the beneficiaries of a long overdue shift in military medical thinking. The reality of the suffering caused by PTSD – Post-Traumatic Stress Disorder – was now acknowledged.

That was not the case in 1982, when Para doctor Captain Steven Hughes returned from the Falklands, his brain refusing to deal with the human destruction he had witnessed at Goose Green. 'On the boat coming back, there was no sense at all about how many people would be affected by their experiences. We didn't realize what was brewing up for the future.'[7] In his own case, he believed he had looked death in the face and stared it down. He was not afraid. But one Saturday night two years later, in a London teaching hospital where he was the casualty surgeon on call, he snapped. 'I suffered a profound, incapacitating, panic attack. For no obvious reason, I was suddenly overwhelmed by a crescendo of blind, unreasoning fear, defying all logic and insight.'[8] The terrors had caught up with him. He was sedated and admitted to a closed psychiatric ward that was all too reminiscent of *One Flew over the Cuckoo's Nest*. After a month of treatment, he went back to work, but the same thing happened again – he panicked to such an extent he thought he was going mad.

It took an old military friend, a Royal Navy psychiatrist who had been on the task force that sailed to the Falklands, to tease out the problem. After they talked, Hughes 'suddenly found myself back at Goose Green, in the rain and the smoke and the horror. I felt again the fear, the despair, the grief, and the anger; an overwhelming maelstrom of emotions long since buried deep in my soul.' The cat was out of the bag. He had PTSD. It was a condition he had begun to identify in other Falklands veterans and even written a paper about for a journal, but he had missed the symptoms in himself. 'I then started to address what I had never acknowledged, let alone come to terms with – the hidden memories and feelings of those black days of 1982. I had never had the time to release the suppressed emotions that I dared not show as I fought to keep alive those gallant young men, Argentinians and Brits, friend and foe. Aware of the eyes of my medics on me, their leader, I had got on, seemingly impassively, with the job at hand, even when the bodies of some of my closest friends lay only yards away. Whatever snapped did so in the burning gorse at Goose Green.'

He now realized that he had never taken the time to come to terms with the death of friends. 'We came home to a society that had simply watched the Falklands as if it were another war movie on television. I never grieved and, as time passed, I supposed and hoped that so had the need. It was as if I had erased the emotion from the tape in my head that records those memories.' The only treatment to return him to mental health was to go back into his past and confront the demons, which he did by talking to those who had had similar experiences. 'Sharing disperses the hurt.'

He realized, too, that what had happened to him must also have struck others who had fought in the Falklands. The psychological damage of that ugly conflict was, he did not doubt, extensive, badly affecting, he calculated, a quarter of the troops, while a further quarter showed milder signs of the hyperactivity or lack of focus that comes from stress. 'Many, like me, will not even be aware that they have a problem.'

He kicked himself for not spotting what, in retrospect, seemed so obvious. The signs had always been there. A few weeks after getting home from the Falklands, he and some army friends had gone to the Farnborough Air Show and found themselves instinctively ducking when the aircraft roared over. In their heads, they were still in a combat zone. A year later, on a posting with the Paras in Belize, the lads were involved in a major punch-up, sparked by unresolved frustration and anger. Hughes looked round at his mates and realized how few of them were managing to have stable family lives or decent relationships. It didn't seem normal, which was why he began to research the issue of post-traumatic stress. From GPs who treated the soldiers' wives, he heard stories about their menfolk disappearing off to the garden for hours on end, drinking a bottle of whisky in one go and then refusing to talk about what was going on in their heads. At work the men were flogging themselves to a ridiculous degree, 'beasting' themselves. 'That and their excess drinking were classic signs of PTSD, though I didn't recognize it at the time.'

Somebody should have. There had been warnings in the past, as this piece of gossip, one army wife about another, indicated. 'Back only a fortnight, and she doesn't know what to do with him. He sits in the back room by himself. Won't speak to anybody, won't go out, won't read. Won't do nothing. She doesn't know what to do. There'll be trouble there.' The year of that observation was 1945, and the anecdote was related in a paper by Lieutenant Colonel T. F. Main, wartime psychiatric adviser to the Director of Military Training at the War Office.[9] He foresaw the serious problems men returning from war would have readjusting and, though the phrase would not be coined for another thirty years (in America, in relation to the Vietnam War), PTSD was part of what he was referring to. Military psychiatry then being a Cinderella discipline, and the country beset by huge social and economic difficulties in the aftermath of a catastrophic world war, Main did not hold out much hope that his advice would be acted on, though he had no doubt that it should be. 'It would be folly to assume that this is a problem too small for consideration and which time will heal,' he wrote.

Folly, however, was to win the day, and the problem was ignored and left unresearched, with the result that four decades later, Steven Hughes was at a loss to work out what was happening to his depressed and out-of-control comrades and had to start virtually from scratch. Nor did he cotton on that any of the behaviour he observed in other Falklands veterans applied to him – not until that night on duty in the casualty department when his past caught up with him.

That his problem identified itself and he was able to have treatment for it may have saved his life. Others simply went under. In the quarter of a century since the Falklands, more veterans of the war have committed suicide than were killed during it. 'It's a horrifying statistic,' Hughes says. 'After all these years, men who fought in the Falklands still seek me out for advice about it. I'll hear down the grapevine that Private X is having a problem, and I'll arrange to see him and try to get him some help. They know I was the doc, and so they'll talk to me, but the truth is that this is a long-term problem, and the military should be taking care of it. Instead they dump the problem over to the NHS once a soldier has left the service, and the NHS facilities for treating PTSD are sporadic.'

There was a further difficulty, in that civilian psychiatrists had little clue about military life and no concept at all of what it was like being in combat. Nor would other patients an ex-soldier might be lumped in with for treatment. In therapy groups, he might find himself with people whose levels of stress in their ordinary lives seemed trifling and inane compared with the hell of battle he had been through, and that would serve only to make him feel more isolated. The solution, as Hughes discovered in his own case, was to open up not to strangers or even to loved ones but to those who had been where he had been, had seen what he had seen and knew how he felt because they had felt it themselves. Who else could comprehend the scenes on the blazing *Sir Galahad* that were burned into the retinas of RAMC sergeant Peter Naya, the last medic off the scorching hulk of the landing ship in Bluff Cove? He could never forget the pain he witnessed that day. The memories still catch him unawares, especially at night, and 'a thousand emotions rage through me. But I bottle it up. Many others who were there do the same. We can't really describe what we went through, not even to our wives. There are certain things I will never talk about.'[10]

The smallest thing can trigger waves of remorse. Medic Andy Poole had to give up watching motorcycle racing, a spectator sport he loved, because the smell of exhaust fumes from the two-stroke engines set off memories of burning flesh on the *Galahad*. 'It was twenty-six years ago, but I still have flashbacks.' He suspects he always will, however hard he tries to put the horror to the back of his mind.

For Bill Bentley, the overriding Falklands' memory was of the hollow sound a dead comrade's head made as it bounced against his knee when he carried the body off the battlefield at Goose Green. He had also been on medical duties in Bluff Cove when the *Galahad* was hit. But it was twenty years later before the stress of these occasions came back to ambush him. He had back problems, one remedy for which was taking long soaks in the bath instead of his usual shower. Lying in the water, he was gripped by the sensation of being on fire. Images of the *Galahad* carnage came flooding back. Then other symptoms appeared. 'I started knocking things over and couldn't concentrate, all classic signs of PTSD.' Unable to work because of sickness, he got into debt and, to raise money, was forced to sell his Military Medal, awarded for saving a man's life at Goose Green. He felt alone with his problem. 'The army doesn't want to help, and the organizations I've been to have been a waste of time. Basically, you just try to get yourself through it.' And he did, but it was tough going.

It was tough too for Simon Weston, the Welsh Guardsman so horribly burnt on the *Galahad* that he wished he had died. The surgeons had worked wonders to keep him alive. He was so damaged he was not expected to survive the journey back to Britain. He did, and then came through scores of operations and skin grafts, fighting off septicaemia and infections. 'I looked like a bubbling mass of scab,' he recalled. 'It was frightening, because you are on your own. The pain is happening to you, and you can't stop it or avoid it. It's just something you have to get through, and it's very lonely.' His career was finished. He was classified as 'P8U8', off the scale for military fitness, or 'physically and totally useless', as he himself describes it. Two years after roasting at Bluff Cove, he was medically discharged from the army, cut adrift into a civilian world where he felt even more frightened for his future. 'I'd lost my face, I'd lost my hands, I'd lost *me*. An officer told me I was totally unemployable, which hurt. I didn't know who I was or where my life would go.'[11]

Not surprisingly, the depression he fell into was profound, and the only remedy liquid. 'I would drink ten or fifteen pints a night, then be back at the pub for opening time next day. I also had a near dependency on hospital drugs and became lazy and lethargic. I hated my looks, my life, everything. I simply stopped caring about myself.'

In the end, it was mates who pulled him back from the brink. Before his injuries, he had played rugby for the regiment. Now his melted hands were so wrecked he could no longer hold a ball, but the team was going on tour and they invited him along. 'For the first time since the war there was no sympathy for me. I was just one of the lads.' They gave him no special treatment but they did make demands of him. 'There was an officer and I went to shake his hand. But I had got into the idle habit of not raising my thumb, and I presented him with what must have felt like a stump. "Shake my hand properly!" he bellowed at me.' Weston was mortified, but stood corrected. 'I was letting myself become disabled in something as simple as a handshake. I was allowing myself to be something I wasn't. It was a moment of truth, a none-too-gentle kick in the pants.'

From that point, his recovery began and he started not only to get his life back on track but to create a new one for himself. He took up charity and media work and became a public figure. More importantly, he came to terms with who he was. And he stopped feeling sorry for himself, remembering that, for all the disfigurement of his face and the stares he sometimes still gets from people in the street, he was alive. 'There were forty-eight guys on that ship who never had that chance. I'm a lucky man, very, very lucky.'

Weston was forced to confront what had happened, and the outcome was good for him. In a sense, the visible nature of his injuries meant he could not hide, and that may have been the saving of him. Stretcher-bearer Tom Onions returned from the Falklands in one piece, but with scars inside that no one could see and which he tried to ignore. His best friend died in his lap on Mount Longdon, and Onions thought he could bury away the experience. 'When I got home, I wouldn't talk about what I'd seen. People asked me what it was like out there, and I'd just say it was something I never discussed.' He kept his silence for three and a half years, until one day he decided to unburden himself to a friend, 'a civvy', over a drink in a pub in Wolverhampton. 'He asked if I wanted to talk about it and I said, yeah, I do actually. I just let it all out, and it was pretty emotional. But my mate couldn't handle it. I was trying to tell him everything that had happened but, after half an hour, he interrupted and suggested we went to another pub. In other words, "Shut up, I don't want to hear it." It was all too much for someone who hadn't been there.'

Now a policeman and a former member of the Royal Protection Squad, he still feels affected by his time in the Falklands. 'I thought I had detached myself from what happened down there, but I hadn't. I still had nightmares and just a mention of the Falklands made me feel incredibly sad and emotional. So, two years ago, I contacted Combat Stress.' He learned to talk about what he had experienced. He also went back to the islands, a 'pilgrimage', as he called it, and was deeply moved by a memorial at Teal Inlet for the Mount Longdon dead.

He has yet to discover whether he is truly on the mend emotionally, whether he has at last managed to bury the past. Time will tell. But he has at least achieved some perspective, because his sympathies lie less in the past and more with the new generation of British soldiers. 'I look at what the guys are doing out there in Afghanistan at the moment. My battle on Mount Longdon was intense, but it lasted only three or four days. These guys are fighting day in and day out over a period of three or four months. I don't know how they cope. I think they have it worse than we did.'

They will, though, get more help than the Falklands veterans did. Some lessons have been learned. When the troops returned in 1982, they were sent instantly on six weeks' leave. This was a mistake, Steven Hughes, the 2 Para doctor, realized later. They simply took their problems home and never dealt with them. He reckoned that, instead of being dispersed, they would have been better staying together as a unit, to readjust together. It is what now happens as a matter of routine. For troops returning from Iraq and Afghanistan, 'decompression' time with their mates, reacclimatizing to reality, is considered crucial.

Whether this will prove to be enough remains to be seen, and Hughes is not over-optimistic. There has indeed been a shift in thinking, and PTSD is no longer necessarily the career-breaker or the sure-fire shortcut to a discharge it once was, but handling the condition is still a major task, and many men and women who have served in Iraq and Afghanistan are in danger of falling through the precarious safety net. 'PTSD is still a very real problem in the military,' says Hughes. 'Today's conflicts could be producing a time-bomb, with psychiatric casualties emerging years after the conflict is over.' He is wary about the notion that stress is now accepted as normal in the services and every bit a war wound as a bullet in the head. He isn't convinced that the connotations of 'shell shock' from the First World War don't still lurk in the military psyche today. 'There is still so much stigma associated with psychiatric illness. Military people at all levels are reluctant to accept these problems, because they don't fit with the image.'

And how long do the after-effects of war last? A lifetime, if the experience of RAMC captain Malcolm Pleydell in the Second World War was anything to go by. He was medical officer on a pleasure steamer that joined the flotilla of ships rescuing the British army from Dunkirk. As it pulled away from the pier with a thousand men crammed on board, he was down in the blacked-out saloon with the wounded, and groping his way between the stretchers filling the floor. 'Crouching down beside a man with an M for "morphia" marked on his forehead, I was trying to make out the dose on the rough notes on his field dressing card when our steamer hit a destroyer head-on as it raced into the harbour at about forty knots.' The collision threw everyone into a heap, the steamer listed dramatically to starboard and panic broke out on the deck above. 'We could hear heavy army boots over our heads, thudding backwards and forwards, this way and that, drumming a mad tattoo.' He feared the sea would come flooding down, 'and we would drown like rats'.

He battled to get the stretchers up the companionway and on deck so the wounded would have some chance to escape. Somehow, the steamer extricated herself from the bows of the destroyer and limped back to Dover and, as she docked, Pleydell realized it was his birthday. 'Not one to forget!' he noted, and he never did, nor could. For months afterwards, his pulse would race and his hands run with sweat if he was in a room and heard the footsteps of people overhead. He would remember the mad drumbeat of boots on the ceiling and feel once again his fear of being trapped and drowning. Writing down his thoughts nearly half a century later, he asked, 'So when did Dunkirk end for me? Was it ten, twenty, or forty years later?' The answer was never. 'Even now, when I go below decks on a ship, the memories come flooding back. The mental scars remain.' From Dunkirk to Afghanistan, much has altered in warfare and in military medicine. But some things never change.

One aspect of post-battle stress is particularly poignant – survivors' guilt, the belief that it is wrong still to be alive when many of those you fought beside are dead. It surfaced years after the end of the Second World War, most notably and publicly when the politician Enoch Powell, whose wartime service saw him rise from private to brigadier, wept on a radio programme when recounting his inability to come to terms with the deaths of comrades. He wished, he said, he had died with them. The prescient army psychologist T. F. Main had spotted this tendency in 1945 and warned of men 'ruminating over the death of comrades or some particularly distressing experience in action that now fills their thoughts and dreams. They reproach themselves for infidelity, neglect of duty or some slight and perfectly unintentional injury they may have done to others. Lapses into alcoholism or acts of delinquency may be not infrequent.'

A generation later, Simon Weston, coming home from the Falklands hideously injured, a man whose survival was a triumph of courage over adversity, nonetheless was at times consumed by the same sense of failure and regret. 'I was haunted by the fact that I couldn't save any of my mates who had died. There were many times I wished I'd died alongside them.'

Self-reproach is still a burden many soldiers bear. Warrant officers in the British army are not prone to breaking down in tears, but that was what one did in 2008 when relating to an inquest in Wiltshire how, during an incident in Afghanistan, he had to choose between two badly wounded friends. A weapon-mounted Land Rover was on patrol in Gereshk when a suicide bomb was detonated against it. Warrant Officer Simon Edgell of the Grenadier Guards was in the vehicle in front and turned back to the wreck, where four men lay badly injured. One of them was in a bad way, his windpipe smashed by ball-bearings that had been packed around the bomb to cause maximum damage, and blood spilling from a ruptured artery in his neck. Edgell knelt beside him, clamping his fingers round the wound and pressing hard to stop the flow before it was too late. Then he realized that another man was missing. Royal Artillery sergeant David Wilkinson, the driver of the Land Rover, had been hurled from it in the blast and was nowhere to be seen.

Edgell had a terrible choice to make. He knew that, unless he got the wounded man to a medic at Forward Operating Base Price ten minutes' drive away, he would die. But that would mean abandoning even trying to find Wilkinson. The time taken looking would probably be a death sentence for the other man, and he decided he couldn't take the risk. He gave the order to head for FOB Price immediately. At the coroner's court, he wept as he recounted how he had had to tell the others in his party, 'I can't find Dave.' Later, Wilkinson's body was found in a drainage ditch. He had died from head injuries. The other man survived and recovered from his wounds, which suggests that Edgell had made the right call. The coroner certainly thought so. Of the warrant officer's conduct, he said: 'In the agony of that moment, he had to make a decision. He had one badly wounded serviceman he knew he must get to the medical centre as quickly as possible, and that he did – understandably in my opinion.'[12]

But no amount of official understanding or rational assessment can ever totally wipe out the sense felt by some soldiers that perhaps, just maybe, in the heat of battle they could and should have done more, or acted differently. Medics, as we have seen in the dozens of individuals whose stories we have told, are particularly prone to this anxiety. Alex Craig, whose shirt, emblazoned with the legend 'Airborne Paramedic', was blown off his back by a mine at Kajaki in Afghanistan and who made it to safety, never stopped wondering if he could have saved the life of his platoon commander, Corporal Mark Wright. 'Should I have gone back in? I'll always wonder.' He knew the guilt was unrealistic and unmerited, 'but it's something that nags at me'. 'Tug' Hartley, another of the Kajaki medics, had a recurrent nightmare of his friends being injured and him not having the bottle to go and help them, even though everything he did in the minefield that day was incontrovertible evidence of the opposite.

There are no quick fixes for these feelings of having let down your mates. Bill Bentley carried a similar cross from the Falklands War, and was plagued by a bad dream in which he was back at Bluff Cove and could see the casualties being brought off the *Galahad*, but could not reach them. 'I would be standing there watching, incapable of helping.' It would be a quarter of a century before his mind released him from this torture of self-flagellation. 'I've pretty well got a grip of it now,' he said, when he spoke to the authors in 2008, 'because I've come to believe that everything I did that day in 1982 was perhaps not perfect but it was the best that was possible in the circumstances. I am utterly convinced of that. At last I've got a clean conscience.' Time, though, does not always turn out to be a healer.

*

It was the twenty-fifth anniversary of the Falklands conflict and, on Horse Guards Parade, the mighty square in the centre of London where military celebrations have been held since the time of Henry VIII, ten thousand veterans of that war were drawn up in ranks in front of Prince Charles, Margaret Thatcher and then prime minister Tony Blair. There was silence as, across to the raised platform in the middle of the square, strode a confident young woman in scarlet high-heeled shoes and a bright yellow dress. All eyes were on Kathryn Nutbeem, a lone figure on a vast dais big enough for a whole choir. Who was she? What was she doing here? On her dress was pinned a campaign medal – her father's. Kathryn was five when RAMC Major Roger Nutbeem died in the smoke and flames of the *Galahad*. He had loved singing and went everywhere with his precious guitar. It was among his effects, sent back from the Falklands and, as she grew up without her dad, she treasured it as her link to him. A professional singer now, she had come to pay homage to a very special man in a very special way. The bandsmen of the Royal Marines and the Guards stood shoulder to shoulder behind her, but their brass and silver instruments were at rest. Instead, a single piano struck up, and she began to sing in a soft, sad voice that rippled around the square and lapped up against the ivy-clad walls of the Admiralty, the Foreign Office, Downing Street. 'Somewhere along the road, someone waits for me . . .'[13] In that place symbolizing power and military might, the tragedy that war brings to human lives was poignantly displayed. Little girls lose their daddies and, just as with Julie Harden, whose medic father won a posthumous VC in 1945, the heartache can never be repaired. Among those battle-heartened veterans listening, throats tightened with emotion and eyes moistened.

Because she was so young when he died, Kathryn's memories of her father are few. 'I remember him in his combat gear, and I have a vague memory of him comforting me after I caught my finger in the front door and cried.' She cried, too, the day her mother told her he was dead, and a new life began for both of them. 'Mum did brilliantly after Dad was killed, and as a result I had a really happy childhood. We talked about him, and there were pictures around the house, so I always had a sense of him.' It was in her teens that she really began to miss him. 'Seeing friends with their dads, I realized there was something I had missed out on.' Music is her point of contact with his memory. 'I remember him playing the guitar. He was into folk music, and that's the music I'm into as well. His battered old guitar means so much to me. It's a tangible part of him, his legacy to me. People also say I have the same smile as him.'

She heard Steeleye Span's 'Somewhere along the Road' when she was nineteen, and the lyrics summed up her feelings perfectly: 'Sometimes when winds are still, unexpectedly/ Perhaps beyond this silent hill, a voice will call to me . . .' – and it still does. 'It's twenty-six years now, and I still think about him. Curious things jolt the memory, such as watching a film with a father in it or reading a book about a father figure. I didn't really know him, but I still really miss him. I think about him when I play his guitar and sing. I find myself wondering, what would he have been like now? I miss what might have been. I've missed a whole lifetime with him. I'd give anything to have him back.'

The same sentiment hangs like a mushroom cloud of grief and regret over the Hampshire village home of Sally Veck, the mother of nineteen-year-old combat medical technician Eleanor Dlugosz, who was killed in 2007 by a roadside bomb in Iraq. This is hero country. A wreath of poppies lies against the rugged stone cross commemorating those villagers who died in the First World War, four of them from one family, a heavy toll. 'Forget them not, O land for which they fell,' reads the inscription.

A skittish colt is led by and stops to crop the grass around the monument. Life goes on in this idyllic setting, where tunnels of trees loop over the lanes and wild roses peep from the hedgerows. The only sounds in the still of a warm summer's day are the cawing of rooks, the screech of swooping swallows and the piping of chaffinches. A poster advertises next weekend's village fête, with stalls and pony rides, to be opened by an admiral. This is the 'English heaven' that Rupert Brooke's soldier, lying in a foreign field, dreamed of. But life has stopped in the cottage where, a year after her daughter's death, Sally Veck spends her days trying to come to terms with a loss so deep it wrenches the heart to see. There are no words to console. Pride in Eleanor's bravery and brilliance is no substitute for a light gone out for ever. Sally struggles to speak, but the words won't flow easily, only tears. The ever-effervescent Eleanor once told her breezily, 'You'll be fine if I'm killed, Mum.' 'But I'm not. They say that the pain lessens, but it doesn't. It will never be the same. I don't think I'll ever be fine again. But I couldn't have stopped her going, and I wouldn't have tried. It was what she wanted to do.' Eleanor's possessions, returned from Iraq in seven large boxes, are in storage, unpacked, the task of sifting through them too painful to contemplate. Her ashes are unscattered. 'I just don't know what to do with them. I don't really know what the future holds at all. The pain is too raw. I try to remember she was out there making a difference. I like to think that she helped some children or some women, improved their quality of life for a bit perhaps . . .'

'She helped.' If epitaphs there must be, then this is a good one, and fitting for a medic. For all those whose deeds we have recorded here, from the dive-bombed beaches of Dunkirk in 1940 to the suicide-bombed alleys of Afghanistan two-thirds of a century later, the personal wish to help others has been what sent them racing into hell with hardly a second thought. Bob Steer speaks for them all when he says, 'I'm proud of being a medic, because you can make a difference. War is designed to wreak death and destruction, but we can actually do some good. Regardless of what the politics are, or the reasons for the fighting, we are in a position to lives and make them better.' Rick Jolly, the Falkl takes pleasure in knowing he has done 's life', words he would settle for on his gravestone. To experienced RAF paramedic Andy Smith, the job he went out to do in Afghanistan this year (2009), flying across the desert to the rescue of wounded troops, was 'the most rewarding I have ever done'. It was, he said, terrible that young Marines were losing limbs, 'but at least we are there for them and we give them the best possible chance'.

Those they rescue are full of admiration too. 'I have nothing but praise for the medics who treated me on the ground, in the helicopter, in the field hospital and afterwards,' says Andy Stockton, the grievously wounded sergeant major with whose story this book began. 'They were all phenomenal. Medics see so much and do so much. I take my hat off to them.' Stu Hale is even prepared to suspend the Paras' traditional contempt for 'crap hats' from other regiments when it comes to medics. They were 'outstanding' in saving him at Kajaki. 'Before that incident I was quite disdainful about them, but now I really admire and respect them.' There is no finer tribute from a red beret – or from anyone, for that matter. Whenever the agonized cry of 'Medic!' went up, it was answered with selfless devotion and courage, and it will continue to bring out the best in humanity as long as wars are fought, lives need saving and wounds need binding. *In Arduis Fideles*, as the motto of the RAMC so rightly says, summing up the essence of all military medics – faithful in adversity.

Glossary

A&E – accident and emergency department
ABC – airway, breathing, circulation
ADS – advanced dressing station
ANA – Afghan National Army
ATO – Ammunition Technical Officer (a mine-clearance team)
cannula – a needle for delivering fluids
casevac – to evacuate casualties
CAT – combat application tourniquet
CCP – casualty collecting post
CPR – cardio-pulmonary resuscitation
FART – Forward Advanced Resuscitation Team
FOB – forward operating base
Hesco – defensive blast walls, designed by Hesco Ltd
IED – improvised explosive device (a bomb)
Intel – Intelligence Corps
IPE – individual protection equipment
KIA – killed in action
MASH – Mobile Army Surgical Hospital
MERT – Medical Emergency Response Team
PTSD – post-traumatic stress disorder
OPA – oral pharyngeal airway
RAP – regimental aid post
REME – Royal Electrical and Mechanical Engineers
RPG – a rocket-propelled grenade
RSM – regimental sergeant major
NBC – nuclear, biological and chemical
SOE – Special Operations Executive
Spencer Wells – artery forceps
Tab – tactical advance to battle
TIC – troops in contact
UAV – unmanned aerial vehicle

Notes

Where a reference is given for an interview, book or document, that reference applies for the remainder of the chapter.

Preface

1. They weren't the only ones to be impressed by the new stretcher. The equipment has now been tested in action and is due to become standard equipment, according to army sources.
2. Medical officer in conversation with JN, April 2009.

Part I: INTRODUCTION

Chapter 1: Saving Sergeant Major Stockton

1. JN interview, 2008.
2. Their detachment was part of OMLT, the Operations Mentoring Liaison Team, and consisted of men from various different regiments. Philippson, for example, was from 7 Parachute Regiment Royal Horse Artillery. Lawrence was from the Royal Army Medical Corps, had been sent to Afghanistan with 16 Close Support Medical Regiment and then been seconded to OMLT.
3. John Reid, then Defence Secretary, in a radio interview after authorizing the deployment of British troops in Afghanistan, explained that its purpose was to help reconstruct a Taliban-free country and to bolster the democratically elected Afghan government. 'If we came for three years here to accomplish our mission and had not fired one shot at the end we would be very happy indeed,' he said. This was generally taken as a reassurance that this was to be a relatively

risk-free operation – though, to be fair to Reid, in the same interview he did also point out its dangers and complexities. 'The terrorist will want to destroy the economy and legitimate trade and the government that we are helping to build up.' It was the reassuring impression that the press chose to go with, and the consummate politician in Reid, if he believed that was wrong, did not rush to correct it.

4. JN interview, 2008, plus interview in *Gunner* magazine, February 2007.
5. JN interview, 2008.
6. JN interview, 2008.
7. Abbreviation for 'casualty evacuation', used as a verb.
8. JN interview, 2008.
9. Quoted in *Combat Surgeons*, John Laffin (Sutton Publishing, 1999).

Chapter 2: Inhumanity

1. 'Tommy', by Rudyard Kipling (1865–1936).
2. *Combat Surgeons*, John Laffin (Sutton Publishing, 1999) – the chief source for the historical overview in this chapter, for which the authors are grateful.
3. Ibid.

Part II: THE SECOND WORLD WAR

Chapter 3: Overwhelmed

1. Private and unpublished diary of Ralph Brooke. Supplied by his grandson, Tom Lenon.
2. See Chapter 12.
3. *Medicine and Victory*, Mark Harrison (OUP, 2004).
4. According to Harrison, ibid., twenty-five field ambulance units were deployed, plus fifteen general hospitals, convalescent depots and medical stores along the lines of communication. These were served

by six ambulance trains and motor ambulance convoys, which were controlled by GHQ. Headquarters was also in direct charge of mobile laboratories, hygiene sections and casualty clearing stations (CCSs). The main medical base was at Dieppe, where there were several specialist hospitals and store depots.

5. 'Ambulance at War': Account by R. H. Montague. RAMC archive, Keogh Barracks. Box 70.

6. *Doctor At Dunkirk*, Ian Samuel (Autolycus Publications, 1985).

7. This process was described in the RAMC journal of December 1940 by Major R. S. Jeffrey. 'All foreign bodies and all devitalized tissue must be removed, particularly muscle. The muscle is cut away until it contracts under the scalpel and is bleeding healthily. Nerves and large blood-vessels are saved if possible, and the infected tissues surrounding. Then dissected off. Fragments of bone which no longer have a periosteal attachment are removed. A minimum of skin is removed, for skin resists infection well and will look after itself. Usually all the skin that needs to be removed is one-eighth of an inch from the wound edge, and this allows approximation without tension, which is so important. As few ligatures as possible are applied to bleeding points, using the finest catgut. In dealing with large nerves that have already been divided, it is a moot point whether one should attempt suture, or simply tie the ends together with silk with a view to making subsequent search for the nerve easier.'

8. *Medicine and Victory*, Harrison.

9. Private memoir. *Captivity*, Trevor Gibbens. Museum of the Oxs and Bucks Light Infantry.

10. Private account. RAMC archive.

11. It was in fact just over the border in Belgium.

12. RAMC journal, LXXVI, February 1941.

13. Such as Major L. J. Long – his memoir, RAMC Archive. Box 70.

14. IWM (Imperial War Museum) archive. Also *Dunkirk*, Hugh Sebag Montefiore, Viking Penguin, 2006.

15. Sebag Montefiore, ibid.

16. Private memoir. *Before I Forget*, W. Simpson. RAMC Archive. Box 70.

17. Simpson went into captivity and was indeed repatriated. But not until 1944.

18. Diary of Captain M. J. Pleydell, IWM 90/25/1.

19. Second World War Experience Centre, Leeds. Tape 1601.

20. Sebag Montefiore, *Dunkirk*.

21. 'Dunkirk Diary', published in the *British Medical Journal*, 1990. Doll was to become one of Britain's most eminent medical experts after the war. His research demonstrated the link between smoking and lung cancer.

22. Estimated at around 14,000.

23. IWM 76/30/1.

24. *Journals of Keith Vaughan* (John Murray, 1989).

25. *Combat Nurse*, Eric Taylor (Robert Hale, 1999).

Chapter 4: Bamboo Surgeons

1. *A Doctor's War*, Aidan MacCarthy (Grub Street, 2006).

2. Private publication. *The Lost Years*, George R. Temple, 2005.

3. 'Massacre and Rape in Hong Kong', Charles Roland, *Journal of Contemporary History*, January 1997.

4. Ibid.

5. *Singapore Burning*, Colin Smith (Viking Penguin, 2005).

6. Major Corbitt, RAMC archive.

7. After the war, it became the QARANC – the Queen Alexandra's Royal Army Nursing Corps.

8. *The Will to Live*, Sir John Smyth (Cassell, 1970).

9. Smith, *Singapore Burning*.

10. Her story was corroborated by Stoker Ernest Lloyd, who had been shot in the massacre of the men further along the beach but survived by diving beneath the water.

11. *Medicine and Victory*, Mark Harrison (OUP, 2004).

12. Much of the detail in this section is from *Surviving the Sword*, Brian MacArthur (Time Warner, 2005).

13. Lieutenant W. W. Tilney, quoted ibid.

14. Lieutenant Colonel Cary Owtram, quoted ibid.
15. His account on *www.cofepow.org.uk*
16. The husks, which contain thiamine (B1), had been removed, leaving just the solid, indigestible grain.
17. Saliva breaks the rice down into sugar, which in turn encourages the growth of yeast.
18. *The Secret Diary of Dr Robert Hardie* (Imperial War Museum, 1983).
19. Ibid.
20. *War Diaries of Weary Dunlop* (Nelson, Australia, 1986).
21. *Survival through Faith in Adversity: The Wartime Diaries of Joe Blythe*, supplied by Cedric Blythe.

Chapter 5: Desert Doctors

1. *Scars of War*, Hugh McManners (HarperCollins, 1994).
2. *Together We Stand*, James Holland (HarperCollins, 2005).
3. See Chapter 3.
4. He was awarded an OBE, the Military Cross and bar and the Distinguished Service Order.
5. *A Doctor at War*, Matthew Hall (Images Publishing, Malvern, 1995).
6. Wartime diary of R. K. Debenham. RAMC archive.
7. *Front-Line Nurse*, Eric Taylor (Robert Hale, 1997).
8. Diary and letters of Captain Malcolm Pleydell. IWM MC 90/25/1.
9. A Health Memorandum for British Soldiers in the tropics spelt out the gruesome details. 'The dysentery germs leave the sick man in his excreta (urine and dung). Flies feed on the excreta and pick up some of those dysentery germs. The infected flies feed on some cooked food and leave some dysentery germs in the food. A healthy man eats that food and those germs. The germs now attack his intestines and make him a case of dysentery. He in his turn passes out dysentery germs which are taken in by some other healthy person in the same manner.' – quoted in *Medicine and Victory*, Mark Harrison (OUP, 2004).
10. *Surgeon At War*, Lieutenant Colonel J. C. Watts (George Allen & Unwin Ltd, 1955).
11. General Sir Ronald Adam – quoted in Harrison, *Medicine and Victory*.

12. Ibid.
13. Mansion House speech, November 1942.
14. Taylor, *Front-Line Nurse*.
15. Hall, *A Doctor at War*.

Chapter 6: Stout Hearts

1. Lieutenant Colonel G. A. G. Mitchell, adviser to the RAMC, in *A Guide to Penicillin Therapy*, 1945.
2. *Combat Nurse*, Eric Taylor (Robert Hale, 1999).
3. Margaret Jackson Browne, quoted in *Front-Line Nurse*, Eric Taylor (Robert Hale, 1997).
4. Quoted in an article entitled 'If your man is wounded, this is how they care for him', in the *Evening News* newspaper, and in *Medicine and Victory*, Mark Harrison (OUP, 2004).
5. Personal diary – family archive. The authors are grateful to the late Dr Helm's family for permission to quote from it.
6. 'First-aid for Fighting Men', RAMC archive.
7. Brigadier E. H. Lessen, commander of No. 21 FDS, 5 Beach Group, quoted in Harrison, *Medicine and Victory*.
8. See Chapter 3. Second World War Experience Centre, Leeds. Tape 1601.
9. Personal Wartime Memoir of Major Charles E. Tegtmeyer, Medical Corps Regimental Surgeon, 16th Infantry Regiment, 1st Infantry Division. Surgeon-General's Office of Medical History. *www.history. amedd.army.mil/booksdocs/wwii/Normandy/Tegtmeyer/TegtmeyerNor mandy.html*
10. Tests had shown they had no serious adverse side effects, according to Harrison, *Medicine and Victory*.
11. Ibid.
12. *All Spirits*, John Vaughan (Merlin Books, Devon, 1988).
13. The Pegasus bridge, as it became known thereafter, taking its new name from the emblem of the airborne forces.
14. *Surgeon At War* by Lieutenant Colonel J. C. Watts (George Allen & Unwin, 1955).

15. *Red Devils*, by members of 224 Parachute Field Ambulance. Private memoir. RAMC archive.
16. *The Doctor's Story*, David Tibbs. Private memoir. RAMC archive.
17. From daily entries in the army book of Colonel Cyril Helm of the King's Own Yorkshire Light Infantry. Private collection.
18. Quoted in Harrison, *Medicine and Victory*.
19. Ibid.
20. Ibid.
21. *The Black Scalpel*, Geoffrey Parker (William Kimber, 1968).
22. *The Battle for Walcheren*, by J. O. Forfar. Proceedings of the Royal College of Physicians of Edinburgh, 1995.

Chapter 7: *Bravest of the Brave*

1. All letters and personal accounts quoted here are from the Harden family archive, collected by Eric's daughter Julia Wells and lodged at the Royal Marine Museum, Portsmouth. The authors are grateful to Mrs Wells for her invaluable assistance with this chapter.
2. Maas, in German and Dutch.
3. She must have imagined that he would be going into battle in the same way as he had on D-Day. In fact, as he told her in a letter, he went by ship from Tilbury to Ostend and reached his unspecified destination after 'seventeen hours on the train, the rest by lorry. The train had wood seats and no steam, very cold.'
4. Personal account, written 1995.
5. *A Doctor's War*, Aidan MacCarthy (Grub Street, 1979).

Part III: THE FALKLANDS WAR

Chapter 8: *A Long Way from Home*

1. Private memoir. RAMC archive.
2. *British Achievement in the Art of Healing*, John Langon-Davies (Pilot Press, 1946): RAMC archive.

3. See Chapter 5.

4. The acronym stood for Mobile Army Surgical Hospital.

5. 1973 in Britain.

6. *Spearhead Assault*, John Geddes (Arrow Books, 2008).

7. JN interview, 2008.

8. They were named in 1690 after Lord Falkland, financial backer of the *Welfare*, the first merchant ship to land there. He was also treasurer of the Royal Navy and later First Lord of the Admiralty.

9. Personal diary and JN interview, 2008.

10. *The Scars of War*, Hugh McManners (HarperCollins, 1994).

11. From *Above All, Courage: Personal Stories from the Falklands War*, Max Arthur (Cassell, 2002). Plus JN interview, 2008.

12. Colonel Paul Parker: Afghanistan dissertation, 2007.

13. See next chapter.

14. Quoted in Arthur, *Above All, Courage*.

15. *The Red and Green Life Machine: A Diary of the Falklands Field Hospital*, Rick Jolly (Red and Green Books, 2007).

16. JN interview, 2008.

17. RAMC journal, Vol. 153, Supplement 1, plus JN interview, 2008.

18. Captain David Hart Dyke of HMS *Coventry*. From his *Four Weeks in May* (Atlantic Books, 2007).

19. *Sod That for a Game of Soldiers*, Mark Eyles-Thomas (Kenton Publishing, 2007). Extracts from *Sod That for a Game of Soldiers* by Mark Eyles-Thomas reproduced by permission of Kenton Publishing.

20. According to Captain John Burgess, medical officer of 3 Para, 'the trench foot was horrendous and every bit as bad as people made out. It's caused by immersion of feet in cold water. It's bloody painful, with huge burning sensations in your feet, especially if you take your boots off, and your feet swell and then you can't get your boots back on. I was giving people morphine for the pain, but even that was ineffective. It's debilitating immediately and also potentially for years afterwards. The vast majority of men had it to some extent. It could have had a really serious effect if the fighting had gone on for much longer. It could have affected the battle for the Falklands. Most definitely, without a doubt, yes.'

21. The same thing – Paras 'tab', Marines 'yomp'. 'TAB' stands for 'tactical advance to battle'.
22. From *Forgotten Voices of the Falklands*, Hugh McManners (Ebury Press, 2007).
23. JN interview, 2007.
24. Hart Dyke, *Four Weeks in May*.

Chapter 9: Battle Stations

1. From Hugh McManners, *The Scars of War* (HarperCollins, 1994) & JN interview, 2008.
2. Private account, plus JN interview, 2008.
3. *Forgotten Voices of the Falklands*, Hugh McManners (Ebury Press, 2007).
4. From McManners, *The Scars of War*.
5. Ibid.
6. Ibid.
7. See Chapter 3.

Chapter 10: Fire Down Below

1. *Spearhead Assault*, John Geddes (Arrow, 2007).
2. *Forgotten Voices of the Falklands*, Hugh McManners (Ebury Press, 2007).
3. Interview on *Kiss the Children*, broadcast on the British Forces Broadcasting Service.
4. *Above All, Courage*, Max Arthur (Cassell, 2002).
5. Ibid.
6. Personal account and JN interview, 2008.
7. *The Red and Green Life Machine*, Rick Jolly (Red and Green Books, 2007).
8. JN interview, 2007.
9. Austrian Formula One racing driver, badly burnt and scarred in a crash at the 1976 German grand prix.

10. Total in Ajax Bay and those shipped the day before to the sick bays of RN vessels in the Sound.
11. JN interview, 2008.

Chapter 11: Gaining the High Ground

1. Private Ernest Douglas. Quoted in *The Soldier's War*, Richard Van Emden (Bloomsbury, 2008).
2. *Sod That for a Game of Soldiers*, Mark Eyles-Thomas. Kenton Publishing, 2007.
3. *Above All, Courage*, Max Arthur (Cassell, 2002).
4. JN interview, 2008.
5. JN interview, 2008.
6. JN interview and Falklands 25th Anniversary issue of RAMC journal, 2007.
7. EylesThomas, *Sod That for a Game of Soldiers*.
8. Not his real name.
9. Not his real name.
10. From Arthur, *Above All, Courage,*. The authors are grateful for permission to quote from this material.
11. Ibid.
12. Personal diary and JN interview, 2008.
13. Argentinian losses were 649 dead and 1,068 wounded.
14. *Scars of War*, Hugh McManners (HarperCollins, 1994).
15. Ibid.
16. Falklands 25th Anniversary issue of RAMC journal, 2007.
17. McManners, *Scars of War*.
18. In a joint paper in the RAMC journal two years later, three senior army doctors were in no doubt that tourniquets had been important in dealing with men in danger of bleeding to death from severe limb wounds. They recommended sanctioning the practice. But another RAMC officer, Colonel R. Scott, professor of military surgery, vehemently disagreed. 'I believe that more limbs and more lives will be lost by the unskilled application of tourniquets . . . Our first-aid

training should continue to stress the value of direct pressure for the control of haemorrhage.' RAMC journal, June 1984.

Part IV: IRAQ

Chapter 12: Bitter Pills

1. Private diary and JN interview, 2008.
2. *Thunder and Lightning*, Charles Allen (HMSO, 1991).
3. JN interview, 2008.
4. See Chapter 5.
5. American academic Francis Fukuyama argued in a famous paper in 1992 that 'what we may be witnessing is not just the end of the Cold War, but the end of history as such: that is, the end point of mankind's ideological evolution, and the universalization of Western liberal democracy as the final form of human government.'
6. 'Emergency Care in Kosovo', by Tim Hodgetts and Gary Kenward. *Emergency Nurse* magazine, February 2000.
7. JN interview, 2008.
8. From *Blood, Heat and Dust*, Lt-Col. David Rew. Private publication.
9. Quoted in 'In Search of Victor Horsley', by Lt-Col. Paul Parker. RAMC journal, 2006.

Chapter 13: Under Siege

1. *Dusty Warriors*, Richard Holmes (HarperCollins 2006).
2. JN interview, 2008.
3. Holmes, *Dusty Warriors*.
4. Ibid.
5. Ibid.
6. Personal account from *In Foreign Fields*, Dan Collins (Monday Books, 2007).
7. Personal account sent to the authors.

Chapter 14: A Woman's Place

1. *Soldier* magazine, June 2006.
2. JN interview, 2008.
3. Her personal story has appeared in interviews in various newspapers, including the *Daily Telegraph* (16 December 2006), and in the book *In Foreign Fields*, Dan Collins (Monday Books, 2007).
4. JN and TR interview, 2008.
5. Interview with Sally Veck, *Daily Mail*, November 2007.
6. A private in the Duke of Lancaster's was historically known as a Kingsman, a rank derived from the King's Regiment, which had joined with the Queen's Lancashire Regiment and the King's Own Royal Border Regiment to form the Duke of Lancaster's a year earlier, in 2006.
7. Report of inquest, BBC News, February 2008.
8. JN interview, 2008.

Part V: AFGHANISTAN

Chapter 15: On Afghanistan's Plains . . .

1. The pyjama-like trousers and loose shirt worn by Afghan farmers.
2. JN interview, 2008.
3. JN interview, 2008.
4. See Chapter 1.
5. JN interview, 2008.
6. Quoted in *3 Para*, Patrick Bishop (HarperPress, 2007).
7. Ibid.

Chapter 16: *Where Angels Fear to Tread . . .*

1. JN interview, 2008.
2. JN interview, 2008.
3. JN interview, 2008.
4. JN interview, 2007.
5. *Defence News*, 8 January 2008.
6. Quoted in *3 Para*, Patrick Bishop (HarperPress, 2007).
7. This was the conclusion of the subsequent inquest into Wright's death. The official MoD line was that the corporal somehow set off the mine himself and the Chinook was not responsible. But 3 Para commander Colonel Stuart Tootal told the inquest that, in his opinion, there was a definite causal link between the helicopter and the detonation.
8. Accounts vary about the timing. These fit the known facts.
9. The winches and hoists on all Chinooks had been withdrawn from service for a routine inspection after a fault was discovered. In returning the winches to service, priority was given to search-and-rescue helicopters in the UK rather than those in use in Afghanistan. The inquiry report added that it was 'disturbing that, in an area of operations where there was such a marked mine threat, there were no UK-equipped, rotary-wing air frames that could provide immediate casualty extraction. If an air frame with hoist capability had been available immediately, the casualty count may well have been less and the need to continue to move in the vicinity of the incident would have been significantly reduced.' *Sunday Telegraph*, 13 January 2008.
10. Inquests were held by the Oxfordshire coroner because it was to Brize Norton air base in Oxfordshire that bodies from Afghanistan and Iraq were flown home.

Chapter 17: Shifting Sands

1. JN interview, 2008.
2. JN interview, 2008.
3. JN interview, 2008.
4. JN interview, 2008.
5. Often maybe, but not always. In 2007. Lt-Col. Paul Parker complained publicly that there had been no serviceable CT scanner for a year and that the blood-testing laboratory had had to be closed for four hours during the hottest part of the day because the air-conditioning system could not cope.
6. *Blood, Heat and Dust*, Lt-Col. David Rew. Private publication.
7. JN interview, 2008.
8. JN interview, 2008.
9. Parker's full list is: aortic cross-clamping during resuscitative laparotomy; simple ligation of any major vessel tear; liver laceration packing; small intestinal perforation stapling; colonic perforation control with terylene tape; arterial injuries shunted/ligated, plus fasciotomy; venous injury ligation; bladder ruptures catheterized and drained; pancreatic bed leaks multiply drained; peritoneal soilage copiously irrigated and contained; abdomen temporarily and/or rapidly closed; visceral compartment syndrome treated with plastic sheet or IV-fluid-bag closure; rapid emergency thoracotomy; non-anatomically stapled lung resection; pulmonary tractotomy; circum-hilar rotation for lung haemorrhage control; e-masse lobectomy; skin staple closure of cardiac wounds; en-masse closure of chest wall muscles; patch closure of thoracic wounds (using an IV-fluid bag); intracranial bleeding – emergent arrest and control; adequate early exposure via 4-into-1 burr hole technique; intracranial haematoma evacuation/limitation of contamination; CNS superficial bone/ metal fragment removal; CNS infection control using early antibiotic therapy; CNS infection prevention with primary dural and scalp closure; post-surgical swelling control with decompressive craniectomy; femoral fracture control with rapid unilateral frame external fixation or Thomas splint; unstable pelvic binding or external

fixation; junctional zone bleed control with urinary catheter tamponade; articular fracture temporization with bridging external fixator; fracture reduction with approximate alignment; pin site skin tenting prevention with wide skin incisions; soft-tissue damage dealt with rapid primary debridement; contamination minimized by pulsed jet lavage; musculoskeletal infection control using appropriate antibiotics; compartment syndrome prevention – wide area fasciotomy; soft-tissue coverage temporary dressing; primary wound management with vacuum drainage packs. From 'Lessons Learnt in Afghanistan', paper by Lt-Col. Paul Parker, Major Nigel Tai, Lt-Col. Peter Hill and Lt-Col. Alan Ray.

Part VI: AFTERMATH

Chapter 18: Scars That Will Not Heal

1. *The Times*, January 2008.
2. Interview. *The Times*, December 2006.
3. *The Times*, January 2008.
4. See Chapter 17.
5. *Independent*, August 2007.
6. See Preface.
7. JN interview, 2008.
8. 'Inside Madness', by Steven Hughes. *British Medical Journal*, 1990.
9. Quoted in *When Daddy Came Home*, Barry Turner and Tony Rennell (Hutchinson, 1995).
10. *Above All, Courage*, Max Arthur (Cassell, 2002).
11. JN interview, *Sunday Express*.
12. *Daily Telegraph*, June 2008.
13. 'Somewhere along the Road'– a Rick Kemp song sung by Maddy Prior. Lyrics from 'Somewhere Along the Road' by Rick Kemp from the Album *Year* by Maddy Prior reproduced by permission of Park records www.parkrecords.com

References

Adkin, Mark, *Goose Green*, Cassell, 1992.

Allen, Charles, *Thunder & Lightning*, HMSO, 1991.

Arthur, Max, *Above All, Courage*, Cassell, 2002.

Bishop, Patrick, *3 Para*, HarperPress, 2007.

Collins, Dan, *In Foreign Fields*, Monday, 2007.

Cooksey, Jon, *3 Para – Mount Longdon*, Pen & Sword, 2004.

Craig, Chris, *Call For Fire*, John Murray, 1995.

Daniel, Paul, *Surgeon At Arms*, Heinemann,1958.

Dunlop, E.E., *The War Diaries of Weary Dunlop*, Nelson, 1986.

Eddy (et al), Paul, *The Falklands War*, Andre Deutsch, 1982.

Eyles-Thomas, Mark, *Sod That for a Game of Soldiers*, Kenton Publishing, 2007.

Fergusson, James, *A Million Bullets*, Bantam Press, 2008.

Geddes, John, *Spearhead Assault*, Arrow, 2007.

Hall, Matthew, *A Doctor at War*, Images Publishing, 1995.

Hardie (Dr), Robert, *The Burma Siam Railway*, IWM, 1983.

Harrison, Mark, *Medicine and Victory*, OUP, 2004

Holland, James,*Together We Stand*, HarperCollins, 2005.

Holmes, Richard, *Dusty Warriors*, HarperPerennial, 2007.

Jolly, Rick, *The Red and Green Life Machine: A Diary of the Falklands Field Hospital*, Red and Green Books, 2007.

Laffin, John, *Combat Surgeons*, Sutton, 1999.

MacArthur, Brian, *Surviving the Sword*, Time Warner, 2005.

MacCarthy, Aidan, *A Doctor's War*, Grub Street, 1979.

MacNalty, Arthur, *Medical Services in War*, HMSO, 1968.

Mather, Carol, *When the Grass Stops Growing*, Leo Cooper, 2007.

McManners, Hugh, *Forgotten Voices of the Falklands*, Ebury Press, 2007.

—, *The Scars of War*, HarperCollins, 1994.

Parker, Geoffrey, *The Black Scalpel*, William Kimber, 1968.

Sebag-Montefiore, Hugh, *Dunkirk*, Viking, 2006.

Shephard, Ben, *After Daybreak*, Pimlico, 2006.

Smith, Colin, *Singapore Burning*, Viking, 2005.

Smyth, Sir John, *The Will to Live*, Cassell, 1970.

Starns, Penny, *Nurses At War*, Sutton, 2000.

Taylor, Eric, *Combat Nurse*, Robert Hale, 1999.

—, *Front-Line Nurse*, Robert Hale, 1997.

Watts, J.C., *Surgeon At War*, George Allen & Unwin, 1955.

Weston (foreword by), Simon, *The Falklands War – A day by day account*, Marshall Cavendish, 2007.

Index

JOHN NICHOL & TONY RENNELL

THE LAST ESCAPE
THE UNTOLD STORY OF ALLIED PRISONERS OF WAR IN GERMANY 1944-45

Hundreds of thousands of British and American servicemen were held as POWs in camps across Nazi Germany by the time of the Normandy landings in June 1944. As winter settled across Europe and the Allied advance threatened German borders, prisoners were moved away from liberating forces. The POWs were forced to march hundreds of miles in appalling conditions. Hundreds died of disease, starvation and exhaustion. Yet when the war was over those who survived found their extraordinary tale was largely ignored and forgotten.

The Last Escape brings the survivors' amazing stories to light telling one of the most courageous and brutal tales of the final months of the Second World War.

'Packed with first-hand testimony and impressive scholarship but with all the pace of a novel, this is a superb memorial of those Allied heroes who thought – wrongly – that for them the war was over' Andrew Roberts

TAIL-END CHARLIES
THE LAST BATTLES OF THE BOMBER WAR 1944-45

Night after night they flew through the flak and packs of enemy fighters to drop the bombs that helped demolish the Third Reich – and they died in their tens of thousands. The airmen of RAF's Bomber Command were heroes who defied Hitler in the early days of the war and continued to sacrifice themselves to shatter the enemy right to the end of the conflict. But with war over they were forgotten, some of their actions seen as crimes.

Tail-End Charlies tells the astonishing and deeply moving stories of the controversial last battles in the skies above Germany, through the eyewitness accounts of the many forgotten heroes who fought them.

'Compelling, powerful, gripping and revealing' *Daily Mail*

JOHN NICHOL & TONY RENNELL

HOME RUN
ESCAPE FROM NAZI EUROPE

The dramatic story of Allied evaders behind enemy lines in World War Two.

They were the few: the stranded soldiers and shot-down airmen who evaded capture in Nazi-occupied Europe and had just one goal – to get back to Britain and to safety. On the run, hunted and desperate, their lives hung constantly in the balance – find the secret escape routes and you might get home, trust the wrong person and the feared Gestapo would scoop you up. A concentration camp, or worse, would be your fate. This is the incredible story of the band of British heroes who made that elusive home run... and those who did not.

'Humanity shines through. A sensitive account of the best and worst of human behaviour' *Daily Telegraph*